BROOKINGS PAPERS ON EDUCATION POLICY

2002

WITHDRAWN

Diane Ravitch
Editor

Sponsored by
the Brown Center on
Education Policy

BROOKINGS INSTITUTION PRESS
Washington, D.C.

Copyright © 2002
THE BROOKINGS INSTITUTION
1775 Massachusetts Avenue, N.W., Washington, DC 20036

Library of Congress Catalog Card No. 98-664027
ISSN 1096-2719
ISBN 0-8157-0269-8

BROOKINGS PAPERS ON
EDUCATION POLICY
2002

ℬ THE BROOKINGS INSTITUTION

The Brookings Institution is an independent organization devoted to nonpartisan research, education, and publication in economics, government, foreign policy, and the social sciences generally. Its principal purposes are to aid in the development of sound public policies and to promote public understanding of issues of national importance.

The Institution was founded on December 8, 1927, to merge the activities of the Institute for Government Research, founded in 1916, the Institute of Economics, founded in 1922, and the Robert Brookings Graduate School of Economics and Government, founded in 1924.

The general administration of the Institution is the responsibility of a Board of Trustees charged with safeguarding the independence of the staff and fostering the most favorable conditions for scientific research and publication. The immediate direction of the policies, program, and staff of the Institution is vested in the president, assisted by an advisory committee of the officers and staff.

In publishing a study, the Institution presents it as a competent treatment of a subject worthy of public consideration. The interpretations and conclusions in such publications are those of the author or authors and do not necessarily reflect the views of the other staff members, officers, or trustees of the Brookings Institution.

BROOKINGS PAPERS ON EDUCATION POLICY contains the edited versions of the papers and comments that were presented at the fourth annual Brookings conference on education policy, held on May 15–16, 2001. The conference gives federal, state, and local policymakers an independent, nonpartisan forum to analyze policies intended to improve student performance. Each year Brookings convenes some of the best-informed analysts from various disciplines to review the current situation in education and to consider proposals for reform. This year's discussion focused on accountability and its consequences for students. The conference and journal were funded by the Herman and George R. Brown Chair in Educational Studies at Brookings. Additional support from the Miriam K. Carliner Endowment for Economic Studies and from the John M. Olin Foundation is gratefully acknowledged.

The papers in this volume have been modified to reflect some of the insights contributed by the discussions at the conference. In all cases the papers are the result of the authors' thinking and do not imply agreement by those attending the conference. Nor do the materials presented here necessarily represent the views of the staff members, officers, or trustees of the Brookings Institution.

Subscription Rates

Individuals $24.95
Institutions $39.95

For information on subscriptions, standing orders, and individual copies, contact Brookings Institution Press, 1775 Massachusetts Avenue, N.W., Washington, DC 20036. Call 202/797-6258 or 800/275-1447. E-mail bibooks@brook.edu. Visit Brookings online at www.brookings.edu.

Brookings periodicals are available online through Online Computer Library Center (contact the OCLC subscriptions department at 800/848-5878, ext. 6251) and Project Muse (http://muse.jhu.edu).

Conference Participants

Leslye Arsht, *Standards Work*
John Barth, *National Education Goals Panel*
Beth Ann Bryan, *U.S. Department of Education*
Sheila Byrd, *Consultant*
Hugh Burkett, *U.S. Department of Education*
Pamela Cherry, *Citizens' Commission on Civil Rights*
Eric Cox, *Cato Institute*
Fritz Edelstein, *U.S. Department of Education*
Lynda Edwards, *U.S. Department of Education*
Chris Etchechury, *University of Virginia*
Lawrence Feinberg, *National Assessment Governing Board*
Chester Finn, *Thomas B. Fordham Foundation*
Fred Frelow, *Rockefeller Foundation*
Dan Goldhaber, *Urban Institute*
Siobhan Gorman, National Journal
Judith Grant, *British Embassy*
Jane Hannaway, *Urban Institute*
Janet Hansen, *Committee for Economic Development*
Gene Hickok, *U.S. Department of Education*
Craig Jerald, *Education Trust*
Richard Kahlenberg, *Century Foundation*
Marci Kanstoroom, *Thomas B. Fordham Foundation*
Carole Kennedy, *U.S. Department of Education*
Jens Ludwig, *Georgetown University*
Julie Lusher, *American Council for International Education*
Robert Maranto, *Villanova University*
Phyllis McClure, *Consultant*
Laura McGiffert, *ACHIEVE*
Margaret McNeely, *U.S. Department of Education*
Sheila Murray, *RAND Corporation*
Susan Neuman, *U.S. Department of Education*
Lynn Olson, Education Week
Robert Rice, *Council for Basic Education*
Michael Ross, *National Center for Education Statistics*
Robin Taylor, *Delaware Department of Education*
Anna Varghese, *Center for Education Reform*
Maris Vinovskis, *University of Michigan*
Martin West, *Harvard University*
Emily Wurtz, *National Education Goals Panel*
Peggy Zelinko, *U.S. Department of Education*

Introduction

DIANE RAVITCH

In May 2001, for the fifth consecutive year, the Brown Center on Education Policy at the Brookings Institution sponsored a conference on a major topic in American education. The discussion focused on the issue of accountability in several leading states and cities, and participants were asked to consider whether students were being helped or hurt by standards-based reforms.

As is now customary, the meeting brought together a distinguished group of educators and policymakers to reflect on the direction of current education reforms. The discussions, as usual, were animated. Some of that animation was due to the fact that the participants were drawn from a range of disciplines and, even more important, from a variety of perspectives. No point of view dominated the discussion; dissent on every issue was welcomed and flourished.

At the beginning of the twenty-first century, American public education was in various stages of standards-based reform. Almost every state had adopted state academic standards in major subject areas. These standards, which differed slightly from state to state, were intended to describe what students were supposed to learn. In addition, almost every state had developed (or purchased) assessments aligned to its standards, to ascertain whether their students had learned what was described in the standards. "Accountability" meant that public officials were supposed to review the results of assessments and establish consequences for students, teachers, schools, or school systems. For students, accountability might mean remedial assistance, summer school, promotion, retention, or a variety of other responses that would provide either help or incentives for better performance. For schools, accountability might mean reorganization, state intervention, even closure. For teachers, accountability might entail merit pay or other rewards or assistance for those in need

1

of it. (In the midst of a national teacher shortage, there was virtually no interest expressed by policymakers or legislators in removing ineffective teachers.)

Standards-based reform has had bipartisan sponsorship. Governors, legislators, and presidents of both major political parties supported it, especially when the possibility of stakes for students was in the distant future. It got its biggest boost in 1983 with the publication of *A Nation at Risk*, a report of the National Commission on Excellence in Education. That report stirred many states to create their own studies and commissions, leading to the bolstering of graduation requirements in many states. Those who support standards-based reform speak of *A Nation at Risk* as a clarion call for action, and those who reject it treat the report as overstated, bombastic propaganda.

In 1989 President George H. W. Bush convened a national summit meeting of governors in Charlottesville, Virginia, to set national goals for education, which included a target of improved student performance in basic subject areas. In 1991 and 1992 the Bush administration supported the development of voluntary national standards. A controversy ensued, because the documents that came forth as national standards represented the aspirations of the professionals that wrote them, not the goals, content, and methods that had been carefully tried and proved successful. In 1994 President Bill Clinton's Goals 2000 program allocated funding to the states to create their own standards and assessments.

By the late 1990s, almost every state was administering tests keyed to its own state standards. In the 2000 election, both major party presidential candidates supported standards-based reform. The Republican nominee and ultimate victor—Texas governor George W. Bush—promoted a program called "No Child Left Behind." Its central theme was testing and accountability, based on the model that had been implemented for more than a decade in the state of Texas. President Bush proposed that every child in grades three through eight should be tested annually. Furthermore, the results of the annual testing should be used to focus attention on those who were lagging, to acknowledge and reward effective schools, and to allow students to leave those schools that had failed to educate them.

Even as a federal initiative on testing and accountability was debated in Washington, D.C., some educators and journalists began to complain about the new emphasis on testing. They charged that testing would harm, not help, children; that it put too much emphasis on trivial matters; that it distorted the curriculum; that it discouraged creative teachers; that it compelled teachers to teach to the test; and that it would standardize education without improving it.

A major goal of the 2001 Brookings conference was to look closely at some of these concerns by analyzing the experience of specific states and localities. The stories from the front lines are complex, with neither great victories nor disastrous defeats to be reported for standards-based reform. In some states, the gains were small but significant (and even those gains were contested by critics). In others, progress toward the original goals appeared to have stalled, as dedicated critics of standards and testing exhibited greater fervor than beleaguered and divided advocates. In a few places, the gains—especially for disadvantaged children—appeared to be indisputable, but the prospects for future advances were nonetheless uncertain.

The overall picture presented at the conference was one in which the dust had not settled. It was a picture of periodic advances and retreats; of steady progress in tiny steps; of conflicts in which educators sharply disagreed, in which business communities rallied behind clear standards, and in which elected officials wavered, as they weighed the interests of their communities, of students, and of their constituencies. For a time, at least when it was no more than a rhetorical cry, almost everyone seemed to favor standards. Almost everyone, however, did not favor testing, because tests often revealed unpleasant facts. As was consistently found, the tests usually uncovered large gaps between children from different racial and socioeconomic groups. Sometimes they showed that a school or a district that was richly endowed with resources had an embarrassingly wide spread of achievement among its students. As testing became more or less institutionalized in the states, the tests attracted opposition in part because they showed how many children were not meeting even the most minimal standards needed to function in the modern world as independent people. It was easier, it seemed, to blame the tests than to figure out why some children in some schools were consistently lagging behind their peers. One may imagine that if the tests brought uniformly good news, they would not likely have been lightning rods for criticism.

As controversy swirled around the issue of testing, the media highlighted the complaints of test critics, especially their hostility to high-stakes testing. The test critics warned that high-stakes tests would damage children's self-esteem and would be especially harmful for poor, minority, and disadvantaged children. Because standards-based reform began as a campaign premised on the belief that all children can learn, this charge of racism and social bias struck at the central hope for the reform effort, calling it a cruel hoax on the very children it was supposed to help.

The reality, however, was that the state tests administered in the 1990s were not truly high-stakes tests. Most people, when they hear the term "high-stakes," take it to mean that students are given a single chance to pass and then retained in grade, failed, or prevented from graduating if they do not reach a certain arbitrary cutoff score. But no state simply gave the tests and then failed kids. In every state that administered tests, students were given multiple opportunities to pass the state tests. If they failed, they received remedial aid in class, in summer school, after school, or on weekends. The advent of state testing became a stimulus for innovative efforts to teach struggling or recalcitrant students.

Only a few months after the 2001 conference, the returns on the standards-and-testing strategy brightened considerably. Massachusetts state officials celebrated in October 2001, when the results of the spring testing were published. State testing began in 1998, but it did not count for students until the spring of 2001, when for the first time students had to pass the tests to qualify for high school graduation. Students take the tests in the tenth grade. If they fail, they then have four more chances to take them before their graduation. For the first three years of testing, the failure rates on the state tests were dismayingly high—as much as 54 percent in mathematics and 34 percent in English. However, the failure rate dropped sharply in 2001, when the tests mattered most. Math failure rates dropped to 25 percent, and English failures dropped to 18 percent. Many of those who failed were close to the passing mark. These manageable figures allow schools to focus remediation on those who need extra help. As each cohort of unsuccessful students becomes smaller, the efforts to prepare them for the tests will become more intense. Teachers will focus on those students who have not yet demonstrated their ability to read, write, and do mathematics at a level that is necessary for higher education and good jobs. Even with this degree of concentrated remediation, some students still might be unable to pass the tenth-grade-level tests of English and mathematics for graduation, and policymakers were debating whether to create exceptions, exemptions, special diplomas, a board of appeals, or some other path to a diploma for students who cannot pass the state tests, without simultaneously gutting their incentive value for the great majority of students.

In some states, students have demonstrated small and steady test score gains. In Virginia and Maryland, for example, eighth-grade scores on the National Assessment of Educational Progress (NAEP) tests increased significantly between 1996 and 2000. Virginia also saw strong improvement in fourth graders' mathematics scores on the NAEP, a federally sponsored test that is given regularly to samples of students across the nation and in most states, and that has achievement levels of advanced, proficient, and basic. The proportion of fourth graders in Virginia that was below basic dropped from 41 percent in 1992 to 27 percent in 2000. Virginia also saw important gains for African American students. In 1992 only 25 percent of black fourth graders reached the basic level of achievement. By 2000, 46 percent of black fourth graders had reached the basic achievement level in mathematics. Nationally, the proportion of fourth graders who were below basic in mathematics dropped from 43 percent in 1992 to 33 percent in 2000.

Virginia has been a national leader in the development of rigorous standards and tests (called the SOLs, or Standards of Learning) and on setting accountability benchmarks for both students and schools. Beginning with the class of 2004, high school students must pass six end-of-course SOL tests to get a diploma. (No limit exists on the number of times that students can retake an SOL test needed for graduation.) Unlike other states, Virginia requires its schools to meet standards. The state Board of Education has promised to remove accreditation from schools, beginning in 2007, in which fewer than 70 percent of students passed the state tests. Despite an aggressive public campaign against the state's standards and tests, students registered steady annual gains on the state tests.

By 2001, Virginia's strategy began to show impressive results in almost every subject tested. In 1998, the first year the SOLs were administered, only 40 percent of students passed Algebra I, but by 2001, 74 percent passed it. In Algebra II, the proportion of students passing jumped from 30 percent in 1998 to 74 percent in 2001. By 2001, growing proportions of students were passing the state tests at every grade level. In 1998 only 20 percent of African American students passed the Algebra I test, a figure that rose to 59 percent in 2001. During the same years, the proportion of African American students who passed Algebra II jumped from 13 percent to 58 percent, and the proportion passing geometry more than doubled from 25 percent to 51 percent. In 1998 only 2.2 percent of schools had met the threshold for accreditation (that is, having at least 70 percent of their students pass the SOL tests); by 2000, that proportion had risen to 23 percent. In 2001 it had increased to 40 percent, and another 30 percent were on track to meet the required benchmark. These gains represented a huge improvement in meeting the state standards and preparing students for higher education and the modern workplace.

Despite a spate of criticism of testing and accountability in the late 1990s, the American public continues to support standards-based reform. Every public opinion poll has found that the public backs standards and testing, wants students who need extra help and time to get them, and wants to continue current efforts to improve student achievement. In an address to the conference, Deborah Wadsworth, president of Public Agenda, posed the question: Do Americans want to hold schools accountable? Among those who know that new standards are being implemented in their communities, 82 percent, according to Public Agenda, believe that the schools are doing so in a "careful and reasonable" manner. Only 9 percent of parents say that teachers are putting too much academic pressure on students; 11 percent, that schools require students to take too many standardized tests; 12 percent, that the standardized tests ask "questions so difficult or unfair that students cannot be expected to answer them"; and 18 percent, that teachers "focus so much on preparing for standardized test that real learning is neglected." That is, most parents do not believe that their children are being overtaxed in school or that teachers are overemphasizing standardized testing. Only 1 percent of parents and less than 1 percent of teachers want local schools to halt their standards-based reform efforts.

Evidence exists that the standards movement is taking hold with the support of teachers, parents, and students. Public Agenda survey data show that social promotion is down; summer school attendance is up; summer school is being taken more seriously by teachers and students; and students (more than 80 percent) see the importance of standardized tests, do not feel overwhelmed by the pressure of having to take them, and find the questions fair. Furthermore, 34 percent of parents in 2001 say public schools have higher standards than private schools, up from 20 percent four years earlier. About one-third of parents give private schools the edge, down from 42 percent in the same time frame. However, as Wadsworth points out, educators and policymakers must consider a number of factors when establishing an accountability system: a good idea poorly implemented or unfairly managed will be criticized and likely will fail; standardized tests should be used in a commonsense manner— for example, graduation from high school should not be predicated on the result of one test; students need behavioral standards as well as academic standards; expectations for parental involvement should be realistic; and no particular policy will have the support of everyone. Wadsworth warns that reform efforts could be derailed by teachers, 70 percent of whom said they felt they did not have a voice in the decisionmaking process regarding standards.

Most teachers believe that when school district leaders do discuss policy matters with them, it is to gain support for the leaders' positions, not to better understand teachers' concerns. And, while teachers back higher standards, they are not a top priority.

If anything is clear about these issues, it is that U.S. public schools are in the midst of a major change. Testing is not new; American schools have always given tests. But what is new is, first, the emphasis on state-administered tests and, second, the increased demand that students demonstrate academic readiness before they can be promoted to the next grade or graduate from high school. Some critics are unhappy with the enlarged role of the state, others are unhappy with the new insistence upon accountability (and overlap exists among both sets of critics).

While some critics wish that they could roll back the entire regime of standards, testing, and accountability and then declare the totality to be an anathema, this does not seem likely to happen. Public officials may feel the hot breath of parents whose children may not get a diploma, but they also know that they need some way to monitor the effectiveness of the education system and of the large public investments in that system. Are new programs working or not? Which schools and which districts are seeing changes in achievement for the better or the worse? Which schools are most effective at narrowing the gap between high-performing and low-performing children and between children from different demographic groups? The polls suggest that parents want to know, too, how their children and how their own district's schools are doing compared with others. Rolling back the standards-and-testing regime would mean depriving public officials, educators, and parents of information about student achievement, which would remove any benchmarks for measuring future gains and losses. Some educators, intently opposed on philosophical grounds to any form of accounting or measurement, would be willing to forgo information and consider it an unwarranted intrusion, but their view remains that of a small minority.

Much of this debate, and certainly much of the uncertainty about the future, is reflected in the papers in this volume. The authors and the discussants of their papers are not of one mind about the status of standards-based reform. Writing about specific localities, they clearly and candidly examine the problems that reformers have encountered. If there is a single story here, it is that the United States is struggling to achieve a national reform despite its unusual and awkward system of decentralized educational authority, dispersed across fifty states, various territories, and thousands of school districts. The schools of the United States are trying to create, adopt, and implement something akin to national education standards without having national authority. The changes described in this volume have not been easy, and their course has not been readily predictable.

If reformers and their critics are often impatient, that impatience is understandable. Children are the future, and educators and policymakers cannot wait forever to improve schools. Schools need well-educated teachers, solid curricula, and up-to-date textbooks, and they also need attentive parents, a clear sense of their own responsibilities, and a readiness to pitch in. Some of these needs are more amenable to public policy than others. The reform of a school system as vast and complicated as that of the United States will not happen quickly. The changes that are under way will likely take many years. The progress of improvement should be checked and the correction of errors should be done on a regular, frequent basis.

The public debates about means and ends to improve schools thus far have been vigorous and will continue to be. The exchanges between public officials, on the one hand, and critics, on the other, have raised hackles, but they have been healthy. The critics have raised some important cautions about the potential misuses of standardized tests, and public officials do well to listen carefully to the critics' concerns. Some schools and districts have undoubtedly become obsessed with test scores and have encouraged teaching to the test. If educators in these schools and districts realize that good teaching of reading, writing, mathematics, and other subjects produces higher test scores, they would shift their emphasis from test preparation to high-quality instruction.

No state has solved all the problems associated with standards-based reform. The quality of standards varies from state to state. Some state standards are vacuous, at best, and provide no guidance to teachers, students, assessment developers, and textbook writers. Over time, the states with flabby and vague standards may learn from those that have excellent standards and that have demonstrated good results over time. So, too, with tests. They vary in quality greatly from state to state. Ironically, Massachusetts, the state with perhaps the best assessments, also contains the most vociferous and unyielding test critics. Unlike many other states, Massachusetts has developed assessments that include not only multiple-choice questions (which can be quickly and objectively graded), but also questions that require students to respond in writing of varying length and complexity. The latter kinds of questions make the exams longer for students as well as more expensive to grade.

Critics complain that tests composed solely of multiple-choice questions are too simplistic. But they also complain that tests containing essays and other open responses take too long. State officials know that they cannot satisfy every critic, but they will be most successful if they are ready to review and address reasonable complaints.

Standards-based reform, as the authors in this volume make clear, is operating in choppy waters. It has encountered resistance and reaction. Yet it has begun to demonstrate significant improvements in such states as Massachusetts and Virginia. With every success, standards-based reform will gain new adherents. Meanwhile, most members of the public and their elected officials see great sense in describing what students are expected to learn with clarity (standards), determining whether the students have learned what they were taught (assessments), and acting on the basis of the information provided by assessments (accountability) in ways that might change the behavior of students, teachers, and others.

The papers in this volume are as follows:

"Grade Retention and Social Promotion in Texas, 1994–99: Academic Achievement among Elementary School Students," by Jon Lorence, A. Gary Dworkin, Laurence A. Toenjes, and Antwanette N. Hill, a team of researchers from the Sociology Department at the University of Houston, asks whether children who are retained in grade (that is, not promoted) were harmed by this policy as compared with those who experienced social promotion. They conclude that, on the whole, they were not. Their discussants, Andrew Rotherham of the Progressive Policy Institute and Lorrie A. Shepard of the University of Colorado at Boulder, debate the paper's conclusion.

Frederick M. Hess of the University of Virginia considers the controversies in Virginia that resulted from its leadership in setting high standards and adopting a commitment to accountability over a ten-year period. The discussants for Hess's paper, "Reform, Resistance, . . . Retreat? The Predictable Politics of Accountability in Virginia," are Alan Wurtzel, a former member of the Virginia State Board of Education, and Iris C. Rotberg of George Washington University.

"School Accountability in California: An Early Evaluation" was written by Julian R. Betts, an economist at the University of California at San Diego, and Anne Danenberg of the Public Policy Institute of California. While acknowledging that the accountability program was in its infancy, the authors sought evidence of its early effects. Their paper is critiqued by Robert Rothman of Achieve and Robert M. Hauser of the University of Wisconsin.

Paul T. Hill and Robin J. Lake of the University of Washington, in "Standards and Accountability in Washington State," vividly portray the political dynamics that first advanced and then stalled the efforts to establish a standards-based system in Washington. Their discussants are Michael J. Petrilli of the United States Department of Education and Michael Cohen of the Aspen Institute and former assistant secretary of education in the Clinton administration.

"Volatility in School Test Scores: Implications for Test-Based Accountability Systems," prepared by Thomas J. Kane of the Hoover Institution at Stanford University and Douglas O. Staiger of Dartmouth College, warns public officials not to base rewards and sanctions on short-term measures because of volatility in test scores related to student-body composition, school size, and other variables. Their discussants are David Grissmer of the RAND Corporation and Helen F. Ladd of Duke University.

"Building a High-Quality Assessment and Accountability Program: The Philadelphia Example" was written by Andrew Porter of the Wisconsin Center for Education Research and Mitchell Chester, executive director of accountability and assessment, Philadelphia school district. Porter and Chester describe the construction of Philadelphia's assessment and accountability program and its consequences to date. Their discussants are Daniel Koretz of the RAND Corporation and Theodore Hershberg of the University of Pennsylvania.

G. Alfred Hess Jr. of Northwestern University, in "Accountability and Support in Chicago: Consequences for Students," reviews the results of Chicago's ambitious accountability reforms in the 1990s and considers their effects on student achievement. His paper is discussed by Stanley S. Litow of the IBM Foundation and Richard Elmore of the Harvard University Graduate School of Education.

These papers demonstrate that "accountability" means far more than rewards and sanctions. In every city and state, the effort to raise achievement by setting standards, administering assessments, and providing accurate information has led to a wide variety of remedial and improvement programs. It has opened up new discussions about the importance of high-quality preschool education and high-quality teacher education.

Information leads to action. As soon as public officials have a clear picture of student performance, their first responsibility is to do something to make it better. This always includes a broad array of programs and activities, but most certainly it entails a focus on improving the academic achievement of low-performing students. Some of this activity bolsters achievement among students who needed some additional prodding and encouragement. Standards-based reform enables public officials to know where they have failed and to know where they have succeeded. It enables them to identify students who are in greatest need of extra assistance. It provides benchmarks for the performance of schools and districts. It is hard to know how the nation can achieve its educational goals without this knowledge.

Grade Retention and Social Promotion in Texas, 1994–99: Academic Achievement among Elementary School Students

JON LORENCE, A. GARY DWORKIN,
LAURENCE A. TOENJES, *and*
ANTWANETTE N. HILL

To make schools more accountable for the performance of students, many school districts as well as entire states have proposed more rigorous standards to help ensure that pupils have the basic skills necessary to be successful in school. Many public and private sector decisionmakers have criticized the common practice of social promotion; that is, allowing students to progress to the next grade level without having already learned the material required for the current grade. The public in general views the practice of social promotion or grade placement as detrimental to low-performing students who are promoted without requisite skills because such students are presumed to fall further behind their more academically proficient classmates. Consequently, some states and school districts have proposed or adopted strict policies of retention that require a low-achieving student to remain in the same grade until meeting a specified level of proficiency.[1] Although these newer standards for promotion may vary across

We thank the Texas Education Agency and its staff for providing the data on which this paper is based. This research was also funded in part by the Texas Education Agency (contract no. 600021000191599). Comments by Lorrie Shepard on earlier versions of this paper are also gratefully acknowledged.

13

different educational boundaries, a common mandate is that students would be allowed to proceed to the next grade only after the retained pupil has demonstrated sufficient understanding of the material appropriate for the present grade. The goal of ending social promotion, although not necessarily replacing it with retention in grade, especially when students return to the same curricula taught in the same manner, was endorsed by President Bill Clinton in 1998 and by the U.S. Department of Education in 1999.[2]

However, unlike many public officials, most educational researchers concur that grade retention practices are ineffective in remediating the academic performance of low-achieving students. For example, Panayota Mantzicopoulos and Delmont Morrison state, "Unlike mixed empirical evidence on other educational issues, research on elementary school nonpromotion is unequivocal. It supports the conclusion that retention is not an effective policy."[3] Some critics of retention policies even contend that retaining students in the same grade will only harm their later academic achievement. For example, Lorrie A. Shepard and Mary Lee Smith argue that "retention worsens rather than improves the level of student achievement in years following the repeat year."[4] Publications in which the intended audiences are educational administrators and practitioners often contain articles highly critical of holding students in grade an additional year.[5] Likewise, a literature review for the National Research Council contends that retaining students another year in the same grade will not yield anticipated educational benefits.[6] The claim against the effectiveness of grade retention is generally based on a few often-cited studies and reviews of research literature that are interpreted as being conclusive evidence that holding students back one year in the same grade will impede academic achievement.[7] More recent analyses of a moderate-size panel of at-risk students still indicate that requiring poorly performing pupils to repeat a grade does not lead to greater academic achievement.[8] The perceived negative effects of grade retention are so entrenched among educational researchers that C. Kenneth Tanner and Susan Allan Galis believe reporting on school retention is often biased and misleading.[9]

Nonetheless, some published research supports the position that grade retention allows low-achieving elementary students additional time to remedy low levels of academic performance.[10] To rebut findings supportive of retention practices, detractors of holding students back a year in grade offer various reasons that such findings should be dismissed. A major criticism is that reported gains among retained students are only temporary; failing students who are promoted to the next grade do as well in the long run, they contend, as the retained students. To illustrate, after reviewing studies on grade retention, C. Thomas Holmes concluded that, among low-achieving students, those who were retained tended to show higher academic achievement than their counterparts who had been promoted, but the initial advantage disappeared after three years.[11] Similarly, Lorrie A. Shepard, Mary Lee Smith, and Scott F. Marion contend that the positive effects attributed to retention among Baltimore public elementary students, as reported by Karl L. Alexander, Doris R. Entwisle, and Susan L. Dauber, were likewise temporary.[12] In addition, Shepard, Smith, and Marion contend that the greater observed gains in academic achievement among retained students in Baltimore resulted from regression-selection artifacts.[13] That is, very low-performing students were selected for retention. A common result of retaining only the lowest scoring pupils is that their test scores would naturally increase in the next year (the year of retention) as these students move to their true mean level of ability. Jay P. Heubert and Robert M. Hauser also suggest that positive results attributed to recently implemented retention practices in the Chicago public schools are likely spurious for similar reasons, because only low-scoring pupils were required to repeat a grade.[14] Similar to the critique of the Baltimore study, the scores of retained Chicago students would also be expected to rise substantially in the next year because of such low scores on the initial test.

Shortcomings of Previous Research

Although considerable research examines the impact of grade retention on student academic achievement, various shortcomings exhibited across these studies make it difficult to derive any concrete generalizations about the effectiveness of requiring students to repeat a grade. Reported effects of retaining students vary across studies because of the differences in sample sizes, the degree to which retained and promoted students were similar, the measures of academic performance, the presence of alternatives to retention, the content of alternative programs, and the extent to which promoted students were socially promoted but given accelerated instruction to bring them up to grade level or simply socially promoted with no additional assistance.[15] Many studies are based on dated samples of students, some of which are many decades old. It is questionable whether old studies based on predominantly white school populations in which 5 percent of the students were retained in grade

are applicable to contemporary urban schools where large percentages of ethnic minorities and economically disadvantaged pupils are retained in grade.
Retention studies are often based on small samples that are unrepresentative
of ethnically diverse educational systems. For example, several recent published analyses by Shane Jimerson and others are based on a panel with less
than thirty students who were retained in grade.[16] Further, many studies indicating that school retention is ineffective are unpublished student master's
theses or dissertations or research reports issued by school districts. The generalizability of such studies are often suspect because of the unknown quality
of the research. With only a few exceptions, another major problem of many
retention studies is that students who were held back were followed for only
a short period of time (for example, only a year or two). Most research on
grade retention focuses only on the short-term effects of being held in grade
and do not study the long-term consequences on students (for example, academic performance three or four years later). In addition, many studies follow
only the performance of retained students without examining the academic
achievement of comparable low-performing pupils who were not required to
repeat the same grade.[17] As a result of these flaws in research design, it is difficult to summarize the extent to which grade retention affects later student
achievement.

Contributions of the Present Study

By utilizing data based on a cohort of all low-achieving elementary students in the state of Texas over a number of years, we can overcome some of
the weaknesses observed in previous studies on grade retention and social promotion. Our purpose is to ascertain whether holding low-achieving students
back a year in grade contributes to enhancing academic performance. We
believe that the findings presented here provide many advantages unavailable
in previous research. First, the state data set analyzed is much larger than
used in earlier studies. Instead of investigating only a small number of students, the data consist of the entire population of elementary students in Texas.
Second, the data include all academically challenged students who were
retained in grade or promoted to the next grade. The academic achievement
of low-performing pupils who were promoted to the next grade can be compared with the educational performance of similar low-performing students
required to repeat a grade. Also, the state data set made available by the Texas
Education Agency (TEA) is detailed enough to enable better comparisons of

the academic achievement of low-performing students of various ethnic backgrounds who were retained with comparable students who were socially promoted. The longitudinal nature of the available data allows us to follow the academic progress of the same students over a six-year period. In sum, the existing state data can be analyzed in a manner that permits better estimation of the effects of retention in grade on student academic performance than has heretofore been possible.

The Texas Educational Accountability System, TAAS, and Retention

The cornerstone of the Texas accountability system has been a state standardized test to assess student achievement. Initial versions of the Texas test assessed only minimum basic skills, but near the end of the 1980s the Texas state legislature mandated a test that would assess both problem-solving and critical skills. Charged with the task, the Texas Education Agency commissioned National Computer Systems and its subcontractors, the Psychological Corporation and Measurement Incorporated, to develop a criterion-referenced test that would assess the reading, mathematics, and writing skills of Texas public school students. The test, known as the Texas Assessment of Academic Skills (TAAS), was intended to deviate from the previous state practice of testing only minimal or basic skills.[18] In 1997 the legislature enhanced the criteria through the creation of the Texas Essential Knowledge and Skills (TEKS), an even more rigorous curriculum, and beginning in 2003 a yet more demanding test, based on additional subjects, will be implemented.

Implementation of the TAAS began in October 1990 with administration of only a limited number of grade levels. Successive grade levels were not regularly tested, thereby making the determination of academic progress over successive grades impossible. However, beginning in 1994, students in grades three through eight and grade ten were tested each year, thus permitting the determination of annual gain scores. Tenth-grade students must pass reading, mathematics, and writing sections of the TAAS, as well as their course-exit exams, before graduating from high school. The TAAS is administered in Spanish for students enrolled in bilingual education programs in grades three through six, but students in the English as a Second Language (ESL) program must take the TAAS in English.

In addition, beginning in 1994 an attempt was made to develop a vertical scale score system for the TAAS, thereby permitting direct comparison of annual student progress. The attempt was partially abandoned and replaced by a metric known as the Texas Learning Index (TLI), which, like a z-score, gives the relative standing of students, year by year, compared with other students. TLI scores have a theoretical maximum of 100, but the empirical maximum at some grade-level tests may be as low as 91. A score of 70 indicates the student meets minimal expectations and is counted as passing the test. A score of 70 should not be interpreted to mean that a student must correctly answer 70 percent of all questions to pass the test. Instead, a score of 70 translates to an equivalent of correctly answering 70 percent of the items on the October 1990 exit-level (tenth-grade) test. Raw scores are adjusted for test item difficulty to maintain a level of proficiency that corresponds to a Texas Learning Index score of 70. The absence of a change in the TLI scores from year to year should not be interpreted as an indication of inadequate progress. Instead, a given TLI score indicates a full year's growth in achievement. Thus, scores of 75 in 1993–94 for third grade, 75 in 1994–95 for fourth grade, and 75 in 1995–96 for fifth grade indicate that the child has made a full year's growth in achievement each year. Increases in TLI scores across years represent greater than a year's growth, while decreases indicate less than a year's growth. More technically, because the TAAS is not a vertical scale test, stability, increases, or decreases in TLI scores correspond to stable, increasing, or decreasing rank order relative to other students. Only the English version of the TAAS utilizes TLI scores. For most of the years we study, the Spanish version of the TAAS contained information on whether a student passed or failed the test and provided a percentile rank comparing the students with others who took the Spanish version of the TAAS.

TAAS performance is an integral component of the state's public school accountability system, with test passage affecting high school graduation of students and passage rates determining the rating of schools and districts. School districts and individual campuses with high TAAS passage rates are offered financial rewards whereas extremely low-performing campuses and districts may face takeover by the state, removal of administrators, and even loss of accreditation. A unique aspect of the Texas accountability system is the disaggregation of passage rates by minority and economically disadvantaged populations. Schools and districts need to have high passage rates among African Americans, Hispanics, and economically disadvantaged children to gain favorable recognition or to avoid sanctions that accompany identification as a low-performing campus or district. Thus, most schools cannot rely only upon their white middle-class students to do well on the state's TAAS test to be recognized. The exception to this generalization is when only a small number of students are in specified accountability groups. The overall rating of a school district or specific campus will not be greatly influenced by the TAAS scores based on accountability groups consisting of less than thirty students. To illustrate, a large school could still receive a high rating by the state if most students obtained high TAAS scores even if twenty-nine economically disadvantaged students performed poorly on average.

One incentive to disaggregate results in the Texas accountability system has been the changing demographics of the state—and the nation as a whole. At the beginning of the twentieth century merely 6.3 percent of the adult population aged eighteen or older nationwide had completed high school; by 1942 the figure had risen to slightly over 50 percent. In the 1970s high school completion remained at about 75 percent; and in the late 1990s it hovered slightly above 80 percent.[19] In the 1940s and 1950s the failure to graduate from high school did not preclude the acquisition of employment that paid an adequate wage. At the beginning of the twenty-first century, jobs that pay well are skill-intensive, while the fastest growing segments of the population and labor force are racial and ethnic minorities. Their attainment of a quality education is imperative. However, academic failure and dropout behaviors are highest in racial and ethnic minority groups.[20]

Many demographic forecasts suggest that the percentages of traditionally underserved minority and economically disadvantaged populations are likely to grow, eventually becoming the majority of the public school population in some states. Such populous states as California, Florida, and Texas are most likely to have a majority of their residents, as well as the school-aged population, drawn from minority groups, particularly Hispanics or Latinos, during the twenty-first century.[21] The Anglo population, which has traditionally dominated the elementary and secondary schools, institutions of higher education, and the high-paying, high-skilled jobs, cannot fill enough of the labor-force positions needed to sustain economic growth. Unless the traditionally underserved populations receive a quality education, national and state economies could well be at risk.

Retention policies in Texas have changed during the 1990s. Initially students could not be retained in grade more than one time between kindergarten and fourth grade or more than once between fifth and eighth grade. Retention in ninth grade was more common because promotion required that students earn a specified number of academic credits before entering grade ten. Retaining ninth graders is not the result of an explicit retention decision by teachers or administrators, but it usually occurs because of an insufficient number of completed courses in specified areas required for promotion to grade ten. Retention in kindergarten or even in prekindergarten is also more common than in other elementary grades and is frequently associated with a child's perceived lack of emotional maturity. Legislation passed in 1999 requires third-grade students to pass the reading section of the TAAS beginning in 2003 before being promoted to the fourth grade. Eventually, all elementary students in specified grades will be required to pass the reading and mathematics sections of the TAAS to avoid retention in grade. Under the new state policy, students failing the TAAS will be required to take an intensive summer school program and pass the test by the end of the summer to avoid being retained in grade. Exceptions to the new promotion standards will be allowed. Pupils with low TAAS scores in third grade can be promoted to the fourth grade if a principal or a specialist, the classroom teacher, and the child's parent(s) all agree that low scores are due to special circumstances and not the child's inability to perform satisfactorily.

Data and Analytical Strategy

This analysis is based upon archival data supplied by the Texas Education Agency, consisting of anonymous student-level TAAS records of every student in the tested grades between 1994 and 1999. We focus on students in third grade because Texas children first take the required TAAS tests in this grade. In addition, the state legislature mandated that students failing the TAAS reading test in grade three will eventually be required to repeat the grade. Students acquired a TAAS record if they were enrolled in a Texas public school in the tested grades during the fall semester or entered a school during the spring semester but before the administration of the TAAS. Scores were not available for all students because of absences during the day of the test or other extenuating circumstances, including cheating and illness during the test. Further, two statutory categories of students were exempted from testing. Special education students who were learning disabled, as determined by a school's Admissions, Review, and Dismissal (ARD) committee, were exempted from taking the test. Students who were of limited English proficiency (LEP status) and enrolled in bilingual education programs did not take the TAAS until a Spanish version was made available in 1996. However LEP students who were in the English as a Second Language program or who were in regular English language classes took the English version of the

Table 1. Social-Demographic Characteristics of 1994 Texas Third Graders
Percent

Social-demographic characteristic	All students	Students with scored tests	Students with scored tests in 1994–99 panel
Female	46.1	47.9	49.2
Male	48.4	47.5	46.5
Non-Hispanic white	47.8	53.1	54.0
Hispanic	33.0	27.8	28.0
African American	12.6	13.3	12.5
Asian	1.0	1.0	1.1
Free or reduced-price lunch	49.8	44.2	41.2
Special education	12.5	6.4	5.1
Limited English proficiency	13.8	6.0	5.3
(Number of students)	(285,019)	(235,199)	(159,218)

Note: Percentages within social-demographic categories do not add to 100 percent because of missing data.

TAAS. The result of the exemptions and other factors reduced the initial pool of students by 17 percent. Table 1 presents the social and demographic characteristics of all 285,019 Texas third-grade students in 1994. Deleting those students who were officially exempted from the TAAS test, or excluded because of absence or other reasons, resulted in 235,199 third-grade pupils with a scored reading test.

The characteristics of third-grade students with scored tests are comparable, in general, with those of the total third-grade population. However, some differences occur because of state test exemption practices. Whereas 12.5 percent of all third graders are classified as being in special education, this group composes only slightly over 6 percent of students with scored tests because such pupils are excluded from the accountability system. Although LEP students are almost 14 percent of Texas third graders, pupils classified as having limited English proficiency represent only 6 percent of third graders with scored reading tests. The exclusion of so many LEP students results in a reduced percentage of Hispanic pupils (the ethnic group with the largest percentage of LEP students) with scored tests. Given that a large percentage of Hispanic students also tends to be economically disadvantaged, the exclusion of LEP students further decreases the proportion of students who qualify for free or reduced-price lunch in the group of pupils with scored reading tests in the spring of 1994.

The number of students on which the majority of analyses were based was further reduced by the nature of the research design adopted. We examined students' reading scores from the spring of 1994 through the spring of 1999. Consequently, students who did not have a scored TAAS reading test in each of the six years examined were deleted from the analyses. Students whose tests were not scored, and especially those who were not in Texas public schools each of the six years, may introduce extraneous factors regarding test performance that cannot be accounted for by either retention or social promotion practices. Many students left the state with their parents. Some students may have entered private schools, while a few pupils were reclassified to LEP or special education status. This stricture further reduced the number of students whose test results could be analyzed to 159,218 third-grade pupils in 1994, or almost 67 percent of the initial group of eligible students with scored tests. The result of these exclusions is that Hispanic and economically disadvantaged students are underrepresented, relative to the third-grade population. However, when compared with the group of students with scored TAAS reading tests in 1994, the social-demographic characteristics of the elementary students who remained in the six-year panel are very similar to the students who provide the basis for the 1994 third-grade accountability measures. The subset of students analyzed appears to be comparable to the eligible tested population.

The general analytical strategy utilized is to compare the test performance of two low-performing groups of students with TAAS reading scores below 70. The first group consists of those third graders with reading TLI scores below 70 who were required to repeat third grade. The reference group includes those 1994 third graders with scored reading tests below 70 who were socially promoted to grade four. Students with a reading TLI score below 70 were selected because this value will be the cutoff score required for promotion to fourth grade in 2003. The type of research design that best summarizes our analysis strategy is a variation of the nonequivalent control group design described by Donald T. Campbell and Julian C. Stanley.[22] Holding students back to repeat third grade is analogous to the treatment condition, and the regular practice of promoting low-achieving pupils to grade four is the control condition. Third-grade students who failed the 1994 TAAS reading test by earning a TLI score less than 70 but were placed into fourth grade are designated as the "socially promoted." The available data can be viewed as a quasi-experiment because low-performing readers were not randomly assigned to the retained (the equivalent of an experimental group) or the promoted group (the control group). The reading score obtained in the spring of 1994 at the end of third grade can be viewed as a pretest measure. Unlike the nonequivalent control group design described by Campbell and Stanley, which entails only a pretest and post-test measurement, additional test scores from 1995 to 1999 provide multiple time points for post-test comparisons between the two focal groups of interest; that is, the low-performing retained and socially promoted third graders.

Although we are primarily interested in the effect of third-grade retention on the two groups of students who failed the third-grade TAAS reading test, based on the cutoff score of 70 soon to be required for promotion, the test scores of two other groups of students are examined briefly. Some pupils with 1994 third-grade TAAS TLI reading scores above 70 were required to repeat third grade. For example, state educational regulations require that students repeat a grade if they miss an excessive number of school days. Consequently, among those pupils with scored reading tests each year between 1994 through 1999, 0.2 percent ($N = 329$) of the third graders were retained in third grade even though their TAAS reading TLI score was 70 or greater. The largest group of students in the panel consisted of those pupils who passed the TAAS reading test and who were promoted to the fourth grade ($N = 127,968$). The social and demographic characteristics of the four groups of students cross-classified by performance on the third-grade 1994 TAAS reading test and their promotion status are shown in table 2. Whereas almost 24 percent ($N = 56,102$) of all the third graders with a scored 1994 reading test would have failed using a cutoff TLI score of 70, the proportion of students in the 1994–99 panel failing the third-grade TAAS reading test is only about 19 percent ($N = 30,921$). The percentage of low-scoring readers in the panel sample is somewhat smaller than in the initial 1994 group of all students with scored test data.

Table 2 displays the demographic composition of the 1994 third-grade cohort followed over time within each of the four TAAS and promotion categories: failed TAAS and retained, failed TAAS and promoted, passed TAAS and retained, passed TAAS and promoted. These data enable examination of possible demographic differences between retained and socially promoted students who failed the TAAS third-grade reading test by receiving a TLI reading score less than 70. Overall few major differences emerge in the demographic composition of the retained and socially promoted pupils. Males were slightly more likely to be retained than females.[23] Non-Hispanic whites were a slightly larger proportion of the promoted low-performing students while African American pupils were less represented among those who were placed into the fourth grade. The largest difference between retained and socially promoted students is observed among the economically disadvantaged. Pupils

Table 2. Social-Demographic Characteristics of 1994 Texas Third Graders by Whether Passed TAAS Reading Test and Retained in Third Grade
Percent

Social-demographic characteristic	Failed TAAS —retained	Failed TAAS —promoted	Passed TAAS —retained	Passed TAAS —promoted	Percentage retained
Female	39.8	43.8	40.1	50.5	0.6
Male	55.7	51.6	54.1	45.2	0.8
Non-Hispanic white	27.4	33.9	48.6	58.9	0.4
Hispanic	39.6	39.5	25.2	25.3	0.9
African American	27.9	21.6	20.7	10.2	1.4
Asian	0.8	0.5	0.3	1.2	0.4
Free or reduced-price lunch	71.8	62.4	55.6	40.0	1.1
Special education	7.6	8.2	5.2	4.4	0.9
Limited English proficiency	8.3	10.4	2.1	4.1	0.8
(Number of students)	(781)	(30,140)	(329)	(127,968)	

Note: TAAS = Texas Assessment of Academic Skills. Percentages within social-demographic categories do not add to 100 percent because of missing data.

qualifying for free or reduced-price lunch composed a greater share of those students who had to repeat third grade. Of those pupils who passed the TAAS but were still retained in grade, 54.1 percent were boys. Only 45.2 percent of those passing the TAAS and promoted to fourth grade were boys. With respect to the ethnic and racial composition of students who received TLI scores equal to or greater than 70 and also were promoted, almost 59 percent were non-Hispanic white. Among pupils who passed the TAAS reading test with scores equal to or above 70, about 25 percent were Hispanic in the higher performing retained group and in the promoted category. About one-half of the students required to repeat third grade, even though their TLI reading score was above 70, were non-Hispanic white. Among students who met the reading cutoff score of 70 and who were promoted to grade four, 10.2 percent were African American. About 21 percent of the students who passed the TAAS but were retained were African American. Greater percentages of economically disadvantaged students were found in the groups of students who failed the reading test and were retained (71.8 percent), failed the reading test but were promoted (62.4 percent), or passed the reading test but were required to repeat grade three (55.6 percent). Only 40 percent of the pupils who were promoted with a TLI score of at least 70 were classified as being on free or reduced-price lunch. About 8 percent of the third graders with TLI scores below 70 were classified as being in special education. Slightly less than 5 percent of the students who passed the reading test and were promoted to grade four were denoted as special education students. Pupils with limited English proficiency were more likely to compose a greater share of all students in the two low-scoring reading groups than in the two groups of students with TLI scores of 70 or higher.

The last column in table 2 shows the percentage of 1994 third-grade students in each of the demographic categories retained in grade. Although Texas legislators in 1999 mandated that TAAS performance eventually be the major criterion for promotion to the next grade, interviews of educational administrators and teachers throughout the state revealed the decision to retain a student during these years was not based upon failing the TAAS.[24] The decision to retain a student was seldom based on TAAS scores because the results of the TAAS exam were not available to schools until about mid-May, near the end of the academic year. Instead of relying on the TAAS grade test, the decision to retain a student was generally made after the end of the fall semester. Results of a practice TAAS may have entered into the decision, but not the results of the spring TAAS. As is evident from the data in table 2, grade retention has been a rare phenomenon in Texas public schools. In 1994, 0.7 percent ($N = 1,110$) of all students were required to repeat third grade. Boys were only slightly more likely to be retained than girls. Compared with non-Hispanic whites, a slightly greater percentage of African American and Hispanic students were required to repeat grade three. However, these two groups of students also had lower reading scores. Even among the economically disadvantaged pupils, only about 1 percent were retained in grade. A slightly smaller percentage of special education students and those classified as having limited English proficiency had to repeat the third grade.

Findings

Several sets of analyses are presented: the academic performance of various subgroups of students in the 1994–99 panel classified by whether they met minimum performance standards and if retained in third grade; the impact of grade retention on all low-achieving students, taking into consideration their initial reading scores relative to the total population of pupils; and test score differences between the retained and socially promoted low-performing students after controlling for differences in social characteristics between the two groups that may affect subsequent TAAS performance.

Initial Comparisons and Subsequent Performances

The data in table 3 reveal the six-year pattern of TAAS performance among students who took the initial reading TAAS in 1994 and were followed through 1999. Average reading TLI scores for four groups of students are presented: (1) third graders with a TLI score greater than or equal to 70 who passed the TAAS reading test and were promoted to fourth grade, (2) students who passed the third-grade reading test but were required to repeat the grade, (3) students with TLI reading scores below 70 who were required to repeat third grade, and (4) students who were placed into grade four even though they did not have a passing score of 70. The table is limited only to students who took the TAAS in each of the six years. Also, data are presented only for students who were promoted annually after the spring of 1995. Students who were required to repeat a grade in later years, or who were promoted more than one grade in a single year, were excluded from the analyses so that only students in the same grades would be compared. For example, there were 127,968 third graders with scored tests in 1994 who were also tested in 1995 when in fourth grade. However, 268 of these students were not in fifth grade when the 1996 TAAS test was given because they had been required to repeat grade four.

Although we are most concerned with the academic trajectories of students who failed the TAAS reading test, examining the performance of those pupils who passed the TAAS reading test is worthwhile. Among third graders in 1994 who received a TLI score greater than 69 and were promoted to grade four (the passed TAAS—promoted group), an overall trend exists of slightly higher mean reading scores. In addition to real gains in learning, an increase in state scores was expected as teachers and students generally became more familiar with the testing procedure and were better able to anticipate the general kinds of questions asked. The exceptions occur during grade four and grade seven when the reading averages decrease slightly. Anecdotal evidence from interviews with teachers and principals suggests that the decline in fourth-grade scores may occur because this test is considered slightly more demanding than the third-grade reading test. The slight decline in reading scores between grades six and seven may occur for the same reason. In addition, the majority of Texas students transfer from an elementary school and move to a larger and more impersonal middle school between sixth and seventh grade. This transition may also help account for the slight decline in test scores between grades six and seven.

Table 3. Mean TLI Reading Scores of Retained and Socially Promoted 1994 Third-Grade Students

Pass/promoted student category	*Year*					
	1994	*1995*	*1996*	*1997*	*1998*	*1999*
Passed TAAS—promoted						
Grade	Three	Four	Five	Six	Seven	Eight
Mean TLI reading score	84.9[a]	84.5[a]	86.3[a]	88.3[a]	87.6[a]	89.0[a]
Standard deviation	6.8	10.0	10.9	9.7	8.9	8.7
Number of students	127,968	127,968	127,700	127,433	126,700	125,585
Passed TAAS—retained						
Grade	Three	Three	Four	Five	Six	Seven
Mean TLI reading score	78.3[a]	81.1[a]	80.9[a]	82.4[a]	83.6[a]	82.1[a]
Standard deviation	6.0	11.1	12.3	12.1	10.9	11.2
Number of students	329	329	327	325	320	312
Failed TAAS—retained						
Grade	Three	Three	Four	Five	Six	Seven
Mean TLI reading score	50.2	68.6	67.1	73.3[a]	73.9[a]	73.5[a]
Standard deviation	11.9	14.5	15.3	13.6	13.5	12.9
Number of students	781	781	777	771	762	732
Failed TAAS—promoted						
Grade	Three	Four	Five	Six	Seven	Eight
Mean TLI reading score	57.4	66.7	67.2	72.5[a]	73.0[a]	76.0[a]
Standard deviation	9.8	13.2	15.3	13.2	13.3	13.1
Number of students	30,140	30,140	29,612	29,328	28,740	27,709

Note: TLI = Texas Learning Index; TAAS = Texas Assessment of Academic Skills.
a. Average score indicates passing the TAAS reading test.

One group of students that has seldom been studied in previous research is the set of pupils who theoretically pass a major examination but who are then required to repeat a grade. There were 329 students who passed the TAAS reading but were retained in grade for another year. Most of these students were likely retained because of an excessive number of missed school days as the average reading score was 78.3, clearly above the passing score of 70. However, almost one-third of the retained third graders who passed the 1994 TAAS reading test had scores below 74. Perhaps their teachers felt these borderline-passing students needed to repeat the grade if they had been struggling throughout the year and had failed one or more other subjects. Regardless of the reasons for retention, overall, the retained third graders who passed the 1994 TAAS scored almost three TLI points higher when they retook the third-grade reading test in the spring of 1995. Eleven percent ($N = 35$) of these retained third graders did not pass the TAAS reading test in 1995, but over 70 percent of the 329 third-grade repeaters obtained TLI scores of 80 or higher. After being promoted to fourth grade in 1995 and taking the grade-level exam in the spring of 1996, about 83 percent of these retained third graders passed the reading test, with 60 percent scoring 80 TLI points or higher. Although the mean 1996 fourth-grade reading score declined slightly from the group's average third-grade score in 1995, this decrease was almost identical to the change observed among those 127,968 students who passed the third-grade TAAS and were promoted to the fourth grade. Those students with a third-grade TLI score above 70, who were required to repeat the grade, demonstrate a pattern of gradually increasing TLI scores over the years, except for a slight decline between sixth to seventh grade, as occurred among the students who passed the TAAS and were promoted. Requiring those third graders who passed the state's third-grade reading test to repeat the grade did not appear to be detrimental to their academic achievement in later years. However, the retained students who met minimum reading expectations may have progressed satisfactorily even if not required to repeat third grade.

Thus far, only students who had third-grade reading scores indicating a pass on the TAAS reading test have been examined. Given that grade retention has been recommended as a form of remediation for low-performing students, we are more concerned with the pattern of academic achievement among those students who did not meet minimum levels of test performance on the third-grade TAAS reading test in 1994. These are the last two groups of students represented in table 3. The 781 third graders with TLI scores below 70 in 1994 who were required to repeat the grade had a mean of 50.2, seven points lower than the average score of 57.4 from the 30,140 low-performing students who were socially promoted to the fourth grade. Compared with their initial 1994 reading score, the retained students gained more than 18 points after retaking the third-grade reading TAAS in 1995, and a net gain of nearly 17 points by fourth grade. On average, the third-grade retainees began passing the reading section of the TAAS by fifth grade in 1997. The socially promoted pupils gained 9 points over their initial score when they took the fourth grade TAAS but did not have an average score indicating TAAS passage until sixth grade, the same year that the retained students passed the fifth-grade exam. On balance, then, the retained students who failed the TAAS initially made greater improvements, but the socially promoted ultimately did as well. The majority of socially promoted students also eventually passed the TAAS. Almost 53 percent of the socially promoted third graders achieved TAAS scores equal to or greater than 70 on both the

1998 and 1999 reading test while 47 percent of them consistently obtained passing scores of 70 or higher on the 1997, 1998, and 1999 TAAS reading test.

Consideration of Regression Artifacts

The third graders who were required to repeat a year had much lower reading TAAS scores on average at the time of retention than the socially promoted pupils. These findings demonstrate that students who were retained catch up and surpass the socially promoted students. Perhaps some of the gain by the retained students was a result of their initially extreme scores on their first taking of the third-grade TAAS; their improved scores more accurately reflect their true ability, which was incorrectly measured in 1994. This phenomenon is referred to as the "regression to the mean effect," a potential threat to the validity of making comparisons that involve a group of students at the extremes of test score distributions.[25] In general, the scores of the highest performing pupils will usually decline somewhat between an initial and second test. Conversely, students with the lowest scores on an initial test will raise their scores when retaking the test. Test scores of the lowest and highest performing students will move, on average, toward the value of the overall population mean of all students. The result of this naturally occurring statistical phenomenon is that observed test scores will automatically change over time, even if the true ability of students has not changed. Statistical regression toward the mean will exist in panel data unless the Pearson correlation coefficient between the two measures is equal to 1.00.[26] Insofar as perfect linear association is never observed between individual student test scores over time, a certain amount of change in student performance over time is due to the regression to the mean effect. This statistical phenomenon has been cited as the major reason for the positive association sometimes found between grade retention practices and the temporary improved academic performance of low-scoring students. For example, Shepard, Smith, and Marion contend that the positive effect of grade retention observed among elementary students in Baltimore was only a statistical artifact of the tendency for exceptionally low-performing pupils (who were retained) to raise their scores on later examinations.[27] The question arises as to the degree to which regression effects may bias the findings shown in table 3, which compare the means of the low-performing Texas third graders who were held back a year with those socially promoted students who also failed the 1994 TAAS reading test.

With respect to the Texas data presented, a stronger case for the positive effect of retention could be made if the retained group still outperformed the socially promoted group after taking into consideration possible regression effects. The mathematical calculations used to estimate expected post–1994 average reading scores of the retained and socially promoted third graders are described in the Appendix. Table 4 contains the predicted means of the two low-performing student groups after taking into consideration regression to the mean effects. For example, the retained low-performing third graders were expected to have an average TLI score of 58.9 when taking the 1995 third-grade TAAS after an additional year in grade. That is, low-performing students required to repeat third grade should automatically experience a gain of almost 9 TLI points (that is, 58.9 – 50.2 = 8.7) as they regress toward the population mean. Given that the third-grade retainees gained about 10 more TLI points than expected (observed mean – expected mean or 68.6 – 58.9 = 9.7), one can conclude that the increased performance observed on the 1995 TAAS test was not due solely to a statistical artifact.

The more important comparisons involve the degree of change observed among the retained third graders relative to the increase in TLI scores produced by the socially promoted low-scoring third graders when both groups of pupils are in the same grade. The difference between the predicted and observed grade four mean TLI scores of the two initially low-performing groups of students is gauged in the following manner. Should the retained third graders regress to the population mean, their expected fourth-grade average should be 58.4. However, their observed mean was higher at 67.1 TLI points. Therefore, the third-grade retainees scored almost 9 points better than anticipated if regression effects occurred (67.1 – 58.4 = 8.7). Conversely, the observed fourth-grade mean reading score among the socially promoted pupils was very close to that expected as students in this group regressed toward the population mean. Their observed grade four mean was 66.7 while the group average anticipated through regression effects was 65.8, a difference of less than 1 TLI point. To determine how much better retained students performed on later TAAS tests relative to the socially promoted pupils, one subtracts the nonregression gain of the latter from the nonregression gain of the former. When both sets of students were in fourth grade, the differential gain of the retained over the socially promoted students was almost 8 TLI points (8.7 – 0.9 = 7.8). That is, after purging the data in both groups of potential regression artifacts between the initial third-grade and fourth-grade test

Table 4. Same Grade Comparisons of Mean TLI Reading Scores of Retained and Socially Promoted 1994 Third-Grade Students after Adjusting for Regression Effects

Retention/ promotion group	Observed mean	Mean expected due to regression	Difference between observed and expected means	Differential gain of retained students	Effect size
Third grade					
Retained	68.6	58.9	9.7	n.a.	n.a.
Socially promoted	57.4	n.a.	n.a.		
Fourth grade					
Retained	67.1	58.4	8.7	7.8	.52
Socially promoted	66.7	65.8	0.9		
Fifth grade					
Retained	73.3	65.5	7.8	5.9	.39
Socially promoted	67.2	65.2	2.0		
Sixth grade					
Retained	73.9	66.6	7.3	4.2	.28
Socially promoted	72.5	69.4	3.1		
Seventh grade					
Retained	73.5	68.1	5.4	2.1	.14
Socially promoted	73.0	69.7	3.3		

Note: n.a. = Not available.

results, the retained students outscored the socially promoted students by almost 8 TLI points in grade four.

A common practice to assess whether a difference between two group means is meaningful is to calculate an effect size. The mean difference between two groups is divided by the standard deviation of the population. The effect size indicates the degree to which two groups differ in standard deviation units. Jacob Cohen recommends the following terminology be used to gauge the magnitude of mean group differences.[28] An effect size of .2 suggests a "small" difference; an effect size of .5 denotes a "moderate" difference; an effect size of .8 implies a "large" difference between two groups. Although TAAS TLI scores were initially constructed in 1994 to have a population standard deviation of 15, the population standard deviations observed in later years vary from about 13 to over 16 (see table A-1 in the Appendix). Nonetheless, for the sake of consistency across all same-grade comparisons, we assumed the population standard deviation of TAAS grade-level reading means is equal to 15. The effect size for the difference between the fourth-grade averages of the retained and socially promoted students is .52 (7.8 / 15.0), suggesting that those pupils retained in grade moderately outperformed those low-scoring students placed into the fourth grade. The findings in the last column of table 4 also demonstrate that the retained third graders obtained relatively higher reading scores than the socially promoted when in grades five, six, and seven. Although the relative gains of the initially retained students decline in each of the later elementary grades, by seventh grade students required to repeat third grade earned reading scores .14 standard deviations greater than the socially promoted students who were never retained in grade. Even after controlling for regression effects, the overall conclusion drawn from the data in table 4 is that retaining the low-performing third graders did not harm their performance on the state's reading test. The retained students repeatedly received higher reading scores than the socially promoted pupils.

These initial analyses do not confirm that retention in third grade leads to negative academic consequences among Texas students or that gains fade quickly, as has been reported in previous studies. Our findings suggest that retaining third-grade students who fail the TAAS helps raise their test scores more than does the practice of social promotion. Although social promotion is eventually associated with improved TAAS performance, the completion of at least one additional grade is required to produce such effects, and test passage rates of the socially promoted students lag behind those of the third-grade retainees.

Adjusting for Social-Demographic Differences

The previous analysis utilized an analytical strategy to correct for possible regression effects that would lead to incorrect inferences regarding the magnitude of differences between the retained and socially promoted students. The next set of analyses examines differences in grade performance between retained and socially promoted students by considering variation in the social-demographic backgrounds of the two groups of students. We use an analysis of covariance procedure to help statistically equalize known differences between the retained and socially promoted students. This analytical strategy enables a more accurate assessment of the effect of grade retention on student academic achievement than was just presented because individual characteristics leading to potential group differences can be taken into consideration as well as differences in the initial level of test performance observed in third grade. The outcome measure will be the TAAS reading score of a selected grade. Seven individual-level variables are used as predictors of student reading scores. Student race or ethnicity is denoted by three binary variables (African American = 1, other = 0; Asian = 1, other = 0; Hispanic = 1, other = 0). Non-Hispanic whites are the omitted reference group. With respect to student sex, females were coded 1 while males were given a score of 0. Students listed as receiving free or reduced-price lunch were classified as economically disadvantaged and assigned a value of 1; all other students were give a value of 0. Students classified as having limited English proficiency received a score of 1 while pupils deemed proficient in English were assigned a value of 0. Special education students were given a score of 1 and non-special-education pupils received a score of 0.[29] The initial 1994 third-grade reading score was also incorporated into the analyses as a covariate when predicting student performance in later test years. After statistically adjusting for potential differences between retainees and those promoted, we assume that any differences in test scores are more likely attributable to the impact of grade retention rather than social-demographic characteristics of the students. The initial average reading scores of the two groups along with the mean averages obtained after controlling for economic and social differences between students in the retained and promoted groups are shown in table 5. The number of students classified as retained or promoted in table 5 differs from the group sizes given in tables 3 and 4. The smaller number of observations results from the lack of social and economic information available for about 6 percent of the low-performing third graders. As was the case in the earlier analyses, mean differences are based only on students in the same grade. Students who were not continually promoted are deleted from same-grade comparisons, as are pupils who were promoted more than one grade in a single academic year.

Data in table 5 show the initial average reading TLI scores by grade for both the retained third graders and those students who failed the third-grade reading section of the TAAS test but were promoted. The first comparison gives the average reading score of third-grade students who were initially retained with the average score of the socially promoted third graders. Note that the "third grade repeated" mean for the retained students was computed from the TAAS test taken at the end of their second year in third grade (that is, their 1995 test score). Scores of those socially promoted in third grade were based on test results in 1994. The small difference between the third-grade adjusted group averages in table 5 are similar to those presented earlier, even though the group of students now being analyzed differs because only students with complete social-demographic information are utilized in the computations. Of those third graders with a reading TLI score below 70 in 1994, the

Table 5. Same Grade TAAS Reading TLI Score ANCOVA Analyses, Third-Grade Retainees versus Socially Promoted Third Graders

Retention/ promotion group	Number of students	Initial mean	Initial difference	Adjusted mean	Adjusted difference	Effect size
Third grade in 1994						
Retained	736	50.3	-7.1***	...	...	...
Promoted	28,351	57.4	...	...	...	...
Third grade repeated						
Retained	736	68.9	11.5***	69.1[a]	11.7***	.78
Promoted	28,351	57.4	...	57.4[a]	...	...
Fourth grade						
Retained	732	67.1	0.4	71.1[b]	4.5***	.30
Promoted	28,351	66.7	...	66.6[b]	...	...
Fifth grade						
Retained	727	73.4	6.2***	77.8[b]	10.7***	.72
Promoted	27,853	67.2	...	67.1[b]	...	...
Sixth grade						
Retained	718	74.2	1.7	77.7[b]	5.3***	.36
Promoted	27,593	72.5	...	72.4[b]	...	...
Seventh grade						
Retained	689	73.8	0.8	77.4[b]	4.5***	.30
Promoted	27,039	73.0	...	72.9[b]	...	...

Note: TAAS = Texas Assessment of Academic Skills; TLI = Texas Learning Index.
a. Means after adjusting for student's race, sex, economic status, limited English proficiency status, and special education status.
b. Means after adjusting for student's 1994 TLI reading score, race, sex, economic status, limited English proficiency status, and special education status.
*** Significant at less than .001 percent.

retained students scored on average 7 points below the socially promoted pupils (that is, 50.3 compared with 57.4). However, the average reading TLI score of 68.9 in 1995 among the 736 retained students was 18.6 points higher than their initial score of 50.3 in 1994. Further, the retained students' average score was almost 12 points higher than the 1994 mean reading score of 57.4 observed among the socially promoted third-grade students. These findings are similar to those presented in table 3. Even after statistically adjusting for differences in student characteristics between the two groups, the adjusted difference of 11.7 is almost identical to the initial difference of 11.5 TLI points. This finding results from the inability to control for the previous year's reading score among the socially promoted students. Whereas those students repeating third grade had a third-grade score in 1994 and 1995, the socially promoted students had only one score for the third grade. The TAAS test is not given in an earlier grade, thus no indicators of earlier academic ability are available for a control variable.

Relative effect sizes of the difference between the retained and promoted third graders were calculated using the procedure described earlier. The adjusted group difference of 11.7 was divided by the presumed population reading standard deviation of 15. The effect size of .78 indicates a strong difference in third-grade test score performance between retained and socially promoted third graders. Upon retaking the third-grade reading exam in 1995, the retained pupils outscored the socially promoted students by almost .8 of a standard deviation. That the students retained in third-grade would do better than those low-performing pupils placed in the next grade is to be expected. Insofar as the retained third-grade students have been tested on third-grade information that has been covered a second time, one would anticipate that the 1995 reading score of the students required to repeat the grade would be higher than the initial 1994 third-grade score of those socially promoted students who covered the material only once. However, examining the same-grade performance of the retained and socially promoted students beyond their third-grade scores suggests that those students who were held back in third grade continued to do as well, if not surpass the academic achievement of the socially promoted. To illustrate, the initial average reading score of the retained third graders was similar to that of the socially promoted third graders when both groups were in fourth grade (that is, 67.1 versus 66.7). But the adjusted group mean of the retained students is 4.5 TLI points greater than that of the socially promoted pupils. Assuming that the fourth-grade reading population standard deviation is 15, the adjusted mean of the retained students was .3 of a standard deviation higher than that obtained among the socially promoted pupils. These findings also indicate that, if the retained and socially promoted students had comparable third-grade reading scores and similar social characteristics, the third-grade retainees, after being retested at the end of the repeat grade, would just exceed the cutoff passing score of 70. The third-grade retainees passed the TAAS reading test by fourth grade while the socially promoted would not pass the test until sixth grade. The retained students achieve an adjusted mean of 71.1 in fourth grade while the socially promoted students do not reach a mean over 70 (that is, 72.4) until two years later in sixth grade.

The gap between retained and socially promoted students was even greater when the low-performing students were tested in grade five. The effect size of .72 indicates an appreciably higher test performance among the retained than the socially promoted students. The retained third-grade students also had relatively higher reading scores in the sixth and seventh grades than the low-performing students placed out of third grade. Although the impact of retention appears to decrease slightly on an annual basis after fifth grade, the magnitudes of these effect coefficients demonstrate that third-grade retention continues to exhibit a substantial positive effect on test performance. Given that the estimated effect sizes are equal to or larger than .30 in grades five through seven, the findings suggest that the retained students had a meaningfully higher level of academic performance than did the socially promoted students. The findings presented in table 5 imply that not only did the retained third graders learn the material they had previously failed to comprehend but they also continued to consistently outperform their socially promoted peers in later grades.

The nature of the gap between the adjusted average TAAS reading scores is graphically depicted in figure 1. This figure illustrates the pattern of reading scores for both the retained students and the socially promoted pupils. Adjusting for initial levels of reading performance and differences in socioeconomic characteristics reveals that the retained students consistently obtained higher reading scores than the socially promoted third graders. Although the mean difference in reading scores was considerably greater on the fifth-grade TAAS test, the third-grade retainees earned about 5 more TLI points in grades four, six, and seven than the socially promoted students.

The analysis of covariance findings presented in table 5 suggests a more positive impact of grade retention than shown in the prior analyses that controlled only for regression to the mean effects. Critics of the covariance analyses, which control for differences in the social characteristics of students, could argue that the higher scores of the retained students are overstated because the tendency for low-scoring students to regress to the mean is not adequately controlled. Insofar as the initial 1994 reading scores of retained students were lower on average than the mean reading score of the socially promoted students, it is not unreasonable to assume that test scores of the retainees may increase at a faster rate than those of students placed into grade four. Because of the fallible nature of test results, students with the lowest scores will likely report improved results upon retaking the test. While such reasoning is plausible, it is highly improbable that the average test score of retained students would significantly surpass the mean test score of the socially promoted students, if the increase in reading scores was due solely to regression effects. The analysis of covariance findings show that those pupils required to repeat third grade had a substantially greater increase in their reading scores than observed among the low-scoring third graders socially

Figure 1. Promoted versus Retained Third Graders: Same Grade Comparisons

Adjusted average TAAS TLI reading score

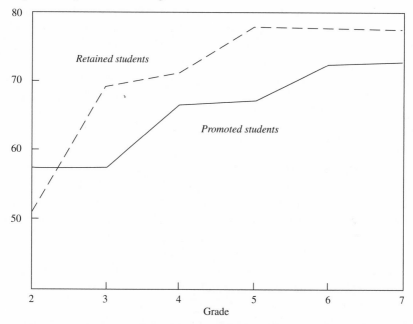

Note: TAAS = Texas Assessment of Academic Skills; TLI = Texas Learning Index.

promoted to grade four. This overall pattern of higher adjusted reading averages among the lower scoring retained students is contrary to the nature of findings expected in the kind of nonequivalent control group design used in this paper to compare low-achieving students. Donald T. Campbell and Albert Erlebacher argue that ex post facto research designs, in which the experimental group has initial lower scores than the matched control group, usually result in findings indicating that the control group outperforms the students receiving an educational intervention.[30] This commonly reported finding results from a statistical regression artifact. According to this logic, the existence of regression to the mean effects in our covariance analyses should yield results in which the socially promoted students demonstrate higher reading scores in each of the test years examined. The fact that the covariance analyses findings are the opposite of those expected lends greater support to the beneficial effect of grade retention on later student test performance.

We recognize that the analysis of covariance results on retention presented here has shortcomings. The covariance analysis assumes that both the retained and socially promoted students regress toward a mean that is common to academically challenged students, instead of the value of the population mean of all test takers. The statistical procedure used here presumes the true reading level of the initially low-scoring students is below the population mean. Such a supposition is reasonable, as the average TAAS reading scores of the two low-performing groups remain at least one-half a standard deviation below the population means. Statistical adjustments made in the covariance analyses have also not been corrected for potential measurement error in the reading scores. Future research that simultaneously adjusts for both differences in student personal characteristics that affect academic achievement and potential regression effects is required to yield a more accurate assessment of the impact of grade retention among these low-performing third graders. At worst, the covariance analysis results shown here may provide an estimated upper boundary of the effect of grade retention among these students.

Alternative Methodological Explanations for the Findings

The overall pattern of results indicates that requiring low-performing students to repeat a grade does not harm their academic performance. The findings support the position that holding low-performing students back an additional year in school provides them more time to obtain the skills necessary for later success in school. Nevertheless, several methodological criticisms could be raised that challenge the interpretation of the reported results. Although we have assumed that the significantly higher scores of the retained students result from students learning the required material during the year of retention, alternative explanations for the improved reading scores focus on the nature of the TAAS reading tests. Critics could argue that the level of difficulty of the reading tests decreased from one year to the next. If the test taken at the end of the repeated year was easier than that of the same grade level in the previous year, one would anticipate higher scores on the test given at the end of the retention year. Support for this argument is weak because the state spends considerable effort to ensure that the level of difficulty for each grade-level test remains constant from year to year. Another alternative explanation for the observed higher scores at the end of the retention year concerns the possibility of testing effects. Insofar as students who retook the reading test at the end of their second year in a specific grade would have a much better idea of what to expect on the second test, one might conclude that the higher scores on the repeated test are spuriously high. However, the state does not give the same TAAS reading examination every year. Again, considerable resources are devoted to preparing a different test, but one that still covers the state's required learning objectives. Further, school districts commonly administer prior versions of the TAAS as practice exercises during the year, thereby familiarizing both retained and socially promoted students with the TAAS format for the specific grade.

Those who doubt the positive effect of grade retention might also question the validity of the findings because analyses are based only on students who had scored tests for each of the years studied. Students not tested each year because of exemptions, absences, or migration were excluded from the analyses. Students with missing information in their records were omitted from many of the analyses. The deletion of such students may raise the suspicion that the exclusion of students with incomplete scored tests or missing social-demographic data might somehow bias the findings. For example, students with complete records may be in a more stable family environment or experience less geographic mobility than students with only partial records. Perhaps the parents of students with complete information are more conscientious in providing requested data to their schools than are the parents of students with missing information. Should the parents of students with complete records also be more concerned about their children's education than are the parents of students with missing information, the effects of retention presented in this report may be biased. Another possibility is that there is a hidden bias in record-keeping. That is, instead of record-keeping errors resulting in missing data being random, certain schools with certain student demographic characteristics would be less likely to have accurate and complete records on their students than others. The Texas Education Agency's sanctioning in 2000 of some districts for inaccurate and incomplete dropout records suggests that hidden biases are plausible. This study's findings would apply largely to students whose parents take a greater interest in the children's education or to students attending schools where record-keeping is more accurate. Data required to address this concern do not exist.

Critics of the present findings might also argue that the importance placed upon TAAS results is so great that teachers and administrators will purposely try to ensure that students likely to perform poorly on the TAAS are omitted from the pool of scored tests used to judge school performance. For example, the test-taking status of many at-risk students may be reclassified to exempt them from the accountability system. Given that the test scores of many special education students are not counted, low-performing students in 1994 or in later years could have been reclassified as being in special education to exclude them from the group of students used to assess school performance. Opponents of grade retention might contend that the higher performance of the students required to repeat a grade is due to greater relative numbers of low-performing retained students being reclassified into the special education category, and hence omitted from the panel of students analyzed.

To ascertain whether changes in the special education classification of students might affect the findings, we examined the change in test-taking status of students from 1994 to 1999. Pupils with a scored test used for the state's accountability system are coded "S" while students classified in special education are usually given a code of "X" and are not to be scored. That is, the reading scores of these special education students will not be used to evaluate a school's educational performance.[31] Analyses revealed that 10 percent of the low-performing retained third graders with a scored test in 1994 had been reclassified to special education status by 1999. Similarly, about 9 percent of the low-scoring socially promoted students with a scored test in 1994 had been reclassified to special education status by 1999. In short, the proportion of students reclassified to the special education category between 1994 and 1999 was about the same for both retained and socially promoted students. Therefore, the higher reported test performance of the retained students over time is not likely due to differential placement of low-performing pupils in the special education category.

To address further the likely effect of panel attrition on the report's findings, we examined the characteristics of students for whom scored tests existed in 1994 but not in 1999. Students for whom annual test scores were available each year were denoted as "panel stayers" while students lacking a test score by 1999 were labeled "panel leavers." Among the 1,386 third graders in 1994 with a TAAS reading TLI less than 70 who repeated third grade, 44 percent had exited from the panel by 1999. This percentage is only slightly larger than the 41 percent of all socially promoted third graders with TLI scores lower than 70 in 1994 who had exited the panel by 1999. Whether students were retained in third grade or placed into grade four had little relationship to their continuation in the Texas educational accountability system.

Another way to help determine if the findings are biased is to examine whether students remaining in the 1994–99 panel differed in reading ability compared with the students who eventually exited the panel. Additional analyses revealed that the reading TLI scores for the panel stayers and leavers were similar. The average reading score among the retained third graders in 1994 who remained in the panel through 1999 was 50.2 while the mean score of the retained third graders who eventually exited the panel was slightly lower at 46.0 TLI points. Likewise, the average 1994 reading TLI scores for the socially promoted third graders who exited and remained in the panel were similar. In 1994 the mean reading score among the socially promoted panel stayers was 57.4 while the average reading TLI for those socially promoted third graders not in the panel by 1999 was slightly lower at 52.6. Although the initial level of reading ability among students who dropped out of the data set was somewhat below that of students incorporated into the analyses, the differences in the reading ability levels of students exiting the panel and those remaining were comparable in both the retained and socially promoted group of third graders.

A final procedure was used to examine whether the effects of grade retention we report apply to students who lacked a scored test in each of the years studied. One panel of students consisted of the low-performing third graders, required to repeat third grade, who had scored TAAS reading tests in both 1994 and 1999, the first and last years of the study period. Although numerous combinations of students with missing test scores across the period of study could be explored, there is little reason to believe that the results would differ from examining test results among pupils missing at least one scored reading test in 1995, 1996, 1997, or 1998. Further, focusing on the first and last year of available data enables us to utilize the largest number of retained third graders with test results. Seventy-nine percent (1,099 out of 1,386) of the initial low-performing 1994 third-grade retainees also had seventh-grade reading results in 1999. The average reading scores of these retained third graders were compared with the reading scores of the socially promoted third graders who also failed the TAAS reading test. To maximize the number of observations among the low-performing third graders, who were not initially retained in grade three, we selected those third graders placed into grade four who had a scored seventh-grade reading test in 1998. Of the initial 50,763 pupils failing the third-grade TAAS who were socially promoted to grade four, 38,665, or 76 percent, of the initial students had usable reading scores in 1994 and 1998. To help ensure that students were in the same grade for comparisons, the number of years required in the panel for the socially promoted third graders is one year less than that needed for the third-grade retainees.

The initial third-grade averages and seventh-grade reading means for the expanded set of students who did not meet the state's minimum reading requirements are shown in table 6. More students are included in the table

Table 6. Mean TLI Reading Scores of Retained and Socially Promoted Students Failing the Reading TAAS in 1994 in Grade Three with Incomplete Records

Retention/ promotion group	1994 Grade three	1995 Grade three	1996 Grade four	1997 Grade five	1998 Grade six	1999 Grade seven
Retained (N = 1,099)						
Mean TLI reading score	50.3	...	...	...	...	72.3[a]
Standard deviation	12.1	...	...	...	...	13.5

	1994 Grade three	1995 Grade four	1996 Grade five	1997 Grade six	1998 Grade seven	1999 Grade eight
Promoted (N = 38,665)						
Mean TLI reading score	56.4	...	...	...	70.9[a]	...
Standard deviation	10.5	...	...	...	14.4	...

Note: TLI = Texas Learning Index; TAAS = Texas Assessment of Academic Skills.
a. Average score indicates passing the TAAS reading test.

because data from only two years were required for the socially promoted and retained third graders. Examining the 1994 average reading scores of the retained and socially promoted third graders shows that the retained students scored about 6 points lower on the TAAS reading test than did the pupils placed into grade four (that is, 50.3 versus 56.4). In 1999 when the third-grade retainees were at the end of seventh grade, their average score of 72.3 was slightly higher than the seventh-grade reading score (70.9) of the low-performing third graders placed into fourth grade at the end of 1994. Those third graders held back a year had increased their reading performance by 22 TLI points while the level of reading ability among the socially promoted third graders increased by almost 15 points. The predicted seventh-grade reading means for the two groups of initially low-achieving readers based upon possible regression effects were also calculated. The expected seventh-grade reading TLI score for the retained students was 68.1 while the socially promoted pupils were expected to have a seventh-grade mean of 69.2. The retained students outperformed the socially promoted pupils by .17 of a standard deviation on the seventh-grade TAAS reading test. The effect size is similar to that reported in table 4 (.15) based on a smaller set of students with scored tests in each of the years between 1994 and 1999. These supplemental analyses indicate that the positive effect of retaining third-grade students is not likely the result of changes in the composition of the student panel.

Summary and Discussion

This study sought to determine the academic effects of retention in grade and social promotion on subsequent school performances, following initial failure on the Texas mandatory standardized reading test. The overall findings suggest that retaining low-performing third-grade students an additional year in grade was not harmful to their later academic performance. Analyses that attempted to control for initial differences between retained and socially promoted pupils revealed that retention appeared to help low-achieving students pass the state reading examination more quickly than students who were socially promoted. The academic performance advantage became even clearer for students who were retained in grade after controlling for initial differences with the socially promoted students. Further, in contrast to some previous studies, we did not find that the gains in learning achieved during the year of retention completely dissipated after several years. Students not meeting grade-level assessment standards, but who were advanced to the next grade level, took longer on average to pass the TAAS reading test.

Nonetheless, the results revealed that, on average, many of the socially promoted low-achieving third-grade students eventually passed the TAAS reading test in a later grade. Critics of grade retention would argue that this finding negates the necessity of holding students back an additional year because most students eventually perform satisfactorily at some time beyond grade three. Some individuals advocating placing low-achieving students in the next grade level believe that these children, if given enough time, will eventually demonstrate satisfactory school performance. Our findings indicate that many of the socially promoted third-grade students in Texas do pass the TAAS test by fifth or sixth grade. Proponents of social promotion would argue that the emotional hardships experienced by retained children and their parents are unnecessary because such children will mature sufficiently in a few years and will then be able to learn the required curriculum. However, we have analyzed all students with a score below 70 because the Texas legislature mandated this value as the cutoff standard for promotion to the next grade. It may be that a TLI score of 70, soon to be required for promotion to the fourth grade, is too high and that students with lower scores (for example, between 60 and 69) might have a high probability of performing satisfactorily in the next academic year. Further analyses are required to ascertain the estimated passage rates of pupils with scores lower than 70.

Before reaching any general conclusions about the impact of retaining low-performing students in grade, several issues should be considered. For example, we have not addressed the psychological impact of requiring students to repeat a grade. Most critics of grade retention argue that holding students back a year, while their classmates advance to a higher grade, lowers the retained students' self-esteem and generates a negative orientation toward school, thereby reducing any positive effect of retention. Retention is viewed as so stigmatizing that social promotion is the option of choice among its advocates. Our access to only institutional academic records precludes us from investigating this argument. Because educational proficiency is most often used to evaluate the effectiveness of educational systems, it is more important from a policy perspective to examine pupil performance instead of their sense of self-worth. Although how students perceive themselves may have some effect on their success in school, the present analyses focus only on student test performance outcomes.

A second concern regarding the generalizability of the findings is whether the positive impact of grade retention observed among Texas third graders applies to students required to repeat a later grade. The present analyses focus only on holding students back in one elementary grade. The beneficial effect of holding students back another year in any subsequent year may be less pronounced in later elementary grades or in middle school. Critics of retention often cite research based on students retained in middle school or high school to support their contention that requiring students to repeat a grade is an ineffective, if not harmful, remediation strategy. Additional analyses examining existing TEA data, indicating whether students held back an additional year in more advanced elementary grades or in secondary grades, are required to address the general question of grade retention effectiveness in Texas.

Another limitation of this study pertains to the lack of knowledge about the educational activities devoted to low-performing readers who were retained in grade and those who were socially promoted to the next grade. Although we have no data indicating the specific instructional services that individual low-performing elementary students received, a related study suggests that Texas educators attempted to provide a similar array of remediation services to all academically challenged elementary students, regardless of whether the children had been retained in grade or socially promoted.[32] In-depth interviews of administrators and teachers in twelve Texas metropolitan school districts indicated that students with TLI scores below 70 who had been socially promoted often received comparable compensatory services (for example, more individualized attention on problem areas and additional staff tutoring) provided to students required to repeat a grade. Educational practitioners stated that many socially promoted students received considerable assistance to help them learn material they had failed in the previous academic year. The interview data suggest that school remediation practices appeared to be the same for low-performing retained and socially promoted students. The fact that both the retained and socially promoted pupils likely received similar additional educational support may help explain why many of the socially promoted Texas elementary students eventually passed the state's mandatory annual examinations. If extra educational support had been provided only to students required to repeat a grade, while the learning needs of socially promoted pupils were largely ignored, the effect of grade retention would probably have been much greater in the current study.

Moreover, schools that are successful in raising the scores of retained students are often successful in raising the scores of the socially promoted, while schools that fail in raising the scores of the retained also fail with the socially promoted. Elsewhere we have noted that schools producing high achievement among economically disadvantaged students resemble schools that cater to the economically advantaged: They have high expectations, they trust the students and teachers, and they begin writing and reading very early.[33] Thus, retained and socially promoted students may both receive access to summer school, extended day programs, pull-out programs, one-on-one instruction, and a broad range of remediation activities designed to help raise academic achievement. There is a limit, however, to how much can be done through these measures. Students whose initial scores are low seem to make significant and sustained improvements if they are retained in grade, but not so clearly when they are socially promoted. Critics of grade retention often contend that requiring students to repeat a grade does little to raise their academic performance because such children will only reexperience a similar negative learning environment responsible for the retention. Conversely, proponents of grade retention usually assume that repeating a grade is the only practice that will ensure children learn the material necessary to be successful in later grades. Our research findings imply that both grade retention and social promotion practices may result in improved academic achievement, if low-achieving students have access to additional instructional resources.

Should educational administrators decide that large numbers of low-achieving students will be better served by repeating a grade, the financial cost associated with retaining elementary school children requires consideration.

Assume that the reported higher TAAS reading scores obtained by retained low-performing readers are attributable to making students repeat third grade. Insofar as the findings indicate that many of the socially promoted low-performing third-grade readers also begin passing the TAAS reading test by grade five, the question arises as to whether the financial cost of retaining all of the students with a TLI score below 70 (the mandated cutoff point for grade retention) is justifiable. TEA data indicate there were 52,159 third graders in 1994 who would have been required to repeat the grade because their TAAS reading score was below 70. Had all of these students been required to repeat grade three, the additional estimated cost to the state would have been about $261 million.[34] This projected cost is based on only one cohort of third graders. The legislature would likely have to increase the state's educational budget should large numbers of third graders be held back every year. The legislative mandate to retain all third graders who fail the state's required reading test may incur further expense.

The data examined in this study show that only a small percentage of low-performing students are retained in third grade. It is uncertain whether the positive effects of holding students back an additional year would be observed if all low-performing elementary students were required to repeat a grade. Whereas school teachers in Texas may have thus far been able to provide failing students the extra assistance needed to help bring them up to grade level, massive grade retention may overwhelm teachers' abilities to remediate academically challenged youngsters. Whether the actual numbers of third graders will explode, as some detractors of the new educational promotional guidelines feel will occur, is questionable. Along with establishing more stringent promotion standards, the legislature increased funding in 1999 to provide additional resources to the early elementary grades, with the hope that additional resources and teacher training would help raise the ability of academically challenged readers before they enter third grade. Before third grade, students are to be tested regularly and given extra assistance so that they will be reading at grade level before entering grade three. The effectiveness of these earlier educational interventions will help determine whether the number of third graders retained in grade increases substantially beginning in 2003.

Another issue that must be addressed is whether the positive effect of grade retention observed in Texas would occur if implemented in other states. Advocates of a stringent grade retention policy may be tempted to use the reported findings to argue that the demonstrated growth in academic achievement among those Texas elementary students required to repeat a grade would emerge in other states. Our sense is that it may be difficult to generalize the findings we observe to other states because of the nature of the Texas educational accountability system. The Texas accountability system, implemented to assess the effectiveness of the state's schools, places considerable emphasis on ensuring that all eligible students are evaluated annually. School districts, principals, and teachers are forced to consider the educational performance of all students within their domain. The state includes the test scores of pupils who have been held back a year in school as well as the scores of socially promoted children in the pool of TAAS examinations used to rank the educational effectiveness of school campuses. A result is that, whether students are retained or socially promoted, teachers are under pressure to raise the performance of all students, even if they are struggling with their studies, to at least a minimal level of competency. Requiring pupils to repeat a grade in school districts lacking an accountability system may not result in pronounced academic gains because teachers would be able to ignore the special needs of pupils required to repeat a grade. Perhaps the weak overall effect on student cognitive performance of making students repeat a grade observed in many prior retention studies resulted from the absence of an educational accountability system. The beneficial academic impact of holding elementary students back in grade a year may be more likely to occur if a structured accountability system exists. Whether academically challenged retained children (or even socially promoted students) in other states would demonstrate the same pattern of learning gains in reading reported here is unknown. Without a similar accountability structure, there would be less incentive (either positive or negative) for elementary teachers to bring low-achieving students up to an acceptable level of educational proficiency. To generalize the findings regarding the benefits of grade retention presented in this study requires replication of the analyses in schools located in other states that have implemented an equally rigorous educational accountability system. The possibility exists then, that to reap benefits from grade retention, states must implement educational accountability systems that have significant consequences for districts and schools that fail to serve all of their children.

To summarize, we concur with the U.S. Department of Education's 1999 observation in *Taking Responsibility for Ending Social Promotion: A Guide for Educators and State and Local Leaders*.[35] Ultimately, neither generic grade retention nor generic social promotion practices by themselves are optimal solutions for the learning problems of children not meeting educational achievement standards. Both strategies represent systemic failures to aid children. Unlike many previous studies, however, our data suggest that the gains made through retention are not lost over time. Still, social promotion also is associated with sustained gains. Both students who were required to repeat third grade and those socially promoted students whose average third-grade scores are higher than those of the retained students will likely pass the TAAS in the same year. This would lead to the conclusion that, while retention may lead to improved educational performance, social promotion reaches the same end in the same amount of time. However, among the socially promoted students whose scores are as low as the average of the retained group, social promotion is less likely to lead to TAAS passage in the same number of successive testings than is retention. In this instance there appears to be an academic advantage to retention.

What then can we conclude about the effects of retention in Texas? First, the data do not support the conclusions of the National Research Council and Lorrie A. Shepard and Mary Lee Smith, who contend that retention fails to produce sustainable growth in academic achievement.[36] Our findings are more congruent with those of Karl L. Alexander, Doris R. Entwisle, and Susan L. Dauber, who concluded that grade retention can sometimes benefit academically challenged students.[37] However, we must qualify our conclusions regarding the effects of grade retention following failure on the state's TAAS reading test. We propose that our findings result from the context of the Texas accountability system. To produce sustainable academic benefits, the practice of requiring low-performing students to repeat a grade may necessitate an accountability system that disaggregates results such that schools are held responsible for the achievement of all groups of students. Long-term beneficial outcomes of grade retention may be more forthcoming if teachers know they will be held responsible for the performance of students who have failed to meet the minimum standards for a specific grade level.

Appendix: Calculation of Regression Effects

Four pieces of information are required to estimate the expected or predicted average reading scores of the retained and socially promoted third graders, if individuals regress toward the overall population mean over time. First needed are the population mean of the initial reading scores in 1994, the population mean of the reading scores at the end of the period being examined, and the 1994 mean reading score of each specific group. The population regression coefficient obtained by regressing the later Texas Learning Index (TLI) reading score on the 1994 reading score is also mandatory to calculate the magnitude of the regression to the mean effect. Although many discussions of regression effects utilize the population correlation to gauge regression effects, Donald T. Campbell and David A. Kenny point out that the population regression slope should be used instead of the correlation if population means and standard deviations change over time.[38] The specific formula used to estimate the predicted average of a group whose members are regressing toward the population mean, obtained from Campbell and Kenny, is[39]

$$\overline{Y}_{jt}' = \overline{Y}_t + \beta_{yx}(\overline{X}_{j1} - \overline{X}_1).$$

The symbol $\overline{Y}_{jt}'$ denotes the average reading TLI score for either the retained or socially promoted group (j) of students predicted for a later grade after adjusting for possible regression to the mean effects. $\overline{Y}_t$ refers to the population mean reading TLI score for all students tested in a specific grade at a later period. The population regression slope β_{yx} indicates the linear relationship between the 1994 reading scores and the reading scores for the later grade of comparison. The average TLI score for either the retained or socially promoted third graders in 1994 is indicated by $\overline{X}_{j1}$ while $\overline{X}_1$ denotes the population mean of the 1994 reading TLI scores based on all third graders with a scored test.

Because the retained third graders are always one grade behind the socially promoted students in each test year after 1994, the respective population grade means for each of the two groups of third graders will vary across test years. For example, the mean fourth-grade score of the third-grade retainees was measured in 1996 while the average fourth-grade score of the socially promoted third graders who failed the Texas Assessment of Academic Skills (TAAS) reading test was observed in 1995. The predicted fourth-grade mean reading score for the retained third graders was based on the population means in 1994 and 1996 whereas the predicted grade four mean of the socially promoted third graders will be derived from the 1994 and 1995 population means. Similarly, the slope coefficient used to estimate the degree of regression to the mean among the retained third graders is based on population data from the 1994 and 1996 reading tests. The slope for the socially promoted low-scoring third graders is derived by regressing the 1995 reading scores of all students in fourth grade on the 1994 test scores of all students. Presumably, a more accurate estimate of the true difference in student achievement between the retained and socially promoted students can be obtained by comparing the adjusted means between the two groups because possible regression to the mean effects have been removed from the data.

The population means, standard deviations, and number of students tested each year in the grades of interest are shown in table A-1. The population means and standard deviations are not based on the same students in each test period because some students leave Texas public schools while others enter the state's public schools. Two sets of means and standards are given in table A-1. Columns three, four, and five present, respectively, the mean, standard deviations, and number of students who took the TAAS reading test beginning in 1994 when they were in third grade. The average reading TLI scores in column three are used to calculate the regression effects for low-performing third-grade readers who were socially promoted in 1994 to fourth grade. Estimated regression to the mean effects for the retained third graders are based on the mean reading TLI scores presented in column seven. The averages in column seven are used for the retained students because they are one grade behind the socially promoted students. To illustrate, the mean used to calculate fourth-grade regression effects among the socially promoted students is 79.5. The retained third graders were not in grade four until 1996. Consequently, the 1996 fourth-grade average of 78.6 in column seven was used to estimate regression to the mean effects among the low-performing readers required to repeat the third grade. The population regression slopes and correlations are presented in table A-2. Given that two test scores are required to calculate the linear relationship between the 1994 and later grade tests, all students with a scored TAAS reading test in each of the two years covered were included in the computations. Incorporating all students with a scored reading test in each of the years examined, instead of limiting the analyses only to students with a scored test in each of the six years, yields a more accurate assessment of the population slopes and correlations.

To illustrate how the information shown in tables A-1 and A-2 was used to obtain the predicted means given in table 4, the following computations were performed. For example, the predicted 1995 third-grade average reading score for those retained third graders was calculated in the following manner:

Retained third graders: Predicted 1995 third-grade mean
$$58.9 = 77.5 + .677 (50.2 - 77.7) \quad N = 781$$

Table A-1. Means and Standard Deviations of Texas Students with Scored Reading Tests

Test year	Grade	Grade mean	Standard deviation	Number of students
TAAS data beginning in 1994				
1994	3	77.7	15.0	235,199
1995	4	79.5	14.0	236,935
1996	5	80.1	16.1	249,809
1997	6	81.9	14.7	265,766
1998	7	81.4	14.1	270,239
1999	8	83.9	13.1	262,408
TAAS data beginning in 1995				
1995	3	77.5	15.6	230,883
1996	4	78.6	16.3	239,868
1997	5	82.4	15.1	251,356
1998	6	82.4	14.3	255,310
1999	7	82.1	13.4	265,126

Note: TAAS = Texas Assessment of Academic Skills. Means and standard deviations were calculated by the authors from Texas Education Agency data files.

Table A-2. Regression Coefficients and Correlations of Texas Students with Scored Reading Tests

Years on which linear associations are based	Regression coefficient	Correlation coefficient	Number of students
1994, 1995	.677	.702	207,044
1994, 1996	.734	.685	201,614
1994, 1997	.614	.659	195,475
1994, 1998	.574	.644	190,045
1994, 1999	.510	.596	183,297

Note: Regression coefficients and correlations were calculated by the authors from Texas Education Agency data files.

The predicted fourth-grade means, respectively, for the low-achieving retained third graders and the socially promoted third graders were calculated as follows:

Retained third graders: Predicted fourth-grade mean
$$58.4 = 78.6 + .734 (50.2 - 77.7) \quad N = 777$$

Socially promoted third graders: Predicted fourth-grade mean
$$65.8 = 79.5 + .677 (57.4 - 77.7) \quad N = 30,140$$

These calculations indicate that those students who failed the 1994 TAAS reading test and were required to repeat third grade would be expected to have an average score of 58.9 when they retook the third-grade TAAS reading test in 1995. Their 1996 fourth-grade reading average should be 58.4 TLI points if they regressed toward the population mean of all students with scored reading tests. Alternately, the socially promoted third graders would have an expected average of 65.8 TLI points on the 1995 fourth-grade TAAS reading exam if they regressed toward the population mean for that test year.

Comment by Andrew Rotherham

Jon Lorence, A. Gary Dworkin, Laurence A. Toenjes, and Antwanette N. Hill provide empirical evidence to help inform the ongoing debate about grade retention and social promotion. Although their study does not put the issue to rest in favor of retention, it should cause participants in the debate to pause. Researchers can argue almost indefinitely about the significance of most findings, and this study is no exception. However, in a debate where ideology frequently trumps evidence, Lorence and his colleagues offer important information for the policy community, particularly because they contradict prevailing beliefs (and other significant studies) with data. I want to frame this discussion more with an eye toward the relevance of the authors' evidence to the policy debate instead of toward the statistical significance of the findings. Regardless of whether or not one supports policies to curtail social promotion, these policies are going to be a fixture of the education policy landscape for some time to come. And, although the authors provide a useful admonition not to generalize from these findings, because they involve only Texas, that will inevitably happen and thus a discussion of some other more general issues is important.

Because this study is based on Texas Assessment of Academic Skills (TAAS) data, it brings a host of other issues into play. Whether one comes to praise or bury Texas, strong feelings arise about the reforms and changes that have occurred and are ongoing there. As the authors point out, one reason for the results they found could be the accountability system in place in Texas. This system is causing attention and energy, as well as resources, to be directed at the group of students who are affected by social promotion policies. In addition, the accountability system's focus on disaggregated results also provides data that are useful for informing this discussion. Finally, Texas has not worked to address teacher professional development and overall teacher quality issues with the vigor of some other states. In light of the results to date, one wonders how much more substantial progress might have been made if, in addition to the other measures that were put in place, the state undertook sustained efforts to address teacher quality.

Unfortunately, the debate is frequently framed as simply about social promotion versus retention, as simply a matter of policy with little nuance. The authors point out the false choice of this dialogue. First, policy must be constructed to address a glaring deficiency. Except perhaps for absurdly low standards, some students will always struggle to meet academic standards, and supports need to be in place to help them. The scale of this challenge in some areas, particularly low-income school districts, is staggering. A larger, related issue is the chronic failure to educate a large number of students, predominately poor and minority students. And, while many will protest that no district has in place a policy of social promotion, the evidence is clear that a de facto policy frequently exists. Second, the polarized nature of the debate belies the fact that evidence does not overwhelmingly support one position or the other. Neither of the stark alternatives offers much educationally. Simply promoting children from grade to grade or just retaining them for second year of instruction that obviously fell short the first time is something of a Hobson's choice for students.

Four policy implications follow from this study, which policymakers must consider as part of the dialogue about grade retention and social promotion. These are time, interventions, school effectiveness, and assessments.

Time is a crucial element because, too often, it is treated as a constant rather than a variable. This is largely an outgrowth of inertia and the antiquated way school districts and schools are organized, for example, in terms of work rules and school calendars. But where it is set down in stone that a student at age X must be in grade Y? Changing this assumption can be difficult, as school superintendents who have tried, for example, to introduce ungraded programs in K–3 have discovered or as the debate over social promotion illustrates. Standards have the potential to move educators and policymakers past this because they focus on what students should know and be able to do in a relatively concrete way. Also, any discussion of time necessarily raises questions about the school day, school year, and so forth. The research on these points, particularly for low-income students, is relatively clear, and that raises the issue of interventions.

As the authors point out, the quality and the quantity of interventions to help struggling students in Texas vary, and the same variation can be found in districts around the country. The crux of an effective promotion policy is the quality of the intervention for students who need extra help. Consider what happens when an airline flight is in distress—the resources that come into play to support and help that plane. Or as Chris Whittle points out, consider a package sent by Federal Express. Its status can be tracked anywhere in the world, and if it gets off-course, assistance is immediately available. But then think about academically at-risk students. Much more often than not, they do not have that sort of comprehensive support. Often their distress (or whereabouts in the Whittle analogy) remains unknown to those charged with their education. Or, too often when a problem is realized, little can be done about it. Any state or community that is considering implementing some sort of policy to curtail social promotion must consider what it will do to help students who are in trouble. The authors discuss the issue of scale in Texas in terms of numbers of retained students, which is an issue for school districts and states nationwide. The quality of interventions is keenly related to the number of students being served and to available resources. Further, in terms of the nature of the interventions, terms such as "research-based" are frequently invoked. Policymakers must, if schools are going to move toward a strategy of focusing on achievement, be relentless in focusing on what works. That is, they must focus on evidence, not ideology. Here, Washington can play a key role by supporting research and ensuring that a rich market of information is available for practitioners and policymakers. Such a leadership role has been abdicated for far too long. With hope, the matter will be addressed in the future.

The third issue is school effectiveness. The public debate on social promotion or retention is often held in the context of how a well-functioning school would respond to the problem of remediating low-achieving students. There seems to be an assumption that if schools know which students need extra help, they will reorient toward helping those students and their teachers, using information, and tackling the problem. Essentially, this argument posits, if policymakers end social promotion, the schools will respond by changing or just working harder. Some schools do adapt. However, many schools simply do not have the capacity to do so. Nor do their school districts have the capacity for large-scale interventions. Not surprisingly, the authors found that schools that were effective in raising the achievement of retained students also frequently succeeded with socially promoted students.

Studies of the allocation of federal dollars at the school level bolster this point. Low-performing schools are providing after-school programs, summer school, and various enrichment activities. But what is happening during this time is apparently not effective. Low-performing students are frequently concentrated in the schools that are having the most trouble. Therefore, this conversation cannot be divorced from other issues, and the assumption cannot be made that all schools, particularly the low-performing subset, are going to be able to adapt a policy of this nature in much more than a haphazard manner. Low-performing schools are facing a deficit situation on so many related issues, including teacher quality, curriculum, resources, and so on. States and school districts must be willing to redirect their attention to these schools in terms of staffing, resources, and attention. Considering how these resources are too frequently allocated (Paul T. Hill's work on teachers, for example, shows that the weakest schools have a disproportionate share of weak teachers), this is a substantial challenge. Therefore policymakers need to take strong action to accompany these policies. The Texas accountability system helps quantify these schools, but as this study illustrates, the large numbers of students who still need extra help indicate the policy is still in its infancy in terms of a comprehensive approach.

Finally is the issue of assessment. The assessments currently in use are still primitive. This does not mean that they should not be used; on the contrary, policymakers should use the best tools at hand while acknowledging their limitations and endeavoring to modernize them. Too often there is far too much lag time in terms of when students are assessed and when teachers and school officials have the information to make decisions. Some progress has been made toward more real-time, online, and computer-based assessment, but this area requires far more support and innovation. The assessments now in use should be merely a way station, certainly not a goal.

The authors conclude their study by outlining some conditions that they argue are essential for effective policy, effective interventions, and disaggregated accountability systems. The importance of an accountability system such as that of Texas to a policy of this nature is clear, as the authors point out, and the federal government has an appropriate role in outlining broad accountability requirements to drive development of such systems. A third condition, more difficult to quantify than the previous two, warrants consideration as well. It is the issue of expectations. For these policies to work for students, policymakers and educators must agree that achievement can be raised, that even students who face challenging circumstances outside of school can learn and achieve on par with other students. The phrase "every child can learn" has morphed into "leave no child behind," but the rhetoric is irrelevant if at the school level, the school district level, in the community, and in the states the key actors do not believe that poor and minority students are able to achieve on par with their more affluent peers. Until policymakers and educators genuinely believe that and reorient the system to accomplish it, the results will continue to come up short.

Comment by Lorrie A. Shepard

Jon Lorence, A. Gary Dworkin, Laurence A. Toenjes, and Antwanette N. Hill begin with a critique of the existing research literature on grade retention. They argue that their study, based on a sample of 736 retained students and 28,351 socially promoted controls, overcomes the weaknesses of previous studies because it is larger, uses a matched comparison group, and follows achievement over a six-year period. In contrast to prior research syntheses showing no academic benefit from retention, Lorence and his colleagues find a positive effect that is striking in the first year following retention (one-half standard deviation achievement gain of retained students over controls). This benefit diminishes over time but still shows a slight positive effect when retained students reach seventh grade. The authors attribute the positive effects of retention as well as the achievement gains found for both retained and socially promoted students to the strictures of the Texas accountability system, which sanctions districts and schools if they fail to raise scores for low-performing students.

Summary of Existing Research

Lorence and his colleagues acknowledge that major research reviews of the literature have found grade retention to be ineffective but cast aspersions on negative findings by referring to the views of educational researchers and their entrenched perceptions. They attempt to explain away negative evidence, calling it biased or flawed. However, their arguments are misleading in several respects. First, the authors quote one or two positive studies and then hold them up against meta-analyses or research reviews that included many dozens of studies.[40] For example, the 1987 S. E. Peterson, J. S. DeGracie, and C. R. Ayabe study was one of many included in the 1989 C. T. Holmes meta-analysis, and the 1994 K. L. Alexander, D. R. Entwisle, and S. L. Dauber study was included in the 1999 J. P. Heubert and R. M. Hauser review.[41] Evidence from these positive studies was considered but outweighed by findings from many more negative studies. Second, the authors imply that new, rigorous studies find positive effects for retention while only old, flawed studies find negative effects. Many of the studies cited in research summaries used statistical controls and matching strategies as good as those employed by Lorence and his colleagues. The Holmes meta-analysis used degree of study control as a variable in examining variation in study findings; and Heubert and Hauser explicitly considered methodological adequacy in weighing findings from Alexander, Entwisle, and Dauber as well as from other studies. Thus, the authors. seem to be going out of their way to build a case for retention instead of trying to evaluate—on balance—where the weight of evidence lies.

Lorence, Dworkin, Toenjes, and Hill have correctly identified me and my colleagues as critics of retention policies based on the evidence. But in their concluding section, they seriously misrepresent our work. They say that "proponents of social promotion would argue that the emotional hardships experienced by retained children and their parents are unnecessary because such children will mature sufficiently in a few years and will then be able to learn the required curriculum." This sounds like our summary of research on kindergarten readiness, kindergarten retention, and within-grade age effects, whereby we showed that kindergarten retention for reasons of social immaturity was unwarranted because within-grade age effects disappear. However, we explicitly distinguished kindergarten retention for reasons of immaturity from retention used as a remedy for poor academic performance. To my knowledge, no one who criticizes the effectiveness of retention as a means to improve achievement would claim that poor achievement can be overcome by ignoring it. Instead, the argument would be to use instructional interventions that are more effective than repeating a grade in school.

Methodological Strengths and Weaknesses

All quasi-experimental studies suffer from some methodological short-comings. Lorence and his colleagues need not claim that their study is impeccable and all other studies seriously flawed. Study limitations should be evaluated in each case to determine whether they are serious enough to call into question the validity of findings. Many other studies in the literature use matched groups or statistical controls as do Lorence and his colleagues. Therefore, I disagree with them that their study is superior because it uses a low-performing comparison group. I agree with the authors that the relative strengths of their study are the large sample size, the availability of concomitant data to allow for both matching and statistical adjustment, and the ability to follow subjects for four years post-retention.

Previously I criticized the authors for exaggerating achievement gains for retained students because they failed to take account of predictable gains due to regression. The paper was revised and the effect sizes in table 4 were reestimated to show relative gains after regression. Although smaller than in the earlier version of the paper, these effect sizes—especially in fourth grade—are still substantial in favor of retention and make the authors' case more credibly. The effect sizes in table 5 were adjusted for differences between the groups in background characteristics but, unfortunately, were not adjusted for regression to the population mean. Therefore, because the magnitude of effect sizes in table 5 is still seriously inflated, they can be used to confirm the finding of significant positive gains but not to report on the amount of gain.

Several issues remain that raise questions about the unusually high gains reported for retention in this study that also have bearing on retention studies more generally. These concerns follow closely several canonical threats to validity of quasi-experimental research designs identified by D. T. Campbell and J. C. Stanley several decades ago.[42] Along with regression to the mean, threats of selection bias, differential attrition (also called experimental mortality), and testing effects can each cause gains in reported achievement that are likely to be mistaken for treatment effects.

In an earlier critique of the Lorence and others study, I pointed out that the overrepresentation of special education students in the control group could be expected to produce greater gains for the retained group over time. Although data on the initial disproportion were not reported in this study, it was documented in a larger study from which this study was drawn.[43] For the 1996 cohort, A. G. Dworkin and others reported that a "higher proportion of special education students who failed the TAAS [Texas Assessment of Academic Skills] reading test are socially promoted."[44] This fact may seem counterintuitive, given that special education students are retained at a higher rate than regular education students and fail the TAAS at a disproportionately high rate. It is not surprising, however, considering that special education students, though low performing, have their own individual education plans and are not typically promoted or retained on the basis of usual grade-level standards.

Data from tables B-1 and B-3 in the Dworkin and others report show that special education students composed only 13 percent of the retained group but constituted 20 percent of the socially promoted group. Because special education students have a much slower growth curve for achievement gains over time, having 7 percent more special education students in the control group would naturally lead to the appearance of greater achievement gains for the retained group without its being the case that retention caused the gains.[45] Lorence and his colleagues address changes in special education classification over the course of the study, with both groups having similar increases in the percentage of students classified in special education, but they did not provide results addressing initial disproportions. They say that they "have attempted to statistically control for a student's special education status." However, these controls presumably were included in the adjusted results reported in table 5 (which lack regression to the mean corrections) but could not have been included in the main analysis of effects reported in table 4.

A second remaining threat to the validity of study inferences is differential attrition. Differential attrition or experimental mortality works like selection bias but occurs after the fact of initial matching between groups. Many retained students likely left the study because their school performance continued to be extremely low. Such selective attrition creates a tautology whereby the benefits of retention are studied among only those students for whom retention was beneficial. In a sense, then, one of the study's strengths—its longitudinal design—is also a serious weakness. Because of the need for complete test data over a six-year period, 44 percent of the original sample of retained students was lost compared with 41 percent lost from the socially promoted group. While this disproportion would not be serious if caused by random effects, it is serious if the study design systematically omitted students for whom retention was the least effective.

Lorence, Dworkin, Toenjes, and Hill attempt to assess the effects of attrition by comparing the initial TAAS scores of leavers from the sample with stayers. Their data confirm that leavers were much lower scoring initially on the third-grade TAAS than stayers (an effect size of about .3 in both groups). However, they point out that this difference was true for both the retained and socially promoted groups. Unfortunately, what this initial comparison cannot reveal is how retained students were performing at the time they left the comparison group. For example, 10 percent of the initial sample of retained students were subsequently referred to special education. Subsequent referral to special education indicates that this 10 percent were worse off after retention than before. How did scores of other study leavers compare with those of stayers in fourth grade or fifth grade at the time when they were lost from the study? Clearly they were seriously behind the retained students who stayed in the sample, but were they also worse off than their relative standing initially? A similar percentage, 9 percent, of socially promoted students were later referred to special education, but were these students as far below their respective group mean at the time of leaving? If they were not, then attrition is systematically biasing the sample in favor of the retained group. Given the huge size of the socially promoted sample compared with the retained group, it is highly probable that attrition was more of a random process in the socially promoted group than in the retained group.

The last serious concern has to do with testing effects and the real possibility that test score gains on TAAS are inflated, especially for low-scoring groups. Over the past two decades, numerous studies have demonstrated the effects of teaching to the test in high-stakes testing environments. For example, to assess whether test score gains in high-stakes settings are real, D. Koretz, R. L. Linn, S. B. Dunbar, and L. A. Shepard used randomized comparison groups and administered independent tests to see if students could do as well on unfamiliar tests covering the same content as on high-stakes, taught-to tests.[46] Student performance dropped on independent tests as much as one-third to one-half standard deviation. This lack of generalization, from familiar to unfamiliar tests, shows that test scores can go up without a true increase in learning.

Pervasive teaching to TAAS in particular, especially in urban districts, was demonstrated in a study by L. McNeil and V. Valenzuela.[47] Although Lorence and his colleagues attribute gains for both retained and control students in their study to an effective accountability program in Texas, serious doubt has been raised regarding the credibility of the "Texas miracle" by a recent study published by RAND researchers S. P. Klein, L. S. Hamilton, D. F. McCaffrey, and B. M. Stecher.[48] One RAND study by D. Grissmer, A. Flanagan, J. Kawata, and S. Williamson praised school reform in Texas because achievement on the National Assessment of Educational Progress (NAEP) was greater than national samples with similar family characteristics.[49] However, the follow-up study by Klein and others showed that gains on NAEP during the 1990s were substantially more modest than gains reported on TAAS.[50] For example, from 1994 to 1998, the effect size for gains in reading on TAAS across racial and ethnic groups ranged from .31 to .49. In contrast, gains on NAEP for the same period ranged from .13 to .15. In this respect, NAEP serves as the gold standard and can be used to evaluate the validity and authenticity of reported gains on TAAS. The differences in these reported gains illustrate that the amount of inflation or falsely reported gains can be substantial.

Inaccurate claims about gains on TAAS were especially serious for students of color, yet Lorence and his colleagues particularly focus on minority student gains as a reason for the apparent success of retention in Texas. In contrast to results on TAAS, however, which show minority students closing the gap between minority and majority students, NAEP results analyzed by Klein and others show that the gap is very large and has widened over this time period. Likely explanations for the discrepancy between the two test patterns are both a ceiling effect on TAAS and rote practice on TAAS provided to low-scoring students.

In the Lorence and others paper, both the retained and control groups show gains in achievement over the six years of the study. Based on previous studies of testing artifacts, it is reasonable to assume that some of the gains for both groups are real but that substantial amounts are spurious. Moreover, some amount of the differential gain for retained students is due to differential testing effects. Given that retained students arrive at each new grade level a year later than socially promoted students, their test scores have the benefit of an extra year of steadily rising test scores, reflecting both true and spurious improvements in achievement.

Taken at face value Lorence, Dworkin, Toenjes, and Hill's longitudinal comparisons in table 3 suggest that retained third graders began the study with devastatingly low achievement (approximately 2 standard deviations below the mean) and that, because of retention, they appear to have made dramatic gains during the repeat year that pushed them ahead of controls and then kept them even with controls even after four years. Once the effects of regression are taken into account, however, this giant boost from retention is no longer so dramatic, though still positive. Other rival hypotheses—selection bias, differential attrition, and testing artifacts—clearly explain some of the remaining gains. Although the data are not available for a straightforward calculation, the magnitude of these types of effects in other studies and specifically with the TAAS reading test have been shown to be as large as the gains and differential gains reported by Lorence and his colleagues. Therefore, the claims of benefits for retention and causal attribution to the accountability system should be advanced more cautiously.

Recommendations for Future Studies

As the authors and I have demonstrated through our exchange over regression estimation procedures, standard quasi-experimental design principles govern interpretation of social science data. Known threats to validity should be controlled as much as possible or (when uncontrolled) taken into account when drawing conclusions. In addition, however, policy analyses and evaluation studies require researchers to consider an expanded set of questions. An evaluator must do more than draw valid causal inferences; he or she must also help policymakers choose among alternative treatments and weigh costs versus benefits. Thus, a wider model to use to evaluate either retention or accountability would be the Federal Drug Administration's standards for judging treatments to be "safe and effective."

A complete analysis of retention's effectiveness should consider whether it is effective in raising achievement (by how much and for how long), whether greater benefits can be obtained from alternative treatments (or the same benefits for less cost), and whether there are any side effects. Lorence, Dworkin, Toenjes, and Hill concluded their study with an analysis estimating what the total cost of retention would be if it were applied to all students who failed TAAS. The resulting $261 million of additional cost to the state is not the main point, however. Presumably it would be a good bargain to spend an extra $5,000 per child to be assured of academic success. The more appropriate debate is whether, given an extra $5,000 for each failing student, the money should be spent on grade retention or on intensive reading instruction or some other treatment. Research syntheses of one-on-one reading interventions and academic tutoring show much more consistently positive gains than do studies of retention. Why should retention be the treatment of choice, especially given that a well-documented side effect of retention is to substantially increase the likelihood of dropping out?[51]

As Lorence and his colleagues have indicated some of the methodological challenges raised here have been encountered in other large-scale studies of retention and can be used to improve the design and analysis of future studies. In particular, the increased use of grade retention as part of high-stakes accountability regimes requires attention. Otherwise, a perpetual debate will ensue between believers and nonbelievers about the credibility of test score gains. As Klein and others have suggested, the evidence of spurious test score gains is serious enough to demand a policy remedy. They note that problems with statewide tests are not confined to the TAAS or to Texas. To lessen the risk of inflated and misleading gains, they recommended that states reduce the pressure associated with high-stakes testing by using different measures for individual students than for school accountability, that traditional paper-and-pencil multiple-choice exams be replaced with large banks of test questions, and that the positive and negative effects of testing programs on curriculum and instruction be directly investigated. Most important, Klein and his colleagues recommended that states periodically conduct audit testing to validate score gains.[52]

These recommendations have bearing on retention research as well. For results to be believable—in Austin, Baltimore, Chicago, or elsewhere—researchers will not be able to use the same test to select students for retention, reward and punish schools, and then measure retention outcomes. Some sort of independent, audit test will be needed to find out whether retention increases learning or merely looks good when measured on an inflationary scale.

Notes

1. For a summary of recent examples, see Jay P. Heubert and Robert M. Hauser, *High Stakes: Testing for Tracking, Promotion, and Graduation* (Washington: National Academy Press, 1999), pp. 114–17.

2. Department of Education, *Taking Responsibility for Ending Social Promotion: A Guide for Educators and State and Local Leaders* (Government Printing Office, 1999).

3. Panayota Mantzicopoulos and Delmont Morrison, "Kindergarten Retention: Academic and Behavioral Outcomes through the End of Second Grade," *American Educational Research Journal,* vol. 29 (Spring 1992), pp. 182–98, quote on p. 183.

4. Lorrie A. Shepard and Mary Lee Smith, "Synthesis of Research on Grade Retention," *Educational Leadership,* vol. 47 (May 1990), pp. 84–88, quote on p. 88.

5. For example, see Linda Darling-Hammond and Beverly Falk, "Using Standards and Assessments to Support Student Learning," *Phi Delta Kappan,* vol. 79 (November 1997), pp. 190–99; William A. Owings and Susan Magliaro, "Grade Retention: A History of Failure,"

Educational Leadership, vol. 56 (September 1998), pp. 86–88; Les Potter, "Examining the Negative Effects of Retention in Our Schools," *Education,* vol. 117 (Winter 1996), pp. 250, 268–70; and Arthur J. Reynolds, Judy Temple, and Ann McCoy, "Grade Retention Doesn't Work," *Education Week,* September 17, 1997, p. 36.

6. Heubert and Hauser, *High Stakes.*

7. Most critics of grade retention practices refer to summaries of research by Gregg B. Jackson, "The Research Evidence on the Effects of Grade Retention," *Review of Educational Research,* vol. 45 (Fall 1975), pp. 613–35; C. Thomas Holmes and Kenneth M. Matthews, "The Effects of Nonpromotion on Elementary and Junior High School Pupils: A Meta-Analysis," *Review of Educational Research,* vol. 54 (Summer 1984), pp. 225–36; C. Thomas Holmes, "Grade Level Retention Effects: A Meta-Analysis of Research Studies," in Lorrie A. Shepard and Mary Lee Smith, eds., *Flunking Grades: Research and Policies on Retention* (London: Falmer Press, 1989), pp. 16–33; as well as other research presented in Shepard and Smith, *Flunking Grades.*

8. Ann R. McCoy and Arthur J. Reynolds, "Grade Retention and School Performance: An Extended Investigation," *Journal of School Psychology,* vol. 37 (Fall 1999), pp. 273–98; and Arthur J. Reynolds, "Grade Retention and School Adjustment: An Explanatory Analysis," *Educational Evaluation and Policy Analysis,* vol. 14 (Summer 1992), pp. 101–21.

9. C. Kenneth Tanner and Susan Allan Galis, "Student Retention: Why Is There a Gap between the Majority of Research Findings and School Practice?" *Psychology in the Schools,* vol. 34 (April 1997), pp. 107–14, especially p. 110.

10. For example, Karl L. Alexander, Doris R. Entwisle, and Susan L. Dauber, *On the Success of Failure* (New York: Cambridge University Press, 1994); Sarah E. Peterson, James S. DeGracie, and Carol R. Ayabe, "A Longitudinal Study of the Effects of Retention/Promotion on Academic Achievement," *American Educational Research Journal,* vol. 24 (Spring 1987), pp. 107–18; and Louisa Pierson and James P. Connell, "Effect of Grade Retention on Self-System Processes, Social Engagement, and Academic Performance," *Journal of Educational Psychology,* vol. 84 (September 1992), pp. 300–07. See also the review in Tanner and Galis, "Student Retention."

11. Holmes, "Grade Level Retention Effects," p. 22.

12. Lorrie A. Shepard, Mary Lee Smith, and Scott F. Marion, "Failed Evidence on Grade Retention," *Psychology in the Schools,* vol. 33 (July 1996), pp. 251–61; and Alexander, Entwisle, and Dauber, *On the Success of Failure.*

13. Shepard, Smith, and Marion, "Failed Evidence on Grade Retention," p. 258.

14. Heubert and Hauser, *High Stakes,* p. 132.

15. Alexander, Entwisle, and Dauber, *On the Success of Failure,* pp. 19–20, cite many other problematic features of the existing research assessing the effects of grade retention.

16. Shane Jimerson, "On the Failure of Failure: Examining the Association between Early Grade Retention and Education and Employment Outcomes during Late Adolescence," *Journal of School Psychology,* vol. 37 (Fall 1999), pp. 243–72; and Shane Jimerson and others, "A Prospective, Longitudinal Study of Correlates and Consequences of Early Grade Retention," *Journal of School Psychology,* vol. 35 (Spring 1997), pp. 3–25.

17. For example, Jane K. Elligett and Thomas S. Tocco, "The Promotion/Retention Policy in Pinellas County, Florida," *Phi Delta Kappan,* vol. 64 (June 1983), pp. 733–35.

18. Although the Texas Assessment of Academic Skills (TAAS) test was developed specifically for the state, this measure of academic achievement is comparable to well-known standardized tests. Recent research indicates that student performance on the TAAS is highly correlated with performance on the Stanford 9 and the Iowa Test of Basic Skills. See Anthony Gary Dworkin and others, *Comparisons between the TAAS and Norm-Referenced Tests: Issues*

of Criterion-Related Validity, report prepared for the Texas Education Agency (University of Houston, Department of Sociology, 1999). The overall validity and reliability of the TAAS is consistent with that of more established standardized tests.

19. Bureau of the Census, *Historical Statistics of the U.S. Colonial Times to 1970 Bicentennial Edition,* Part 1–2 (Government Printing Office, 1974); and Bureau of the Census, *Statistical Abstracts of the United States: 1998* (Government Printing Office, 1998), table 262.

20. For a discussion of these issues, see Margaret D. LeCompte and A. Gary Dworkin, *Giving Up on School: Student Dropouts and Teacher Burnouts* (Newbury Park, Calif.: Sage, 1991).

21. Texas state demographer Steve H. Murdock and his colleagues have forecast that between 1990 and 2030 the percentage of Hispanic students enrolled in Texas elementary and secondary schools will grow from 32.2 to 53.4 percent, while the African American and Anglo American percentages will fall from 13.2 and 53.3 to 10.9 and 30.5 percent, respectively. The percentages of school children who are economically disadvantaged, who drop out of school, who need to participate in bilingual or English as a Second Language classes are likewise expected to double or triple. Steve H. Murdock and others, *The Texas Challenge: Population Change and the Future of Texas* (Texas A&M Press, 1997).

22. Donald T. Campbell and Julian C. Stanley, *Experimental and Quasi-Experimental Designs for Research* (Chicago: Rand McNally, 1966), pp. 47–50.

23. The percentages in table 2 are based on all students, including those with missing demographic data. To illustrate, among students who received a Texas Learning Index (TLI) reading score below 70 and who were required to repeat grade three, the sex classification of 4.5 percent of these pupils was missing.

24. Antwanette N. Hill and others, *Educational Practices Applied to Texas Elementary Students Retained in Grade,* report prepared for the Texas Education Agency (University of Houston, Department of Sociology, 1999).

25. Donald T. Campbell and David A. Kenny, *A Primer on Regression Artifacts* (New York: Guilford Press, 1999).

26. Campbell and Kenny, *A Primer on Regression Artifacts,* p. 11.

27. Shepard, Smith, and Marion, "Failed Evidence on Grade Retention."

28. Jacob Cohen, *Statistical Power Analysis for the Behavioral Sciences,* 2d ed. (Hillsdale, N.J.: Lawrence Erlbaum Associates, 1988), pp. 24–27.

29. Shepard, Smith, and Marion, "Failed Evidence on Grade Retention," recommend deleting special education students from retention studies because such pupils may be less likely to be retained in a grade even if they do poorly on a grade level test, as they can still be promoted if they met individual education plans. Consequently, low-scoring special education students may be more likely to appear in the socially promoted group and pull down the average test score of the promoted students, thereby inflating the gap between the gains made by retained and socially promoted students. To maximize the number of students in the analyses, we statistically control for the special education classification of students in the retained and socially promoted group. Additional analyses not shown here were conducted in which special education students were deleted from computations. The findings presented here are very similar to those obtained from the more restricted sample. See Jon Lorence, Anthony Gary Dworkin, and Laurence A. Toenjes, *Longitudinal Analyses of Elementary School Retention and Promotion in Texas: A Second Year Report,* report prepared for the Texas Education Agency (University of Houston, Department of Sociology, 2000).

30. Donald T. Campbell and Albert Erlebacher, "How Regression Artifacts in Quasi-Experimental Evaluations Can Mistakenly Make Compensatory Education Look Harmful," in Jerome Hellmuth, ed., *Compensatory Education: A National Debate,* vol. 3: *Disadvantaged Child* (New York: Brunner/Mazel Publishers, 1970), pp. 185–210.

31. Some students classified as being in the special education category have limitations that do not preclude them from being incorporated into the groups of pupils used to assess how good a job schools do in educating their pupils. Therefore, special education students with scored tests have been incorporated into all of our analyses. We have attempted to statistically control for a student's special education status. Although it would be useful to know the nature of a special education student's limitation, we did not have access to information identifying a child's specific disability.

32. Hill and others, *Educational Practices Applied to Texas Elementary Students Retained in Grade.*

33. Anthony Gary Dworkin and others, *Evaluation of Academic Performance in the Houston Independent School District*, final report prepared for the Center for Houston's Future—Greater Houston Partnership (University of Houston, Department of Sociology, 1998).

34. To estimate the cost of retaining a student in grade, we assume that all retained students are held back only one year and that all of them eventually graduate from high school in thirteen instead of twelve years. We also assume that the cost of holding back a single student for one year is $5,000, the minimum amount of money Texas school administrators often report as being required to educate one student for an academic year. Because we have focused extensively only on students with scored annual tests between 1994 and 1996, the data in table 3 show that 30,921 low-scoring third graders were not allowed to proceed to grade four. However, 52,159 third-grade students in 1994 with reading TLI scores below 70 remained in Texas public schools in the 1994–95 academic year. Therefore, the estimated cost of retaining all low-performing 1994 third graders would be 52,159 x $5,000 or approximately $260,795,000 for this one cohort alone. Although a large absolute sum of money, this cost would amount to only about a 1 percent increase in the state's current education budget.

35. Department of Education, *Taking Responsibility for Ending Social Promotion.*

36. Heubert and Hauser, *High Stakes;* and Shepard and Smith, *Flunking Grades.*

37. Alexander, Entwisle, and Dauber, *On the Success of Failure.*

38. Campbell and Kenny, *A Primer on Regression Artifacts*, pp. 25–28.

39. Campbell and Kenny, *A Primer on Regression Artifacts*, p. 28.

40. Favorites are K. L. Alexander, D. R. Entwisle, and S. L. Dauber, *On the Success of Failure* (New York: Cambridge University Press, 1994); and S. E. Peterson, J. S. DeGracie, and C. R. Ayabe, "A Longitudinal Study of the Effects of Retention/Promotion on Academic Achievement," *American Educational Research Journal*, vol. 24 (1987), pp. 107–18.

41. Peterson, DeGracie, and Ayabe, "A Longitudinal Study of the Effects of Retention/Promotion on Academic Achievement"; Holmes, "Grade Level Retention Effects"; Alexander, Entwisle, and Dauber, *On the Success of Failure*; and Heubert and Hauser, *High Stakes.*

42. Campbell and Stanley, *Experimental and Quasi-Experimental Designs for Research.*

43. A. G. Dworkin and others, *Elementary School Retention and Social Promotion in Texas: An Assessment of Students Who Failed the Reading Section of the TAAS* (University of Houston Sociology of Education Research Group, 1999).

44. Dworkin and others, *Elementary School Retention and Social Promotion in Texas*, p. 7.

45. Those not familiar with regression and selection artifacts may be confused by seemingly contradictory challenges claiming, on the one hand, that lower scoring groups could be expected to gain more (hence predicting greater gains for the retained group due to regression to the mean) and claiming, on the other, that very low-scoring special education students would be expected to gain less. The difference methodologically has to do with the reliability of the initial selection decision. Retained and socially promoted controls were selected for low performance from much larger populations of students on the basis of a single test score; hence

the mean of both groups would be expected to be higher on any subsequent test. Special education subgroups within these larger samples, however, are more reliably low performing because they are placed based on multiple test scores and evidence, not a single test score. Their scores therefore would not rebound on subsequent testings because of regression.

46. D. Koretz and others, "The Effects of High-Stakes Testing: Preliminary Evidence about Generalization across Tests," paper presented at the annual meeting of the American Educational Research Association, Chicago, April 1991.

47. L. McNeil and V. Valenzuela, *The Harmful Impact of the TAAS System of Testing in Texas: Beneath the Accountability Rhetoric* (Harvard University Civil Rights Project, 2000).

48. S. P. Klein and others, *What Do Test Scores in Texas Tell Us?* (Santa Monica, Calif.: RAND, 2000).

49. D. Grissmer and others, *Improving Student Achievement: What State NAEP Test Scores Tell Us* (Santa Monica, Calif.: RAND, 2000).

50. The two RAND Corporation studies are often cited as if they contradicted each other. However, both can be true. There can be real improvements in Texas as measured by NAEP (see Grissmer and others, *Improving Student Achievement*), but these gains might be modest compared with the euphoric gains reported on the Texas Assessment of Academic Skills (see Klein and others, *What Do Test Scores in Texas Tell Us?*).

51. Heubert and Hauser, *High Stakes.*

52. Klein and others, *What Do Test Scores in Texas Tell Us?*

Reform, Resistance, ... Retreat? The Predictable Politics of Accountability in Virginia

FREDERICK M. HESS

In the 1990s, Virginia launched one of the nation's most ambitious standards-based reform efforts. Encouraged by a budding national accountability movement and motivated by conservative distrust of the public school establishment, state officials sought to clarify what students needed to know and to hold students and educators accountable for demonstrated performance. The effort to launch and then implement the state's nationally hailed Standards of Learning (SOLs) program would provide an exemplary case study of the political tensions that imperil any push for high-stakes accountability. By 2001, determining with certainty which program elements were the result of educational considerations and which were a response to political challenges would prove difficult.

These developments were particularly illuminating given Virginia's earlier experiences with high-stakes reform. In the 1970s, and again in the 1980s, Virginia adopted widely supported testing programs that called for students to master particular skills and content before graduating. On each occasion, large numbers of children failed to meet the standards initially set, but only a handful of children were ever denied diplomas. While some proponents chalked this pattern up to dramatic improvements in school quality, it can be more usefully and fully understood as a story of political accommodation and compromise. I use Virginia's extensive experiences with high-stakes accountability to examine the politics and prospects of standards-based

I am obliged to Amber Winkler and Chris Etchechury for their invaluable research assistance.

69

reform.[1] I consider the history of Virginia's experiences with standards-based reform, the effect of the Standards of Learning on student performance, and their impact on the broader culture of schooling.

The allure of standards-based reform is straightforward. Standards are a statement that—at a minimum—schools ought to teach children certain knowledge and skills and that the state should ensure that both children and schools meet minimal standards. The challenge posed by this prosaic goal is equally clear. Setting minimal performance standards means that some students, teachers, and schools will be deemed unacceptable. This poses a daunting political dilemma in a democratic society where the low-performers will have a powerful incentive to question the legitimacy of the system.

High-stakes accountability systems link rewards and punishments to demonstrated student performance in an effort to transform the quality of schooling. Such systems press students to master specified content and require educators to effectively teach that content. In such a regime, school improvement no longer rests upon individual volition or intrinsic motivation. Instead, students and teachers are compelled to cooperate by threatening a student's ability to graduate or a teacher's job security. Such transformative systems seek to harness the self-interest of students and educators to refocus schools and redefine the expectations of teachers and learners.[2]

High-stakes efforts are fundamentally different from standards-based reforms that reject the coercive force of self-interest. Gentler, less threatening standards-based approaches seek to improve schooling through informal social pressures and by using tests as a diagnostic device.

In practice, the two visions of standards represent two points on a continuum. Most programs start with substantial commitment to the transformative high-stakes ideal. Over time, however, implementation begins to reveal the costs implied by such change. Support for coercive accountability then erodes while opposition coalesces. In the face of such pressure, transformative systems are generally weakened in one of five ways. Conventionally, officials (1) lower the stakes, (2) make the test easier, (3) reduce the thresholds required to pass, (4) permit some students to sidestep the required assessment, or (5) delay the implementation of the stakes. While each alteration is a response to legitimate programmatic concerns, the common thread is the manner in which it eases political resistance at the cost of weakening the coercive impact of accountability.

Ironically, the accountability systems that are the most sophisticated and most commonly hailed for their careful design are the most susceptible to the inevitable political backlash. It is far simpler for officials to publicly explain, defend, and hold the line on a simple system (for example, one based upon a handful of straightforward multiple-choice tests, accompanied by blunt, self-explanatory sanctions) than on a system dependent on subtle instruments or complex systems of measurement and enforcement. The very nuance that characterizes the most carefully crafted systems serves to multiply possible negotiating points and create grounds for possible compromise, while opening the door to the notion that accountability systems require refinement. The result is public officials find it difficult to defend the abstract merits of a technically desirable system against the claims of discrete groups.

High-stakes accountability systems generally get off to a promising start, but the political dynamic inexorably leads to a weakening of the high-stakes component. High-stakes accountability is symbolically appealing in the abstract, but the implementation of such regimes produces visible costs that tend to be more politically salient than the accompanying educational benefits. The benefits are diffuse and long-term while the costs are immediate and concentrated, creating a political dynamic that tends to aid critics of high-stakes accountability.[3]

The Allure of Outcome Accountability

In seeking to ensure school quality, policymakers have two fundamental methods at their disposal. The traditional approach has been to govern by focusing on the inputs, instead of on the outcomes, of schooling. Policymakers often seek to ensure school quality by requiring that schools spend specified amounts of money per pupil, have facilities that meet set criteria, employ teachers with certain certifications, and so on. Because inputs may not be used in a way that translates into results, input monitoring is characterized by regulation and micromanagement.

Public schools and school personnel have traditionally been judged on the basis of whether or not they comply with regulations and mandates governing inputs. Policymakers have evaluated schools based upon their fealty to policy directives, not upon student performance or progress. In large part, this approach emerged as a lowest common denominator compromise among policymakers reluctant to resolve disputes about the relative merit of competing goals or how to gauge school outcomes. Instead of pursuing an elusive consensus on such questions, educators adopted a "shopping mall" ideal in which schools provided a heterogeneous population with a smorgasbord of services.[4]

Regulating schools on the basis of inputs and compliance with rules gives rise to obvious and well-documented problems. Consequently, the suggestion that students and educators ought instead to be held to a performance standard has a natural appeal. Such an outcome-based approach would focus on how effectively schools are educating students by establishing performance criteria and then checking to see that they are met.

Conceptually, outcome accountability is alluring. First, it promises to provide educators, officials, and the public with clear measures of educational performance. Second, it enables educational administrators to determine what is working and what is not. Third, performance information enables administrators to gauge teachers' effectiveness, to take steps to assist or motivate less effective teachers, and to reward and recognize effective teachers. Fourth, clear information on performance allows public officials and educational administrators to target resources more efficiently. Finally, an outcome focus can offer workers more operational freedom, because supervisors can forgo regulation and concentrate on monitoring outcomes.

In practice, substantive accountability can push educators to focus on teaching the required content and skills, set clear performance expectations, and ensure that all students are mastering essential competencies. However, such changes come at a price. High-stakes accountability may marginalize many of the other roles that schools play, reallocate educator energy and resources, and narrow the scope of instruction. Whether this is good or bad depends not just on the size and specifics of the resulting changes, but also on normative notions of what schools are for and what constitutes good teaching.[5]

The Politics of Accountability

Meaningful standards-based reform requires a series of decisions that often give proponents pause. First, a prescribed body of content and skills to be tested must be designated. This decision will marginalize content and skills that are not included. Second, assessments must be administered that render clear indications as to whether students have or have not mastered the requisite skills and content. Third, such assessment requires policymakers to specify what constitutes mastery. Fourth, policymakers must decide what to do with students who fail to demonstrate mastery. Finally, if accountability is to significantly alter what the educational system provides, educators must be rewarded or sanctioned on the basis of student performance. Making these decisions is especially difficult because each tends to produce passionate opposition among those who bear the costs of each choice. Hesitant to make the necessary choices and facing opposition to the unpleasant consequences, proponents of standards-based reform often compromise on program design. In the end, the substantive promise of accountability is often sacrificed, so that the primary benefits of reform are the diagnostic support offered by testing and the informal social pressures that follow public testing.

Concentrated resistance to high-stakes reform arises due to four prominent tensions. First, while accountability may yield significant long-term and systemic benefits regardless of individual losses or specific inequities, it does require denying diplomas to some students. The current system also takes a high toll on students who perform poorly, permitting many to graduate with meaningless diplomas.[6] The difference is that existing inequities can be attributed to impersonal social forces, while high-stakes accountability requires public officials to visibly sanction vulnerable children. Those students denied diplomas suffer clear and immediate costs, while the benefits of effective accountability tend to be diffuse and to emerge over the longer term. The losers, with more immediately at stake, will tend to be passionate, while the larger mass of winners will find the issue less pressing. Moreover, children in minority and low-income communities are disproportionately likely to fare poorly, leaving officials vulnerable to charges of callousness and racial bias. As a result, officials will find themselves pressured to reduce the number of losers or minimize the severity of losses.

Second, in the most highly regarded school systems, and those serving some of the highest performing populations, concern arises about the impact of high-stakes accountability. In these communities, the parents and educators do not fear that students will be sanctioned, but that an emphasis on state-mandated tests will hurt local schools by forcing them to shift their attention to state-dictated curricula and content. In particular, parents and educators in highly regarded districts fear that the pressure to teach baseline skills and content will disrupt high-level classrooms and squeeze out valued lessons. They are also concerned that the test scores are an inaccurate proxy for the broader quality of schooling and that an emphasis on test scores may have a variety of negative consequences, such as understating school performance, impeding students' future prospects, and reducing local property values.

Accountability proponents may claim that any disruptions are an indication that all students were previously not mastering necessary skills and content or that disappointing test scores may be an indication that elite districts are not as effective as parents would like to think. However, these are academic claims unsupported by a coherent constituency. Meanwhile, the educated, wealthy, and politically involved residents of high-performing suburban districts have a visceral desire to protect the practices and the reputations of their schools. When these communities view high-stakes accountability as sufficiently intrusive and damaging, they seek to weaken them. No alternative constituency helps public officials resist such pressures.

Third, teachers have a passionate aversion to being subjected to sanctions on the basis of student performance, while the broader public has a much less immediate stake in the matter. Again, public officials will have difficulty standing up to the concerted opposition of teachers, especially given the lack of a natural pro-sanction constituency. In addition, children vary in ability and preparation from community to community and school to school, confronting some educators with greater challenges than others. This raises concern over whether test scores can equitably determine teacher performance, forcing advocates of high-stakes accountability to defend sanctions in the face of heated criticism from teachers and their allies.

Teachers also have a second complaint, one more geared to the culture of schooling. American schools have been built on a premise of professional, autonomous teachers who operate out of a sense of duty and commitment.[7] The premise of high-stakes testing challenges this culture by pressing teachers to teach the content and skills mandated by the state, regardless of their personal preferences. In doing so, high-stakes testing challenges the low-pressure culture that educators have traditionally embraced. Educators have incentives to resist a system that challenges their autonomy, holds them accountable, and forces them to engage in practices they may not favor. No similarly motivated constituency exists to advocate on behalf of standards.

Finally, the multiple agendas that coexist within public schooling ensure that the push for high-stakes accountability will provoke conflict from those whose agendas may be marginalized. A deep-rooted disagreement exists in the United States as to what schools are for, what a good education includes, and what skills and content children need to know. Efforts to impose statewide agreement will inevitably offend some constituencies. The aggrieved parties will oppose efforts to narrow the curriculum and marginalize their concerns, while the broader public will have little cause for action.

In each of these cases, proponents of standards must marshal diffuse support in response to criticism from aggrieved, passionate, coherent constituencies. The temptation for proponents is to compromise on the elements of accountability, slowly softening the coercive threat posed by high-stakes regimes.

The American political system is notoriously bad at pursuing collective goods when it requires imposing concentrated costs on select groups. American government is highly permeable, making it relatively easy for small but passionate factions to block or soften adverse legislative or bureaucratic decisions.[8] Because visible and vocal groups such as teachers and minorities are likely to feel that they are suffering large costs under high-stakes accountability, and given that the presumed benefits are generally diffuse and long term, the political calculus is rendered difficult.

However, if an accountability system survives implementation, the political calculus can start to reverse. First, as is the case in Japan or Western Europe, accountability systems come increasingly to be seen as central to legitimate schooling; they become intrinsic to the "grammar of schooling."[9] Second, the existence of a widely accepted assessment regime can be useful to educators and public officials, as it offers a lever by which educators are able to demonstrate performance, strengthening their claim on public support and resources. What becomes clear is that the political pressures pinch more tightly as accountability morphs from vague precept to a concrete reality. The result is a cyclical dance, in which officials garner support for the notion of standards and then struggle to hold firm as implementation produces pressure to ease standards, shrink the number of at-risk parties, or lessen the consequences of failure. At its most basic, the politics of accountability is a desperate contest in which proponents race to institutionalize the regime before resistance leads officials to gut the system.

The dance of accountability will be heavily shaped by the political context in which it takes place. States vary immensely in their social makeup, culture, institutions, and educational systems, confronting proponents of high-stakes accountability with substantially different challenges from one locale to the next. Because acceptance and legitimacy are so critical to efforts to institutionalize transformative accountability, the existing architecture of state testing will also prove significant. Unfortunately, space constraints and the desire to focus at length upon a single state make it impractical to address these important questions of interstate variability here.

Virginia's Early Experience with Standards

The Virginia push for standards in the 1990s is a story of broad support for the abstract notion of accountability, but increasing public queasiness with the measures required to define quality or sanction poor performance.[10] That same story line played out in the Graduation Competency Test in the 1970s and the Literacy Passport Test (LPT) in the 1980s.

Early Efforts: Minimum Competency Testing

Before 1976, in Virginia, as in most states, high school graduation required only that students accumulate the specified number and type of course credits. In July 1976, however, Virginia became one of the first states to embrace minimum competency testing. The powerful state Board of Education required graduates to demonstrate functional literacy, basic computational skills, knowledge and understanding of American history and culture, and the ability to pursue higher education or to gain employment.[11] The decision enjoyed significant political support from elected officials, including Republican governor John Dalton. The change was made over the opposition of established civil rights and educational organizations such as the Virginia Education Association (VEA), the National Association for the Advancement of Colored People (NAACP), and the Virginia Association of School Administrators (VASA).[12] In 1978 the General Assembly put teeth into the board's decision when it passed a Graduation Competency Test to ensure that students had acquired basic proficiency in reading and math before being permitted to graduate.[13] The test required students to demonstrate that they had mastered survival skills such as how to balance a checkbook or fill out a job application.[14]

Initially, the standards that accompanied minimum competency testing were billed as an innocuous effort to clarify the state curriculum.[15] Proponents were careful to play down the changes that the new standards would bring. They hoped that simply adopting standards and initiating testing, regardless of the substantive consequences, would infuse the educational process with heightened rigor. As Linton Deck, superintendent of high-profile Fairfax

County, said in 1979, "Because of the test programs it seems pretty obvious that students and teachers and everybody else associated with the schools, including parents, have taken schooling more seriously."[16]

The launch of the testing program was delayed because state officials were unable to agree on what the passing score should be.[17] The passing score was finally set at 70 percent in October 1978, before the Board of Education had seen the results from the initial round of testing.[18] Starting with the class of 1981, students would have to pass both parts of the test to receive their diploma. Those who failed one or both parts were to be given remedial work and three more opportunities to pass.

When the 159-question test was first administered in 1978, 17.8 percent of the seventy-one thousand tenth-grade test-takers failed either the reading or mathematics component.[19] Forty-two percent of black students failed at least one component, prompting the executive director of the Virginia NAACP, Jack Gravely, to blast the test's discriminatory impact.[20] There was particular concern that some students who fared poorly on the test would be denied a diploma as a consequence. Diana Pullin, a lawyer for the federally funded Center for Law and Education, maintained that the test "would be wrong if [just] one student didn't get his diploma."[21] Criticism subsided, however, as the passing rate of black students rapidly rose—with just 0.5 percent of black students failing in the spring of 1981.[22]

Opposition to the test quieted as passage rates skyrocketed. In 1981 the state denied diplomas to just 87 of the 62,236 seniors who took the test. In other words, 99.86 percent of seniors passed the test.[23] Some said the standard was so low that it failed to ensure that students were equipped to attend college or enter the work force.[24] State delegate George Grayson said the results showed the test to be "ridiculously easy." The high pass rates, said Virginia NAACP executive director Jack Gravely, had caused the issue to be "put on the back-burner." He observed that the NAACP, "Just d[oesn]'t hear very much about it anymore."[25]

Between 1978 and 1981, schools took a number of steps to raise test scores. One common tactic was to reallocate time and energy away from broader educational goals and toward test-specific preparation. Scores were boosted by remedial support tailored to the test; by schools incorporating test-specific content into their lessons, especially in the lower tracks; and by state efforts to provide sample lessons, practice questions, and reports on individual weaknesses. The larger significance of these behaviors was unclear. Critics said they demonstrated that schools were focusing on test preparation instead of education, while proponents were pleased that schools were finally focusing on ensuring that low-performing students were mastering basic skills.

As minimum competency testing grew, so did concern that it imposed a state curriculum on localities. While some degree of centralized standardization is inherent in any move toward statewide accountability, legislators were hesitant to acknowledge this fact. Consequently, while the Board of Education had unanimously approved the development of statewide Standards of Learning in 1979, the legislature, in 1980, refused to fund the effort.[26]

In 1981 Democrat Charles S. Robb was elected governor. At the time, statewide Scholastic Aptitude Test (SAT) scores were flat and Virginia teacher salaries ranked thirty-fourth in the nation. In his inaugural address, Robb called for renewed attention to educational improvement, a push that benefited from the 1983 report *A Nation at Risk*. The report decried the state of the nation's schools and called for radical reform, including a dramatic commitment to standards and accountability.[27] During Robb's 1982–86 tenure, per-pupil education spending grew by 33 percent.[28] By the end of Robb's term, standards for new teachers had been raised and Virginia teacher salaries had climbed to twenty-sixth in the nation. Robb also advocated tougher academic standards, such as requiring high school students to take more academic classes.[29] The Robb years set the stage for another comprehensive accountability-based reform.

The Literacy Passport Test

In March 1986 Governor Gerald Baliles, a Democrat who had formerly served as Robb's lieutenant governor, convened a sixteen-member Commission on Excellence in Education. In October of that year, the commission reported that 25 percent of Virginia ninth graders were not completing high school. Moreover, while Virginia's students exceeded the national averages on nationally administered tests, nearly half of all school divisions were scoring below average.[30] The report illustrated how readily a state school system can be characterized as either effective or ineffective, depending on which benchmarks are selected and how the data are presented.

The commission endorsed a Literacy Passport Test to ensure that all sixth graders were performing at an acceptable level in reading, writing, and arithmetic. The proposed LPT would include multiple-choice tests in mathematics and reading and a required writing sample. Students who failed the test would receive remediation and be retested in seventh and eighth grade. No student would be promoted to ninth grade without passing the test. In October 1987, the Board of Education adopted the LPT, estimating the associated costs for remedial programming would run $25 million a year. The legislature wrote the LPT into law in 1987. Special needs students were exempted from the LPT program, largely as a result of concerns voiced by the influential community of special education parents and teachers.

The first round of LPT testing took place in 1990. In that year, 71 percent of white students passed the LPT while 46 percent of black test-takers did. In 1991 the passage rate among black students improved from 46 percent to 53 percent, but the black passage rate still lagged the white rate by 26 percentage points. Even in Fairfax County, an elite district where four of five sixth graders passed the entire LPT, black and Hispanic students lagged about 20 percentile points behind their white peers. The results drew outrage. Robert Frye, who held the at-large minority seat on the Fairfax school board, said, "I would have to characterize myself as still outraged by the scores." He said efforts to increase test preparation and to target minority students with a new summer school program were just "a Band-Aid on a tremendous problem." Minority leaders, including NAACP president L. Marie Guillory, called for Fairfax's superintendent to resign. Guillory declared, "If there hasn't been any change in the scores, then maybe there should be a change in the administration."[31]

From 1990 to 1998, the rate at which students passed the LPT would fluctuate between 64 percent and 72 percent, showing no clear trend.[32] In the early years, officials were not unduly alarmed about the passage rates, because students could continue to retake the test. By 1992, of the initial cohort of test-takers, five thousand had been promoted to eighth grade without passing the LPT. In theory, these students would not be permitted to begin high school until passing the test. That restriction was waived, however, meaning that the real squeeze would not come until 1996, when students who had failed the test were about to graduate from high school.

Struggling to address the pressures produced by the LPT, public officials demonstrated the same basic array of behaviors that would be evident in the 1990s. First, officials softened the sanctions implicit in the LPT system. The premise of the LPT called for keeping these students in middle school until they mastered the essential skills. However, as state board member Alan Wurtzel explained, "We blinked."[33] Under pressure from parents and other advocates, the board decided to allow students who had failed the test to enter high school as ungraded students. The only sanction was the determination that these students would not be eligible to engage in interscholastic activities or sports until they passed the LPT. Even this relatively weak no-pass, no-play sanction was deemed overly punitive by some. Moreover, the policy was less significant than it appeared, because many of the affected students were already banned from interscholastic activity due to academic performance requirements governing eligibility.

Second, officials sought to remove or lower the testing bar for some students who would have difficulty passing the exam. Some students were exempted from the LPT, while others were permitted to postpone the test's first administration by a year or more. In 1993 the legislature addressed concerns that the LPT was unfair to English as a Second Language (ESL) students by allowing these students up to three years after enrolling in a Virginia high school to pass all three sections of the exam.

Third, schools devoted resources and energy to help ensure that students passed the LPT exam. Across the state, school systems began to launch efforts intended to ensure that students who had failed portions of the LPT passed the remaining sections. Such efforts included requiring remedial classes, providing additional tutoring, and holding special test preparation classes.

In 1993 and 1994, as consequences loomed for students who failed the LPT, allegations of cheating—involving both students and teachers—emerged in several school districts. Some local superintendents started to publicly question the credibility of the scores and appealed results to the state Department of Education. While allegations of cheating were uncommon, they offered critics anecdotes to support their claim that testing was inimical to the ethos of schooling.

After the fall 1994 administration of the LPT, state figures showed that 982 students taking tenth-grade classes had not passed, with 60 percent of those students needing to pass just one of the three tests. The ninth-grade cohort included 2,824 ungraded students who had not yet passed the entire LPT.[34] High school teachers from the period recall that they engaged in extensive tutoring and test preparation to ensure that low-scoring students passed all parts of the LPT.[35] While policymakers had initially intended for the LPT to be a hurdle that students had to jump before entering ninth grade, the board would not enact that policy until 1995. Superintendent of Public Instruction William Bosher explained the delay as a failure of nerve on the part of the board. He observed, "Someone blinked [and] instead of a barrier there was accommodation. . . . A policy decision was made to let them go to high school."[36]

The class of 1996 was the first class in which students who failed a portion of the LPT could be denied a standard diploma and instead issued a certificate of program completion. Meanwhile, Individualized Education Program (IEP) committees had the right to waive the LPT for special education students, resulting in the award of a special diploma to those children. In the end, the number of students denied diplomas due to the LPT was negligible. In 1996, 83 students were denied diplomas because of their LPT scores. In 1997, 148 students were denied diplomas. The 99+ percent pass rate was reminiscent of the experience fifteen years earlier with minimum competency testing. In spring 1998, the Board of Education requested that the General Assembly phase out the LPT. It was deemed unnecessary in light of the newly adopted Standards of Learning.

During 1987–96, officials had created enough slack, provided enough assistance, and kept the group of failing students small enough that the LPT was a political success. The problem for standards proponents was that the compromises needed to help LPT survive, including the decision not to link student performance to any consequences for educators, ensured that the LPT carried only a faint tinge of coercive accountability. Instead of trying to gradually strengthen the LPT, proponents rallied behind Republican gubernatorial candidate George F. Allen's 1993 call for an ambitious new program.

Allen and the Fight to Define Quality, 1994–98

Republican gains in the state legislature increased the muscle behind efforts to advocate standards and accountability. Republicans made substantial gains in Virginia during the 1980s and 1990s. As late as 1975, Republicans held just seventeen of the one hundred seats in the Virginia House of Delegates and five of the forty seats in the Senate. By the time Republican George Allen was elected in 1993, Republicans held forty-one seats in the House and eighteen in the Senate.[37] Whereas Democratic legislators enjoyed substantial support among the groups most likely to critique or oppose high-stakes testing—for instance, the fifty thousand-member Virginia Education Association and NAACP—these groups were generally seen as hostile by Republicans. Republican legislators were therefore more willing to support measures these groups found objectionable.

In 1990, under the leadership of State Superintendent Joseph Spagnolo, the Department of Education sought to broaden the state curriculum by adopting an expansive common core of learning as part of a World-Class Education initiative. The initial premise—that competence ought to be broadly defined—was relatively unobjectionable. However, conservatives eventually attacked the program as a value-laden, costly effort to dumb-down academic standards. Stung by the attacks, Democratic governor L. Douglas Wilder directed the Department of Education to pull the plug on the common core of learning in 1993.[38]

In his 1993 campaign, Allen attacked Spagnolo's initiatives as outcome-based education and contrasted it with his call for higher standards and more accountability.[39] The focus on accountability permitted Allen to champion education while facing a Democratic opponent who had a warm relationship with the public school teachers union and despite the fact that Allen, as a member of Congress, had proposed cutting federal education spending.[40]

Reformers can often find evidence to support their claim that educational performance is inadequate, though the effectiveness of such an appeal will depend on public receptiveness and whether the evidence is seen as reliable and significant. In Virginia in 1993 and 1994, roughly one in three sixth graders was failing the LPT.[41] The 1994 National Assessment of Educational Progress (NAEP) reading test showed that Virginia scores had declined against the national averages and that 46 percent of Virginia fourth graders ranked below the basic level.[42] From 1984–85 to 1993–94, average SAT scores slid from 908 to 893.[43] Whether or not these data constituted a fair indictment of Virginia's schools, they proved an effective way for reformers to stir up popular concern with the status quo.[44]

Allen took office in 1994 facing a legislature with Democratic majorities in both houses. Allen's call for standards enjoyed widespread but shallow support, with a lack of agreement about what they ought to include or how they should be enforced. In May 1994, shortly after taking office, Allen appointed a Governor's Commission on Champion Schools. The commission was intended to educate the public and marshal support for a coherent program. Chaired by Allen's secretary of education, Beverly Sgro, the commission included a number of Allen supporters and public school critics.[45] One of its key goals was revising standards that critics assailed as vague, undemanding, and immeasurable. The Allen administration also moved aggressively to reshape the Board of Education as seats became open.[46]

Designing the SOLs

The commission held seven public hearings, visited schools, and solicited input from experts and citizens. Although it did not issue its final report until

January 1996, the commission's leadership provided substantial support for SOLs and spurred extensive activity on standards and testing during 1994 and 1995.[47]

In May 1994 the Board of Education initiated the development of statewide standards in math, science, English, and history. Beset by ongoing cutbacks that trimmed its size from 500 to about 250 employees, the Department of Education lacked the resources to develop the standards internally. Needing to tap the capacity that some of the leading school districts could provide, and seeking to win over local educators, the state moved to develop the standards in concert with four leading school districts.[48] In June 1994 the Department of Education finalized agreements with these Lead School Divisions, specifying that the standards were to be academic, rigorous, and jargon-free.

The standards were devised during summer 1994 by local teams of teachers, parents, and other community residents. In the fall, they were sent to State Superintendent of Instruction William Bosher, an Allen appointee. Bosher employed writing teams to revise the standards developed by the pilot communities, particularly in the case of social studies, before he sent the standards on to the board. Critics, including the Virginia Education Association and the Virginia Association of School Superintendents, accused Bosher of having rewritten the standards to reflect a conservative perspective and of fostering social studies and language arts standards that promoted the "regurgitation of isolated facts" and "lower-level thinking skills."[49] Bosher and his defenders viewed such attacks as inaccurate and politically motivated. Michelle Easton, Allen's first appointee to the Board of Education, defended Bosher and the standards that emerged from the process. She said, "In asking students to master a concrete body of knowledge, we are setting academic goals whose achievement we can measure rather than calling for the establishment of vague and highly subjective behaviors and attitudes."[50]

In June 1995 the board enacted new Standards of Learning in the core academic subjects of English, math, science, and history/social sciences. Little controversy arose over the math and science standards. The math standards were strengthened so that graduates, who previously had only been required to master consumer math, were also expected to understand algebra.

During 1994 and 1995, SOL proponents engaged in a delicate dance. They tried to tout the virtues of meaningful standards without inflaming opponents who worried that SOLs would stifle the classroom autonomy of teachers or result in educators being held accountable for student test performance. For instance, in an effort to reassure SOL critics who worried that teachers might be held accountable for student test scores, Board of Education president James Jones said at a November 1995 board meeting that no board member had ever suggested "hold[ing] any teacher accountable for any test score." Similarly, board member and passionate SOL proponent Lil Tuttle said the board had no intention of using the results punitively against school divisions or individuals.[51]

Under the leadership of hard-charging Allen appointees such as Michelle Easton and Lil Tuttle, the board had initially moved aggressively to impose standards. Remarked one journalist who covered the board, "They didn't compromise at all, they just rammed [the SOLs] through. And in the process, they upset a lot of people and made a lot of enemies. Some of the more radical Board members were out there calling the schools 'fundamentally flawed,' attacking school counselors, and calling teachers 'incompetent.' They got the reforms they wanted, but they sparked a lot of opposition." This backlash influenced Allen's successor, Republican James Gilmore. Gilmore, who had been Allen's lieutenant governor, did not reappoint the more militant board members that Allen had named. Instead, seeking to quell the opposition sparked by aggressive efforts to push full-speed ahead on SOLs, Gilmore sought more compromising personalities.

A July 1998 editorial in the *Richmond Times-Dispatch* succinctly captured the ambivalence that characterized the moderate proponents of the SOLs. The editorial quoted Governor Gilmore reassuring educators, "Some people have said that the test results are going to be used to punish low-performing schools. … Nonsense! You have my word; I won't let that happen." The *Times-Dispatch* reasonably asked, "Why not? If ineffective policing were giving criminals free rein, would the Governor side with negligent cops? . . . The 10-year results of the Literacy Passport Test showed Virginia what does not work. More money, more teachers, and smaller classroom size did not boost academic achievement. . . . [U]ntil someone is willing to ask teachers hard questions, the learning curve may well remain stagnant."[52]

A Comprehensive Accountability System

The proposed accountability program included four key components. First, it required the creation of demanding academic standards in grades K–12. The new Standards of Learning were adopted in June 1995. Second, it called for criterion-referenced tests that were aligned specifically with Virginia's SOLs to measure student progress in learning the new standards. The tests were officially administered for the first time in spring 1998. Third, student test achievement was linked to school accreditation and to student graduation. Finally, school performance was to be reported to parents on a broad range of indicators—from test results to school safety—in annual School Performance Report Cards. The report cards were first issued in March 1999, providing public information on school safety, student performance, and a variety of other measures.

The SOL tests are criterion-referenced tests designed to measure whether students had mastered the specific content laid out in the state curriculum. The tests are short and consist entirely of multiple-choice questions in all subject areas except English. The English test also includes a writing component. A total of twenty-seven individual SOL tests are administered in a variety of subjects in grades three, five, and eight and at the end of high school.[53] The tests range in length from thirty to sixty-three multiple-choice questions. To earn their diploma, students would have to earn verified course credits by passing six of the twelve end-of-course (EOC) exams offered at the high school level. From the inception of the tests, proponents lauded them as clear, manageable, and concise. Meanwhile, critics argued that the tests were simplistic and overly focused on trivia. Said one critic, "With so few questions available to measure so many, often elaborate SOLs, it is impossible to reference the scores to specific skills or even to the standards themselves."[54]

In October 1996 Virginia chose Harcourt Brace Educational Measurements to develop the SOL test questions. At Harcourt Brace, about five thousand test questions were initially drafted by test-question writers who sat down with the SOLs and test guidelines for a period of six months. The questions were given to twenty-seven content-review committees—one for each exam—that included public educators from across Virginia. The revised questions were field-tested in 1997 and the content-review committees examined the results to flag problem questions.[55] Through the end of 1999, Virginia paid Harcourt Brace approximately $18 million for developing, printing, and scoring the SOL tests.[56]

STANDARDS AND CONTENT. Determining the precise material that the Standards of Learning ought to include provoked substantial controversy. While proponents tried to suggest that the standards would simply provide a floor to ensure that certain fundamental content would be covered, the decision to prioritize some content inevitably served to marginalize other content. This issue was relatively manageable in areas such as math, where wide-

spread consensus existed regarding what children ought to know, but provoked fierce debate in, for example, social studies.

During 1994, some conflict arose over the relative emphasis that the language arts standards ought to devote to phonics, but most conflict centered on
social studies.[57] Critics complained that the social studies standards had been
heavily revised by Bosher's rewrite committee to include too much specific
content. James Jones, the Board of Education president and a Baliles
appointee, said, "I think [the complainants] are concerned that there was such
a great change in the work that professional educators did and the draft that
has come from the commission."[58]

A series of ten public hearings held across Virginia in March and April
1995 drew nearly five thousand speakers. Most of the speakers criticized the
proposed standards, with public educators and academics particularly
opposed. Critics assailed the standards as unrealistic, trivia-oriented, lacking
in coherent intellectual or developmental direction, and fundamentally mis-
guided. Proponents contended that the new standards were specific, rigorous,
would ensure that students learned significant content, and would raise the bar
for acceptable performance. Speakers could readily point to the same proposed standards—for instance, the requirement that fourth graders be able to
summarize the purpose and content of documents such as the Mayflower
Compact, the Virginia Declaration of Rights, the Virginia Statute of Religious
Freedom, the Declaration of Independence, and the Federalist Papers—to
justify either perspective. Bosher observed in April 1995 that "positions seem
to be polarized" and promised ongoing revisions.[59] After the spring hearings,
he convened a team that altered 124 of the 138 social studies standards.

Initial efforts to resolve the disputes over social studies standards were
inconclusive. In 2000 a Board of Education committee revised the social studies standards again. Conservatives accused the board of easing the standards
and making them more politically correct. For instance, the revisions reduced
the number of historically significant individuals that students were expected
to know from ninety-five to fifty-four, eliminating Thomas "Stonewall" Jackson, J.E.B. Stuart, and Paul Revere.[60]

The controversial Virginia history SOLs gained national acclaim for their
rigor and clarity; they were cited during the 1990s as exemplary by groups
including the American Federation of Teachers and the Thomas B. Fordham
Foundation. However, much of the purported breadth and depth of the history
standards was the result of accommodations among the agendas of multiple
constituencies and camps. The standards may look imposing on paper but

prove less than solid in practice. For example, Virginia's tenth-grade standards called for students to analyze the regional development of Africa, Asia, the Middle East, Latin America, and the Caribbean in terms of physical, cultural, and economic characteristics and historical developments from 1000 A.D. to the present. Few of Virginia's social studies teachers—or professors of history, for that matter—could meet the plain meaning of the standards. Moreover, the standard does not make clear what would constitute acceptable mastery of the content or what kind of assessment is appropriate. The resulting ambiguity is politically useful to those who support high standards in principle but makes it difficult to implement standards in practice or to use them as a basis for sanctioning students or educators.

When officials write narrow, specific standards they increase the risk of offending those who see cherished skills, ideas, or content left out. However, efforts to broaden the standards undermine their ability to drive systemic change. Such conflict will be more common in subjects and grade levels in which more disagreement exists regarding the skills and content that children should learn. This tension is not due to any particular program design, but to the varied demands that multiple constituencies place upon American schooling.

TESTS AND STUDENT CONSEQUENCES. At the heart of the SOL accountability system was the promise that students would not graduate from high school until they had demonstrated acceptable performance. Graduation requirements contingent on acceptable SOL performance were slated to take effect for the first time in 2004. Fully implementing the SOLs required the board to establish passing scores for the tests, to decide which students to exempt from the tests, and to determine what to do with students who failed to pass the tests.

In October 1998, with the first administration of the SOLs looming, the Board of Education had to set passing and proficient (advanced) scores for the SOL tests. To assist in this task, the board convened eight twenty-person advisory committees, each composed primarily of teachers and administrators. State delegate James Dillard II, the Republican cochairman of the House Education Committee, observed, "The board was in a real box. If they set the scores too high, they were dooming school systems to failure. If they set them too low, they would be accused of dumbing down the curriculum. It's really difficult to say at this time whether they made good or bad decisions. They're kind of locked into what they did and we'll see whether the schools can make the necessary adjustments."[61] In setting the passing scores, the board tended to favor the high end of the recommended ranges. The recommended passing scores for the twenty-seven tests ranged from 23 percent to 75 percent. The scores adopted by the board ranged from a low of 52 percent for high school biology to a high of 73 percent for fifth-grade English. The board set proficient standing on the SOLs at 90 percent or above on most tests.

The board voted 7-1 to establish standards for all twenty-seven tests, with only Lil Tuttle dissenting. Tuttle, an ardent critic of public school performance, argued that the high school standards were too low. The bar-setting exercise provoked fierce conflict in pro-SOL ranks, as some Allen appointees were criticized by former allies for having gone soft. Those favoring moderate thresholds attacked the hard-liners, in turn, for demanding unreasonable standards that would produce backlash and demoralize students and educators. After defeating a Tuttle proposal to raise the eighth-grade requirements, board president Kirk Schroder said, "I know people out there would love to blow up the reform movement. I for one don't want to give them the ammunition to do so. We have to be on credible, solid ground." Board member Mark Christie, who had previously served as Allen's top lawyer, added, "If we don't have a rational basis, we're going to lose the legal attack. We've got to be able to defend it legally and politically."[62]

Meanwhile, SOL opponents were worried about how the cutoff scores were developed and the manner in which the data on student passing rates would be used. As one critic argued, "Even if the scores have respectable reliability and the benchmarks were divinely inspired, the potential for misclassifying students scoring near the benchmarks is great. For most tests the 'proficient' bar was placed near the middle of the score distribution. As a result, many students will miss the mark by a mere score point or two."[63] SOL critics asked whether proponents intended to deny a diploma to a student who was a few points short of passing a single SOL test. By opting to set high thresholds, the board raised the stakes of its subsequent decisions regarding who would have to take the tests and what the penalties would be for students who failed.

A crucial test for a system of coercive accountability is what happens to students who fail the required exams. SOL proponents sought to deflect this question by arguing that "SOLs will lift performance across the board" and that "ill-prepared students should not be graduating." However, such responses did not address the problem that would exist when flesh-and-blood students who had completed twelve years of schooling were about to be denied diplomas. The decision to set high passing scores produced some calls for a safety valve to assist students who failed the tests. Pressure for such a course grew when early test results showed the vast majority of students had failed the SOLs.

In February 2000 board president Schroder proposed a basic diploma that the state could issue to students who passed the English and math tests and to demonstrate that they possessed job skills but did not pass the half-dozen high school SOLs required for a standard diploma.[64] Critics worried that the Schroder proposal would create a two-tiered educational system and might lead to tracking for basic diploma students.[65] The basic diploma proposal was dropped in the summer of 2000. Cheri James, president of the Virginia Education Association, captured the ambivalence that infused this discussion when she observed, "When we first talked about [the basic diploma], we were talking about how do we build a safety net for those gap kids, and we thought this basic diploma route would be an option. But at the same time, we were having double conversations. While we said it could be a safety net, others said people could be tracked into it."[66]

While the board dropped the basic diploma, in summer 2000 it did create a modified standard diploma allowing the 14 percent of students enrolled in special education to bypass the SOL tests.[67] Special education students could receive course credit simply for passing their high school courses. As had been the case with the LPT, officials were lobbied intensively by special educators and special education families. This formidable coalition was concerned about the use of inappropriate tests, interfering with individualized instruction, and creating an insuperable barrier for many children.

The issue of how to handle students with limited English proficiency (LEP) also arose. While such students made up only about 2 percent of Virginia's 1.1 million students, nearly half of Virginia's LEP students were located in influential Fairfax County. After several years of discussion and delay, the board decided in early 1999 that students with limited English skills could opt out of one year of SOL testing and could take the tests using a bilingual dictionary and that the scores of such students would not count toward the school composite for two years.

In 2000 the board also responded to protests from some high-achieving districts by allowing high school students to substitute such board-approved tests as the Advanced Placement (AP), International Baccalaureate (IB), or SAT II for the appropriate SOL test. The board noted that more than fifteen hundred Virginia students took IB exams and more than fourteen thousand took an AP course in 1999–2000. This approach has the particular appeal of offering succor to those high-performing teachers and students most likely to feel straitjacketed by the SOLs and to mobilize in opposition. They are not resistant to IB or AP because they are used to it—the same way teachers get used to high-stakes testing. Teachers and students have chosen these classes, and teachers perceive them as more teacher-friendly and less threatening. Supporters said that the move indicated appropriate flexibility, while critics worried that it undermined the SOL tests.

ACCREDITATION AND MULTIPLE CRITERIA. Recognizing that holding educators responsible for student test performance would provoke heated opposition, reformers at first showed little inclination to link school evaluation to student performance. Eventually, in accord with a 1992 legislative directive that instructed the Board of Education to devise performance-linked Standards of Accreditation for schools, the board in 1997 adopted a performance-based accreditation system.[68] The new accreditation requirements were scheduled to take effect in 2006–07, ten years in the future. In adopting the standards, the board made clear that school accreditation would depend upon student performance on the SOLs, but then it explicitly ducked the question of what losing accreditation would mean for a school.[69] SOL proponents did not begin to routinely acknowledge the system's coercive intent in their public rhetoric until after 1997.[70]

To be fully accredited, 70 percent of a school's eligible students would have to pass the SOL tests in each of the four core academic areas. An exception was crafted for the third- and fifth-grade levels, where the board set the required English pass rate at 75 percent and determined that science and history/social science scores would not be used to calculate a school's accreditation rating. Critics of this policy argued that not counting science or history/social science scores in elementary accreditation would send a message that these subjects were not important and could hurt instruction.

In response to public feedback, the more moderate board dominated by appointees of Allen successor James Gilmore revised the proposed regulations in September 2000. Answering concerns that the test-driven focus was too narrow, the board broadened the elements that would be considered to include input-based considerations such as facilities, staffing patterns, and course offerings. Seeking to alleviate concerns that standards would be punitive, inequitable, or otherwise unbalanced or unfair, the board traded the clarity and focus of test-driven accreditation for an amorphous approach that would not provide similar clarity in evaluating performance.[71] Meanwhile, the only specified consequence for schools that failed to meet accreditation standards in

2005–06 was that they adopt a three-year School Improvement Plan. The board did not specify what would occur if the plan failed to produce the desired results.[72]

In discussions of school-level accountability, critics argued that student performance is largely a function of factors beyond the control of the teacher. One 1999 analysis argued that two-thirds of the variation across school districts in the first-year SOL results could be explained by just three measures of community socioeconomic status.[73] Moreover, critics argued that schools vary dramatically in their resources, meaning that some educators labor under unfair handicaps. Given these concerns, SOL critics argued against evaluating schools on the basis of student test performance and called for more holistic measures of performance.[74] While the adoption of such measures threatened to undermine the clarity of focus essential to transformative accountability, the case for using multiple criteria was reasonable and hard to resist.

In the 2001 legislative session, several multiple criteria proposals emerged and were adopted by the House Education Committee, although none made it beyond that point. These proposals sought to base graduation on criteria other than SOL test performance. The bills were prompted by complaints from administrators, teachers, and parents who thought their schools were being unfairly labeled as low-performing. One bill, sponsored by Democratic delegate and public school speech pathologist L. Karen Darner, would allow local school boards to substitute at least one alternative criterion for the SOL exams in determining whether a student qualified for a diploma. A second bill, backed by Republican delegate and SOL proponent James Dillard, would permit a small percentage of students who failed a test by a narrow margin to boost their test score by factoring in their classroom grade. Board of Education president Kirk Schroder criticized the legislative proposals, terming them, "Simply a back door to help students who otherwise should have failed the tests."[75] However, as 2006–07 creeps closer, along with the prospect of some schools losing accreditation, the question remains open whether reformers will continue to be successful at beating back such efforts.

The Early Results: 1997–2001

The first school report cards, issued in January 1999, showed that Virginia's schools had performed abysmally in the 1998 testing. Just thirty-nine of Virginia's eighteen hundred public schools had satisfied the 70 percent passing rate required for school accreditation. More than 97 percent of the state's schools were out of compliance with the new standards. How was this to be interpreted? Lawrence Cross, former president of the Virginia Educational Research Association, spoke for many critics in May 1999 when he asserted that "the SOL test results misrepresent the condition of public schools in Virginia."[76] Virginia school board president Michelle Easton countered, "The standards are high—much higher than what was previously required for promotion and graduation. But wasn't that the purpose of raising standards? . . . Schools would prefer a perpetual 'improvement model' that allows schools to retain accreditation as long as they show an improvement each year in test scores—even if it took decades for a school to reach a 70 percent pass rate. . . . But this would make state accreditation meaningless as it has been until now."[77]

In 1999 test results improved substantially—though they remained abysmally low—as 6.5 percent of schools had at least 70 percent of students pass. Of the 1,791 schools administering tests, 116 cleared the bar. Officials and educators wrestled with whether they ought to celebrate the tripling in the percentage of satisfactory schools or bemoan the fact that more than 93 percent of the state's schools were still failing. In one widely hailed 1999 development, black student performance improved on twenty-six of the twenty-seven SOL exams and the black-white gap shrank on sixteen of them. Nonetheless, while 41 percent of white students failed at least one SOL exam, three quarters of black students did.

The 1999 scores also fostered continued debate about the validity of the results, given that some thought the performance of Virginia's schools was not reflected in the scores. State delegate Kenneth Plum, a Fairfax Democrat, observed, "When you look at our schools relative to nationally normed tests, we do reasonably well. An accountability program that says 94 percent failure suggests there's something about the accountability program that we ought to review. Something doesn't add up."[78]

In 2000 test results jumped significantly, with 406—or 22 percent—of Virginia's 1,824 eligible schools meeting the 70 percent threshold. Another 38 percent of schools met provisional benchmarks, meaning 60 percent of schools were thought to be performing acceptably. In addition, black student performance improved again, with scores increasing on twenty of the twenty-seven exams. SOL advocates seized on the results as evidence that standards were working as intended.[79] Meanwhile, SOL critics rejected that interpretation and said the improved results did not necessarily mean educational quality was improving.[80]

As they had in 1999, the results in 2000 included some evidence of erratic movement in school scores. This enabled critics to argue that the reliability of the tests was a concern, that the tests were poor proxies for instructional performance, and that they ought not be used as the sole criterion for graduation or accreditation decisions. SOL proponents countered that the reported results either reflected real performance changes or were blips that would even out in the trend data.[81]

Reasons for Improvement

In Virginia, as in a number of other states, the introduction of high-stakes testing was followed by steady test score gains. What was the source of the gains? Three forces seem to be at work, but the relative significance of each is not yet clear.

First, high-stakes standards put pressure on educators to more effectively teach the required material. Teachers who pursued private agendas, disregarded curricular guidelines, or worked less diligently than they might have and administrators who had overlooked such activity are compelled to alter their behavior.[82] The result is greater adherence to curricular guidelines; more pressure to find ways to help students improve their performance; and a greater investment in some of the essential—if less enjoyable—aspects of teaching, such as checking homework and working with low-performing students. The system also encourages administrators to focus on identifying and offering appropriate assistance to high- and low-performing teachers and to find ways to remove teachers who continue to be ineffective.[83] The SOLs also provide a common language and goal that can unify school personnel and enhance administrative focus.[84]

Second, high-stakes testing leads educators to shift time and energy away from untested content and skills and toward the specified standards. Teachers increasingly focus on teaching tested content and on developing test-taking skills. This enhances curricular coordination within a school and across the schools in a system, increases the focus on material that has been deemed central, makes it less likely that teachers will use their classroom as a personal forum, and helps to ensure that all students are being educated to a specified level. However, these benefits bear a cost, as nontested content is marginalized and as teachers abandon more complex and elaborate lesson plans to focus on the tested content and on test-taking skills.

Finally, there are some pernicious effects. Students and educators are confronted with incentives to cheat. Incidents of cheating were reported in 2000 and 2001 in a number of locales across the state, including Chesapeake, Fairfax, Herndon, Petersburg, and Vienna.[85] Moreover, especially in the case of students having difficulty, test preparation and intense drilling could displace more substantive instruction or training in necessary skills.

These three dynamics have very different implications for educational quality. Thus far, no effort has been made to determine their relative significance in producing SOL test score improvement. However, determining how much of the improvement in student performance can be credited to each dynamic is essential to understanding the costs and benefits of coercive accountability.

Public Opinion and Backlash

The SOLs were launched in 1998. Implementation brought on substantial resistance, even though it would be 2004 before student results had consequences and 2007 before school results did. In March 1999 SOL critics launched Parents Across Virginia United to Reform SOLs. By fall 1999, its membership numbered twenty-two hundred. In November 1999, thirteen southwest Virginia superintendents argued that SOL scores alone should not prevent students from graduating and called for changes in the administration of the SOLs. The fall 1999 Virginia Parent Teacher Association (PTA) convention packed a room with members complaining about the SOLs.[86]

In November 1999 the Board of Education held five statewide meetings on SOLs and drew close to one thousand attendees to the largely hostile hearings.[87] Critics argued that SOL scores did not reflect real gains or were due to an unhealthy focus on testing and test preparation. As Mickey VanDerwerker, cofounder of Parents Across Virginia United to Reform SOLs, argued in September 2000, "What are we losing in our quest, above all else, for higher test scores? Parents can see that besides the increased stress and anxiety for children, this test mania is hurting real teaching and learning."[88] SOL critics took pains to explain that they were not opposed to accountability in principle— only to the SOLs as they were currently designed.[89]

In late 1999, in response to a letter from Schroder, a number of influential statewide education associations jointly expressed their concerns about the

SOLs and called for reforms.[90] Most significantly, the group opposed using SOL test scores as "the sole criterion, or even the primary criterion, for determining promotion and retention, graduation and school accreditation" and called for a "multiple criteria" system. Schroder argued that the current state system did base promotion and graduation on multiple criteria, because it took into account student course performance, attendance, and other conventional obligations. In the case of accreditation, the board ultimately did add input measures to the accountability plan.

Whatever the merits of the individual remedies proposed by the critics, each would result in a less precise and more complex test, one less able to render clear-cut signals regarding school or student performance.[91] In other words, each of their reform proposals would render the SOLs less suitable for the purpose that the proponents of transformative accountability wanted it to serve.

Meanwhile, at the urging of the pragmatic Gilmore appointees, the Board of Education sought to demonstrate flexibility and a willingness to compromise. As one reporter said of board president Kirk Schroder in early 2001, "He's the reason the program is doing as well as it is. He's out there selling it and listening to the critics and promoting compromise, and he's not ramming it down people's throats."

Even as test scores increased between 1998 and 2000, the coalescing opposition and the costs of change fostered growing public concern about the SOLs. An August 2000 *Washington Post* survey of 1,031 registered Virginia voters found that 51 percent said that the SOL testing program "is not working" and 34 percent said it "is working." Asked what should be done about the tests, 43 percent said they should be substantially changed and 21 percent said they should be "ended entirely." Just 24 percent of respondents said they should remain "as is." Many respondents worried that the fact-based exams force too much time to be spent on drills and quizzes and that the tests were too difficult, while others objected to linking graduation or school accreditation to test score performance.[92]

An October 2000 *Richmond Times-Dispatch* poll of 507 registered voters found similar discontent with the SOLs, with 66 percent saying that SOLs were not the best way to measure student performance and 68 percent that they were not the best way to measure school performance. Those surveyed were much more critical of SOLs than were respondents to a similar poll conducted in December 1999, when 58 percent had deemed the tests a good measure of student performance.[93]

Not surprisingly, students also appeared to dislike the SOLs. A spring 2000 survey of more than twelve hundred area seniors conducted by the *Norfolk Virginian-Pilot* found that 76 percent thought the SOLs had hindered their education and that only 18 percent thought the SOLs helpful. In addition, 77 percent said the SOLs reduced creativity in the classroom.[94]

The protests and poll results highlighted the delicate challenge facing SOL proponents. While Virginians supported accountability in the abstract, they were sometimes uncomfortable with the larger changes implicit in a high-stakes approach.

Efforts to Support Implementation

The state government has launched or supported several efforts designed to increase educator comfort with the SOLs. In 2000 the legislature approved a $114 million initiative to develop online SOL testing and to provide World Wide Web-based materials for teachers. The initiative was intended to cut test costs, simplify the testing process, and help teachers to better prepare students. In 2000–01 the state gave $1.2 million to 189 schools where children performed 20 or more percentage points below the English or mathematics benchmarks so that schools could support additional staff development.

In another effort, James Madison University launched a summer SOL Academy. The university designed the course in partnership with the Department of Education, which supported two regional centers and provided content specialists. In the summer of 2000 the academy attracted 615 teachers from across Virginia to focus on SOL areas of particular concern.

Changing the Culture of Schooling

Observers and school personnel report that neither students nor educators initially took the SOLs seriously. This was due largely to the Board of Education's decision to leave sanctions vague and to delay their implementation until well into the next decade. Many educators reportedly viewed the first wave of SOL tests as another passing fad. Over time, however, especially as school-specific data became available, as educators were given a chance to have more input, and as they felt more involved in the system, they started to recognize that the tests and the potential consequences were real elements of the educational landscape.[95]

High-stakes accountability is effective to the degree that it is coercive. When jobs or working conditions are at stake, educators can no longer close their classroom doors and wait out reforms. Educators are compelled to cooperate by relentless monitoring and concrete threats. School improvement is no longer contingent on the good will or intrinsic motivation of educators. This approach infringes on the prerogatives of teachers and imports a bottom-line sensibility into the traditionally forgiving culture of public schooling.

However, outcome-based management also has the ability to offer employees tremendous operational latitude. Traditionally, because schools monitor inputs instead of outcomes, they rely heavily upon paperwork and procedures. This can be a distraction, impeding creativity and rendering the profession less alluring to talented and energetic individuals. High-stakes accountability can alleviate this problem, permitting administrators to rely upon outcomes while cutting back on more intrusive monitoring.

Scant evidence exists that administrators are moving toward outcome-based management.[96] They have done little to use SOLs as a managerial tool, instead demanding that teachers generate extensive paper trails documenting their lessons and insisting that teachers scrupulously follow standardized curricular guides.[97] Instead of targeting intrusive measures on low-performing teachers, administrators in many locales are requiring all teachers to abide by uniform directives. Such an approach increases stress, reduces operational freedom and job satisfaction, and stifles entrepreneurial energy, resulting in heightened resistance to standards.[98]

The Clash between New and Old

The most obvious, and perhaps the most significant, clash over cultural change in schools takes place within the ranks of the teachers. Initially, veteran teachers resented the intrusion of SOLs. They viewed the new standards as interfering with their ability to do their job effectively and with their professional autonomy. Administrators reported a number of teachers taking early retirement rather than adjust to the SOLs. The SOLs, for good and ill, shaped classroom practice and the culture of teaching.[99]

While evidence shows that many teachers feel anxious and under siege, an unscientific online survey of thirty-one thousand teachers conducted by the state in spring 2000 found that most reported having been provided substantial support with which to meet the new demands.[100] Similarly, interviews with new teachers suggest that they are generally comfortable with the Standards of Learning. What accounts for the ease with which new teachers have accepted the system? Why does resistance among veteran teachers seem to have softened? It appears that several reinforcing factors are at work.

First, inexperienced teachers do not sense the loss of freedom bemoaned by veterans. New teachers accept the standards and expectations as routine, seeing the obligation to cover specific content—regardless of their own content preferences—as a condition of the job.

Second, new teachers express an enhanced sense of purpose and security. The autonomy of the typical American classroom teacher confronts novices with the problem of determining just what they are supposed to be doing and with trying to adapt to a fragmented, isolating culture. New teachers suggest that the common pressures and expectations of the SOLs make them feel like they are part of a team. As such, especially compared with the typical novice teacher, new teachers seem unusually certain of what they are supposed to be doing and of how they can assess their performance.[101]

Third, new teachers see the SOLs as a pragmatic and moderate approach to managing schools. They point out the value of having all students leave school with a common set of experiences and a common base of knowledge. They explain that such standardization makes it easier on both students and teachers when students move from one school to another and when students are promoted. Several teachers also suggested that the SOLs are not all that rigid. New teachers view the paperwork that districts have adopted to track SOL lesson plans as routine. These teachers are used to putting the SOL numbers in their lesson plans and on papers, while veteran teachers view the paperwork as an unnecessary headache.

Fourth, new teachers generally appear to feel more prepared for the SOLs. Teacher preparation familiarizes student teachers with the exams, acclimates them to the dictates of the SOLs, trains them to write a unit for the various standards, and helps them to build a portfolio of SOL lesson plans.

Finally, given the ambiguity of their job description, teachers tend to create a personal philosophy of teaching. Veteran teachers often feel that their personal philosophies are at odds with the expectations implicit in the SOLs. Meanwhile, inexperienced teachers are able to embrace an approved code of professional purpose and then get on with the business of teaching.

Veteran teachers talk about losing control, power, and professionalism. They also suggest that administrators have become less accommodating and less flexible, further reducing teacher autonomy. Teachers feel as though they have less freedom to use their judgment to select themes, design lessons, administer tests, or pace their classes.[102] Said one veteran teacher, "I feel rushed, like I have to just keep plowing ahead. When the kids don't get it, I get frustrated and just want to scream, 'Get it!' " Veterans also suggest that the changes make teaching less fun. Said one veteran, "It's taken the joy out of teaching." Another fretted, "There's a pit in my stomach when the scores come in; I think I'm going to get yelled at." Explained a third, "It gets to you. There is this constant worry. I swore I wasn't going to get sucked into it. But I started getting really nervous and afraid."[103]

Veteran educators were particularly bothered by having to curtail activities that they enjoy and believe to be educationally rewarding. Especially at low-performing schools, teachers reported cutting field trips, the amount of time spent on creative exercises, the number of fun or celebratory class activities, and the number of movies they showed to students.[104] Fierce disagreement has arisen over whether these changes are problematic or are evidence that the SOLs are forcing educators to focus on more serious education. The very stress reported by teachers suggests that teachers are feeling compelled to work harder or to teach differently than they might otherwise choose to.

As indicated by the responses to the state's spring 2000 Internet survey, even veterans are becoming acclimated to the SOLs. Many of the most resistant teachers were among the first to leave. Teachers also suggest that their comfort with the standards and tests has grown with time and with additional opportunity for input.[105] Moreover, three years after the launch of SOL testing, veteran teachers ascribe some concrete benefits to the program. They praise the increased consistency in what children are learning, think it helps transfer students, and like the fact that it reduces parental concern about varied teacher assignments and workloads. The SOLs are also credited with forcing some previously weak teachers to work harder and with helping to force others out of the schools. The SOLs also were prompting teachers to engage in more joint planning and collaboration.[106]

By early 2001, Virginia schooling was being transformed by the SOLs. In a particularly telling development, largely in response to parental requests, preschools were beginning to incorporate SOL-related material into their programs. Seeking to prepare students for kindergarten, some schools added units on recognizing coins and making change, identifying the planets and the moon, finding the directions and key on a map, and learning about prominent historical figures. Some preschool administrators believed it sensible to introduce students to these concepts, while critics, such as one preschool director, argued, "It upsets me because I believe the SOLs are pushing the first-grade curriculum into the kindergarten. You don't prepare a child for inappropriate material by being inappropriate sooner. I think it's setting them up to have school problems."[107]

The benefits produced by accountability are rooted in the assurance that teachers and schools will be compelled to provide students with an education of a certain minimal quality. Over time, clear expectations, employee accountability, and the ability to identify and terminate ineffective educators have the potential to improve education in those places where a reliance on good will alone has proven inadequate. Naturally, such a promise is most relevant to those children served by poor schools or poor teachers.

Conclusions

The decision to embrace high-stakes accountability represents a choice to trade the strengths and frailties of an education system reliant on good will and intrinsic motivation for one anchored in the firmer ground of self-interest. Policymakers no longer need to rely on students being driven by enthusiasm or teachers by a personal or moral commitment. While vaguely alluring in the abstract, however, this trade-off threatens the values that permeate traditional public schooling and inflicts heavy costs on particular constituencies. The result is a tendency to recoil from the reality of standards, resulting in a series of well-intentioned compromises that leave the façade of accountability intact but strip its coercive power.

It is hard for proponents to stand firm on the details of any particular accountability system because essential components related to content, testing, passing scores, and sanctions are inherently arbitrary. The closer one gets to crafting and enforcing standards, the less defensible specific program elements can appear. In the end, standards are an artifice. They are a powerful way to summon accountability from the ambiguity that shrouds child development, but they can seem problematic when lives and futures are at stake. A commitment to coercive reform requires embracing a system of accountability with all of its flaws, recognizing that any significant standards-based reform will inevitably include arbitrary and unpopular elements.

Determining what students need to know, when they need to know it, and how well they need to know it is an ambiguous and value-laden exercise. Neither developmental psychologists nor psychometricians can prove that specified content ought to be taught at particular grade levels. Such decisions are imperfect, publicly rendered judgments about the needs and capacities of children. Because public schooling requires public officials to make these judgments and impose them statewide, these difficult questions inevitably become political ones.

Under pressure, policymakers make several compromises as they seek to design and then implement high-stakes accountability systems. Each of these can be readily justified on practical or educational grounds, but the larger point is that each marks a retreat from the transformative premise of coercive accountability.

One common compromise is to lower the stakes of the tests for students, for educators, or for both. When sanctions are weak or nonexistent, teachers, low-performing students, and others have little incentive to worry much about test results. Virginia adopted this approach when it permitted students who failed the LPT to continue on to the next grade. When the scores have little or no impact, neither students nor teachers have an incentive to change their behavior.

A second compromise is to simply make the test easier, either by lowering content standards or by adopting easier test questions. The Board of Education did this when it streamlined the history SOL curricular guidelines in 2000. While some content softening may take place, this is a politically perilous course because it signals a public retreat from the notion of school quality.

Instead of easing the test, officials can reduce the thresholds required to pass the accountability assessments. If weakening test content is difficult, the decision to lower the score required to pass the tests is at least equally so. Once passing scores are established, officials have trouble lowering the bar.

If officials choose not to weaken the sanctions and find it difficult to weaken content or lower the bar, they may adopt two other strategies. They can permit some students to sidestep the required assessment. Officials find it hard to refuse a diploma to a student who has attended school and passed the requisite courses for twelve years. They can be equally uncomfortable requiring that teachers of advanced classes alter their teaching, especially when the changes may hurt student performance on recognized and high-visibility assessments such as IB or AP exams. One solution is for officials to provide opt-out provisions to substantial numbers of students. Provisions are often made for special education students, permitting these students to receive a basic diploma if they complete the required high school courses. In the case of minimum competency testing and the LPT, such accommodations minimized the number of students denied diplomas. Similarly, high-performing students are permitted to substitute other assessments for SOL exams, though this means no assurance can be made that they will master the SOL content.

Officials can also reduce opposition by delaying the implementation of sanctions. Virginia officials decided that no student would face the threat of being denied a diploma until seven years after the LPT was launched or nine years after the SOLs were approved. While solid educational and organizational reasons could be cited for these decisions, the delays push the necessary day of reckoning off into the distant future. During the period between enactment and implementation, meanwhile, changes in the political climate or among public officials can offer critics a chance to modify the proposed program.

While the push for coercive accountability generates fierce opposition, evidence shows that the political dynamic may reverse if these systems can be institutionalized. The experiences of Western Europe or Japan, of Texas with the Texas Assessment of Academic Skills (TAAS) or of New York with the Regents exams, suggest that once high-stakes exams are in place for a sufficient period they become part of the grammar of schooling for educators, parents, and voters. By the end of the 2000–01 school year, tentative signs were seen that the SOLs might be inching toward such a status in Virginia. Both gubernatorial candidates supported the SOLs during their 2001 election campaign, the tests were becoming part of the public school lexicon, and the majority of teachers appeared to be gradually accepting the tests and adjusting to them. Over time, the diffuse benefits of the test become more evident and more salient. When high-stakes accountability is institutionalized, the tests become accepted as the unquestioned gold standard for measuring performance, and all involved parties adjust their behavior accordingly. Opponents of high-stakes testing thus find themselves in the unenviable position of attacking an established system that seems to ensure that students are learning, teachers are teaching, and that the state's schools are serving their public purpose.

Coercive accountability can only drive behavior and change cultural norms if high-stakes regimes survive the long odds against full implementation. Given the political challenges to implementation, proponents of high-stakes reform have used four techniques to bolster their legislative prospects.

The first and most common approach is compromise. Reformers can reduce the size and scope of losers by shrinking the number of students, teachers, and schools that will be labeled inadequate by a test or reducing the real consequences of being deemed inadequate. This builds comfort with accountability, but it does so by lowering standards and by rendering them less significant—a price that reformers may not be willing to pay.

A second approach is to start by initially setting passing thresholds at a low level and then gradually ratcheting them up. Such an approach gives all parties a chance to gradually become acclimated to standards. It also serves to dull the effectiveness of critics, as they have little incentive to respond sharply to the minimal standards first put in place. By the time that standards are raised to more significant levels, critics will have difficulty overcoming the more accepting position they have staked out. This gradualist approach is the route that was followed in Texas during the 1990s.

A third approach is to make the status quo appear so frightening that voters will demand change and will reward educators and legislators who oppose the determined efforts of groups that lose out under reforms. Allen sought to employ this *A Nation at Risk* strategy during his 1993 campaign, with mixed success, and it generally is alluring to high-stakes reformers because it has the potential to alter the fundamental dynamic of the accountability debate. However, whipping up a widespread sense of crisis is difficult. Sustaining it for any length of time is even harder, limiting the effectiveness of this approach.

Finally, proponents can seek to make standards more palatable to educators by tamping down the leading source of opposition. One way to do this is to accelerate teacher turnover while ensuring that new teachers are familiarized with standards and high-stakes testing as a condition for their entry into the field. This will serve to increase the percentage of teachers who were trained and acculturated in an environment where high-stakes accountability is an established fact of life. A related strategy focuses more on administrators, encouraging districts to recruit more entrepreneurial administrators and to train them in the strategies of outcome-based management. Both approaches promise to reduce educator opposition to standards, to make the transition to standards-based schools an easier one, and to foster the ranks of public educators who are supportive of transformative accountability.

The effectiveness of high-stakes accountability rests upon the decision to institutionalize a number of subjective and arbitrary decisions. Linking real consequences to these decisions has the power to fundamentally transform education, especially in those schools where a reliance on educator magnanimity has failed to serve the interests of the students. Harnessing this power, however, requires making and then standing behind a series of difficult decisions, even though this posture will necessitate visiting some harm upon schools and some inequities upon students and teachers. The success of such an approach depends on whether the proponents of standards can convince the populace to commit to a system of accountability long enough for the accompanying benefits of reform to take hold. In practice, the effort to enact high-stakes accountability is often met by compromising key elements of the reform. While each compromise is reasonable and softens the negative effects of coercive accountability, each also marks a retreat from the transformative promise of accountability, diluting the potential benefits. The question is whether proponents of high-stakes accountability are willing and able to sustain the support required to institutionalize the proposed reforms, or whether their efforts will prove more symbolic than substantive.

Comment by Alan Wurtzel

Frederick M. Hess presents an excellent analysis of the politics of high-stakes accountability. I think standards, assessments, and consequences are useful, necessary ingredients to improving public education.

The issue is not whether, but how, to achieve high-stakes accountability in a manner that is fair and effective and that achieves both public and political support. I agree with the fundamental premise of Hess's paper that high-stakes accountability is popular in the abstract, but that losers, as well as winners, inevitably emerge during implementation. The losers are likely to be more effective politically in watering down the stakes than the advocates of accountability are in persuading politicians to stay the course. So how an accountability system is set up and whether it gives the potential losers a greater opportunity to influence politicians to water down the high stakes are important considerations in the design. Hess has done a persuasive job in showing how the system is working in Virginia.

While Virginia has not given up the basic thrust of accountability, the school board, under pressure from the legislature, has delayed or watered down the process of implementation, carved out exceptions for students with learning disabilities and for whom English is a second language, and reduced the graduation requirements. And it is likely to move to make something else, in addition to high-stakes testing, a factor in the criteria for graduation. This is to meet the criticism of people who maintain, with some justification, that a child's future should not rest on a single high-stakes test. The struggle is to find something else that is useful and relevant to add.

While Hess points out that the failure of earlier efforts of standards-based reform in Virginia was significant—the Literacy Passport Test, for example—he does not discuss the historical context in which the current Standards of Learning (SOLs) efforts were and are being played out. History may be relevant to an understanding of how the whole design makes the standards more or less politically immune to attack.

The modern effort at standards, or SOL reform, began in 1989 under Democratic governor L. Douglas Wilder and his superintendent of public instruction, Joseph Spagnola. When I joined the Virginia Board of Education in 1991, which was halfway through Governor Wilder's term, an effort was well under way to create a new and challenging standard under the rubric of outcome-based education (OBE). OBE was attacked by, for example, Peg Lusick, an outspoken critic of outcomes-based education, the American Eagle Forum, and other right-wing groups.

The members of the board, most of whom were Democrats, and all of whom had been appointed by either Wilder or his Democratic predecessor, came to agree that the methodology that Spagnola and his advisers were following was too politically correct (PC). Not that it was wrong in theory, or basically flawed, but that the tone of it was too PC and was, therefore, subject too easily to political attack. Under political pressure Governor Wilder pulled the plug before the board could act to correct and depoliticize the standards. It is not unlike what happened with the national history standards, which some board members thought were fundamentally good, although the exemplars were too PC.

Republican George F. Allen, elected governor in 1993 over weak Democratic opposition, declared OBE "dead and buried." But once in office, he began the process of creating education standards that were different in tone, but I would argue not fundamentally different in substance. They were grade by grade. They were concrete, specific, and measurable. They were focused on the fundamental core subjects, and they were premised on high standards.

He appointed Bill Bosher as superintendent of public instruction. Bosher, who led the standards process, was far more politically savvy than his predecessor. He had, for the first two years, to juggle a tough-talking Republican governor who, in large part, owed his election to the religious right and a school board, a majority of whom were Democrats, appointed by Governor

Wilder. Virginia's Board of Education has staggered terms, so that it takes two years before the new governor appoints a majority. Two of Allen's three initial appointments to the board were hard-core right-wing, religious right appointees. So Bosher was juggling some hard-core board members, the right leaning but pragmatic governor, and a majority of the board who were initially five Democrats and one Republican, all of whom were moderates on education policy.

He treaded this minefield by first co-opting the leading school districts of Virginia to design the standards. Fairfax County led the effort for math, a different county was chosen for social studies and English, and so on. And each district created for its discipline a committee that was composed of teachers and educators from other well respected districts throughout the state. As a result, the standards that came to the board had broad support within the education and the teacher community of Virginia.

Bosher also set four basic guidelines, which served Virginia well: (1) the standards would be limited to four core subjects: math, English, history, and science; (2) they would be grade by grade; (3) they would be written in plain English so that parents, students, and teachers could understand them; and (4) they would be measurable.

The Democrats on the board insisted that, in addition to these requirements, the standards be benchmarked to current national standards in those four key subjects, such as the history standards or math standards, which were in circulation at that time, in those four key subjects. They also insisted that the standards include a strong element of critical thinking, reasoning, and creative thinking, as well as basic computer literacy.

As the board went through this process over a two-year period, math and science were not political problems. Some efforts were made to broaden them in the critical thinking elements, but there was easily consensus.

English was a bit of a battleground, particularly over phonics. The board ultimately agreed in the end that phonics was essential, but not the only essential element in teaching reading.

History was the big battleground. Republicans insisted on more challenging material in the early grades. They, for example, wanted Greek, Roman, and Egyptian civilizations covered at the second- or third-grade level and in a comprehensive manner: from Mesopotamia to Macedonia, from the beginning of time until yesterday; and with a much greater emphasis on facts as opposed to interpretation. After some considerable give and take, and with the help of former U.S. assistant secretary of education Diane Ravitch, the board adopted quite decent standards, with a fair emphasis on historical thinking and reasoning.

On June 30, 1993, two or three days before the board became majority Republican appointees, the five-to-four Democratic majority passed these compromised standards, with three of the four Republicans voting in favor. This was a good start, with wide bipartisan support.

What happened then? Why did the standards start getting watered down?

Before answering those questions, let me point out that the game is far from over. While some continue to call for the abandonment of high-stakes accountability, particularly those involving the loss of school accreditation or diploma denial, consequences are still on the books. No school has yet lost its accreditation, and no kid has been denied graduation. The original basic framework, with some significant modification of the details, still exists.

Furthermore, Governor Jim Gilmore, a conservative Republican elected in 1997, has appointed to the school board people who are moderates on educational theory and politically centrist, replacing, as soon as he could, the right-wing ideologues that Governor Allen had initially appointed to the board.

The biggest problem in gaining wholehearted support of parents, teachers, and the public has been poorly designed assessments and a failure to implement an effective remediation program. There has been criticism from both ends of the political spectrum. Parents and teachers in the low-income schools are afraid that the standards are too high and their kids will never reach them. People in the affluent suburbs, and Fairfax in particular, are saying that the curriculum is being dumbed down, that the tests are too factual and simple minded, and that since teachers inevitably teach to the test, the material being taught is no longer challenging.

The argument over standards plays out in three areas: assessments, school accreditation, and the diploma requirements.

Regarding assessments, considerable opposition to standards is based on the belief that assessments are designed with too little emphasis on thinking skills. I agree with this view. The Allen Board of Education selected the test developer and set the guidelines for almost exclusively multiple-choice, fact-based questions with clear right and wrong answers. This reflects in part an ideological bias of the religious conservatives. The right wing does not like gray areas, uncertainty, and room for interpretation.

There is also a significant financial component. Testing with multiple choice is far cheaper than other alternatives. Multiple choice much more easily lends itself to yes or no, true or false, facts or factual questions, rather than to judgment, interpretation, and critical thinking. More sophisticated exams, particularly essay questions, cost more and take longer to score. This means that if an exam is administered at the end of the school year, the results likely will not be available until school begins the following fall.

Because assessments are largely confined to factual material and largely ignore the critical thinking skills that are also embedded in the standards, considerable concern and opposition has arisen, particularly in the affluent suburbs.

With respect to school accreditation, the Allen board decided that within seven years a school would lose its accreditation if 70 percent of all the students, including students with learning disabilities and for whom English is a second language, failed to get a passing score of 70 on the high-stakes exam. So, one size fit all. Seventy percent of the students in the highest achieving high school in Fairfax County or the lowest achieving inner-city or rural school elsewhere in the state had to get a grade of 70 or the school would lose its accreditation. I think that was a mistake.

I and others on the board urged that accreditation be based on continuous improvement so that particularly low-performing schools had some chance over seven years to meet the standards. Asking low-performing schools to do a five-foot high jump from a standing start, when other schools have many students who were already jumping three or four feet, was an unrealistic standard. But the board rejected continuous improvement and said it was one size fits all. Seventy percent of the kids have to get a grade of 70 or the school loses its accreditation.

Another disadvantage of the 70 percent cutoff score is that the Fairfax high schools and the schools with 80 percent passing have no incentive to make any improvement. Kentucky, for example, rewards schools with 80 percent passing that go to 81 or 82. That was absent from the Virginia system.

In the case of high school graduation with a standard diploma, the board has created a constantly shifting set of complex criteria based on the number of courses and high-stakes exams. From the beginning, students had to demonstrate mastery by passing end-of-course exams that had some curriculum diversity. The mix is changed, however, and the number of tests that a student is required to pass has been reduced over time. Today, a student is expected to pass three English, two math, and one lab science course to graduate. No passing score in history or social studies is required.

I believed, and I think Bosher believes, that it would have been far more politically acceptable to set the tenth-grade curricular standard as the standard for high school graduation. If the board had stipulated that every kid had to read at the tenth-grade level, do math at the tenth-grade level, and know some basic science and history at the tenth-grade level, I think the public would have accepted the standards much more easily. If children did not pass a subject in tenth grade, they still had two more years to master the material. If at the end of twelve years a kid could not read or write or do other basic high school material at the tenth-grade level, it would have been far more acceptable to say, "You are not going to get a standard diploma." The student might get a basic diploma, or a certificate of attendance, but not a standard diploma.

A clearer standard that is more politically understandable is needed, particularly because rigorous tenth-grade skills are what most employers are looking for in the work force from kids who do not go to college. If they can do English and math at the tenth-grade level, most employers would find that a reasonable level of accomplishment to hire them on at an entry-level job. The board did not set such a standard, however. Complex, hard-to-understand, and constantly shifting standards have drawn criticism that a clear tenth-grade standard would have avoided.

What are the lessons learned? The first lesson is that even a contentious political process—and the political process in Virginia was definitely contentious under Governor Allen—can develop meaningful standards on a bipartisan basis.

The second lesson is that to gain acceptance, especially among teachers and better educated parents, assessments need to be geared to critical reasoning and creative aspects of the standards, as well as to the more rote and traditional, manipulative, fact-oriented elements.

The third lesson is that standards for school accreditation must involve a challenge to poorly performing schools that is perceived to be realistically within their grasp. The standards should require continuous improvement or perhaps something like in the Texas model, where students from low-income or other disadvantaged groups are disaggregated and school expectations are adjusted accordingly.

The fourth lesson is that high school graduation standards need to be clear so that parents and the public can understand and accept them, such as tenth-grade literacy and proficiency in English, science, math, and history.

Hess has done an excellent job in describing the political dynamic of what is happening in Virginia and why. His basic analysis of the political challenges is absolutely correct. However, he has not discussed or examined whether the political backlash could have been mitigated or avoided if Virginia had done a better job of designing the consequences. In short, could it have achieved most, if not all, of the advantages of high-stakes accountability with much less political flak? I think so.

Comment by Iris C. Rotberg

I began as a research psychologist. When I changed fields and went into public policy, I assumed that I could apply the research methodology, but not the subject matter itself, to policy formulation. Now it has come full circle: I find that the research methodology used in psychology has little relevance to policy studies, but the psychological and behavioral analyses have become especially salient.

In formulating policy, lawmakers and educators pay little attention to how human beings might respond to any given intervention. Frederick Hess's paper on the politics of accountability presents an excellent and highly informative analysis of how those responses affect the likelihood that an accountability plan will be implemented as originally intended.

I would like to suggest that how human beings respond to test-based accountability will determine not only whether or not it gets implemented but also, if implemented, whether it ultimately helps or hurts children. That is, the tests themselves can have little impact one way or another. What matters is how educators, parents, and students change their behaviors in response to the tests and whether these behavioral changes are productive or counterproductive. My comments will focus on educators.

I assume that people on both sides of the test-based accountability debate share the same goal: to strengthen academic programs and reduce the gap in achievement. Testing programs will affect the way students are sorted. Those who support test-based accountability believe that it will provide the clarity and structure needed to enable students from low socioeconomic backgrounds to participate fully in educational opportunities. Those who oppose it believe that basing promotion and graduation decisions on test scores will magnify the adverse effects of poverty and unequal educational resources, thereby increasing the gap.

Educators' behavioral changes in response to the testing programs will play a major role in determining whether or not the programs produce positive outcomes. A small amount of research has been conducted on some of these behavioral changes; for most, there is anecdotal evidence or conjecture. I will give a few examples of arguments on both sides, beginning with potentially positive changes.

First, test-based accountability plans might change behavior by giving states and school districts a greater incentive to direct their energies to those students who have previously been ignored. Thus, if teachers and principals are held accountable for test results, they might devote more attention to low-achieving students. Moreover, the increased public attention given to student achievement might encourage policymakers to target additional resources to these students. In recent interviews with policymakers and researchers about the Bush administration education proposals, one respondent noted: If reporting disaggregated scores provides accurate information, which, in turn, "directs money to the right places, it would have a positive effect on educational equity."[108]

Second, the plans might change behavior by encouraging school systems to focus on the subject matters that are stressed in the tests and thereby reduce the time devoted to less academic activities. A respondent described it this way: "If schools are given sufficient time to develop standards, realign curricula, and ensure that teachers are trained in the new requirements, test-based accountability requirements could improve programs. In the absence of these elements, testing will weaken programs because it will force teachers to teach to the test because the consequences for not improving test scores are too high."[109]

Third, the tests might change behavior by providing the structure that many teachers, particularly those with less expertise, need to present material competently. For example, a respondent commenting on the Bush administration education plan stated: "Some teachers need structure, especially those coming from the second and third tiers of teacher preparation or those teachers who are teaching out of field, which happens quite often in the poorest inner-city schools. In these cases, standards and tests may be helpful in getting them through. In theory, the idea is not to have those kinds of teachers. But we don't have a deep bench when it comes to teaching."[110]

The argument, therefore, is that behavioral changes in response to test-based accountability plans can potentially strengthen education, particularly for those students who are at greatest risk of falling behind. On the less optimistic side, many believe that test-based accountability will provide incentives that are counterproductive—for the same students.

First, the pressures on educators to raise test scores might encourage them to make decisions that are not necessarily in the best interest of the child. These decisions affect student assignments, grade retention, and dropout rates. For example, students with disabilities or language-minority students might be assigned to special programs to exclude them from the test results rather than to improve their educational experience. Or, conversely, principals and teachers might be reluctant to recommend their highest achieving students for gifted programs in other schools because they would then lose the benefits of those students' high scores. There also are incentives to retain students in the grade immediately preceding the test-administration year, a practice that raises average test scores but also increases dropout rates, particularly if students are retained in middle or high school. Recent reports have described this problem, for example, in Kentucky and Texas—states that emphasize test-based accountability.[111] This practice was not invented in response to the current round of test-based accountability. Similar practices were reported in Ireland as early as the 1940s and in China and Kenya more recently.[112]

Second, the incentives implicit in accountability systems might lead to different responses from educators in low-income communities than they do from educators in higher income neighborhoods, thus exacerbating the current two-tier system. For example, teachers in the lower scoring schools might experience more pressure to teach to the test and to exclude subject matter that is not directly relevant to the test than teachers in higher income schools. Teachers in the more affluent schools might feel they have the flexibility to continue to teach a wider range of subject matter and even, as reported in Hess's paper, get permission to substitute other tests for the ones that are part of the accountability plan.

Third, test-based accountability, particularly when combined with low salaries and difficult working conditions, might discourage the most qualified teachers and principals from entering and remaining in the profession. There already are reports of educators choosing not to teach in the grades tested or in low-income communities, where the pressures to raise test scores are strongest.[113] Shortages of teachers and principals have become more severe, particularly in the lowest income communities. In comments on the Bush administration education proposals, one respondent stated: "The result will be that the best teachers will leave teaching or perhaps migrate to private schools where they are not subject to this. Why would the best and brightest want to deliver a script?"[114] The point is that accountability plans cannot be more or less effective than the educators who ultimately must carry them out. Another respondent put it this way: "It's getting to the point where the question is, Will the last real teacher in an urban district turn out the lights?"[115]

Finally, the focus on test-based accountability might detract attention from poverty, the most significant correlate of low educational achievement. A respondent commenting on that issue noted: "We believe that schools solve the problem of poverty, and now this program assumes that tests solve the problem of schools. By implication, that means tests are supposed to solve the problem of poverty."[116]

While educators might have different views about the potential trade-offs and net result of test-based accountability, whatever position they take, the behavioral responses to the testing program will determine whether the policy is or is not wise. It is to that issue, therefore, that I suggest attention be directed in formulating policy and conducing research.

Notes

1. The research is based on archival research; examination of state legislative and administrative documents, communications, and reports; a number of unpublished studies; and interviews with more than thirty-five public officials, observers, and educators.

2. See Frederick M. Hess, *Revolution at the Margins: The Impact of Competition on Urban School Systems* (Brookings, 2002), chapter 9.

3. For a general discussion of the political and practical challenges that confront high-stakes accountability, see Frederick M. Hess and Frederick Brigham, "None of the Above: The Promise and Peril of High-Stakes Testing," *American School Board Journal*, vol. 187 (2000), pp. 26–29.

4. For a particularly effective discussion of this point, see Arthur G. Powell, Eleanor Farrar, and David K. Cohen, *The Shopping Mall High School: Winners and Losers in the Educational Marketplace* (Boston: Houghton Mifflin, 1985).

5. Surveys find that adults overwhelmingly support standards and accountability in the abstract, but doubts emerge when high-stakes standards are put into practice. For instance, Public Agenda has reported that roughly eight in ten Americans believe it wrong to base grade promotion or graduation on standardized tests. This hesitance is due to the fact that two-thirds or more of Americans express concern that some students do not test well, that testing cannot measure all the skills children should learn, and that too much reliance on testing will cause teachers to focus too heavily on tested material. See Public Agenda, *Questionnaire and Full Survey Results: National Poll of Parents of Public School Students* (New York, 2000).

6. The fact that so many minority and low-income children are ill-served by their current schools helps to explain how leaders of these groups can emerge on both sides of the high-stakes accountability discussion. While some leaders voice concerns about the inequitable impact of sanctions, others like that educators are being forced to effectively serve students they previously overlooked.

7. For the classic treatment of the resultant "school house" culture, see Dan C. Lortie, *Schoolteacher: A Sociological Study* (University of Chicago, 1975).

8. See John E. Chubb and Terry M. Moe, *Politics, Markets, and America's Schools* (Brookings, 1990), pp. 26–47, for a particularly nice discussion of this point in the context of education.

9. See David B. Tyack and William Tobin, "The Grammar of Schooling: Why Has It Been So Hard to Change?" *American Educational Research Journal*, vol. 31 (1994), pp. 453–79.

10. This account focuses on the challenges that confront efforts to enact substantive accountability. Consequently, it inevitably gives short shrift to many of the technical and legal elements of the accountability debate. For an exceptionally clear and thorough explication of these issues, see Kathleen G. Harris, "The Standards of Quality" (Richmond, Va.: Virginia Division of Legislative Services, 1999).

11. Much of Virginia's educational policymaking is delegated to an appointed nine-member Board of Education. Board members serve staggered four-year terms, ensuring that the membership is composed of appointees named by both the incumbent and preceding governor.

12. In his 1978 address to the legislature, Republican governor John N. Dalton announced, "I favor the ideas of requiring students to show proficiency in the basic skills before they are granted diplomas." See "A Text of Dalton's Address to the General Assembly," *Richmond Times-Dispatch*, January 18, 1978, p. A5. For discussion of opposition to the effort, see Marvin E. Winters, "S. John Davis: A Thematic History of Public Education in Virginia as Interpreted through the Professional Career of the Sixteenth Superintendent of Public Instruction," Ed.D. dissertation, Virginia Polytechnic Institute, 1995, pp. 205–07.

13. Both tests were developed commercially; the reading test by Instructional Objective Exchange of Los Angeles, and the math test by Illinois-based Scholastic Testing Service.

14. For discussion of the minimum competency push in Virginia and its link to the national movement, see James C. Impara, "Virginia's Approach to Minimum Competency Testing," in Richard M. Jaeger and Carol Kehr Tittle, eds., *Minimum Competency Achievement Testing* (Berkeley, Calif.: McCutchan, 1980), pp. 284–309. See also Richard L. Needham, "An Analysis of Minimum Citizenship Competency Statements of Local School Divisions in Virginia," Ed.D. dissertation, University of Virginia, 1982, pp. 1–4, 22–32.

15. In 1978, two years after adopting minimum competency testing, the state adopted a standard K–6 curriculum. Using the curriculum, the Division of Elementary Education proceeded to develop 252 educational objectives covering math, communication, and reading skills. The approach was modeled on a similar K–12 curriculum that had been adopted in Fairfax County in 1971 when state superintendent S. John Davis had served as superintendent of the influential northern Virginia district. See Winters, "S. John Davis," pp. 94–98.

16. See Kerry Dougherty, "New Superintendent in Fairfax Discusses His Educational Views," *Washington Post*, November 29, 1979, Virginia Weekly 5.

17. State Board of Education member Hank Tulloch explained that this was a problem because, "If we don't give the test soon, then we're not going to have time to remedy the problems of those who fail by the time they're supposed to graduate in 1981." See Maggie Locke, "Fairfax Postpones Minimum Competency Tests in Math, Reading," *Washington Post*, October 12, 1978, Virginia Weekly 16.

18. See Lawrence Feinberg, "Competence Test Score of 70% Set in Virgnia," *Washington Post*, October 28, 1978, p. C3.

19. The untimed test included sixty questions in reading and ninety-nine in mathematics.

20. See Gary Robertson, "Competence Tests Scored," *Richmond Times-Dispatch*, August 7, 1979, p. B1; and Lawrence Feinberg, "18% of Virginia 10th Graders Fail Reading, Math Tests," *Washington Post*, January 17, 1979, p. C1.

21. The black community expressed substantial enthusiasm for the promise of equal treatment. In 1981 the *Washington Post* reported that "many black teachers seem to have become

ardent supporters of competency testing." As the chair of the English department in one predominantly black school noted, "All the way through life there are competency standards everywhere you go. Our kids have to learn to pass them." See Lawrence Feinberg, "High School Competency Tests Viewed as Too Easy," *Washington Post*, December 8, 1981, p. A1. This tension, between black leaders concerned about inequities resulting from the denial of a diploma and those concerned about inequities stemming from "the bigotry of low expectations," would continue to characterize the discourse during the next twenty years. In general, however, in Virginia as nationally, the visible and official black leadership tended to focus on the former.

22. See Feinberg, "High School Competency Tests Viewed as Too Easy," p. A1.

23. These results mirrored the results of every previous state to adopt minimum competency testing. In every case, less than 1 percent of students failed the test when high school graduation was at stake. See Needham, "An Analysis of Minimum Citizenship Competency Statements of Local School Divisions in Virginia."

24. See, for instance, Feinberg, "High School Competency Tests Viewed as Too Easy," p. A1.

25. See Feinberg, "High School Competency Tests Viewed as Too Easy," p. A1.

26. The proposed Standards of Learning (SOLs) represented Superintendent S. John Davis's effort to integrate the elementary-level Basic Learning Skills (BLS) program and the Graduation Competency Testing (GCT) program. Denied additional funding by the legislature, Davis funded the effort by reallocating Department of Education resources. To build broad support for the effort, he sought to include educators from all levels in a statewide process. The standards were widely distributed as they were being devised to maximize input. However, because they had no significance beyond the symbolic, critics had limited incentive to mount extensive efforts. The board approved the initial SOLs in 1981. See Winters, "S. John Davis," pp. 195, 210–15.

27. As state Board of Education member Margaret Marston said in early 1983, the commission's report bore "out all our fears" and suggested that "our very future as a nation and a people" is threatened by the "rising tide of mediocrity" in public schools. Marston was the state board representative on the national commission that crafted the report. See Nancy Scannell, "Improving the Schools; Arlington Member of National Commission Suggests Ideas for Better Education in State," *Washington Post*, May 4, 1983, Virginia Weekly 1.

28. This amounted to about $864 per student.

29. For a brief account of these events, see Craig Timberg, "Robb Legacy Is Popular with Teachers," *Washington Post*, September 29, 2000, p. B1.

30. See the report of Governor's Commission on Excellence in Education, *Excellence in Education: A Plan for Virginia's Future* (Richmond, Va.: Commonwealth of Virginia, 1986), pp. 5–6.

31. See Peter Baker, "Test Scores Are High but Show Some Stubborn Gaps," *Washington Post*, July 5, 1990, Virginia Weekly 1.

32. The 1990 pass rate was 65 percent, climbed to 72 percent in 1991, fell to 64 percent in 1992, and was at 67 percent in 1998.

33. See Robin Farmer, "Ungraded Policy Is Ended," *Richmond Times-Dispatch*, February 24, 1995, p. A1.

34. Another sixty-six hundred high school students had yet to pass the test because of absence, disability, limited English proficiency, or having just transferred to Virginia schools since the test administration.

35. In fall 1994, 58,833 students took one or more Literacy Passport Tests (LPTs). That included 18,200 high school students. Slightly more than half of the test-takers passed the components they took—the pass rate ranged from 54 percent to 61 percent.

36. See Farmer, "Ungraded Policy Is Ended," p. A1.

37. See Frederick M. Hess and David L. Leal, "Republican Party Growth in Southern Legislative Elections," *Virginia Newsletter*, vol. 75, no. 4 (1999), pp. 1–4.

38. See Michael Hardy, "Wilder Scuttles Outcome-Based Education Plan," *Richmond Times-Dispatch*, September 16, 1993, p. A1.

39. The George F. Allen effort was interpreted by political opponents as an intentional assault on public schooling. As Virginia Education Association president Rob Jones would say in February 1995, "I think there's been a deliberate attempt to make public schools the battleground. People have defamed the public schools for political gain." See Ruth S. Intress, "Education Battle Waged for Money, Control," *Richmond Times-Dispatch*, February 26, 1995, p. A10.

40. See Craig Timberg, "Allen Shook Up Va. Education," *Washington Post*, September 30, 2000, p. B1.

41. For discussion, see Mark Christie, "Standards of Learning: Why Virginia's Education Reform Is Working," *Virginia Issues and Answers*, vol. 6, no. 2 (1999), pp. 32–37. The 1994 LPT results showed 51.1 percent of black students failed at least one section of the test, compared with 21 percent of white students. In 1994, 478 ungraded ninth- and tenth-graders took the test—18.4 percent of these passed all three sections of the LPT.

42. See Timberg, "Allen Shook up Va. Education," p. B1.

43. See Governor's Commission on Champion Schools, *Final Report to the Governor* (Richmond, Va.: Commonwealth of Virginia, 1996), pp. 8–9.

44. Robley S. Jones, the president of the Virginia Education Association, seized on the same data—especially the two-thirds of Virginia sixth graders who passed the LPT and the fact that Virginia scored above the national average on the National Assessment of Educational Progress (NAEP) tests—to argue that the results "belie the general perception that public schools are failing." See Jon Glass, "30 Percent Fail Test of Basics," *Norfolk Virginian-Pilot*, June 29, 1994, Local 1.

45. Of the fifty-two members of the commission, seven were Allen political appointees, former Reagan-Bush appointees, or leaders of the conservative Network of Politically Active Christian Women; seven were state legislators; twenty-eight were a mixture of local elected officials, private educators, academics, and other private citizens; and ten were current or recent public school teachers or administrators.

46. Allen's first board appointee was Michelle Easton, an outspoken social conservative who had served twelve years in the Reagan and Bush administrations and was an uncompromising proponent of high-stakes accountability. Allen's second appointment was Lil Tuttle, another active social conservative. By summer 1995, three of the board's nine members were Allen appointees.

47. See Governor's Commission on Champion Schools, *Final Report to the Governor.*

48. Each of the four districts took the lead in one content area. Fairfax County assumed the lead in math, Prince William County in science, Virginia Beach in English, and Newport News in history. The first two districts were both in wealthy and suburban northern Virginia; the second two in the state's dense southeastern beach and naval community. None of the districts in the interior or more rural southwest corner of the state was involved in these preliminary efforts.

49. See Teresa Lemons Coleman, "Social Studies: 'A Long Shot,' " *Richmond Times-Dispatch*, June 18, 1995, p. A1.

50. See Robin Farmer, "Revision Battle Lines Formed," *Richmond Times-Dispatch*, June 18, 1995, p. A1.

51. See Gary Robertson, "Testing, Counselors Get More Study," *Richmond Times-Dispatch*, November 17, 1995, p. B7.

52. See editorial, "Stagnation," *Richmond Times-Dispatch*, July 28, 1998, p. A6.

53. Students in grades three, five, and eight are tested in English, history and social science, mathematics, and science. Fifth and eighth graders are also tested in technology applications. To earn certified credits for their standard high school diploma, students are required to pass at least six of the twelve end-of-course (EOC) SOL exams offered in grades nine through twelve. The high school EOC exams are in courses such as Algebra I, Algebra II, English writing, biology, chemistry, world history to 1000 A.D., and world geography. Aside from the English writing exam, the high school exams range in length from forty-two to sixty-three questions.

54. See Lawrence H. Cross, "The Standards of Learning (SOL) Reform: Real Consequences Require Real Tests," *Virginia Issues and Answers*, vol. 7, no. 1 (2000), p. 24.

55. The mechanics of the system suggest that Virginia has made a determined effort to anticipate and respond to concerns about the validity and possible bias of test questions. The Department of Education has twenty-seven content-review committees—one for each SOL exam—that are composed of teachers from across the state. The panels are assisted by representatives from the department and test-developer Harcourt Brace, but only the teachers vote on test items. Each summer the committees meet in Richmond to review questions proposed by Harcourt Brace's professional test-writers or questions that have been field-tested. The review committees were charged with examining test items for appropriateness, the match between the questions and the standards they are intended to measure, the match between the questions and intended student mastery, and possible cultural bias or stereotyping. Virginia also uses bias-review committees that include groups such as the National Association for the Advancement of Colored People (NAACP); all proposed test items are screened for correlation with the SOLs, age and reading-level appropriateness, material importance, and possible gender or ethnic bias. The committees have the authority to eliminate proposed test items. In October 1998 the Board of Education decided to create an SOL Assessment Program Advisory Committee to help monitor the SOL testing program. The committee included a collection of public educators, business officials, academics, and elected officials. The larger point is that such programmatic efforts to address these issues can lessen—but cannot eliminate—the existing concerns and political conflicts.

56. State officials report that the contract cost Virginia $4 million in 1997, $6 million in 1998, and $10 million in 1999.

57. The social studies standards encompassed the disciplines of civics, geography, economics, and history, but history was the source of most conflict.

58. See Robin Farmer, "New Learning Standards Draw Early Criticism," *Richmond Times-Dispatch*, February 17, 1995, p. B14.

59. See Farmer, "Revision Battle Lines Formed," p. A1.

60. The discussions also included thorny political topics, such as whether the 1915 killings of Armenians in the Ottoman Empire ought to be taught as genocide and whether they ought to be included in the standards. Dozens of Virginians of Armenian and Turkish descent testified before the Board of Education or otherwise contacted the board, urging members to approach the 1915 killings from one perspective or another.

61. See Pamela Stallsmith, "SOL History, Algebra Failure Rates Are High," *Richmond Times-Dispatch*, November 3, 1998, p. A1.

62. See Pamela Stallsmith, "Board Leaning to Higher Scores," *Richmond Times-Dispatch*, October 30, 1998, p. B1.

63. See Lawrence H. Cross, "Are Virginia's Public Schools Failing? Assessing the Assessments," *Virginia Issues and Answers*, vol. 6, no. 1 (1999), p. 5.

64. Ironically, this proposal was reminiscent of the minimum competency measures first enacted by the board in 1976.

65. The executive director of the Virginia chapter of the NAACP, Salim Khalfani, said, "Our concerns are that [black students are] going to be steered and tracked into that kind of thing. It flies in the face of their SOL effort if our young people aren't getting what they need to meet the work force of the 21st century." See Pamela Stallsmith, " 'Basic Diploma' May Be Revised," *Richmond Times-Dispatch*, July 23, 2000, p. C1.

66. See Stallsmith, " 'Basic Diploma' May Be Revised," p. C1.

67. For a more extended discussion of the effort to accommodate special needs students under the SOLs, see Frederick M. Hess and Frederick J. Brigham, "How Federal Special Education Policy Affects Schooling in Virginia," in Chester E. Finn Jr., Andrew J. Rotherham, and Charles R. Hokanson Jr., eds., *Rethinking Special Education for a New Century* (Washington: Thomas B. Fordham Foundation and Progressive Policy Institute, 2001), pp. 161–81.

68. Historically, accreditation had been based entirely on standards regarding criteria such as pupil-teacher ratios and the provision of specified programs.

69. A happenstance that proved politically helpful to SOL advocates was the manner in which the state supervised and accredited private schools served to exempt these schools from the SOL regime. Since 1985, when the Board of Education stopped accrediting private schools and turned over the task to the Virginia Council for Private Education, the state body had enjoyed no regulatory authority over private schooling. Substantively, this practice was a setback for ardent accountability proponents, as it meant that a substantial pocket of Virginia schools and students would escape the reach of standards. Politically, however, it was desirable because it eliminated a potential source of coherent opposition. It also created the possibility of a safety valve for some who found the SOLs particularly objectionable.

70. As Virginia Board of Education member Mark Christie argued in the spring of 2001, "[SOL critics believe] that objective tests should not be used for accountability purposes. I—and other SOL supporters—believe that without objective data about students' achievement derived from standardized tests and real consequences tied to that data, accountability in our schools will be nothing more than a Potemkin village." See Mark Christie, "The Standards of Learning Work Because the Tests Count," *Virginia Issues and Answers*, vol. 7, no. 2 (2001), pp. 30–31.

71. The board also adopted some revisions called for by educators, such as determining that accreditation scores could be based on either the percentage of students passing the current year's SOL tests or the school's trailing three-year average, whichever was higher.

72. For the regulations regarding school accreditation, see Virginia Board of Education, *Regulations for Establishing Standards for Accrediting Public Schools in Virginia* (Richmond, Va.: Virginia Department of Education, 2000).

73. See Cross, "Are Virginia's Public Schools Failing?" p. 6.

74. Virginia had already struggled, unsuccessfully, to develop a holistic tool for assessing school performance. In 1990 the Virginia Department of Education launched a program intended to compare the performance of school systems and individual schools. The Educational Performance Recognition, conceived in 1987, was to use sixty-three categories of data to derive composite evaluations. Proponents argued that the proposed approach was exemplary because it went "beyond test scores"—also including measures such as Advanced Placement offerings, attendance, vocational education enrollment, dropout rates, and physical fitness test results. Critics argued that the approach was "bureaucratic," overly complex, and ultimately "useless." In the end, the highly regarded and expensive approach had little impact, largely as

a result of its very sophistication and complexity. See Alice Digilio, "New Rating Plan for Va. Schools Viewed as Overly Bureaucratic," *Washington Post*, July 14, 1990, p. B5.

75. See Pamela Stallsmith, "'Proposal to Modify SOL Tests' Role Advances," *Richmond Times-Dispatch*, January 27, 2001, p. A8.

76. See Cross, "Are Virginia's Public Schools Failing?" pp. 2–6.

77. See Michelle Easton, "Virginia Can Become No. 1 in Education," *Richmond Times-Dispatch*, March 29, 1999, p. A15.

78. See Pamela Stallsmith, "Many Schools Gain, Near Goal," *Richmond Times-Dispatch*, August 14, 1999, p. A1.

79. Governor James Gilmore said, "The fact that the number of schools receiving full accreditation more than tripled and the overwhelming majority of our schools reached full or provisional accreditation is excellent news." See Pamela Stallsmith, "Schools Triple Passing Rate," *Richmond Times-Dispatch*, October 26, 2000, p. A1.

80. Roxanne Grossman, a spokeswoman for Parents Across Virginia United to Reform SOLs, argued, "Our concern is we focus more and more on whatever it takes to make standardized test scores rise while shortchanging anything that won't be tested. That's not necessarily the same thing as improving overall education." See Stallsmith, "Schools Triple Passing Rate," p. A1.

81. Kirk Schroder, president of the state Board of Education, said, "The bottom line is, the trend is in the right direction. You cannot look at a single year. You have to look at the pattern." See Pamela Stallsmith, "Blacks Post Higher Gains," *Richmond Times-Dispatch*, September 23, 2000, p. B1.

82. For instance, Pine Spring Elementary, which had been targeted by the Fairfax County superintendent as one of the district's low-performing schools, boosted its passage rates across the board from 1999 to 2000. Teachers were promised cash bonuses if the school met the district's target and sanctions—such as staff terminations—if it failed to do so. In 2000 the passage rate for fifth graders on the SOL math test increased from 64 percent in 1999 to 96 percent in 2000, while the number passing the history test grew from 29 percent to 89 percent. The school had not changed principals and had not adopted new reforms. One teacher at the four hundred-student school said, "I wish I could say there were these 10 magic strategies. But the fact is it was a lot of people pulling together—teachers really came together and helped each other out." Another teacher said, "[The rewards and sanctions] certainly played a part. Hey, when someone says you have three years to improve, that's definitely going to jump-start things." Faculty analyzed student test scores by grade and by child, sometimes adjusting groupings as a result. The school lowered student-teacher ratio by putting the reading specialist and special education teachers into the classrooms for more hours, while teachers sought to reinforce lessons by presenting the same material in different forms and across subject areas. Quizzes were designed to replicate the standardized exams, but teachers said they did not feel that this stifled their creativity. The faculty sought to make lessons more engaging, to pay more attention to student strengths and weaknesses, and to provide more collegial support. In essence, teachers worked harder, cooperated more, and focused on teaching the skills and content the state required. Meeting the improvement goal netted each teacher a $2,000 bonus and the school a $10,000 bonus. Overall, including Pine Spring, nine of the twenty schools Fairfax targeted met the performance goals. See Victoria Benning, "Va. School Overshoots Goal," *Washington Post*, August 11, 2000, p. B1.

83. For instance, the West Point school division, which was one of three districts to have all of its schools qualify for accreditation in 2000, had its teachers focus on specific subjects and increased staff development with such activities as bringing in consultants to teach teachers how to analyze test data. In another case, one Richmond-area high school with low SOL

math scores fired four tenured math teachers during 1999–2000 and 2000–01. The administrators identified several teachers with low student scores, conducted a burst of extensive observations of those teachers, and used the negative evaluations and poor test results to fire established teachers.

84. A number of school administrators, particularly in low-performing rural schools, seized on SOL compliance as a goal with which to motivate their faculties. Common were visible gestures such as school banners reading "SOL Compliance by 2001." See Liz Seymour, "SOL Program Gives Rural Schools a Boost," *Washington Post*, September 25, 2000, p. B1.

85. For example, there were several reports during summer 2000 of teachers being disciplined for improperly aiding students and of students themselves stealing test copies or otherwise seeking to cheat on the test. See Victoria Benning, "More Students Must Retake SOL Tests," *Washington Post*, June 8, 2000, p. B1; Leef Smith, "Va. Tests Still Too Strict, Educators Say," *Washington Post*, July 29, 2000, p. B1; Liz Seymour and William Branigin, "Theft Forces School to Give State Test Again," *Washington Post*, June 2, 2001, p. B3; Matthew Cella, "'Irregularities' Force Hundreds in Virginia to Retake SOL Exams," *Washington Times*, June 6, 2001, p. C3; Amy Jeter, "Chesapeake Students Gear Up to Retake SOLs: Teachers Question Preparation Boundaries," *Norfolk Virginian-Pilot*, June 7, 2001, p. B1; and Matthew Bowers, "Students at 3 More Schools Must Retake SOL's," *Norfolk Virginian-Pilot*, June 8, 2001, p. A12. For a good discussion of the larger issue, see Gregory J. Cizek, *Cheating on Tests: How to Do It, Detect It, and Prevent It* (Mahwah, N.J.: Lawrence Erlbaum, 1999).

86. In courting public opinion, SOL critics did suffer from association with a wing of anti-repression protestors who were widely viewed as extreme. See Pamela Stallsmith, "Coalition Offers Ways to Improve SOL Program," *Richmond Times-Dispatch*, February 25, 2000, p. B1.

87. See Rhea R. Borja, "Anti-SOL Concerns Growing," *Richmond Times-Dispatch*, November 22, 1999, p. B1; and Rhea R. Borja, "Comments: SOLs Raise Concern, Little Support," *Richmond Times-Dispatch*, December 1, 1999, p. A1.

88. See Rhea R. Borja, "Statewide Test Scores Rise," *Richmond Times-Dispatch*, September 8, 2000, p. A1. In February 2000, Melvin D. Law, the former chair of the Richmond School Board, attacked the SOLs as "punitive and anti-child" and said the SOL system was "illogical, unfair, and borders on disgraceful." Law had previously called the SOLs the "Standards of Lunacy."

89. Roxanne Grossman, a spokeswoman for Parents Across Virginia United to Reform SOLs, said in early 2001, "We're not opposed to including standardized testing scores in the criteria [for determining graduation and accreditation], but what needs to be gotten at is that the criterion of the test scores should not be given the most weight." See Pamela Stallsmith, "Lawmakers Seeking SOL Changes," *Richmond Times-Dispatch*, January 24, 2001, p. C1.

90. The group, dominated by traditional public school organizations, included the Virginia Association of Elementary School Principals, Virginia Association of Secondary School Principals, the Virginia Association of School Superintendents, the Virginia Congress of Parents and Teachers, the Virginia Education Association, and the Virginia School Boards Association.

91. As prominent opponent Lawrence H. Cross noted in spring 2000, "I had hoped that the technical concerns that I and many others had raised about the SOL tests and their intended uses would have caused our leaders in Richmond . . . to abandon this test-driven reform of public schools." See Cross, "The Standards of Learning (SOL) Reform," p. 25.

92. See Jay Matthews, Victoria Benning, and *Washington Post* staff writers, "Va. Voters Negative on SOLs," *Washington Post*, September 11, 2000, p. B1.

93. See Jeff E. Schapiro, "Survey: SOL Tests Lose Public Support," *Richmond Times-Dispatch*, October 6, 2000, p. A1.

94. See Philip Walzer, "In Survey, Seniors Give Thumbs-Down to SOLs," *Norfolk Virgin-ian-Pilot*, June 18, 2000, p. B1.

95. See Margaret Grogan and Pam Roland, "A Study of Successful Teachers Preparing High School Students for the Standards of Learning Tests in Virginia," paper presented at the annual University Council for Educational Administration conference in Albuquerque, N.M., November 3, 2000, p. 13.

96. For a discussion of how principals have approached the new system, see Daniel Duke, Walter Heinecke, and Pamela Tucker, *Initial Responses of Virginia High Schools to the Accountability Initiative* (University of Virginia, Thomas Jefferson Center for Educational Design, 2000).

97. In some systems, principals are routinely requiring teachers to file more detailed lesson plans that explicitly spell out classroom activities and time on various tasks for high, average, and slow learners. Teachers report being required to file five or six pages of lesson plans a day where they used to file one. See Denise Watson Batts, "Emphasis on SOLs Brings Added Stress to Teachers," *Norfolk Virginian-Pilot*, November 14, 1999, p. B1.

98. The fact that SOLs do not necessarily imply continuous fact-based drilling or memorization is brought home by visits to classrooms where teachers are finding creative ways to design more elaborate lessons around the required content. For a depiction of a few such efforts, see Emily Wax, "New Ways to Make the Past a Blast," *Washington Post*, March 6, 2000, p. B3.

99. Two scholars who had studied the reaction of nine teachers to SOLs concluded in early 2000 that, "Teachers considered test preparation to be synonymous with teaching. In most of the classroom, teachers had displayed the relevant SOL for every lesson." See Grogan and Roland, "A Study of Successful Teachers Preparing High School Students for the Standards of Learning Tests in Virginia," pp. 6–7.

100. In the survey, teachers expressed satisfaction with the assistance they had received in implementing the SOLs. About thirty-one thousand of Virginia's eighty-seven thousand teachers responded to the anonymous survey. The unscientific survey cannot provide reliable estimates of actual teacher attitudes, but it provided strong anecdotal evidence that teachers felt they were receiving the necessary support and training. Ninety percent of respondents said they had the necessary knowledge about the SOL subject area they were teaching to be effective, 84 percent said teachers and administrators protect classroom instructional time to ensure that students can meet the SOL objectives, and 69 percent agreed that "high quality and relevant instructional materials" had been provided to help school employees teach the standards.

101. A number of teachers in a variety of school circumstances expressed this feeling. Said one, "Without the SOL, I'd feel like I was second-guessing myself." Another said, "The SOL makes me feel safe." A third suggested, "[The SOL] let's me know here's where I am and here's where I have to go."

102. One seventeen-year veteran teacher who resigned in 1999 rather than continue to teach under the SOLs said, "I'm sad about the fact that I needed to leave Norfolk to feel better about myself as a teacher. The new standards and the tests are fine. It's the indirect pressure the teaches are feeling from the administration." Another veteran teacher said, "Teachers are taking medication to cope with the stress. Teachers are quitting because of the stress. Teachers are crying in the hallways and 'snapping' at one another because of the stress." See Denise Watson Batts, "Emphasis on SOLs Brings Added Stress to Teachers," *Hampton Roads Virginian-Pilot*, November 14, 1999, p. B1.

103. For an extensive look at the effects of the SOLs on the teacher work force, see Liz Seymour, "SOL Tests Create New Dropouts," *Washington Post*, July 17, 2001, p. A1.

104. As one English teacher who had revised her American literature class to focus on grammar explained, "I spend anywhere from 10 to 15 minutes reviewing the standards of grammar usage. Our plan is for 11th grade to continue to review all English SOLs until the test in May. So some students complain we don't have enough time for creative activities, and that is a concern of mine." Similar concerns were expressed by some critics who feared that SOLs were squeezing the time devoted to other activities, such as arts instruction or weekend recreation. See Kristen Noz, "Arts Groups Cite SOL-Related Woes," *Richmond Times-Dispatch*, May 19, 1999, p. B7; and Kristen Noz, "Saturdays for SOL Review Sessions," *Richmond Times-Dispatch*, April 5, 2000, p. M1.

105. One Roanoke County teacher explained in August 2000 that she was originally suspicious about the SOLs but changed her mind after serving on a committee of teachers who reviewed test questions for the eighth-grade writing test. "I was unaware of how much effort and revision went into the testing process until I worked on the tests myself. I did not previously know that classroom teachers were allowed to revise test items or that teachers have the final say-so about whether test items were approved or rejected." See Joel Turner, "Teachers Test SOL Questions," *Richmond Times-Dispatch*, August 4, 2000, p. B2.

106. See Duke, Heinecke, and Tucker, *Initial Responses of Virginia High Schools to the Accountability Initiative*.

107. See Holly Carroll, "Mixed Reviews: Parents Want Preschool to Teach Standards of Learning Concepts," *Richmond Times-Dispatch*, February 28, 2001, p. J1.

108. Iris C. Rotberg, Kenneth J. Bernstein, and Suzanne B. Ritter, *No Child Left Behind: Views about the Potential Impact of the Bush Administration's Education Proposals* (George Washington University, 2001), p. 14.

109. Rotberg, Bernstein, and Ritter, *No Child Left Behind*, p. 13.

110. Rotberg, Bernstein, and Ritter, *No Child Left Behind*, pp. 16–17.

111. Richard F. Elmore, Charles H. Abelmann, and Susan H. Fuhrman, "The New Accountability in State Education Reform: From Process to Performance," in Helen F. Ladd, ed., *Holding Schools Accountable: Performance-Based Reform in Education* (Brookings, 1996), pp. 65–98; and Marguerite Clarke, Walter Haney, and George Madaus, "High Stakes Testing and High School Completion," *NBETPP Statements* (Boston College, 2000), pp. 1–11.

112. George F. Madaus and Vincent Greaney, "The Irish Experience in Competency Testing: Implications for American Education," *American Journal of Education* (February 1985), pp. 268–94; and Vincent Greaney and Thomas Kellaghan, *Equity Issues in Public Examinations in Developing Countries*, Technical Paper 272 (Washington: World Bank, 1995).

113. See, for example, Iris C. Rotberg and others, "Nation's Schools Struggling to Find Enough Principals," *New York Times*, September 3, 2000.

114. Rotberg, Bernstein, and Ritter, *No Child Left Behind*, p. 16.

115. Rotberg, Bernstein, and Ritter, *No Child Left Behind*, p. 15.

116. Rotberg, Bernstein, and Ritter, *No Child Left Behind*, p. 11.

School Accountability in California: An Early Evaluation

JULIAN R. BETTS *and* ANNE DANENBERG

O ver the last decade, virtually every state has launched a school accountability program in response to public concern over failing schools. A state accountability program ideally consists of at least three components: a content standard or framework that stipulates what students should know and when they should know it, an assessment system that tracks student progress against the content standards, and a menu of responses by the state. These responses are typically directed both at schools that excel and at those that lag behind, but sometimes rewards are given to students who excel and extra educational resources are provided for students who are struggling.

Assessments and accountability are not new. As Robert L. Linn notes, they have been included in many education reform programs over the last fifty years. He also points out that what is new in the current reform effort is the emphasis on content standards, setting challenging content standards while including all students, and the element of high-stakes accountability.[1]

Proponents of school accountability argue that standards can energize school systems, by putting pressure on schools to help all students. The public release of test scores can bring attention to bear upon schools that lag behind. A carefully designed system of consequences related to state assessments can in turn focus additional resources and oversight on those schools that are struggling the most. After almost a decade of accountability reforms, content standards and testing remain very popular in opinion polls.

At the same time, detractors of the standards movement point to a number of failings of typical accountability programs. First, opponents charge, the sys-

We thank Robert Hauser and Robert Rothman for helpful comments.

tem of incentives and consequences can be unfair if it does not take into account the predominant role of family socioeconomic status (SES) in determining student achievement. A system that channeled all the financial rewards to schools in the suburbs, while imposing financial sanctions on inner-city schools, could be an example. The opportunity-to-learn movement claims that holding all schools accountable to the same content standards makes sense only if schools serving disadvantaged students first receive an infusion of resources. Second, the assessment system must be closely aligned with the content standards. Otherwise, teachers and students receive mixed messages about what students are expected to learn during the course of a year. Third, many critics worry that states' accountability systems will lead to significant changes in both school resources and the curriculum that may not benefit all students. For instance, Julian R. Betts and Robert M. Costrell note that in some states the most vociferous complaints about standards and testing have come from well-to-do suburbs, apparently on the grounds that state accountability systems interfere with schools that were already meeting affluent parents' goals for their children.[2] Inner-city parents in the same cities often strongly support standards and testing.

We address these issues in the context of California public schools. California has recently implemented an accountability system that encompasses the three fundamental components: content standards, student assessments, and a system of responses for schools at both ends of the achievement spectrum. We pay particular attention to trends in overall student achievement and school resources and the distribution of student achievement and school resources since the introduction of the accountability system. We call our analysis an early evaluation because it is far too soon to know whether the new system will succeed. However, a retrospective of the accountability reforms a decade or more from now, while valuable, is of little use to policymakers who are changing the accountability recipe on a year-by-year basis. It is essential that neutral outside observers monitor early trends in achievement and school resources to inform this policy debate.

The Challenges Facing California Schools

California's schools and students differ from those in the rest of the country on a number of dimensions. Each of these variations arguably heightens both the need for uniform educational standards and the risks of imposing

Figure 1. Real Expenditures per Pupil, United States and California

Dollars

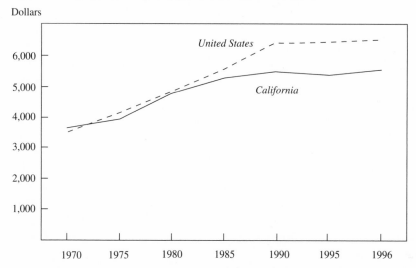

Source: National Center for Education Statistics, *Digest of Education Statistics* (1999), table 171, 1976 table 75, 1971 table 78.
Note: Data are adjusted to 1997 prices using the consumer price index, obtained from the Department of Labor, Bureau of Labor Statistics.

them. First, California school expenditures have grown over time but beginning in the 1980s began to lag behind national averages. Figure 1 illustrates this trend. Jon Sonstelie, Eric Brunner, and Kenneth Ardon argue that a combination of legislative responses to the *Serrano* v. *Priest* school finance equalization case and the 1979 passage of Proposition 13, a voter initiative that effectively removed the ability of local authorities to raise property taxes for local needs, caused the growth in school spending in California to begin to trail the national average.[3] This suggests that standards in California, if they were pitched too high, might fail because of the relatively low levels of resources devoted to public education in California.

Second, California's student population differs from that in the rest of the nation. The state has a far higher number of limited English proficiency (LEP) students than other states. This heterogeneous population implies that performance on standardized tests will be equally heterogeneous. Figure 2 presents the percentage of California's public school students scoring at or above national norms in math during the first (spring 1998) administration of the new state test. The middle line shows that in most grades the percentage of all students at or above the national median in math was in the low forties. (If California students were identical to those in the nation as a whole, then

Figure 2. California Students above National Median in Math Based on Statewide Summary Data, 1998

Percent

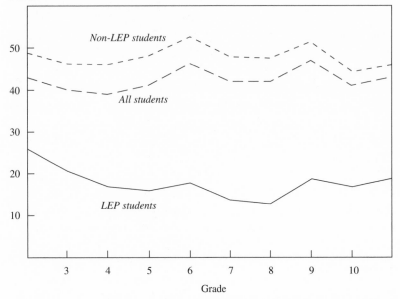

Grade

Source: Julian R. Betts, Kim S. Rueben, and Anne Danenberg, *Equal Resources, Equal Outcomes? The Distribution of School Resources and Student Achievement in California* (San Francisco: Public Policy Institute of California, 2000), figure 7.1.
Note: LEP = limited English proficiency.

exactly 50 percent should have been at or above national norms.) However, the other two lines in the figure show that LEP and non-LEP students scored differently from each other at each grade. Non-LEP students in California still lagged behind national norms but only by a few percentage points, while LEP students were far below national norms. Limited experience with English poses considerable academic challenges for many of California's students. (The gap between LEP and non-LEP students in reading is, understandably, even larger than the gap in math.)

The considerable gap in achievement between non-LEP and LEP students in California increases the importance of setting educational standards in a bid to bring up the achievement of California's LEP students. At the same time, this heterogeneity poses serious risks for the integrity of educational standards.

Which of these two variations from national averages, in spending per pupil or in students' ability in the English language, matters more in the design of educational standards? While both are potential landmines, we believe that variations in language pose the greater difficulty. If California's educational standards did not take into account variations in the number of LEP students in each school, the system could in theory unfairly penalize schools that served unusually large numbers of English learners.

Lower spending per pupil in California probably also drives a wedge between average student achievement in California and other states. This could lead to perennial underperformance of California's schools. However, it is important not to overestimate the impact of spending on student outcomes.[4] In the California case, Julian R. Betts, Kim S. Rueben, and Anne Danenberg find that variations in school resources explain only a small portion of the variation in achievement among the state's schools that existed in 1998.[5] Throughout this chapter, the school resources to which we refer are school-level teacher characteristics as measured by experience, education, and credentials; average class size; and high school curriculum as measured by the percentage of college prep class sections across all subject areas. Although per-pupil spending is often the measure of resources that researchers use, in California the lowest available level of per-pupil spending is at the district level. Another reason to prefer our nonfinancial measures of school resources is that variations in spending per pupil to some extent mirror variations in the cost of living across the state.

A remarkable variation exists in both test scores and certain school resources among California's schools. For example, schools, when ranked into quintiles by the percentage of students receiving free or reduced-price lunch, varied radically in student achievement in spring 1998 (see figure 3). The figure shows the percentage of non-LEP students scoring at or above national norms among schools in each quintile. Even setting aside the issue of LEP students, disadvantage is strongly related to variations in student performance across schools.

Variations in teacher characteristics and, at the high school level, curriculum also appear among California's schools. Table 1 illustrates this point using data from California high schools. Teachers without full credentials, inexperienced teachers, and teachers with at most a bachelor's degree are distributed highly unequally among schools. For instance, when we rank schools by the percentage of teachers without a full credential, at the 10th percentile school and the 90th percentile school 0 percent and 17.6 percent of teachers lack a full credential, respectively. Curriculum measures in the table include the percentage of classes that are Advanced Placement (AP) and the percentage of courses

Figure 3. Non-LEP Students Scoring at or above National Medians in Math and Reading by School SES Quintile Based on Percent Receiving Free or Reduced-Price Lunch

Percent

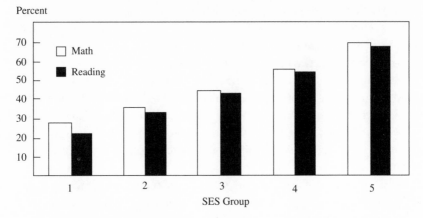

SES Group

Source: Julian R. Betts, Kim S. Rueben, and Anne Danenberg, *Equal Resources, Equal Outcomes? The Distribution of School Resources and Student Achievement in California* (San Francisco: Public Policy Institute of California, 2000), figure 7.3.
Note: LEP = limited English proficiency; SES = socioeconomic status. The lowest SES group = 1.

that help students to meet the "a-f" requirements for admission to the University of California and the closely related requirements for the California State University system. The data in the table show meaningful variations in these measures of high school curriculum. Betts, Rueben, and Danenberg show that these variations in teacher characteristics and high school curriculum exhibited in the table are strongly related to student disadvantage.[6]

In summary, in the 1997–98 school year in California, both LEP students and students fluent in English lagged behind national norms. California's spending per pupil fell behind the national average in the 1980s, and in 1997–98 considerable inequalities in school resources, especially teacher qualifications, existed among schools. Schools also varied dramatically in average student achievement at this time. However, variations in poverty and the percentage of students who were LEP at each school explained far more of the variations in student achievement across schools than did variations in teacher preparation and other resources.

The large variations in student achievement among schools and the gap between California students' performance and national norms both suggest that the rationale for statewide educational content standards, assessment, and intervention is strong. At the same time it raises important questions about the capability of schools to bring all students up to common norms of achievement, especially in light of variations in resources among schools.

Table 1. Percentiles of California High School Characteristics, 1997–98, Weighted by Student Enrollment

Variable	Distribution percentile				
	10th	*25th*	*50th*	*75th*	*90th*
Class size	20.0	21.6	23.3	26.1	31.6
Percent "a-f" classes	40.8	47.2	54.9	61.1	67.0
Percent AP classes	0.6	1.4	2.2	3.4	4.8
Percent teachers with 0–2 years of experience	5.2	8.4	12.2	16.8	21.7
Percent teachers with at most BA	2.4	5.4	10.4	20.6	37.5
Percent teachers not fully certified	0.0	2.3	6.3	12.2	17.6

Source: Julian R. Betts, Kim S. Rueben, and Anne Danenberg, *Equal Resources, Equal Outcomes? The Distribution of School Resources and Student Achievement in California* (San Francisco: Public Policy Institute of California, 2000), table A.2.
Note: AP = Advanced Placement; BA = bachelor's degree.

Compounding matters, even if resources could be equalized across schools, this equalization by itself would do little to close the test score gap related to variations in student disadvantage.[7]

For these reasons, it becomes essential to understand how the accountability system sets standards, what allowance the accountability system gives to existing differences across socioeconomic strata in initial variations in achievement, the allowances made for LEP students, and the way in which school resources have changed at schools over the last few years.

The School Accountability System in California

The standards being set in California today come in the form of a series of measures enacted at the state level.[8] Matrix tests that assessed average achievement at the school level were used in the 1980s; in the early 1990s a written test was introduced statewide, only to be cancelled in 1994. In 1997, legislation based on Senate Bill (SB) 376 passed, by which California reinstituted a statewide test in spring 1998. The new testing system, the California Standardized Testing and Reporting program (STAR), initially relied on one test—the Stanford 9. The Stanford 9 is a nationally normed multiple-choice achievement test. School districts are required to administer the Stanford 9 to all students in grades two through eleven, except for those students whose individual education plans (IEPs) explicitly exempt them or those students whose parent or guardian submits a written request to exempt the child. (Exemption rates to date have been very low.) In grades two through eight, students are tested in reading, spelling, written expression, and mathematics. In grades nine through eleven, testing is required in reading, writing, mathematics, science, and history/social science.

At roughly the same time, the state developed a series of content standards stipulating what students should learn in a variety of subjects, on a grade-by-grade basis. Specifically, California adopted English/language arts and mathematics standards in late 1997, science and history/social science content standards in late 1998, and content standards in visual and performing arts in early 2001. The state Board of Education typically has published two companion volumes for each subject, a set of content standards that lists skills that should be mastered in each grade, and a much longer volume containing a content framework that provides specific examples of each type of content.[9]

Given the inability of an off-the-shelf test such as the Stanford 9 to reflect these content standards fully, beginning in 1999 additional test items in language arts and in mathematics were included as part of the STAR program. These additional items, known collectively as the California Content Standards or the STAR Augmentation, are intended to address California content standards that are not addressed by the Stanford 9. Also beginning in 1999 Spanish-speaking English language learners (ELLs), also known as LEP students, who have been in California public schools fewer than twelve months must be administered the Spanish Assessment of Basic Education, Second Edition (SABE/2).

The Public School Accountability Act of 1999

The reintroduction of statewide testing and the creation of content standards paved the way for a statewide accountability system. Such a system was approved through SB 1X, known as the Public Schools Accountability Act (PSAA) of 1999, as well as amendments and additions to it in SB 1552 in 2000. The PSAA is motivated by the fact that many of California's students are not progressing academically at a satisfactory rate, and it contains three key elements to reform assessment and accountability: (1) the Academic Performance Index (API), (2) the Immediate Intervention/Underperforming Schools Program (II/USP), and (3) the High Achieving/Improving Schools (HA/IS) program, which includes the Governor's Performance Award Program (GPAP).

THE API. The API provides a method for indexing and ranking schools on a number of indicators, including performance-based indicators.[10] In the 1998–99 and 1999–2000 academic years, the performance component of the

API was based solely on the norm-referenced Stanford 9 test published by Harcourt Brace Inc., which is administered in the spring. Other measures, such as criterion-referenced standards-based tests (that is, the STAR Augmentation), a high school exit exam, attendance rates, and graduation rates are to be phased into the API in subsequent years.

Achievement scores constitute at least 60 percent of the value of the API and exclude the test scores of students enrolled in a district for less than one year. Only comprehensive high schools, middle schools, and elementary schools with more than one hundred students are included in the index.[11] All "numerically significant ethnic and socioeconomically disadvantaged subgroups" are included in the API for the purpose of measuring the progress of these student groups within schools. The legislation defines "numerically significant" as "a subgroup that constitutes at least 15 percent of a school's total pupil population and consists of at least 30 pupils." In addition, the API disaggregates pupil data collected from the tests by gender, ethnic or racial group, English language learners, socioeconomic status, and special education status.

The API has been used to establish two types of performance targets. First, annual growth targets for schools were set based on the July 1999 API baseline score. The minimum growth target is 5 percent annually. However, the state Board of Education may set differential targets for schools at the top and bottom of the distribution, with particular attention paid to those at the bottom "because they have the greatest room for improvement."[12] Second, statewide performance targets are being developed as the state content standards are implemented. This type of target represents a basic proficiency level as deemed appropriate by the board.

Elementary, middle, and high schools are ranked into deciles based on the API. In recognition of the role that socioeconomic status and language ability play in determining student achievement, the state also ranks schools into ten deciles after first grouping schools together with other schools with similar characteristics. The similar characteristics used to derive each school's Similar Schools Rank include student ethnicity, student SES, student mobility, percentage of students who are ELLs, average class size, percentage of teachers who are fully credentialed, percentage of teachers on emergency credentials, and whether the school is on a multitrack, year-round calendar. Beginning in June 2001 schools are also ranked by their growth rates and how their growth rates compare with schools with similar characteristics.

THE II/USP. The II/USP provides a carrot-and-stick method for helping schools not performing well. In fall 1999 any school performing below the

50th percentile on the STAR program in both 1998 and 1999 was eligible to participate in the II/USP, which provides for both a state planning grant of $50,000 and a federal Comprehensive School Reform Demonstration (CSRD) implementation grant of at least $50,000. External evaluations and an action plan arising from the evaluation are requirements for participants in the II/USP. Improving academic performance, involving parents or guardians, and providing effective and efficient allocation of resources and school management are among the key elements of the action plan.

Among the possible consequences of an II/USP school's failure to meet performance goals and to show substantial growth within two years are state reassignment of school management, reorganization of the school, or closure of that school.[13] In addition to these direct state actions, the state may allow parents to apply for the creation of a charter school at the existing school site. Before any of these actions may be taken, however, a public meeting must be held and the state must publicly find the school to be a failure. In the 1999–2000 academic year, a first cohort of 430 schools was chosen for external evaluation, and in 2000–01 a second cohort of 430 schools participated in II/USP.

THE HA/IS AND GPAP. HA/IS and its subsection, GPAP, provide mechanisms for rewarding schools that meet or exceed their growth targets or state performance targets. All schools, including those in the II/USP, are eligible to participate in the GPAP, because the monetary rewards of up to $150 per pupil are based on meeting or exceeding growth targets, not on the school's absolute rank in the API. Other nonmonetary awards such as classification as a distinguished school, placement on a public list of honor roll schools, and public commendations from the governor or legislature may be made in addition to or in lieu of monetary awards.

This emphasis on rewarding schools based on their rate of improvement, instead of their absolute level of achievement, represents a sensible solution to concerns that accountability systems could automatically funnel all the rewards to schools with the highest level of achievement. These schools typically are in affluent areas, have fewer LEP students, and often have more highly educated and experienced teachers. A second factor somewhat mitigates problems in comparing schools with high and low percentages of students who are LEP: The API calculation excludes scores of students who are new to a district in a given year.

In 1999 only the STAR program test results were used to identify II/USP and HA/IS schools. Since June 2000 the growth and statewide performance target components of the API have also been used to identify schools that are underperforming and those that are high achieving. Beginning in June 2001 the additional component of similar schools is used to rank and identify schools for II/USP and HA/IS. Because our analysis compares outcomes across years including the year before the API was introduced, for issues of consistency we focus our analysis on the Stanford 9 test results only. However, the need to measure outcomes consistently across time is important for any researcher or policymaker to consider when analyzing the API rankings and their implications for schools and children.

Recent Legislative Initiatives

The II/USP program channels additional funds to schools with low test scores, but in a limited way. Several other education bills passed during the 1999 emergency session of the legislature or in 2000 pay particular attention to funneling additional resources to the schools that have the lowest test scores or high proportions of low SES students. For example, section 52247 of the California Education Code provides funding to increase college-going rates in high schools that have low college participation rates. In addition, the Awards and Evaluation Unit of the Policy and Evaluation Division administers a series of monetary incentive-based reward programs.

Incentive Programs for Schools and Staff

The PSAA and related legislation contain three monetary-based incentive programs for schools and staff: (1) chapter 3 of the PSAA of 1999—the Governor's Performance Awards (GPA), (2) SB 1667, chapter 71 of the 2000 amendments—the School Site Employee Performance Bonus (SSEPB), and (3) Assembly Bill 1114, chapter 52 of the 2000 amendments—the Certificated Staff Performance Incentive Act (CSPIA). These pieces of legislation appropriated monetary rewards to schools and staff totaling $677 million.[14]

The GPA rewards a school that has an API ranking if it meets all of the following conditions: The 2000 API shows 5 percent growth, 80 percent of the growth target is met by each subgroup, K–8 schools have 95 percent and grade nine through twelve schools have 90 percent Stanford 9 participation rates, and schools already at or above 800 on the API have at least a 1-point gain. Schools meeting all of these conditions are eligible for rewards based on student enrollment at $63 per pupil, and the funds are for schoolwide use to be determined by the site governing team and ratified by the local school board.

The SSEPB rewards all staff at a school site that has an API ranking and meets the same conditions that apply to the GPA. It is funded at $591 per full-time equivalent (FTE), all staff receive it based on their FTE, and an equal amount of money is to be given to the school and used under the same determination as the GPA. In other words, if a school's staff consists of ten FTE, the school receives $5,910 for the staff and matching funds for the school. This matching amount is in addition to any monies received under the GPA.[15]

The CSPIA rewards certificated staff in schools with API rankings in deciles 1 to 5 (that is, low rankings) in 1999 who meet the following conditions: Stanford 9 test scores grew from 1998 to 1999 (unspecified amount), the 2000 API is twice the annual growth target of the school (10 percent), in K–8 schools 95 percent and in grade nine through twelve schools 90 percent of the teacher's students are tested, and all subgroups make 80 percent of the growth target. The monies are distributed across the state as follows: 1,000 staff in schools with the largest gains receive $25,000 each, 3,750 staff receive $10,000 each, and 7,500 staff receive $5,000 each. The district and teachers union jointly decide which personnel receive the rewards at each school site. To put this latter program in perspective, more than 292,000 teachers taught in the classroom (as opposed to holding administrative positions) in California in the 1999–2000 academic year, so that just over 4 percent of teachers are likely to win awards under this program in any given year.

Clearly these three incentive programs do provide additional motivation for schools and staff to raise test scores in their schools and classrooms. However, such high stakes may also lead to abuses of the system. For example, the popular media have reported on teachers changing answers on the test forms to create fraudulent gains in their students' test scores. And the latest API scores on the California Department of Education website list a small number of schools at which testing irregularities were reported.

In early 2001 the legislature began to consider additional means by which it might improve resources at schools with low test scores. In April the legislature's education committees considered bills that would attract highly qualified teachers to schools with low test scores. For instance, Senate Bill 572 would pay a $15,000 salary bonus to credentialed teachers who teach in schools that rank in the bottom fifth of the state in test scores.[16]

Accountability for Students

Testing is nothing new in education. There is now, and has been for many years, a battery of tests students face throughout their educational careers. In California, the Stanford 9 is not alone, although it has garnered much of the recent attention from the press, the public, and researchers. The new accountability system prompts the question: Just how high are the high stakes for students in California?

There are two other statewide tests—the Golden State Exam (GSE) and the newer High School Exit Exam (HSEE). The GSE was established by Senate Bill 813 in 1983 and was reauthorized twice during the 1990s. This rigorous exam is given in key academic areas in grades seven through eleven. Unlike the HSEE, which tests for basic proficiency in particular content areas, the GSE is used to recognize students for outstanding academic achievement and to determine student eligibility for the Golden State Seal Merit Diploma.[17]

In April 1999 Senate Bill 2 authorized a new graduation requirement: Seniors, beginning with the class of 2004, must pass an exit examination to receive a high school diploma. The HSEE was administered statewide for the first time in spring 2001 after a trial run in 2000. Only students in grade nine could volunteer to take the test in 2001. Beginning in the 2001–02 academic year, students in grade ten are required to take the exam. Because the test is so new, it is uncertain what the effects of this requirement will be. Jay P. Heubert and Robert M. Hauser find that little research has been done on the specific effects of graduation testing, but they caution that possible links to consequences such as a rise in the dropout rate must be considered by a well-designed accountability system.[18]

Similar to the incentives for schools and staff, specific monetary rewards are given for high test scores in California. Senate Bill 1688 (Ch 404, 2000) established the Governor's Scholarship Programs. The legislation appropriated $118 million for 2000–01, to be divided between two programs—the Governor's Scholars Program and the Governor's Distinguished Mathematics and Science Scholars Program.[19] The former awards $1,000 scholarships based on high test scores on the Stanford 9 and may be earned up to three times, for grades nine, ten, and eleven. The latter awards $2,500 scholarships to students who both win a Governor's Scholars Award and earn high test scores on a math and science AP test, GSE test, or International Baccalaureate (IB) test. This award may be earned only once.

Given the incentives and penalties that the PSAA and related legislation place in California's new accountability system, much clearly is at stake—for school, for staff, and for students at either end of the performance distribution.

Trends in California's Test Scores and Gaps between Groups

We begin our analysis of achievement trends in California with test scores for all students, LEP students, and non-LEP students in the state. Because the state test has been administered only since spring 1998, we examine three years of test scores. The PSAA was passed just before the spring 1999 test was given, and most of its elements were not implemented until after the 1999 test. We therefore focus much of our attention on differences between the 1997–98 and 1999–2000 academic years, interpreting this as a before-and-after analysis of the reforms.

Figures 4, 5, and 6 illustrate the three-year trend in math scores for the percentages of students scoring above the national 75th percentile, at or above the national median, and above the national 25th percentile, respectively. The data for these figures as well as corresponding scores in reading are in appendix tables A-2, A-3, and A-4. There, we take a simple average across grades as well as an average across grades weighted by the numbers of students who were tested in each grade level; the figures show the latter. We tested the significance of the difference—that is, that the one-year changes in test scores were zero.[20] The tables show the test results by individual grades as well.

The largest absolute gain from spring 1998 to spring 2000 is for LEP students scoring above the 25th percentile of national norms, and the difference of means is statistically significant. In fact, all of the differences of means for math are statistically significant for all three groups. It appears that math achievement has risen significantly over the three years in question. As the data in the appendix tables show, the results for reading are not as strong. Two-year gains in the share of students scoring at or above the 25th percentile of national norms are significant, but gains in the share at or above the median or 75th percentiles are not statistically significant.

Before concluding that reading and especially math achievement have risen in California, we should note that test scores commonly rise in the first few years after the introduction of a new test, independently of trends in the true underlying achievement of students. Daniel Koretz recounts evidence that rising test scores in one school district reflected growing student (and

Figure 4. Average Percentage of California Students Scoring in Top Quartile in Math, 1997–98 to 1999–2000

Percent above 75th percentile

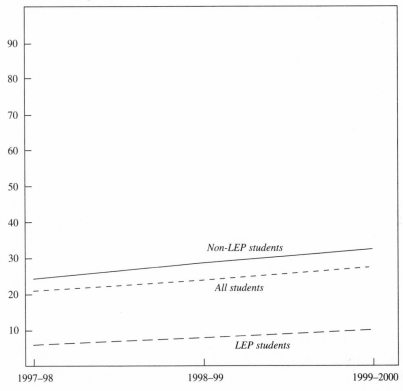

Source: Authors' calculations using California Department of Education data sets.
Note: LEP = limited English proficiency.

teacher) familiarity with the test form over several years.[21] He and others found that when they administered an older test form, test scores reverted to the levels observed in the first year that the current test form was adopted. Because California has used the same test form since spring 1998, at least some of the improvement in test scores likely reflects growing student and teacher familiarity with the format of the test and—a more serious possibility—growing teacher familiarity with the specific questions that are asked on the test form for a given grade. We doubt that all of the improvement in scores reflect growing knowledge of the Stanford 9 test form, but it certainly is likely to explain a portion of the gains.

Figure 5. Average Percentages of California Students Scoring at or above National Median in Math, 1997–98 to 1999–2000

Percent above 50th percentile

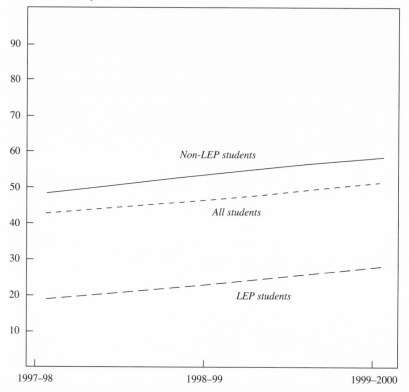

Source: Authors' calculations using California Department of Education data sets.
Note: LEP = limited English proficiency.

Changes in Inequality in Student Achievement

The same achievement data are presented in a slightly different way in table 2. Here, we have the overall percentage of students across all grades in each quartile of national norms for reading and math. In both subjects, for all students, LEP students, and non-LEP students between 1997–98 and 1999–2000 in all cases but one, the percentage point drop in the number of students in the bottom quartile of national norms exceeded the percentage point rise in the share of students in the top quartile of national norms.[22] In other words, at the same time that average achievement has been rising, the distribution of test

Figure 6. Average Percentage of California Students Scoring above National 25th Percentile in Math, 1997–98 to 1999–2000

Percent above 25th percentile

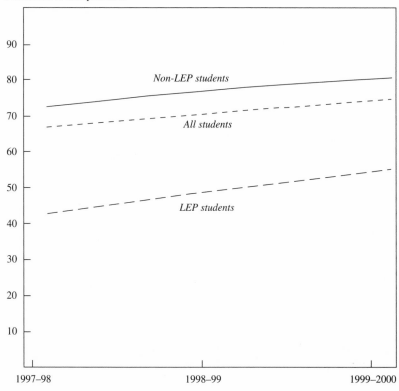

Source: Authors' calculations using California Department of Education data sets.
Note: LEP = limited English proficiency.

scores has been compressed. To restate this a third way, students who were the furthest behind national norms have improved more quickly than students who were initially above national norms.

Test Score Growth in Schools at the Bottom and Top

In addition to examining overall trends in student achievement, it is crucial to study whether the test score gap between the bottom-performing and top-performing schools has narrowed or widened over time. The legislature passed the PSAA specifically to address the large variations in student performance across schools.

Table 2. Students in Each Quartile of National Norms, by Student Group, 1997–98 to 1999–2000
Percent

Subject and quartile	All students				LEP students				Non-LEP students			
	1997–98	1998–99	1999–2000	Change, 1997–98 to 1999–2000	1997–98	1998–99	1999–2000	Change, 1997–98 to 1999–2000	1997–98	1998–99	1999–2000	Change, 1997–98 to 1999–2000
Math												
Quartile 1	34.78	30.87	27.02	-7.76	58.21	51.80	46.03	-12.17	29.27	24.34	21.24	-8.02
Quartile 2	22.85	22.74	21.83	-1.02	23.22	25.48	26.35	3.13	22.76	21.84	20.71	-2.05
Quartile 3	21.67	22.91	23.81	2.14	12.87	15.10	17.65	4.78	23.74	25.23	25.64	1.90
Quartile 4	20.70	23.47	27.34	6.65	5.70	7.63	9.96	4.26	24.23	28.59	32.40	8.17
Reading												
Quartile 1	37.67	35.87	33.18	-4.49	74.00	69.70	65.58	-8.42	29.49	25.61	23.67	-5.82
Quartile 2	22.90	23.42	23.75	0.85	17.85	20.39	22.32	4.47	24.04	24.23	24.53	0.49
Quartile 3	21.45	21.88	23.01	1.55	6.40	7.76	9.39	3.00	24.85	26.43	26.74	1.89
Quartile 4	17.97	18.82	20.06	2.09	1.75	2.15	2.70	0.95	21.62	23.74	25.06	3.44

Source: Authors' calculations using California Department of Education data sets.
Note: LEP = limited English proficiency. Quartile 1 is the lowest achievement group.

The vast differences between the proportion of LEP students in California and the nation make comparisons of California's all student and LEP student categories with student performance in the nation as a whole problematic. In the national norming sample for the Stanford 9 test only 1.8 to 2 percent of students were LEP, while California has approximately 20 percent LEP students. Therefore, for a more accurate comparison we examine the percentage of non-LEP students scoring at or above the national median from this point forward. We ranked schools by the percentage of non-LEP students scoring at or above the national median in the Stanford 9 math test results at each school in 1997–98, and we identified the schools that ranked in the bottom quintile, or fifth, of performance and those in the top quintile of performance in that year. We then followed these schools through 1999–2000. We also identified the bottom and top quintiles of schools when ranking was based on reading scores. We ranked elementary, middle, and high schools separately.

Table 3 presents the percentage of students at or above the 25th, 50th, and 75th percentiles of national norms in these two samples of schools in 1997–98 through 1999–2000. The top panel shows results for math; the bottom panel, reading. The three rightmost columns show changes in the percentage of students at or above each cutoff point between 1997–98 and 1999–2000 for schools that initially had low and high test scores and the change in the test score gap over the two-year period.

The results are clear. The percentage of students at or above the 75th percentile of national norms has grown in both types of schools—those that were low performing in 1997–98 and those that were high performing. The gains are broadly similar in the two types of schools, although in most cases the gains have been modestly higher in the top-performing schools. One major exception to this rule occurs for reading achievement among high school students. Here, the percentage of students in the top quarter of national norms surged upward by 16.1 points in the top schools compared with a rise of only 1.9 points in the bottom schools.

When we examine the percentage of students scoring at or above the 50th and 25th percentiles of national norms, the story is reversed. That is, typically the bottom-performing schools in 1997–98 appear to have improved considerably faster than the top-performing schools. The percentage-point increase in the share of students above these two cutoff points in bottom-performing schools is typically at least twice as big as the corresponding increase in top-performing schools. Again, there is one exception to this overall pattern: In top-performing high schools the increase in the percentage of students at or

Table 3. Average Percentage of Non-LEP Students in 1997–98 Cohorts of High and Low Test Score Schools Scoring at or above National Norms in Reading and Math, 1997–98 to 1999–2000

Subject and grade-span	Percentile	1997–98		1998–99		1999–2000		Changes, 1997–98 to 1999–2000		Gap change[a]
		1997–98 Low-score schools	1997–98 High-score schools	1997–98 Low-score schools	1997–98 High-score schools	1997–98 Low-score schools	1997–98 High-score schools	1997–98 Low-score schools	1997–98 High-score schools	Change in gap between high- and low-score schools
Math										
K–6	Above 75th	5.04	46.79	10.62	53.49	15.24	59.80	10.2	13.01	2.81
	At or above 50	18.28	74.09	28.97	78.67	36.74	83.14	18.47	9.05	-9.42
	Above 25	40.74	89.46	53.09	92.07	61.45	94.18	20.71	4.71	-16.00
(Number of observations)		(853)	(869)	(853)	(869)	(853)	(869)	(853)	(869)	
6–8	Above 75th	5.65	47.77	9.18	51.05	10.80	54.34	5.15	6.57	1.43
	At or above 50	20.76	74.74	28.04	76.92	31.09	79.65	10.33	4.91	-5.42
	Above 25	45.88	89.91	55.28	90.94	58.03	92.48	12.15	2.57	-9.59
(Number of observations)		(191)	(192)	(191)	(192)	(191)	(192)	(191)	(192)	
9–12	Above 75th	5.80	43.76	9.37	46.17	10.36	48.10	4.56	4.34	-0.21
	At or above 50	23.72	72.61	31.15	73.70	33.09	75.78	9.38	3.17	-6.20
	Above 25	55.25	88.79	62.45	89.11	63.92	89.84	8.67	1.06	-7.61
(Number of observations)		(151)	(157)	(151)	(157)	(151)	(157)	(151)	(157)	

Reading

K–6									
Above 75th	4.00	44.31	7.45	48.66	8.91	51.76	4.91	7.45	2.55
At or above 50	17.00	73.85	25.59	77.81	29.79	80.49	12.79	6.65	-6.15
Above 25	40.64	90.25	52.04	92.81	58.17	94.44	17.54	4.19	-13.35
(Number of observations)	(854)	(863)	(854)	(863)	(854)	(863)	(854)	(863)	
6–8									
Above 75th	5.77	44.11	8.22	44.69	8.66	46.98	2.89	2.87	-0.02
At or above 50	22.64	75.86	29.22	76.38	30.45	78.56	7.82	2.69	-5.12
Above 25	50.55	92.06	59.77	92.41	61.72	93.74	11.16	1.68	-9.48
(Number of observations)	(192)	(193)	(192)	(193)	(192)	(193)	(192)	(193)	
9–12									
Above 75th	3.82	32.17	5.65	46.29	5.76	48.27	1.94	16.1	14.16
At or above 50	16.23	62.43	20.75	73.76	21.20	75.83	4.98	13.4	8.43
Above 25	43.41	84.70	50.26	89.12	51.09	89.83	7.68	5.12	-2.56
(Number of observations)	(152)	(153)	(152)	(153)	(152)	(153)	(152)	(153)	

Source: Authors' calculations using California Department of Education data sets.
Note: All t-tests, probability > |t| for the average differences between 1997–98 and 1999–2000 levels are significant at the 0.001 level. LEP = limited English proficiency.
a. Calculated as (1999–2000 high-score schools – low-score schools) – (1997–98 high-score schools – low-score schools).

above the 50th percentile in reading exceeded the increase in the schools that were initially low performing. Apart from this exception, schools that initially had the lowest achievement do appear to have had more success in increasing the share of students in the top half and top three quarters of national norms. For example, in elementary schools, the percentage of students at or above the national median in the bottom-performing schools for math increased from 18.3 percent to 36.7 percent, an increase of 18.5 percent. In contrast, the schools that were top performers in 1997–98 increased their percentage of students at or above national norms from 74.1 percent to 83.1 percent, an increase of just 9.1 percent.

The bottom-performing schools had more room for improvement, so one might have expected results such as this even if the school accountability reforms had not directly caused the narrowing in the gap in achievement among schools. This argument is not persuasive though. It is mathematically possible that top-performing schools could have matched the gain in the percentage of students at or above the 50th or 75th percentile of national norms at bottom-performing schools. For instance, in the case of elementary school math results, the 18.5 percent gain in the share of students at or above the national median at the bottom schools could theoretically have been matched at the top-performing schools. This would have required an increase in the share at or above the national median at the top schools from 74.1 percent to 92.6 percent. In reality, the share of students above the median grew from 74.1 percent to only 83.1 percent. Schools originally in the bottom fifth of achievement clearly have had more success at increasing the share of students in the top 50 percent and 75 percent of national norms than have the top-performing schools. This finding strongly supports claims that testing and accountability may help to narrow the achievement gap among schools. The fact that low-performing schools have multiple incentives to raise performance through eligibility for II/USP, GPAP, GPA, SSEBP, and CSPIA funds lends even more credibility to this argument.

Is the Narrowing of the Test Score Distribution Genuine?

Although this conclusion appears strong, we were concerned that a statistical oddity known as "regression to the mean" might have driven the narrowing in the achievement gap. To understand regression to the mean, consider the following extreme hypothetical example. Suppose that all schools in California have equally proficient students, but a great deal of random variation exists from one year to the next in the test scores. Then our top-performing and bottom-performing schools in 1997–98 would be identical, but some had better random shocks than others. If this were true, then by 1999–2000 the two sets of schools should have reverted to the mean on average, producing roughly equal student achievement. We would have incorrectly interpreted this as a complete elimination of a real test score gap in the two-year period, when the test score gap was not meaningful in the first place.

We undertook three steps to test this possibility. First, if the schools in our low- and high-performing groups simply had bad or good luck in spring 1998, then we should see no evidence that compression has occurred in the overall distribution of student test scores. As the discussion of table 2 showed, for the state's overall student population, clear evidence exists that the number of California students who moved out of the bottom quartile of national achievement exceeded the number who moved into the top quartile. This pattern corroborates the claim that student achievement in California has grown relatively more quickly at schools that initially had the lowest test scores.

As a second test for regression to the mean, we identified fresh samples of schools in the bottom and top fifth of achievement in each school year. This procedure is different from what we did in table 3, where we selected these schools just once, in 1997–98, and followed the same subsets of schools over time. If regression to the mean were driving our result of convergence in student achievement, we would expect to see essentially no narrowing of the achievement gap between the bottom and top schools over time when we choose fresh samples of bottom and top schools each year.

Table 4 has the results, using the same format as for table 3. The overall patterns we reported in table 3 persist: There has been a slightly higher increase in the share of students at or above the 75th percentile of national norms at the top schools, but the increase in the share of students at or above the 50th or 25th percentiles of national norms has been considerably larger in the bottom fifth of schools than the top fifth of schools. In other words, when we focus on students performing in the top half or top three quarters of national norms, there has undeniably been a narrowing in the achievement gap among schools.

It is noteworthy that the gains made by bottom-performing schools relative to top-performing schools are much greater when we follow the same schools over time, as in table 3, instead of allowing the schools making up the top and bottom groups to change each year, as in table 4. This fact suggests that there could be some regression to the mean at play in table 3.

Table 4. Average Percentage of Non-LEP Students in High and Low Test Score Schools Scoring at or above National Norms in Reading and Math, 1997–98 to 1999–2000[a]

Subject and grade-span	Percentile	1997–98 Low-score schools	1997–98 High-score schools	1998–99 Low-score schools	1998–99 High-score schools	1999–2000 Low-score schools	1999–2000 High-score schools	Changes, 1997–98 to 1999–2000 Low-score schools	Changes, 1997–98 to 1999–2000 High-score schools	Gap change[b] Change in gap between high- and low-score schools
Math										
K–6	Above 75th	5.04	47.22	9.53	55.27	13.50	62.06	8.46***	14.85***	6.39
	At or above 50	18.34	74.38	26.75	80.63	33.67	85.24	15.33***	10.86***	-4.47
	Above 25	40.94	89.56	51.35	93.09	59.20	95.19	18.26***	5.63***	-12.63
(Number of observations)		(895)	(896)	(888)	(890)	(914)	(926)			
6–8	Above 75th	5.66	48.36	8.00	52.02	9.78	55.39	4.12***	7.03***	2.91
	At or above 50	20.57	75.18	25.44	78.08	29.03	80.97	8.46***	5.79***	-2.66
	Above 25	45.38	90.11	52.36	91.76	55.76	93.32	10.38***	3.2 ***	-7.17
(Number of observations)		(202)	(203)	(199)	(205)	(212)	(222)			
9–12	Above 75th	4.98	43.74	7.10	46.77	7.50	47.96	2.52***	4.22***	1.71
	At or above 50	21.86	72.70	25.28	74.97	27.34	76.51	5.48***	3.81***	-1.67
	Above 25	52.33	88.83	57.19	90.00	58.18	90.40	5.85***	1.57***	-4.28
(Number of observations)		(168)	(169)	(158)	(162)	(175)	(186)			
Reading										
K–6	Above 75th	4.04	44.89	7.15	50.22	8.30	53.61	4.26***	8.72***	4.46
	At or above 50	17.03	74.20	23.85	79.46	27.71	82.37	10.67***	8.17***	-2.50
	Above 25	40.68	90.29	50.59	93.48	56.11	95.23	15.43***	4.95***	-10.49

(Number of observations)	(895)	(896)	(884)	(892)	(907)	(917)			
6–8									
Above 75th	6.03	44.85	7.51	46.21	8.15	48.65	2.13***	3.8***	1.67
At or above 50	23.03	76.35	27.25	77.89	28.95	79.97	5.91***	3.62***	-2.29
Above 25	50.22	92.17	57.28	93.11	58.95	94.39	8.73***	2.23***	-6.50
(Number of observations)	(202)	(203)	(200)	(205)	(212)	(215)			
9–12									
Above 75th	3.66	32.58	4.42	32.53	4.71	33.77	1.06***	1.19	0.14
At or above 50	15.73	62.81	17.62	63.53	18.35	64.91	2.61***	2.1*	-0.51
Above 25	42.17	84.91	44.71	85.83	47.15	86.51	4.97***	1.6***	-3.37
(Numer of observations)	(168)	(169)	(157)	(161)	(177)	(183)			

Source: Authors' calculations using California Department of Education data sets.

a. This table, unlike table 3, defines low-score and high-score schools based on the test score rankings from the stated school year. Thus, the identity of schools in each of these quintiles varies by year, whereas in table 3 the composition of the low-score and high-score cohorts is identical across years and is based on 1997–98 rankings. All differences of means are statistically significant at <0.05 except reading in high test score high schools, which is not significant. Difference of means t-test: probability > |t|: * = 0.05, ** = 0.01, *** = 0.001.

b. Calculated as (1999–2000 high-score schools – low-score schools) – (1997–98 high-score schools – low-score schools).

However, another interpretation could be made more favorable to the view that school accountability provides strong incentives to those working in the bottom-performing schools to improve student achievement. Specifically, schools at the very bottom of the 1997–98 test score results could have implemented various reforms to improve over time. That means that by 1999–2000 many of these schools had overtaken other schools that were originally ranked higher. If the public release of test scores creates stronger incentives to improve at the very weakest schools, then we should expect exactly what is observed in the two tables. First, schools that were originally bottom performers should have gained markedly relative to the top schools. Second, because these bottom schools should have overtaken some other schools, the overall variation in test scores statewide from one year to the next should have narrowed, as shown in table 4, but not as much as did the variation in test scores for the original bottom-performing schools.

As a third test of the possibility that the apparent narrowing in achievement among schools merely represents regression to the mean, we should see the opposite pattern—a widening in the test score gap—if we define our cohorts of low- and high-scoring schools using end-of-period scores instead of beginning-of-period scores. [23] To understand this, suppose that random errors affect each year's data on student achievement at each school and that these random errors are the only reason that two schools' rate of improvement might differ between years. One way of detecting this is to reanalyze the school data after defining low- and high-scoring schools using end-of-period test scores. If all that were different between these schools were the amounts of random luck in the final year, then at the start of the period their test scores should have been similar to each other. Figure 7 illustrates with hypothetical data, under the assumption of regression to the mean and, for simplicity, no real growth in average achievement. According to this theory, the narrowing in test scores across schools would be reversed if instead we defined high- and low-scoring schools based on their end-of-period scores. This is shown by the solid lines in figure 7.

Most important, the gap between low- and high-scoring schools should move in opposite directions, depending on whether we defined these schools using beginning- or end-of-period test scores. If there is no correlation in the errors over time, the change in the gaps should be of opposite sign but equal in absolute value. (Note that even if all schools are truly improving at the same rate over time, but with random errors that regress to the mean, then this statement should still be true.)

Figure 7. Hypothetical Illustration of Regression to the Mean

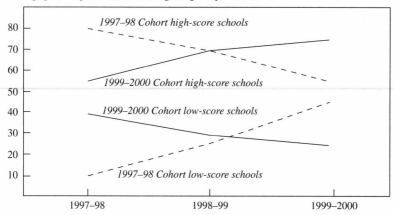

Average percentage of students scoring at a given percentile

Table A-6 performs this exercise using samples of high- and low-performing schools selected based on 1999–2000 test scores. The results are similar to the results in table 3, where we selected the subsamples based on 1997–98 scores. First, and most important, we do not find that the change in the gaps between low-scoring and high-scoring schools are equal and opposite to those found in table 3. Thus, pure regression to the mean without any genuine changes in achievement gaps can be ruled out. Second, as our second test suggested, some regression to the mean probably is at work along with genuine changes in achievement gaps across schools. The narrowing in the gap in the percentage of students at or above the 25th percentile of national norms in table 3 also occurs, but to a lesser extent, in every case in table A-6, suggesting that the narrowing achievement gap is real. In most cases in table A-6, the change in the percentage of students scoring at or above the national median is very close to zero, while in table 3 the gap narrowed substantially in five out of six cases. The most logical interpretation is that there is both genuine narrowing in the achievement gap between low- and high-performing schools and regression to the mean, which work in opposite directions, nearly canceling each other out. That is, the estimates of test score compression in table 3 overstate the true extent of narrowing while the estimates in table A-6 understate the narrowing. Finally, table 3 suggested that when we measure achievement by the share of students at or above the 75th percentile of national norms, in two cases the gap did not change and in four cases it rose by modest to meaningful amounts. The changes in this test score gap in table A-6 are all positive and, in most cases, are a few percentage points higher than in table 3. Together, these results suggest that a modest but genuine widening in the test score gap may have occurred at the 75th percentile of national norms.

In sum, these three tests suggest that although regression to the mean is present to some extent in the data, a genuine narrowing of the test score gap took place when measured by the gap in the percentage of students scoring at or above the 25th or 50th percentile of national norms, and a slight widening of the test score gap was apparent when measured as the percentage of students scoring at or above the 75th percentile of national norms.[24]

Trends in School Resources and Dropout Rates

More than 270,000 teachers were in the classroom (that is, not in administrative positions) in California in the 1997–98 academic year. By the fall of 1999, that number had risen to more than 292,000. At the same time, the numbers of AP courses increased in high schools pursuant to a 1999 order by Governor Gray Davis. By these measures, school resources did increase pre-PSAA to post-PSAA. However, California's student population also increased from more than 5.7 million to more than 5.9 million during that time. The question of how these additional resources are distributed across California and how measures such as average class size and teacher characteristics have changed in recent years naturally follows.

Table 5 presents statewide averages for each of the three grade-spans, weighted by student enrollment at each school in each of the three years. To facilitate comparison with the earlier samples of schools, we limit our sample to the schools with valid math or reading data. (In practice, only about 3 percent of schools and approximately 1 percent of students in regular schools statewide were excluded from our sample by this restriction.) Resource levels are virtually identical whether we limit the sample to either schools with math or reading scores. Thus, any trends we observe are evident across all schools for which math and reading data exist. Asterisks in the final column in the table indicate whether the change in each resource level between fall 1997 and fall 1999 is statistically significant. Corresponding columns of asterisks to the right of the earlier columns show the results of tests that the one-year changes in resources were zero; we focus our attention on tests of the two-year changes shown in the final column of the table. Although the average student in elementary and middle schools attends a school in which class size did go down, the change between 1997 and 1999 is so small as to be virtually unnoticeable and is not statistically significant. In high schools, class size also went down, and this change is significant at the 0.01 level.

In all three grade-spans, the average student attends a school in which average teacher experience and the percentage of teachers with a master's degree have declined, while the percentages of teachers with at most a bachelor's degree and lacking full credentials have risen. In elementary schools the percentage of teachers with at most two years of teaching experience has decreased; however, in middle and high schools it has increased. Of these five resource measures, in elementary and middle schools all differences in the means from 1997 to 1999 are significant except the percentage with at least a master's, while in high schools all of these measures are significant at levels equal to or less than 0.05.

Because low experience and lack of credentials are relatively highly correlated (with a correlation of 0.46 in 1997–98), we would expect the percentages to change in the same direction, not inversely as they do in elementary schools. This finding suggests that it may be taking teachers longer to earn a full credential in the elementary schools and that middle and high schools may be hiring novice teachers who begin teaching without full credentials, but who earn their credential before they reach their third year of teaching.

In high schools we also examine the levels of college-prep and AP course offerings and look at changes since the PSAA of 1999. The data in table 5 show that the average high school student attends a school in which the percentages of both types of curricula have increased, but the difference in the averages from 1997 to 1999 is significant only for the "a-f" series of courses.

In addition to course-taking patterns, we also examine recent trends in the dropout rate in California. Theoretical work suggests that any increase in academic standards is likely to cause students on the borderline of success to give up or even drop out, unless the increase in standards is accompanied by additional resources targeted at the students at risk.[25] With the introduction of rigorous new content standards in the late 1990s and the new statewide test that began in spring 1998, with results going both to a student's teachers and parents, one might wonder whether the dropout rate has increased in California. Figure 8 illustrates official calculations by the California Department of Education on the annual dropout rates among California high school students. If anything, the trend in dropout rates appears to be downward.

**Table 5. Weighted Average School and Teacher Characteristics for Subsamples of
Schools with Reading and Math Test Scores, 1997–98 to 1999–2000**

Subject and grade-span	School or teacher characteristic	1997–98 Mean	1998–99 Mean	1999–2000 Mean
Math				
K–6	Percent free or reduced-price lunch	56.66	56.23	55.79
	Average class size	24.85***	24.28*	24.60
	Average teacher experience	12.30***	11.87	11.84***
	Percent at most BA	21.08***	23.24	22.87***
	Percent at least MA	26.23	25.95	25.96
	Percent low experience (0–2 years)	21.13***	19.78***	16.73***
	Percent lacking credential	12.10***	13.20	13.63***
(Number of observations)		(4,477)	(4,442)	(4,587)
6–8	Percent free or reduced-price lunch	47.81	48.52	47.53
	Average class size	28.68	28.98	28.64
	Average teacher experience	13.70***	13.14*	12.81***
	Percent at most BA	18.33***	21.05	22.38***
	Percent at least MA	33.14	32.49	32.41
	Percent low experience (0–2 years)	14.13***	15.67	16.40***
	Percent lacking credential	10.27**	12.03***	14.66***
(Number of observations)		(1,011)	(1,012)	(1,071)
9–12	Percent free or reduced-price lunch	30.86	32.30	32.27
	Average class size	29.70	29.76**	28.77**
	Average teacher experience	15.27***	14.73***	14.24***
	Percent at most BA	15.60***	18.15*	19.63***
	Percent at least MA	39.73	38.70	37.85**
	Percent low experience (0–2 years)	12.98	13.63*	14.52***
	Percent lacking credential	8.35**	9.75***	12.40***
	Percent "a–f" classes	59.42*	60.89	61.46**
	Percent AP classes	2.97	3.11	3.21
(Number of observations)		(843)	(794)	(896)

Although the development of the statewide test and content standards does
not seem to have adversely affected the dropout rate, it may take a decade to
see the full effects of the accountability reforms on the dropout rate. We say
this because the component of the reforms that is most likely to affect dropout
and graduation decisions is just now being phased in. The class of 2004 is the
first that is required to pass a new state high school exit examination before
graduation. Thus, if this new graduation requirement lowers the probability of
high school graduation for marginal students, it may take several years to
become apparent.

Table 5. Weighted Average School and Teacher Characteristics for Subsamples of Schools with Reading and Math Test Scores, 1997–98 to 1999–2000 (continued).

Subject and grade-span	School or teacher characteristic	1997–98 Mean	1998–99 Mean	1999–2000 Mean
Reading				
	Percent free or reduced-price lunch	56.66	56.21	55.79
K–6	Average class size	24.85***	24.28*	24.60
	Average teacher experience	12.30***	11.87	11.84***
	Percent at most BA	21.08***	23.25	22.87***
	Percent at least MA	26.23	25.94	25.96
	Percent low experience (0–2 years)	21.13***	19.79***	16.74***
	Percent lacking credential	12.10***	13.21	13.63***
(Number of observations)		(4,477)	(4,437)	(4,585)
6–8	Percent free or reduced-price lunch	47.81	48.52	47.53
	Average class size	28.68	28.98	28.64
	Average teacher experience	13.70***	13.14*	12.81***
	Percent at most BA	18.33***	21.05	22.38***
	Percent at least MA	33.14	32.49	32.41
	Percent low experience (0–2 years)	14.13***	15.67	16.40***
	Percent lacking credential	10.27**	12.03***	14.66***
(Number of observations)		(1,011)	(1,013)	(1,071)
9–12	Percent free or reduced-price lunch	30.86	32.34	32.27
	Average class size	29.70	29.77**	28.77**
	Average teacher experience	15.27***	14.73***	14.24***
	Percent at most BA	15.60***	18.14*	19.63***
	Percent at least MA	39.73	38.72	37.85**
	Percent low experience (0–2 years)	12.98	13.63**	14.52***
	Percent lacking credential	8.35**	9.74***	12.40***
	Percent "a-f" classes	59.42*	60.88	61.46**
	Percent AP classes	2.97	3.11	3.21
(Number of observations)		(843)	(795)	(896)

Source: Authors' calculations using California Department of Education data sets.

Note: BA = bachelor's degree; MA = master's degree; AP = Advanced Placement. The t-tests are for one-year changes in the columns labeled 1997–98 and 1998–99. They are for a two-year change in the column labeled 1999–2000. Probability > |t|: * = 0.05, ** = 0.01, *** = 0.001.

Furthermore, the measurement of dropout rates in California has become a highly contentious issue, mainly because the state has not adopted a longitudinal database that tracks students as they move between schools, leave the state, or in the case of immigrants reverse migrate to their country of origin. We have reported the one-year dropout rates calculated by the state. Using enrollment and graduation data, Julian R. Betts shows that the ratio of high school graduates to grade nine enrollment three years earlier in California has consistently hovered around 0.69–0.74 throughout the last half of the 1990s,

Figure 8. One-Year Dropout Rates in California

Proportion

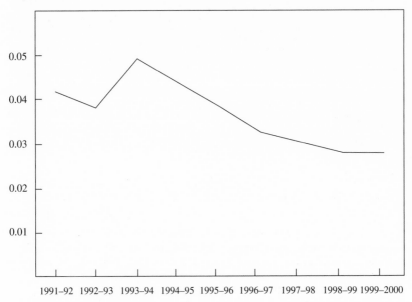

Source: California Department of Education.

suggesting a four-year dropout rate of about 25–30 percent.[26] This stands in stark contrast to the one-year dropout data in figure 8, which imply a dropout rate over the four years of roughly 12 percent.[27] For this and the other reasons already mentioned, it is too soon to conclude whether the new school accountability program has affected the dropout rate.

The Gap in School Resources and Course Offerings

In 1997–98, how did resources vary between schools with unusually high and low test scores? Since California began its accountability program, are low test score schools receiving more resources and high test score schools receiving fewer resources? We calculate the size of the resource gap between high and low test score schools and measure how much the gap has changed from 1997 to 1999. We also test whether any changes in the resource gap between schools are statistically significant. Because the PSAA was implemented in early 1999, we view the analysis of changes as a before-and-after analysis.

Resource Levels across Years

We rank schools by the percentage of students scoring at or above the national median in math and reading tests in spring 1998. We then choose a cohort of low test score schools and a cohort of high test score schools in each grade-span and follow them across the three years for which data are available. In the interest of saving space, we discuss only the resource levels for schools ranked by math tests. However, the results for reading, which are shown in the tables, are similar.

The data in table 6 show that students in high test score schools in each of the three years attend schools, on average, with lower percentages of students receiving free or reduced-price lunch. Students in these schools also have higher levels of experienced teachers and more highly educated teachers than do students in low test score schools. The average student in a low test score school attends a school with higher percentages of teachers with low education, low levels of experience, and who lack a full credential. We can observe these patterns in all three years in all grade-spans. Average class size appears to differ little between low and high test score schools but is slightly higher in high test score schools. In high schools in each of the three years, the average student attending a low test score school has a lower percentage of college-prep and AP courses than the average student in a high test score school.

An analysis of 1997–98 data showed that relationships between student socioeconomic status and resource levels are similar to the relationship between average test scores and resource levels.[28] This is not surprising given the high correlation between SES and test scores.

Average Resource Differences across Years

We now examine whether the gap in resources between schools that in 1997–98 had low and high test scores has changed meaningfully. Table 7 presents several measures that compare the 1997–98 and 1999–2000 academic years. The first two pairs of columns in the table explore whether the changes in levels of resources at low and high test score schools before and after the PSAA are likely to be random or systematic. The last three columns of the

Table 6. Comparison of Average School and Teacher Characteristics in 1997–98 Cohort of High and Low Test Score Schools for Reading and Math, 1997–98 to 1999–2000

Subject and grade-span	School or teacher characteristic	1997–98		1998–99		1999–2000	
		1997–98 Low-score schools	1997–98 High-score schools	1997–98 Low-score schools	1997–98 High-score schools	1997–98 Low-score schools	1997–98 High-score schools
Math							
K–6	Percent free or reduced-price lunch	86.35	17.72	85.66	17.22	85.00	16.95
	Average class size	24.34	25.38	23.83	24.85	24.31	25.41
	Average teacher experience	11.16	13.43	10.37	13.18	10.27	13.28
	Percent at most BA	30.46	12.69	33.35	14.74	32.93	14.58
	Percent at least MA	23.37	30.76	22.89	30.96	22.34	31.48
	Percent low experience (0–2 years)	24.89	17.47	25.25	15.13	21.75	12.38
	Percent lacking credential	20.97	4.82	23.56	4.53	24.10	5.39
	(Number of observations)	(853)	(869)	(853)	(869)	(853)	(869)
6–8	Percent free or reduced-price lunch	76.51	16.37	78.69	15.60	76.17	14.96
	Average class size	27.88	30.35	28.09	30.18	27.51	29.82
	Average teacher experience	12.64	14.96	11.72	14.72	11.25	14.60
	Percent at most BA	27.95	10.89	30.56	14.14	33.53	14.83
	Percent at least MA	29.96	37.21	29.18	36.88	27.87	37.65
	Percent low experience (0–2 years)	16.59	11.71	19.78	12.24	21.72	11.80
	Percent lacking credential	19.21	5.42	22.35	4.74	26.31	6.73
	(Number of observations)	(191)	(192)	(191)	(192)	(191)	(192)
9–12	Percent free or reduced-price lunch	53.31	11.05	57.83	10.68	59.16	10.16
	Average class size	28.43	30.32	28.47	29.53	28.03	28.82
	Average teacher experience	14.42	16.63	13.92	16.04	13.36	15.61
	Percent at most BA	24.99	11.40	28.26	12.71	30.73	13.78
	Percent at least MA	38.03	45.72	36.66	45.02	35.59	44.52
	Percent low experience (0–2 years)	13.88	11.08	14.64	11.71	16.70	12.07
	Percent lacking credential	13.93	6.13	15.79	5.20	20.28	7.13
	Percent "a–f" classes	53.88	66.43	57.26	69.08	57.59	68.28
	Percent AP classes	2.14	4.29	2.31	4.54	2.51	5.08
	(Number of observations)	(151)	(157)	(151)	(157)	(151)	(157)

Reading

K–6

Percent free or reduced-price lunch	88.45	14.59	87.91	14.12	87.15	13.63
Average class size	24.60	25.48	23.85	24.91	24.31	25.36
Average teacher experience	11.01	13.51	10.31	13.28	10.13	13.41
Percent at most BA	32.26	12.54	35.42	14.14	35.19	13.67
Percent at least MA	23.60	30.02	22.95	30.21	22.22	30.65
Percent low experience (0–2 years)	25.51	16.99	25.78	14.61	22.48	11.87
Percent lacking credential	22.20	4.04	24.80	3.79	25.33	4.54
(Number of observations)	(854)	(863)	(854)	(863)	(854)	(863)

6–8

Percent free or reduced-price lunch	78.73	14.64	81.06	14.28	77.99	13.51
Average class size	27.87	30.09	28.19	29.73	27.60	29.62
Average teacher experience	12.81	14.90	11.94	14.65	11.41	14.56
Percent at most BA	29.72	10.76	32.55	13.85	35.40	14.17
Percent at least MA	30.05	36.26	29.09	35.72	27.75	36.77
Percent low experience (0–2 years)	16.00	11.37	19.06	12.08	21.59	11.23
Percent lacking credential	18.66	5.20	21.81	4.64	25.99	6.13
(Number of observations)	(192)	(193)	(192)	(193)	(192)	(193)

9–12

Percent free or reduced-price lunch	53.95	9.17	58.26	8.84	59.44	8.39
Average class size	28.28	29.95	28.44	29.66	28.19	28.86
Average teacher experience	14.67	16.48	14.12	15.87	13.51	15.50
Percent at most BA	24.45	10.29	27.66	10.58	30.24	12.08
Percent at least MA	38.36	45.47	37.11	44.73	35.66	44.43
Percent low experience (0–2 years)	13.45	11.07	14.45	11.68	16.77	11.75
Percent lacking credential	13.33	5.35	15.10	4.73	19.81	6.53
Percent "a–f" classes	54.74	67.96	58.10	69.36	58.13	68.84
Percent AP classes	2.27	4.40	2.41	4.65	2.60	5.00
(Number of observations)	(152)	(153)	(152)	(153)	(152)	(153)

Source: Authors' calculations using California Department of Education data sets.
Note: Weights used for means in each year are that year's enrollment. BA = bachelor's degree; MA = master's degree; AP = Advanced Placement.

Table 7. Average Change in School and Teacher Characteristics between 1997–98 and 1999–2000 for 1997–98 High and Low Test Score Schools, Gaps between These Schools, and Change in Gap Size, for Reading and Math

Subject and grade-span	School or teacher characteristic	Average resource level change from 1997 to 1999 for 1997–98 high and low test score schools[a]		Gap between low and high test score schools' average resources[b]		Change in size of gap, fall 1997 and fall 1999[c]
		Low-score schools	High-score schools	Fall 1997 gap	Fall 1999 gap	1999 Gap minus 1997 gap
Math						
K–6	Average teacher experience	-0.85***	-0.09	2.28	3.00	0.73
	Percent at most BA	2.22***	1.81***	17.76	18.35	0.59
	Percent at least MA	-1.06***	0.76**	7.39	9.14	1.75
	Percent low experience (0–2 years)	-3.17***	-5.27***	7.42	9.37	1.95
	Percent lacking credential	2.91***	0.53	16.15	18.71	2.57
	Average class size	-0.02	0.00	-1.04	-1.10	-0.05
6–8	Average teacher experience	-1.43***	-0.35**	2.32	3.35	1.03
	Percent at most BA	5.59***	3.84	17.06	18.71	1.64
	Percent at least MA	-2.18***	0.39	7.26	9.78	2.53
	Percent low experience (0–2 years)	5.11***	0.03	4.88	9.91	5.03
	Percent lacking credential	7.16***	1.22	13.79	19.58	5.79
	Average class size	-0.37	-0.29	-2.47	-2.31	+0.16
9–12	Average teacher experience	-1.04***	-0.99***	2.20	2.25	0.04
	Percent at most BA	5.45***	2.50*	13.59	16.95	3.36
	Percent at least MA	-2.61***	-1.25*	7.70	8.93	1.23
	Percent low experience (0–2 years)	2.76***	0.97	2.79	4.64	1.84
	Percent lacking credential	6.14***	1.12	7.80	13.15	5.34
	Percent "a–f" classes	3.24*	1.72	12.54	10.69	-1.85
	Percent AP classes	0.36***	0.79***	2.14	2.57	0.43
	Average class size	-0.48	-1.39*	-1.89	-0.79	+1.10

Reading

K–6				
Average teacher experience	-0.86***	2.49	3.28	0.79
Percent at most BA	2.78***	19.72	21.52	1.80
Percent at least MA	-1.39***	6.42	8.43	2.00
Percent low experience (0–2 years)	-3.10***	8.51	10.60	2.09
Percent lacking credential	2.97***	18.17	20.80	2.63
Average class size	-0.25	-0.88	-1.05	-0.17
6–8				
Average teacher experience	-1.45***	2.09	3.16	1.07
Percent at most BA	5.63***	18.96	21.23	2.27
Percent at least MA	-2.40***	6.21	9.02	2.82
Percent low experience (0–2 years)	5.60***	4.63	10.36	5.73
Percent lacking credential	7.36***	13.46	19.86	6.39
Average class size	-0.27	-2.23	-2.02	+0.20
9–12				
Average teacher experience	-1.16***	1.81	2.00	0.18
Percent at most BA	5.60***	14.16	18.16	4.00
Percent at least MA	-2.86***	7.10	8.77	1.67
Percent low experience (0–2 years)	3.27***	2.39	5.01	2.63
Percent lacking credential	6.34***	7.98	13.28	5.31
Percent "a–f" classes	3.06*	13.21	10.71	-2.50
Percent AP classes	0.34***	2.13	2.40	0.27
Average class size	-0.14	-1.66	-0.67	+1.00

Source: Authors' calculations using California Department of Education data sets.
Note: BA = bachelor's degree; MA = master's degree; AP = Advanced Placement. Probability > |t|: * = 0.05, ** = 0.01, *** = 0.001.
a. Mean differences are between fall 1997 and fall 1999, and the weight is fall 1999 enrollment.
b. Data derived from table 6. Gaps are calculated so that a positive gap indicates that low test score schools have less resources.
c. Data may have 0.01 rounding error.

table calculate the 1997 high-low gap, the 1999 high-low gap, and the change in the size of each gap for each resource between 1997 and 1999.

We perform a paired t-test on the average difference between the resource levels observed in the 1997–98 (pre-PSAA) data and the resource levels observed in the 1999–2000 (post-PSAA) data for the two cohorts of schools. The first two columns compare enrollment-weighted mean differences between the resource level in 1997–98 and 1999–2000. We weight the average difference by 1999 enrollment to illustrate the average change over the last three years at a school attended by the average student attending a school of either type in 1999. This weight results in slightly different results than if we simply calculate the difference between 1997 and 1999 resources in table 6.

TEACHER CHARACTERISTICS IN ELEMENTARY SCHOOLS. The patterns of change in teacher characteristics at the elementary schools with the highest and lowest test scores in spring 1998 are complex. Overall, the patterns suggest that schools with high scores have fared better over the two-year period. The average K–6 student attends a school in which the average experience level of teachers has declined slightly, but the decline is significant only in low test score schools. At the same time, the percentage of teachers with very low levels of experience has also decreased by 3 percent in the bottom-scoring schools and 5 percent in the top-scoring schools; the decrease is significant in both types of schools. However, the percentages of teachers with low education levels and lacking full credentials have increased at both types of schools, and the changes are significant for all but credentials in the high test score quintile. The percentage of highly educated teachers has decreased in the low quintile and is significant, while in the high quintile it has increased slightly but is insignificant, suggesting that in the low quintile the change is systematic, while in the high quintile it is random. Of the five measures of changes in teacher preparation that we focus on, all are significant in the low quintile of schools, while only three are in the high quintile.

TEACHER CHARACTERISTICS IN MIDDLE SCHOOLS. We see a similar pattern to that observed for K–6 schools, with the exception that of the five measures of change, only one—declining average teacher experience level—is significant in the high quintile of schools. All five changes are significant at the 0.001 level in the low quintile of schools. These changes at schools that initially had low test scores are uniformly disturbing: Teacher experience, education, and credentials have deteriorated over time in a statistically significant fashion.

TEACHER CHARACTERISTICS AND COURSE OFFERINGS IN HIGH SCHOOLS. We examine the above teacher characteristics in high schools as well as the percentage of classes that are college-prep and AP. The average high school student in these groups of schools attends a school in which average teacher experience and the percentage of teachers with at least a master's degree have declined slightly, whereas the percentages of teachers with at most a bachelor's degree, with at most two years of experience, and who lack full credentials have risen. In the low test score quintile of schools, changes in all of these measures are statistically significant. In the high quintile of schools, changes are statistically significant for only three of the five measures of teacher preparation and, when significant, are less significant than in the low quintile of schools.

The change in the percentage of classes that are AP at either type of school is significant. This last finding that the increase in AP classes is unlikely to be by chance is unsurprising, given Governor Davis's order in 1999 to increase the proportion of AP classes in the state.

AVERAGE CLASS SIZE. The mean differences in the table suggest that average class size has changed very little for the average student attending elementary and middle schools at either end of the test score spectrum and that any changes that have taken place are likely to have been by chance. For the average high school student in a low test score school, there has been an average decrease of less than one student per class, and the change is not statistically significant. However, in high schools with high test scores, class size has decreased by slightly more than one student per class with significance of 0.05. Thus, the change in class size is likely to be systematic only in high test score high schools.

Overall, these results suggest that several of the changes in resources are unlikely to be by chance and are more likely the result of systematic changes in the composition of the teaching force in these schools.

Gaps between High and Low Test Score Schools

The last three columns of table 7 compare the average resource gaps between low and high test score schools in 1997–98 and 1999–2000 and the change in the gap measured as the high-low gap in 1999 minus the high-low gap in 1997. Remarkably, all resource gaps in all grade-spans have widened, with the exception of average class size in middle and high schools and the percentage of college-prep classes in high schools.

These findings, together with data on the levels of resources from table 6, suggest that resources are not being taken away from high test score schools to increase resources at low test score schools. Nor does it seem to be the case that resources are increasing at low test score schools while resources are maintained at the top-scoring schools. Low test score schools appear to be receiving lower levels of teacher resources over time despite additional funds being directed toward raising the quantity of highly qualified teachers. At high test score schools, the rise in the proportion of teachers who are unqualified is many times less than that seen in low test score schools for many of the measures. For example, in middle schools, the increase in the share of uncredentialed teachers is almost six times as high at low test score schools as at high test score schools. In elementary and high schools, a similar divergence in trends appears. Given the high correlation between student SES and test scores, these findings imply that the resource gaps are also rising between low SES and high SES students.

What is unclear from these data is what causal mechanisms for these patterns are operating in California. However, the widening gap in resources between schools that initially had low and high test scores is related primarily to various measures of teacher preparation, and not class size or high school curriculum. Therefore it seems plausible that teacher mobility between schools and perhaps different exit rates from the teaching profession across schools are the driving forces behind the increase in resource inequality. One possibility is that the accountability system, with its sanctions for bottom-performing schools, has discouraged highly educated and experienced teachers from moving to, or staying at, such schools. Another possibility is that the class size reduction initiated in 1996 in elementary schools has lured highly qualified elementary teachers from low-performing schools to high-performing schools. However, this second hypothesis does little to explain why we find the same disturbing trends in not only elementary schools but also middle and high schools.

Policy Implications and Outlook

Our analysis of test scores suggests that since the introduction of the state test in the spring of 1998, student achievement in California has grown overall and among LEP and non-LEP students. Determining the cause or causes of this gain is difficult. Some of the gains could reflect growing familiarization with the test form, and some of the gains among LEP students might be related to the ending of bilingual education in California, although it is too early to know yet whether the latter is the case. It seems plausible that the introduction of testing itself, combined with publication of school rankings and reports to schools and parents about individual students' performance, might itself have spurred some of the improvement.

Patterns in the test scores over time can also inform the debate about who might be helped most by school accountability and who might be hurt by it. A plausible scenario is that the implementation of school accountability could aggravate inequality in test scores, because schools in relatively affluent areas likely have greater resources—both in the school and in the home—to bring to bear upon improving student achievement. We compared growth in test scores among the schools that ranked at the bottom fifth and the top fifth of achievement in spring 1998, and we found that the bottom-performing schools increased their shares of students above the 25th and 50th percentiles of national norms significantly more than did the top-performing quintile of schools. This finding is meaningful because mathematically the top schools had just as much room for improvement but did not improve to the same extent. Turning to the share of students at or above the 75th percentile of national norms, this measure of elite performance grew at both types of schools, but growth was slightly higher at the schools that were originally top performers. We undertook three checks to determine whether these trends in achievement gaps merely reflect regression to the mean. We found some evidence of regression to the mean but the overall patterns appear to be genuine.

Another concern about raising standards is that it can discourage students who hover at the borderline between success and failure. It is far too soon to know for sure if such effects will occur to a large extent. We note, however, that one-year dropout rates in California high schools have been declining in recent years. Thus no evidence yet exists of a significant negative impact of the new system on dropout rates. California also needs to improve its measurement of the dropout rate if this hypothesis is to be tested accurately.

A second set of issues surrounds resources and curriculum. A number of programs were designed to bring additional resources to schools with low test scores. Have the schools that initially had the lowest test scores enjoyed a measurable increase in resources? At the top end of the test score distribution, at schools that are largely in affluent areas, have resources gone up? One concern that seems plausible is that the need to devote additional time to test preparation might have diluted the curriculum, especially in the top-performing schools. Has this happened?

Our analysis of trends in school resources and curriculum reveals some important patterns. Most disturbingly, we find that the level of preparation of teachers in the bottom-achieving quintile of schools has declined between 1997–98 and 1999–2000, both relative to teacher preparation among the top fifth of schools and, in most cases, in absolute terms. For instance, in the bottom-performing middle schools, between 1997–98 and 1999–2000 the percentage of teachers lacking a teaching credential rose from 19.2 percent to 26.3 percent, while in the top-performing fifth of schools, the percentage of teachers lacking a credential barely budged, rising from 5.4 percent to 6.7 percent.

However, we cannot be sure of the reason for this and other trends in teacher preparation, and whether they are related to the school accountability program. Betts, Rueben, and Danenberg voiced the concern that after the passage of the PSAA, teachers at the bottom-performing schools might leave these schools because of the additional public scrutiny such schools would receive. The state has taken several steps to improve the level of resources at schools with low achievement. But it seems highly possible that these measures might be swamped by movements of teachers between schools in response to the sanctions that await bottom-performing schools that fail to improve adequately. Further research into this question is urgently needed. Unfortunately, it is difficult to examine this issue at the state level due to the lack of a longitudinal database on California's teachers.

On the issue of possible dilution of the curriculum, we were able to gain some insights into this question by examining trends in the percentage of high school courses that were Advanced Placement or college preparatory. Statewide, the percentage of courses that fit either description has risen between 1997–98 and 1999–2000, although only the increase in the share of courses that are AP is statistically significant. We also looked for divergences in curriculum between the schools that were initially in the bottom or top fifth of the test score distribution in spring 1998. In both types of schools the percentage of classes that were AP rose significantly, and by roughly the same amount. If anything, the percentage of courses that were college preparatory seemed to rise more at the schools that initially had the lowest test scores. We conclude that at least by these measures, testing and the related aspects of accountability have neither diluted the high school curriculum nor widened inequality in the curriculum between top- and bottom-performing schools.

The following conundrum has been raised: How could low-scoring schools have done more to improve student achievement at the 25th and 50th percentiles of national norms at the same time that their teacher resources have been declining both in absolute terms and relative to high-scoring schools? We cannot answer this question with any certainty, but two possibilities spring to mind. First, Betts, Rueben, and Danenberg find that teacher qualifications are related to student achievement, but only weakly.[29] Second, it seems somewhat plausible that less experienced teachers might have adapted to the new regime of testing and content standards more quickly than did their more experienced colleagues. For example, inexperienced teachers who have not yet fully prepared lecture notes and class materials might be able to adjust their teaching more closely to the new standards.

In sum, we have found two important trends in the data. Test scores in California have risen significantly, especially for schools that originally had the lowest test scores. At the same time, teacher resources have declined, especially at low-scoring schools. Given that student achievement in these low-performing schools has risen while resources have decreased, and given the monetary incentives for individual teachers in the low-performing schools, a skeptic could argue that these patterns reflect teaching to the test or, at the very least, growing test familiarity. An alternative interpretation is that the growth in achievement in spite of the significant drop in a number of measures of teacher preparation in low-performing schools reflects genuine achievement growth spurred by the accountability reforms and public scrutiny. We think that the latter hypothesis deserves to be taken seriously. It certainly should surprise critics of the standards movement who claim that additional resources are the only way to improve achievement at the bottom schools to learn that the bottom-achieving schools have shown the most pronounced improvement in spite of a reduction in average teacher preparation.

Overall, we cannot know for sure which of these two explanations—teaching to the test or genuine improvement—is the more important. One method of distinguishing between these divergent hypotheses is to analyze California's results on the National Assessment of Educational Progress (NAEP) over the next decade. If test scores on the state test continue to surge while NAEP scores do not improve significantly, it would suggest that our first, less sanguine, hypothesis was the dominant explanation for rising test scores on the Stanford 9.

The Outlook for the Future of School Accountability in California

After several years of rapidly introduced accountability reforms, what has California achieved, and what are the prospects for the future? California has probably made the most progress in defining content standards, with a detailed set of standards of what students should know in each grade, with sample questions to guide teachers, students, and parents alike. On the other two foundations of reform—testing and intervention—California has also made significant progress, although significant problems clearly remain.

First, the current Academic Performance Index, by relying solely on an off-the-shelf test, ranks schools based on subject matter that is not particularly closely aligned to the new content standards. By introducing supplementary test questions that specifically target the content standards, the state has advanced in this regard. However, the state now faces a difficult dilemma. While it seems apparent that at least theoretically all tests should link directly to the content standards, if California abandons the Stanford 9 test completely, it will once again have canceled an existing statewide test, making it extremely difficult to know whether student achievement is truly improving over time. Another problem with abandoning the Stanford 9 test is that it provides the lone nationally normed test used by the state. It makes sense to provide some external yardstick against which to compare student achievement in California. Officials in Sacramento seem to be acutely aware of these issues. In late April 2001 the Senate Education Committee began considering a proposal from the governor to shorten the Stanford 9 test in all subjects but language arts, while increasing the length of new tests in various subjects that are more closely linked to the state's content standards.[30] The proposal has been approved and will apply to testing in 2002. The key to such a reform is to ensure that a statistically valid cross-walk exists between the streamlined Stanford 9 tests in math and science that are being implemented and the more detailed test given in 1998 through 2000.

In this unsettled environment, it becomes extremely difficult to know what sort of testing system, if any, will be in place ten or even five years from now. If what emerges is a new testing system that links questions closely to the state's detailed subject framework, while providing a means of estimating whether student achievement is changing meaningfully over the years, it would represent an improvement on the current system. Clearly, the high school exit examination, already in place, also becomes an important content-specific gauge of achievement for high school students.

The most difficult question facing the state's accountability system now is whether it has the right mix of responses for schools where student achievement lags. The most compelling dilemma here relates to the high school exit examination. If the experience of other states is any guide, no matter what passing grade the state decides on, a large percentage of students in California will fail the test initially. To prevent this almost certain outcome from spiraling into higher dropout rates in California, it becomes imperative to target additional assistance to students at risk and to their teachers. There is some reason to be optimistic. Both the legislature and the governor's office have taken steps recently to increase further the assistance going to the bottom schools. To give one example, in late April 2001 the governor's office announced that a plan to extend the school year across all middle schools would be scaled back, with the savings being devoted to additional resources, of an unspecified nature, for schools in the lowest two deciles of student performance.[31]

While the future of the school accountability system in California is not yet assured, it would be a mistake to underestimate the scope of what has already been achieved. In the space of half a decade, rigorous content standards have been developed. A statewide testing system has been introduced, which is being used to help schools identify weaknesses in the preparation of individual students and to help administrators identify schools that are underperforming given the resources they receive and the socioeconomic status of their students. A high school exit examination will be given and provides incentives for schools, parents, and students to focus on mastery of basic skills. This test provides a worthwhile complement to the Golden State Exams and scholarships that currently reward students at the top end of the achievement spectrum. This effort to create a system of multiple incentives for students at different points in the achievement distribution represents a move toward the sort of multiple credential system that Betts and Costrell espouse as a way of improving incentives for all schools and all students.

At the same time, many measures have been enacted to improve teacher training and enrich the curriculum at bottom-performing schools. This trend represents a sea change in political thinking. Title I and similar state programs have for many years directed additional resources to schools in disadvantaged areas. But the multiple new programs in this vein represent significant movement beyond the notion, embodied in the 1971 *Serrano* v. *Priest* court decision, that all that California needed was equal access to funding across districts. Time will tell whether the current reforms in spending, together with the newly created incentives for teachers, administrators, and students, suffice to bring meaningful and lasting changes to the level of student achievement and the dispersion in achievement in California.

We close by reiterating what may be our most important finding, that inequality in teacher preparation as measured by teacher credentials, education, and experience has risen between the bottom- and top-performing schools in California. California needs to continue the search for powerful new incentives to retain highly qualified teachers at the schools in the greatest need. Meeting this challenge could prove pivotal to the long-term success of school accountability in California.

Appendix

CBEDS

The California Basic Educational Data System (CBEDS) is maintained and supported by the Educational Demographics Unit in the California Department of Education. It contains individual-level credentialed-personnel data and summary student and program data at the school and district levels. These data are collected through three report forms each October: the Professional Assignment Information Form (PAIF), the School Information Form (SIF), and the County/District Information Form (CDIF).

Variables available at the individual level (PAIF) include education level, experience, and types of credentials held for personnel in California's public schools. The PAIF also collects information on specific classes taught and student counts per section for each teacher. From these data we calculate average class size and course offerings and then take school-level, weighted means of these measures and overall teacher characteristics, such as the proportions for experience, education, and credentials for each school.

The school-level data (SIF) contain variables of two general types: (1) staff and student counts, and (2) program types. Staff and student counts include classified staff counts and student enrollment, including student counts in specific types of programs, as well as graduate and dropout counts. These variables are enumerated by gender and ethnicity. Program types include variables such as technology, educational calendar, magnet programs, and alternative education.

CalWorks

CalWorks, a school-level data set, contains counts and percentages of California children in families receiving Aid to Families with Dependent Children (AFDC) and children enrolled in free and reduced-price meal programs. According to the California Department of Education, these AFDC data are collected each October through the cooperative efforts of the schools, districts, county offices of education, and the county offices of health and welfare. Schools report their meal program enrollment data annually, based on their

October meal program enrollment files. (Both sets of data are collected on the California Department of Education, Education Finance Division Form No. CFP-2, School Level AFDC Report.)

STAR Test Results

The Standardized Testing and Reporting (STAR) program file is maintained by the Standards, Curriculum, and Assessment Division of the California Department of Education. It contains results from the *Stanford Achievement Test* Series, Ninth Edition, Form T (Stanford 9) test series administered by Harcourt, Brace & Co. These results are reported at school level in two ways for each subject area and grade level (grades two through eleven only): first, for all students tested in the group, and second, for limited English proficiency (LEP) students tested. From these two measures, we also calculated non-LEP students' test scores.

There are six subject-test areas: (1) reading, (2) math, (3) language (written expression), (4) spelling, (5) science, and (6) history/social science. Students in grades two through eight are required by Senate Bill 376 to take tests in the first four subject areas.[32] Students in grades nine through eleven were required take tests in areas 1, 2, 3, 5, and 6. Our analysis focuses on the first two subject tests.

The following six statistics were reported at the school, district, county, and state level: (1) total number valid in each subject and grade, (2) mean-scaled score, (3) percent of normal curve equivalency, (4) percent scoring above the 75th percentile (based on national norms), (5) percent scoring at or above the 50th percentile, and (6) percent scoring above the 25th percentile. We focus on the last three measures.

Using the SIF, we identified different types of schools and then focused on schools that have regular academic programs. Thus, our analysis excludes students in special education schools, juvenile hall, continuation schools, and adult schools. The sample also excludes schools for which Stanford 9, SIF, and PAIF information were missing. We grouped the selected schools into four grade-span categories, based on similar characteristics of the schools. Each of the K–6, 6–8, and 9–12 groups included all schools where the enrollment fell entirely within one of these grade-span boundaries.[33] Schools where the enrollment crossed the boundaries were placed into an "Other" category, which we do not analyze in this research.

Table A-1 presents the numbers of schools, teachers, and students in the state and in our sample in each year. Our math sample includes over 75 percent of all schools, comprising over 88 percent of all students in each of the three years.

Data Tables

Tables A-2, A-3, and A-4 present the underlying data and t-test significance levels for figures 4, 5, and 6 and table 2.

Test Score Quintile Ranges

Table A-5 contains the boundaries of the five test score quintiles for math and reading in each of the three grade-spans in the 1997–98 academic year.

Table A-6 provides an alternate test for regression to the mean using a 1999–2000 subset of high- and low-scoring schools.

Table A-1. Schools and Students in State and in Math Test Sample, 1997–98 to 1999–2000

Academic year	Statewide	Sample	Percent
1997–98			
Schools	8,179	6,331	77.41
Students	5,727,303	5,145,831	89.85
1998–99			
Schools	8,331	6,248	75.00
Students	5,844,111	5,150,133	88.13
1999–2000			
Schools	8,563	6,554	76.54
Students	5,951,612	5,381,890	90.43

Source: Authors' calculations using California Department of Education data sets.

Table A-2. Students Scoring above 75th Percentile in Math and Reading, 1997–98, 1998–99, and 1999–2000
Percent

Subject and grade	All students			LEP students			Non-LEP students		
	1997–98	1998–99	1999–2000	1997–98	1998–99	1999–2000	1997–98	1998–99	1999–2000
Math									
Grade two	21	27	33	9	13	18	25	33	40
Grade three	19	24	31	7	10	14	23	31	38
Grade four	20	23	29	5	7	10	25	29	36
Grade five	20	22	27	4	5	7	25	28	33
Grade six	25	28	32	5	7	9	30	35	39
Grade seven	21	22	25	4	5	6	25	27	30
Grade eight	20	22	24	4	5	5	23	26	28
Grade nine	22	23	25	5	5	5	25	27	28
Grade ten	17	19	20	5	6	6	19	22	23
Grade eleven	22	24	25	7	9	8	24	27	28
Simple average across grades[a]	20.7	23.4	27.1	5.5	7.1	8.8	24.2	28.5	32.4
	(2.11)	(2.59)	(4.09)	(1.65)	(2.81)	(4.24)	(2.72)	(3.72)	(5.68)
Weighted average across grades[b]	20.7	23.5	27.3	5.7	7.6	10.0	24.2	28.6	32.4
Change	1998 to 1999	1999 to 2000	1998 to 2000	1998 to 1999	1999 to 2000	1998 to 2000	1998 to 1999	1999 to 2000	1998 to 2000
Significance	1999	2000	2000	1999	2000	2000	1999	2000	2000
t-test	*		***	*	*	*	**	**	**

Reading

Grade two	18	21	24	4	5	7	23	28	32
Grade three	17	18	20	2	2	3	22	25	28
Grade four	21	22	23	2	3	3	27	29	31
Grade five	20	21	21	2	2	2	25	27	27
Grade six	21	22	23	1	2	2	26	27	29
Grade seven	21	21	23	1	1	2	25	26	28
Grade eight	19	20	21	1	1	1	22	24	25
Grade nine	12	12	13	0	0	0	14	15	15
Grade ten	13	14	14	1	1	1	15	16	17
Grade eleven	17	16	17	1	1	1	19	19	19
Simple average across grades[a]	17.9	18.7	19.9	1.5	1.8	2.2	21.6	23.6	25.1
	(3.25)	(3.56)	(3.93)	(1.08)	(1.40)	(1.93)	(4.54)	(5.08)	(5.99)
Weighted average across grades[b]	18.0	18.8	20.1	1.8	2.2	2.7	21.6	23.7	25.1
Change	1998 to 1999	1999 to 2000	1998 to 2000	1998 to 1999	1999 to 2000	1998 to 2000	1998 to 1999	1999 to 2000	1998 to 2000
Significance t-test	1999	2000	2000	1999	2000	2000	1999	2000	2000

Source: Authors' calculations using California Department of Education data sets.
Note: LEP = limited English proficiency. Probability > |t|: * = 0.05, ** = 0.01, *** = 0.001.
a. Standard deviation is in parentheses.
b. Weighted by numbers of students taking tests in each category and grade.

Table A-3. Students Scoring at or above National Median in Math and Reading, 1997–98, 1998–99, and 1999–2000

Percent

Subject and grade	All students			LEP students			Non-LEP students		
	1997–98	1998–99	1999–2000	1997–98	1998–99	1999–2000	1997–98	1998–99	1999–2000
Math									
Grade two	43	49	57	26	33	40	49	57	65
Grade three	40	48	56	21	28	37	46	57	65
Grade four	39	44	51	17	21	27	46	52	60
Grade five	41	45	50	16	19	24	48	54	59
Grade six	46	50	55	18	22	26	53	59	63
Grade seven	42	45	48	14	16	19	48	52	55
Grade eight	42	45	48	13	15	17	48	52	55
Grade nine	47	48	51	19	19	21	51	55	57
Grade ten	41	44	46	17	20	21	44	49	50
Grade eleven	43	45	47	19	22	23	46	50	51
Simple average across grades[a]	42.4	46.3	50.9	18.0	21.5	25.5	47.9	53.7	58.0
	(2.50)	(2.21)	(3.90)	(3.68)	(5.40)	(7.51)	(2.56)	(3.27)	(5.37)
Weighted average across grades[b]	42.4	46.4	51.2	18.6	22.7	27.6	48.0	53.8	58.0
Change	1998 to 1999	1999 to 2000	1998 to 2000	1998 to 1999	1999 to 2000	1998 to 2000	1998 to 1999	1999 to 2000	1998 to 2000
Significance									
t-test	**	**	***	***	***	**	***	*	***

Reading

Grade two	40	44	49	15	19	25	48	56	61
Grade three	38	41	44	9	12	15	47	53	57
Grade four	40	41	45	9	11	13	49	53	56
Grade five	41	42	44	8	9	10	50	53	55
Grade six	42	44	46	7	9	10	50	54	55
Grade seven	44	44	46	7	7	9	52	53	55
Grade eight	46	47	49	7	8	9	53	57	58
Grade nine	34	34	35	3	3	4	39	41	41
Grade ten	32	33	34	3	3	3	36	38	39
Grade eleven	36	35	36	4	4	4	40	41	41
Simple average across grades[a]	39.3	40.5	42.8	7.2	8.5	10.2	46.4	49.9	51.8
	(4.37)	(4.84)	(5.67)	(3.55)	(4.86)	(6.51)	(6.06)	(7.02)	(8.13)
Weighted average across grades[b]	39.4	40.7	43.1	8.1	9.9	12.1	46.5	50.2	51.8
Change	1998 to 1999	1999 to 2000	1998 to 2000	1998 to 1999	1999 to 2000	1998 to 2000	1998 to 1999	1999 to 2000	1998 to 2000
Significance t-test									

Source: Authors' calculations using California Department of Education data sets.

Note: LEP = limited English proficiency. Probability > |t|: * = 0.05, ** = 0.01, *** = 0.001.

a. Standard deviation is in parentheses.

b. Weighted by numbers of students taking tests in each category and grade.

Table A-4. Students Scoring above 25th Percentile in Math and Reading, 1997–98, 1998–99, and 1999–2000
Percent

Subject and grade	All students			LEP students			Non-LEP students		
	1997–98	1998–99	1999–2000	1997–98	1998–99	1999–2000	1997–98	1998–99	1999–2000
Math									
Grade two	65	71	77	50	58	65	70	77	83
Grade three	64	71	77	45	55	64	70	78	83
Grade four	62	66	73	39	46	54	69	74	80
Grade five	61	65	70	35	41	48	68	73	78
Grade six	67	71	74	40	46	51	73	78	81
Grade seven	65	68	71	37	41	45	71	75	77
Grade eight	64	68	71	34	38	42	70	75	77
Grade nine	71	73	75	48	50	53	75	78	80
Grade ten	68	70	71	46	50	50	71	75	75
Grade eleven	66	68	69	43	48	49	69	73	73
Simple average across grades[a]	65.3	69.1	72.8	41.7	47.3	52.1	70.7	75.6	78.7
	(2.91)	(2.51)	(2.86)	(5.53)	(6.31)	(7.43)	(1.96)	(2.01)	(3.30)
Weighted average across grades[b]	65.2	69.1	73.0	41.8	48.2	54.0	70.7	75.7	78.8
Change	1998 to 1999	1999 to 2000	1998 to 2000	1998 to 1999	1999 to 2000	1998 to 2000	1998 to 1999	1999 to 2000	1998 to 2000
Significance	1999	2000	2000	1999	2000	2000	1999	2000	2000
t-test	**	**	***	*	**	***	***	*	***

Reading

Grade two	61	66	71	33	42	50	70	76	81
Grade three	59	63	68	28	34	41	69	76	80
Grade four	62	64	68	29	34	38	72	76	80
Grade five	63	64	67	26	29	32	73	76	78
Grade six	66	68	70	28	32	34	75	78	80
Grade seven	66	67	69	24	27	30	75	77	79
Grade eight	70	72	73	29	31	34	78	81	82
Grade nine	59	60	62	16	17	19	65	69	70
Grade ten	55	55	56	12	13	14	61	64	64
Grade eleven	62	61	62	17	19	20	67	69	69
Simple average across grades[a]	62.3	64.0	66.6	24.2	27.8	31.2	70.5	74.2	76.3
	(4.27)	(4.71)	(5.13)	(6.86)	(8.95)	(10.97)	(5.06)	(5.16)	(6.24)
Weighted average across grades[b]	62.3	64.1	66.8	26.0	30.3	34.4	70.5	74.4	76.3
Change	1998 to 1999	1999 to 2000	1998 to 2000	1998 to 1999	1999 to 2000	1998 to 2000	1998 to 1999	1999 to 2000	1998 to 2000
Significance t-test			*			*			*

Source: Authors' calculations using California Department of Education data sets.

Note: LEP = limited English proficiency. Probability > |t|: * = 0.05, ** = 0.01, *** = 0.001.

a. Standard deviation is in parentheses.

b. Weighted by numbers of students taking tests in each category and grade.

Table A-5. Math and Reading Test Score Quintile Ranges for the Percentage of Non-LEP Students Scoring at or above National Median, 1997–98

Subject and grade-span	Quintile 1	Quintile 2	Quintile 3	Quintile 4	Quintile 5
Math					
K–6	0 to 25.9	26.0 to 37.2	37.3 to 49.4	49.5 to 63.2	63.3 to 100
6–8	0 to 28.2	28.3 to 39.5	39.6 to 51.3	51.4 to 64.7	64.8 to 100
9–12	0 to 31.3	31.2 to 43.1	43.2 to 52.7	52.8 to 62.9	63.0 to 100
Reading					
K–6	0 to 24.6	24.7 to 37.0	37.1 to 49.7	49.8 to 63.6	63.7 to 100
6–8	0 to 31.7	31.7 to 43.9	44.0 to 56.3	56.4 to 67.4	67.5 to 100
9–12	0 to 22.8	22.8 to 33.2	33.3 to 42.3	42.4 to 52.4	52.5 to 100

Source: Authors' calculations using California Department of Education data sets.
Note: LEP = limited English proficiency.

Table A-6. Average Percentage of Non-LEP Students in 1999–2000 Cohorts of High and Low Test Score Schools Scoring at or above National Norms in Reading and Math, 1997–98 to 1999–2000

Subject and grade-span	Percentile	1997–98		1998–99		1999–2000		Changes, 1997–98 to 1999–2000		Gap change[a] between high- and low-score schools
		1999–2000 Low-score schools	1999–2000 High-score schools	1999–2000 Low-score schools	1999–2000 High-score schools	1999–2000 Low-score schools	1999–2000 High-score schools	1999–2000 Low-score schools	1999–2000 High-score schools	
Math										
K–6	Above 75th	6.39	45.17	10.54	53.76	13.21	61.71	6.83	16.54	9.71
	At or above 50	21.09	72.15	28.67	79.00	33.41	84.97	12.32	12.82	0.50
	Above 25	43.33	88.28	52.60	92.31	58.75	95.11	15.42	6.83	-8.59
(Number of observations)		(842)	(848)	(842)	(848)	(842)	(848)			
6–8	Above 75th	6.42	47.03	8.79	50.56	9.72	55.07	3.30	8.04	4.74
	At or above 50	22.21	73.90	27.32	76.70	29.03	80.64	6.82	6.74	-0.08
	Above 25	47.25	89.48	54.44	91.00	56.25	93.11	8.99	3.62	-5.37
(Number of observations)		(187)	(198)	(187)	(198)	(187)	(198)			
9–12	Above 75th	6.25	42.29	7.82	45.50	8.39	48.19	2.14	5.90	3.76
	At or above 50	24.51	71.01	28.75	73.31	29.59	76.24	5.08	5.22	0.15
	Above 25	55.46	87.84	60.45	88.97	60.90	90.31	5.45	2.47	-2.98
(Number of observations)		(129)	(169)	(129)	(169)	(129)	(169)			
Reading										
K–6	Above 75th	4.96	43.83	7.54	49.07	8.16	52.91	3.21	9.08	5.87
	At or above 50	19.09	73.02	25.39	78.30	27.52	81.95	8.43	8.92	0.50
	Above 25	42.55	89.75	51.53	93.07	55.98	95.14	13.43	5.39	-8.03
(Number of observations)		(845)	(834)	(845)	(834)	(845)	(834)			

Table A-6. Average Percentage of Non-LEP Students in 1999–2000 Cohorts of High and Low Test Score Schools Scoring at or above National Norms in Reading and Math, 1997–98 to 1999–2000 (continued)

Subject and grade-span	Percentile	1997–98		1998–99		1999–2000		Changes, 1997–98 to 1999–2000		Gap change[a] between high- and low-score schools
		1999–2000 Low-score schools	1999–2000 High-score schools	1999–2000 Low-score schools	1999–2000 High-score schools	1999–2000 Low-score schools	1999–2000 High-score schools	1999–2000 Low-score schools	1999–2000 High-score schools	
6–8	Above 75th	6.18	43.52	7.68	44.95	7.83	47.79	1.65	4.27	2.62
	At or above 50	23.55	74.99	28.11	76.39	28.65	79.40	5.11	4.41	-0.70
	Above 25	51.29	91.37	58.47	92.50	59.85	94.20	8.56	2.83	-5.73
(Number of observations)		(185)	(191)	(185)	(191)	(185)	(191)			
9–12	Above 75th	3.92	31.62	4.53	31.66	4.50	33.63	0.58	2.00	1.42
	At or above 50	16.75	61.47	18.66	61.86	18.61	64.29	1.86	2.82	0.97
	Above 25	43.66	83.89	47.77	84.66	47.93	86.37	4.27	2.49	-1.78
(Number of observations)		(135)	(158)	(135)	(158)	(135)	(158)			

Source: Authors' calculations using California Department of Education data sets.

Note: In 1999–2000, approximately 18 percent of 9–12 schools were in the bottom quintile of the test score distribution, while almost 21 percent were in the top for both math and reading. This appears to be due to multiple schools with the same test score for numerous test score values within the test score rankings in the top quintile. All t-tests, probability > |t| for the differences between 1997–98 and 1999–2000 levels are significant at the 0.001 level

a. Calculated as (1999–2000 high-score schools – low-score schools) – (1997–98 high-score schools – low-score schools).

Comment by Robert Rothman

Julian R. Betts and Anne Danenberg have done an admirable job both in explaining the complex California accountability system and in analyzing its initial effects. They offer sound evidence to support two strong conclusions: that student performance, as measured by the state test, improved substantially, particularly for the lowest performing schools; and that teacher quality, as measured by a number of dimensions, declined, particularly in those same schools.

At one level these two findings pose a paradox: How can student performance increase in schools with less-qualified and less-experienced teachers? There are several possible explanations. Maybe teacher quality does not matter as much as other research suggests it might.[34] Maybe the gains in achievement are inflated, as Daniel Koretz suggests may have been the case in other states.[35] Betts and Danenberg pose a third possibility—that the incentives created by the accountability system were sufficient to encourage low-performing schools to overcome the shortcomings in teacher preparation and raise performance anyway.

I will suggest a fourth possibility: the lack of coherence in California's education policy. To be sure, coherence in education policy is much easier to wish for than achieve in a system of widely dispersed authority, and California is far from alone in falling short of the ideal. But standards-based reform was aimed, at least by its architects, at imposing some coherence by placing standards for student performance at the core of policy around curriculum, teacher development, and testing.

California is not there yet. In part, this is because, more so than in most other states, many actors have hands in setting education policy in the state—the governor, the elected state superintendent of public instruction, the state Board of Education, the legislature, and the voters, through the widely used initiative process. And that is only at the state level; districts set their own policies as well. Achieving coherence is difficult under any circumstances with that kind of governance structure. Even acting with the best of intentions, these actors can adopt policies that do not support, or may conflict with, other policies.

For example, in 1996, as the state was beginning to embark on its standards-based strategy by developing content standards and implementing a statewide test, the legislature, with the strong support of Governor Pete Wilson, mandated a substantial reduction in class sizes in the early grades. This initiative in principle supported the notion of standards-based instruction by enabling teachers to interact with young children. But in practice the law produced a scramble to hire new teachers to staff the smaller classes, and many schools—particularly those serving low-income and minority children, which tended to be low performing—were forced to hire underqualified teachers. This outcome, which undermines the vision of standards-based reform of teachers prepared to teach the content standards, could help explain the lower levels of teacher qualifications in low-performing schools that Betts and Danenberg found—at least in the early grades.

Are Betts and Danenberg correct that the accountability system was powerful enough to overcome this trend? Unfortunately, no one knows, and California's lack of coherence makes it difficult to make judgments. In a more coherent system, someone might be able to do so. The theory of action underlying the reform suggests that the standards communicate the expectations for instruction and learning, assessments measure the extent to which schools and students are meeting those expectations, and accountability creates incentives for schools to improve performance against the standards and directs resources to schools that are falling behind. This theory rests on assumptions that may not have proven true, such as the availability of high-quality professional development. But the theory suggests that the incentives encourage schools to focus on the standards and that improvements represent progress toward those standards.[36]

California's system, at least so far, does not match that ideal. The state has all the elements, but they do not work together as the architects of standards-based reform envisioned.

The standards the state has adopted are strong. They have won acclaim from a number of observers. Achieve, for example, an organization formed by governors and business leaders to support state standards-based reform efforts, uses the California English language arts standards as benchmarks against which to compare other state standards. The mathematics standards, meanwhile, won praise from researchers involved with the Third International Mathematics and Science Study.

However, California implemented a statewide test before the state standards were adopted, and the test it has used—the Stanford Achievement Test, Ninth Edition (Stanford 9)—is a commercially available test that was not designed to match California standards. California has acknowledged the mismatch between the standards and tests, and the state in 1999 began administering an augmentation to the Stanford 9 aimed at filling the gaps between the standards and tests and providing information on student progress toward the standards. However, until 2001, schools under the accountability system were answerable for progress only on the Stanford 9.

This situation meant that schools could earn substantial cash bonuses or be subject to intervention as underperforming schools solely on the basis of performance on a test that was not aligned to the state standards. What would schools do? Focus on the standards and hope that the improved instruction would lead to higher performance on the test? Some schools must have acted that way. But more likely, schools focused on what they needed to do to raise Stanford 9 scores, and these actions may or may not have improved instruction. Moreover, the information schools received on performance, such as how students compared with other schools and with national norms, did little to guide them on the areas of the standards they needed to address to improve performance.

Thus the mismatch between the tests and the standards makes it difficult to know whether the accountability system helped improve instruction and learning to compensate for lower levels of teacher quality in low-performing schools. But the California system is evolving and is moving toward a more coherent system. The augmented test in English language arts, known as the California Standards Test, is being used for accountability purposes in 2001. And the state legislature is considering legislation to implement a standards-based test in other subjects in 2002.

However, even if the alignment between the standards and tests is tight, it will still be difficult to know from aggregate data if instruction is improving and whether the accountability system is producing such improvements. Research in Texas, for example, has shown that schools respond in very different ways to accountability pressures, even on a test that is designed to match state standards. While some schools focus on short-term efforts to boost scores, by teaching test-like materials, others have made more concerted efforts to improve instruction by redesigning their curriculum and improving teachers' abilities to deliver high-quality instruction.[37]

These studies suggest that, to get a better handle on the effects of accountability on instruction, researchers need to get inside of classrooms and examine the kind of work teachers are assigning and students are performing on a regular basis. Surveys of teachers help, but surveys do not always capture the true nature of classroom practice. Teachers may respond in socially acceptable ways, or they may indicate that their instruction has changed substantially when a closer examination may reveal otherwise. Recent research in Maryland, Michigan, and New Jersey has shed a good deal of light on instructional practice and the extent to which state policies are affecting what teachers do in classrooms.[38]

Researchers also should examine the influence of state accountability policies on school practice. The extent to which the incentives created by the accountability measures drive change must be determined, and teachers and principals can indicate whether their actions were spurred on by the need to show improvement on state measures or to earn cash awards. California, at least, shows some indication that teachers were not even aware of the possibility of rewards, so such incentives may not have had the desired effect.

But accountability is more than an incentive structure. In California's case in particular, the accountability system directs substantial resources and assistance to low-performing schools. As Betts and Danenberg note, in the first two years of the program 860 schools qualified for such assistance. But the aggregate data do not disclose whether such assistance made a difference. To judge the effects of accountability, more must be known about what kind of assistance the state provided, how it was implemented, and what schools did in response. Only then can the claim be made with some confidence that the accountability system helped improve student achievement in California.

Comment by Robert M. Hauser

The central question is whether children are hurt or helped by standards-based reform. Despite their commendable effort to bring together data about school reform, school resources, and student performance in California, Julian R. Betts and Anne Danenberg provide few valid clues about the direction of change in that state. Their analyses of trends and differentials in student performance are fatally flawed. The one persuasive set of new evidence in the paper suggests that high- and low-performing California schools grew less equal in teacher quality between the academic years 1997–98 and 1999–2000. However, the available data cannot reveal whether growing inequality is simply a persistent trend or whether the trend might be worse in the absence of educational reform.

The goals in standards-based reform are severalfold: to set high standards, to raise student achievement, to ensure equal educational opportunity, to foster parental involvement, and to increase public support of the schools.

What Betts and Danenberg Report

Betts and Danenberg describe the California reforms as consisting of content standards, an assessment system, and a menu of responses by the state. In the context of those reforms, the aim of their paper is to assess overall trends in student achievement, in school resources, and in the distribution of student achievement and resources.

Betts and Danenberg assess trends and differentials in achievement in mathematics and reading on the Stanford 9, by grade level, from 1997–98 to 1999–2000. They summarize achievement levels and changes in achievement levels with percentages and changes in percentages, above or below selected national norms on the Stanford 9—the 25th, 50th, and 75th percentiles.[39] Sometimes the data are tabulated by population group—total, limited English proficient (LEP), and non-LEP. At other times, achievement and changes in achievement are tabulated by grade level (elementary, middle, or secondary) for groups of schools with high or low achievement levels in a particular academic year.

Resources are all measured at the school level, and they cover median teacher experience, low teacher experience, teachers with a bachelor's degree or less, teachers with a master's degree or more, teacher certification, average class size, college prep classes, and Advanced Placement (AP) classes. There is a single, crude measure of socioeconomic status at the school level—the percentage of students who sign up for free or reduced-price school lunches.

The rationale for educational reform in California is compelling. First, students in California perform below national norms. This is largely, but not entirely, accountable to the large share of LEP students in California schools. Second, large differences exist in resources and achievement among schools. Betts and Danenberg hold that "the rationale for statewide educational content standards, assessment, and intervention is strong." However, there are "important questions about the capability of schools to bring all students up to common norms of achievement, especially in light of variations in resources among schools. Compounding matters, even if resources could be equalized across schools, this equalization by itself would do little to close the test score gap related to variations in student disadvantage."[40]

What have been the major educational reforms in California in the 1990s? First, content standards were adopted in late 1997 in English, language arts, and mathematics. They were adopted in late 1998 in science, history, and social science. Early in 2001, content standards were established in individual and performing arts. Second, the Stanford 9 has been administered from the spring of 1998 forward. The Stanford 9 was presumably chosen in part because of its compatibility with nascent state content standards, but several variations in the exams have been introduced since 1998 to bring the test into greater conformity with the standards. A new high school exit exam will be phased in for students scheduled to graduate in 2004 and later years. Third, in 1999 and 2000 the state established three mechanisms to support school accountability: an Academic Performance Index (API) for each school and for subpopulations within each school; a set of positive and negative responses to poor school performance (defined relative to the API); and a set of rewards for schools and students with exceptional growth or performance levels. Thus, according to Betts and Danenberg, California has implemented each of the components of a state accountability program, and other new support mechanisms, for example, higher salaries for teachers in low-performing schools, have recently been created.

Betts and Danenberg noted four main findings. First, test scores rose across the two-year period from 1997–98 to 1999–2000. That is, growth was evident in the percentages of students above the selected cutoff points in the normative distribution of the Stanford 9 examinations in mathematics and reading. Betts and Danenberg consider the possibility that the score gains may be attributable to greater familiarity with the new test, but, they say, "We doubt that all of the improvement in scores reflects growing knowledge of the Stanford 9 test form."

Second, inequality of academic achievement declined over this period, in the overall test score distribution and between initially high-scoring and low-scoring schools. Growth in achievement was greatest at the low end of the distribution. For example, referring to mathematics and reading achievement among LEP and non-LEP students, Betts and Danenberg report that, "in all cases but one, the percentage point drop in the number of students in the bottom quartile of national norms exceeded the percentage point rise in the share of students in the top quartile of national norms." And similarly, "Typically the bottom-performing schools in 1997–98 appear to have improved considerably faster than the top-performing schools. The percentage-point increase in the share of students above [the 25th and 50th percentiles] in bottom-performing schools is typically at least twice as big as the corresponding increase in top-performing schools."

Third, while some have worried that higher, test-based academic standards would increase the number of dropouts, California's dropout rates at the end of the 1990s continued a decline that began before the educational reforms of the late 1990s.[41] Fourth, the school resources measured by Betts and Danenberg were either stable or declined from 1997–98 to 1999–2000, but school resources typically became less equal between high- and low-scoring schools.

How Good Is the Evidence?

Have Betts and Danenberg provided a full and accurate description of educational reform and its initial successes and problems in California? No. Their exposition does not say whether standards-based educational reform has been implemented in California, and few of their empirical findings are supported by their data and analysis.

Betts and Danenberg describe accountability systems as consisting of a framework of content standards, an assessment system, and annual responses by the state. This leaves out a key factor—implementation at the school and classroom level. How are standards delivered to teachers down to that level? Do they have the knowledge and resources to deliver the content to students? The answer: No one knows.

There is a closely related problem of timing: Cause should precede effect. How could the California reforms—variously enacted from 1997 to 2000—have affected performance across the period 1997–98 to 1999–2000? Even the earliest of the reforms—content standards in English, language arts, and mathematics (adopted in late 1997)—were unlikely to have affected achievement in the following academic year, that is, led to achievement growth between 1997–98 and 1998–99. It takes time, effort, and money to translate standards into actions. More doubtful is that the content standards adopted in 1998 and thereafter could have affected academic achievement in 1999 or growth between 1998–99 and 1999–2000.

The same holds, yet more strongly, for the new state educational reporting system and sanctions attached to it. The Academic Performance Index was first reported after the end of the 1998–99 academic year. Change in the API could not have been observed until after the end of the 1999–2000 academic year. How could sanctions tied to change in the API have affected growth in academic achievement from the end of the 1997–98 academic year to the end of the 1999–2000 academic year? The achievement data tabulated by Betts and Danenberg come too early to establish any credible connection between the California reforms and their possible effects on academic achievement.

Betts and Danenberg report achievement in mathematics and reading on the Stanford 9 by grade level for 1997–98 to 1999–2000, but they focus on change across the entire two-year period, not from one year to the next. Why and when would anyone expect to see change in a measure that is not linked to the new standards and accountability system? The obvious candidate—the expected trajectory of test score growth following the introduction of the Stanford 9—was simply brushed aside by Betts and Danenberg on the basis of no evidence.[42] Further, why should older students care about the reforms, and how much effect could any reform—however energetically introduced— make up for years of schooling under the previous regime? It is only the students in the ninth grade in 2001 and later years for whom the high school exit exam will matter. Perhaps, but only perhaps, evidence of differential change by grade level would help address this issue.

Betts and Danenberg focus their attention on the achievements of all students and of non-LEP students classified by the test score levels of their schools. However, despite their own earlier finding that the socioeconomic composition of schools dominates school resources as a source of school-to-school variation in achievement, their analysis does not disaggregate achievement growth by socioeconomic status among non-LEP students. If socioeconomic inequality is a key factor in unequal educational outcomes, educational reform should alter its effects. However, given the severe methodological flaws in the Betts and Danenberg analysis, it is perhaps just as well that they did not pursue this elaboration.

What Is the Null Hypothesis?

Betts and Danenberg describe differentials and changes in achievement test score distributions using percentages, or changes in percentages, above or below selected national test norms—fixed cutoff points in each test score distribution—sometimes tabulated by population groups and other times by grade and school performance levels. The analytic problem is that it is impossible, given the form of these data, to look at changes in overall test score distributions or to separate changes due to overall test score gains from changes in the shape of the distributions. The data in Betts and Danenberg's tables just do not tell them what they want to know about changing inequality in the test score distributions. Another way to put the matter is that, through most of Betts and Danenberg's analysis of test score changes, there is no null hypothesis.

Leaving aside, for the moment, what might have led to higher test scores, my null hypothesis is that there was a gradual increase in mean achievement levels affecting all schools, but no change in variance or in the shape of the distribution. That is, the null hypotheses are that achievement gains occurred uniformly across the test score distribution from 1997–98 to 1999–2000 and that they occurred uniformly in schools whose test scores were initially high and in schools whose test scores were initially low. A very simple set of assumptions, consistent with this hypothesis, is that student achievement levels are distributed normally with constant variance. Under these assumptions, it is possible to fit the Betts and Danenberg data, and the fit is excellent. There is no need to believe, as Betts and Danenberg appear to find, that inequalities in academic achievement declined among students in California, even as inequality of resources grew.

Consider, for example, the distribution of reading achievement among all California students in 1997–98—0.3767 below the first (national) quartile, 0.2290 between the first quartile and the median, 0.2145 between the median and the third quartile, and 0.1797 above the third quartile (as shown in the first column of Betts and Danenberg's table 2). Assuming a unit normal distribution, this distribution may be reexpressed as three unit normal deviates, -0.314, 0.268, and 0.916, corresponding to the quartiles of the national test score distribution. Similarly, the distribution of reading achievement among all students in 1998–99 (0.3587, 0.2342, 0.2188, 0.1882) may be reexpressed by the unit normal deviates -0.362, .235, and 0.884. If there were a shift in mean achievement, but no change in variance, the differences between corresponding unit normal deviates would each reveal the mean shift in achievement. There are three estimators of this shift, one for each cutoff point on the distribution: $-0.362 - (-0.314) = -0.048$, $0.235 - 0.268 = -0.033$, and $0.884 - 0.916 = -0.032$. The near agreement among these estimators confirms the possibility that there has simply been an increase in mean achievement; the estimators would not agree if the shape of the distribution had changed relative to the three cutoff points. I estimated the unit normal deviates for the annual cutoff points under the model of constant variance by least squares. Then I translated the estimated unit normal deviates back into estimated test score distributions.

To extend the example, table 1 gives the same information as Betts and Danenberg's table 2, except the reported figures are my estimates, not the

Table 1. Model Estimates of the Percentage of Students in Each Quartile of National Norms by Student Group, 1997–98 to 1999–2000

Subject and quartile	All students				LEP students				Non-LEP students			
	1997–98	1998–99	1999–2000	Change, 1997–98 to 1999–2000	1997–98	1998–99	1999–2000	Change, 1997–98 to 1999–2000	1997–98	1998–99	1999–2000	Change, 1997–98 to 1999–2000
Math												
Quartile 1	34.67	31.01	26.99	-7.68	58.01	51.98	46.05	-11.96	29.16	24.45	21.23	-7.93
Quartile 2	22.92	22.58	21.92	-1.01	23.49	25.18	26.37	2.87	22.76	21.77	20.79	-1.98
Quartile 3	21.82	22.82	23.74	1.91	12.82	15.21	17.58	4.76	24.02	25.05	25.52	1.50
Quartile 4	20.59	23.59	27.36	6.77	5.67	7.63	10.00	4.33	24.05	28.73	32.46	8.41
Reading												
Quartile 1	37.24	35.83	33.63	-3.61	73.50	69.89	65.95	-7.55	28.81	25.72	24.18	-4.62
Quartile 2	23.43	23.39	23.26	-0.17	18.30	20.17	22.05	3.75	24.83	24.21	23.82	-1.01
Quartile 3	21.57	22.03	22.71	1.14	6.53	7.77	9.19	2.67	25.25	26.16	26.57	1.32
Quartile 4	17.75	18.75	20.39	2.64	1.67	2.17	2.81	1.13	21.12	23.91	25.43	4.31

Note: LEP = limited English proficiency. Quartile 1 is the lowest achievement group.
Source: Authors' calculations from Julian R. Betts and Anne Dannenberg, "School Accountability in California: An Early Evaluation," table 2.

observed data. Remarkable agreement exists between the model estimates for each year and the observed data. No estimated percentages or changes in percentages deviate by more than 1.5 from the figures reported by Betts and Danenberg. Just as in their table 2, the declines in the shares of cases below the bottom (national) quartile are larger than the gains in the shares of cases above the third quartile, except in the case of mathematics among non-LEP students. The only substantial difference between the two tables is that the estimates in my table 1 are based on the assumptions that test scores are normally distributed and that mean test scores may change, while the variance of test scores is constant.

In short, the real empirical observations to which Betts and Danenberg refer as evidence of declining inequality provide almost no substantiation of the claim that inequality has changed. However, a hint of such evidence appears in the deviations between observed and estimated score distributions. For example, in the case of reading among non-LEP students, growth is slightly less than estimated—about 1 percentage point—both below the first (national) quartile and above the third quartile.[43] However, that pattern is much weaker or nonexistent in the other populations for which score distributions are reported in Betts and Danenberg's table 2. Moreover, if that pattern were real, it would suggest an overall reduction of variance, not a larger improvement in performance at the lower than at the upper end of the distribution.

Table 2 displays my model-based estimates of change in mean achievement in reading and in mathematics for LEP and for non-LEP students. I report these separately for each interyear period to highlight the lack of evidence that California's reforms produced the observed changes. Specifically, in three of four possible comparisons, growth in mean achievement was larger from 1997–98 to 1998–99 than from 1998–99 to 1999–2000. That is, test score growth was, if anything, faster before the reforms could take effect than afterward. Again, this suggests that artifactual improvement in scores on the newly introduced Stanford 9 is the far more plausible explanation of the Betts and Danenberg data.

One might argue the implausibility of my assumptions that test scores were distributed normally with constant variance. It is surely wrong—but the question is, how wrong? And those assumptions strike me as far more plausible than the claim of strikingly large, uncaused effects advanced by Betts and Danenberg.

Table 2. Model Estimates of Mean Change in Achievement on the Stanford 9 by Student Group, 1997–98 to 1999–2000

	LEP students			Non-LEP students		
Subject	Change, 1997–98 to 1998–99	Change, 1999–98 to 1999–2000	Change, 1997–98 to 1999–2000	Change, 1997–98 to 1998–99	Change, 1999–98 to 1999–2000	Change, 1997–98 to 1999–2000
Mathematics	0.152	0.149	0.301	0.143	0.106	0.250
Reading	0.107	0.110	0.217	0.093	0.048	0.141

Note: LEP = limited English proficiency. Estimated changes are in standard deviation units.
Source: Authors' calculations from Julian R. Betts and Anne Dannenberg, "School Accountability in California: An Early Evaluation," table 2.

Under the same assumptions, I have constructed estimates of change in test score distributions for non-LEP students using Betts and Danenberg's table 3, which classifies schools in each grade range by academic achievement in 1997–98.[44] The findings are essentially the same in mathematics and in reading at each grade level, whether schools are classified by achievement at the beginning or at the end of the period of observation. The observed data are fitted closely under the null hypothesis that the test scores are normally distributed with constant variance, but possibly changing means within each grade level and group of schools. Consequently, all of the major features of the observed data are reproduced under this null hypothesis, including the findings to which Betts and Danenberg refer as evidence of reduced inequality between high- and low-performing schools. For example, "The percentage of students at or above the 75th percentile of national norms has grown in both types of schools—those that were low-performing in 1997–98 and those that were high-performing. The gains are broadly similar in the two types of schools, although in most cases the gains have been modestly higher in the top-performing schools. . . . Typically the bottom-performing schools in 1997-98 appear to have improved considerably faster than the top-performing schools."

However, these models permit growth (in means) to differ by group of schools within type of test and grade level. Perhaps not surprisingly, then, the estimated score distributions display the patterns described by Betts and Danenberg. For this reason, I reestimated the models, averaging the estimated growth in achievement across high- and low-scoring schools within type of test, grade level, and period. These models did not fit particularly well, but the estimates still showed features that were highlighted by Betts and Danenberg, especially larger growth high in the distribution among initially high-scoring schools and larger growth low in the distribution among initially low-scoring schools. That is, these features of the observed data follow from the original locations of the test score distributions in high- and low-scoring schools, not from differential growth.

However, the best-fitting analyses do yield differing estimates of mean growth, depending on the period (1997–98 to 1998–99 versus 1998–99 to 1999–2000), type of test (math versus reading), grade level (primary, middle, or secondary), and initial performance level (low-scoring schools versus high-scoring schools). These findings are summarized in table 3. Unlike the percentages reported by Betts and Danenberg, the trends and differentials reported here are not confounded by the initial locations of achievement distributions.

As in table 2, growth in mean achievement was as large or larger from 1997–98 to 1998–99 than from 1998–99 to 1999–2000. Again, this casts doubt on the possibility that California's educational reforms could be responsible for the observed growth in test scores. In most, but not all, cases, growth is larger in the lower grade levels than at higher grades; the one large and glaring exception is growth in reading achievement in grades nine through twelve from 1997–98 to 1998–99. One might offer a variety of speculations about greater effects of reform at lower grade levels, but the occurrence of the differential in the first interval as well as the second suggests that reform has little to do with the matter. Last, the table provides inconsistent evidence that growth occurred faster in low-performing than in high-performing schools. This occurred in seven of the twelve independent comparisons in table 3, which is scarcely convincing, but several of the observed differences were large (in standard deviation units).

One strong point of Betts and Danenberg's paper is the data on change in school-level resources. It is especially convincing—with multiple indicators—that teacher quality has not increased and that differentials in teacher quality between low-scoring and high-scoring schools have increased. But if it is impossible to credit California's test score increases to its educational reforms, it is equally inappropriate to blame perverse incentives in the reform package for the changes in teacher quality.

What Is to Be Done?

Educational reforms cannot be established overnight, and their effects cannot be measured by morning. The first lesson I would draw from the problems faced by Betts and Danenberg is that careful thought must be given to whether

Table 3. Model Estimates of Mean Change in Achievement on the Stanford 9 by 1997–98 School Achievement Level: Non-Limited English Proficiency California Students, 1997–98 to 1999–2000

Schools and grades	Reading			Mathematics		
	Change, 1997–98 to 1998–99	*Change, 1999–98 to 1999–2000*	*Change, 1997–98 to 1999–2000*	*Change, 1997–98 to 1998–99*	*Change, 1999–98 to 1999–2000*	*Change, 1997–98 to 1999–2000*
Low-performing schools in 1997–98						
K–5	0.30	0.13	0.42	0.35	0.22	0.57
6–8	0.21	0.04	0.25	0.24	0.08	0.33
9–12	0.18	0.02	0.19	0.22	0.05	0.27
High-performing schools in 1997–98						
K–5	0.13	0.10	0.23	0.16	0.16	0.32
6–8	0.02	0.08	0.10	0.07	0.09	0.16
9–12	0.30	0.05	0.35	0.04	0.05	0.09

Note: Estimated changes are in standard deviation units. Components of change may not add to total change because of independent rounding.

Source: Authors' calculations from Julian R. Betts and Anne Dannenberg, "School Accountability in California: An Early Evaluation," table 3.

policy changes have taken hold and whose lives they should be expected to change. Experimenters carry out manipulation checks. Has a reform been enacted at the classroom level? How much can a reform be expected to affect students at different grade levels?

A second lesson is that, when the measurement of achievement tests is based on new, or newly introduced, tests, no change is not an appropriate null hypothesis. Test scores must be expected to go up in the absence of improved learning. Based on Betts and Danenberg's data, I believe that expectations of artifactual test score growth should depend on who is being tested at what stage of the educational process. This leads to a third lesson—that comparison is the essence of valid inference. States must understand that, however much data they may produce, universal, high-stakes assessments must be complemented, from the outset of the educational process, with independently developed, sample-based, low-stakes assessments.

A final lesson is that states must produce data that are worth analyzing. The fatal flaws in Betts and Danenberg's data analysis began with the unfortunate way in which the state of California released its test score data—in aggregate distributions at the school level. I find fault in Betts and Danenberg's failure to recognize the rich possibilities for artifact and error in analyzing data in that form, but truly I doubt that the same problems would have occurred if the state had released student record data for the evaluation of educational reform.

Notes

1. Robert L. Linn, "Assessment and Accountability," *Educational Researcher*, vol. 29, no. 2 (2000), pp. 4–16.

2. Julian R. Betts and Robert M. Costrell, "Incentives and Equity under Standards-Based Reform," in Diane Ravitch, ed., *Brookings Papers on Education Policy 2001* (Brookings, 2001), pp. 9–74.

3. Jon Sonstelie, Eric Brunner, and Kenneth Ardon, *For Better or Worse? School Finance Reform in California* (San Francisco: Public Policy Institute of California, 2000).

4. For a review of the limited impact of school resources on student test scores, see Eric A. Hanushek, "School Resources and Student Performance," in Gary Burtless, ed., *Does Money Matter? The Effect of School Resources on Student Achievement and Adult Success* (Brookings, 1996), pp. 43–73. For a review of the link between school resources and years of education obtained and earnings after leaving school, see Julian R. Betts, "Is There a Link between School Inputs and Earnings? Fresh Scrutiny of an Old Literature," in Gary Burtless, ed., *Does Money Matter? The Effect of School Resources on Student Achievement and Adult Success* (Brookings, 1996), pp. 141–91.

5. Julian R. Betts, Kim S. Rueben, and Anne Danenberg, *Equal Resources, Equal Outcomes? The Distribution of School Resources and Student Achievement in California* (San Francisco: Public Policy Institute of California, 2000).

6. Betts, Rueben, and Danenberg, *Equal Resources, Equal Outcomes?*

7. For evidence, see Julian R. Betts and Anne Danenberg, "Resources and Student Achievement: An Assessment," in Jon Sonstelie and Peter Richardson, eds., *School Finance and California's Master Plan for Education* (San Francisco: Public Policy Institute of California, 2001), pp. 47–79.

8. The next three paragraphs are drawn in large part from the California Department of Education website: www.cde.ca.gov/psaa.

9. For example, the content standards for math stipulate in Item 2.1 under Algebra and Functions that in grade three students should be able to "Solve simple problems involving a functional relationship between two quantities (e.g., find the total cost of multiple items given cost per unit)." California Department of Education, *Mathematics Content Standards for California Public Schools, Kindergarten through Grade Twelve* (Sacramento, 1999). The more detailed mathematics framework gives the following example of this content item: "John wants to buy a dozen pencils. One store offers pencils at 6 for $1. Another offers them at 4 for 65 cents. Yet another sells pencils at 15 cents each. Where should John purchase his pencils in order to save the most money?" California Department of Education, *Mathematics Framework for California Public Schools, Kindergarten through Grade Twelve* (Sacramento, 1999). The entire content standards and subject frameworks can be found at www.cde.ca.gov/ci/.

10. For a complete discussion of the Academic Performance Index (API) calculation in 2000, see the California Department of Education website: www.cde.ca.gov/psaa/api/yeartwo/base/apicalcb.pdf.

11. The legislation provides for an "alternative accountability system" for schools with fewer than one hundred students, alternative and continuation high schools, independent study programs, community day schools, and other schools that are excluded from the API.

12. See article 2, section 52052 (c) of the Public Schools Accountability Act of 1999.

13. Senate Bill 1552 provided an additional year of funding for schools making significant progress toward their growth targets without meeting them.

14. The next few paragraphs rely heavily on the description on the California Department of Education website. See "Side-by-Side Comparison of PSAA Award Programs" (www.cde.ca.gov/psaa/awards/compare.htm [April 25, 2001]).

15. Kathleen Seabourne, California Department of Education consultant, personal communication clarifying website language, April 25, 2001.

16. Associated Press, "Qualified Teachers Sought for State's Worst-Off Schools: Legislative Bills Offer Incentives," *San Diego Union Tribune*, April 19, 2001.

17. Golden State Examination website: www.cde.ca.gov/statetests/gse/gse.html [April 25, 2001]).

18. Jay P. Heubert and Robert M. Hauser, eds., *High Stakes: Testing for Tracking, Promotion, and Graduation* (Washington: National Academy Press, 1999).

19. California Department of Education website: www.cde.ca.gov/sfsdiv/budgetact/implementation300.htm [April 25, 2001].

20. For the difference between 1998 and 2000 test score means, we are comparing a two-year change.

21. Daniel Koretz, "Using Student Assessments for Educational Accountability," in Eric A. Hanushek and Dale W. Jorgenson, eds., *Improving America's Schools: The Role of Incentives* (Washington: National Academy Press, 1996).

22. The exception was math scores for non-limited English proficiency (LEP) students where the gains in the share of students in the top quartile very slightly outweighed the decrease in the share in the bottom quartile.

23. We thank Lorrie Shepard for this third way of testing for regression to the mean.

24. Also, note that the low-scoring schools do not display a decline in achievement in table A-6, as predicted in our hypothetical model in figure 7 under the assumption that regression to the mean without any true change in test score gaps was at play. While a significant finding, it is important to remember that figure 7 implicitly assumed no real growth in average achievement over time. If there has been growth in average achievement, then we would not necessarily expect low-scoring schools as defined at the end of the period to show declining test scores, but, rather, slower growth than high-scoring schools.

25. Robert M. Costrell, "A Simple Model of Educational Standards," *American Economic Review*, vol. 84, no. 4 (1994), pp. 956–71; and Julian R. Betts, "The Impact of Educational Standards on the Level and Distribution of Earnings," *American Economic Review*, vol. 88, no. 1 (1998), pp. 266–75.

26. Julian R. Betts, *A Critical Path Analysis of California's K–12 Sector* (Irvine, Calif.: California Council on Science and Technology, forthcoming).

27. Analysis of decennial census data for California by Julian R. Betts finds that between 1970 and 1990 the percentage of nineteen to twenty-four-year-old natives living in California who lacked a high school diploma was about 16.5 percent, while among immigrants in California in the same group the percentage rose from 40.6 percent in 1970 to 50.3 percent in 1990. Further, in 1990 among young California immigrants, 58.7 percent who had lived abroad in 1985 were high school dropouts compared with 46.7 percent of those who had lived in California in 1985. Overall, this suggests that the true dropout rate among teenagers who attend school in California is around 20–25 percent, given that 26.2 percent of adults in California by 1990 were immigrants. See Julian R. Betts, *The Changing Role of Education in California* (San Francisco: Public Policy Institute of California, 2000), chapters 2 and 3.

28. Betts, Rueben, and Danenberg, *Equal Resources, Equal Outcomes?*

29. Betts, Rueben, and Danenberg, *Equal Resources, Equal Outcomes?*

30. The proposal would also eliminate the Stanford 9 social science test currently given to high school students. See Sarah Tully Tapia, "Davis Proposes Streamlining Tests," *Orange County Register*, April 25, 2001.

31. See Julie Tamaki, "Davis Scales Back Plan to Lengthen School Year," *Los Angeles Times*, April 25, 2001.

32. California Department of Education website: www.goldmine.cde.ca.gov [March 24, 1999].

33. Some sixth-grade students are in elementary schools, and some are in middle schools. Because approximately half of elementary schools are K–5, approximately half are K–6, and the rest comprise some combination of grades between kindergarten and sixth grade, our elementary school category comprises grades K–6. The majority of middle schools have grades six through eight, whereas others have grades seven and eight, and a few are single-grade. Sixth-grade-only schools were included in K–6 schools instead of the grade six through eight schools.

34. National Commission on Teaching and America's Future, *What Matters Most: Teaching and America's Future* (Columbia University, Teachers College, 1996).

35. Daneil Koretz, "Using Student Assessments for Educational Accountability," in Eric A. Hanushek and Dale W. Jorgenson, eds., *Improving America's Schools: The Role of Incentives* (Washington: National Academy Press, 1996).

36. National Research Council, *Testing, Teaching, and Learning: A Guide for States and School Districts*, edited by Richard F. Elmore and Robert Rothman, Committee on Title I Testing and Assessment (Washington: National Academy Press, 1999).

37. Linda McNeil, *Contradictions of School Reform: Educational Costs of Standardized Testing* (New York: Routledge, 2000); and Charles A. Dana Center, *Equity-Driven, Achievement-Focused School Districts* (University of Texas at Austin, 2000).

38. Suzanne Lane and Clement Stone, "Consequences of Assessment and Accountability Programs," paper presented at the annual meeting of the American Educational Research Association, Seattle, Washington, April 2001; James P. Spillane, "External Reform Initiatives and Teachers' Efforts to Reconstruct Their Practice: The Mediating Role of Teachers' Zones of Enactment," paper presented at the annual meeting of the Association for Public Policy Analysis and Management, Washington, D.C., November 1997; and W. A. Firestone and others, "State Standards, Socio-Fiscal Context and Opportunity to Learn in New Jersey," *Educational Policy Analysis Archives,* vol. 8, no. 35 (2000) (epaa.asu.edu/epaa/v8n35 [July 26, 2000]).

39. The percentages above each cutoff point are reported only at the school level, and Julian R. Betts and Anne Danenberg weight them appropriately to estimate population characteristics. Unfortunately, this reporting scheme leads to serious problems in the analysis of changes and differentials in achievement.

40. Betts and Danenberg later wonder, appropriately in my judgment, whether compensatory resource allocation, not equalization of resources, is the right policy.

41. I will not discuss the dropout statistics in detail, but they are of limited value. They do not meet the standards of the federal-state cooperative program established by the National Center for Education Statistics, and their trend differs from state-level estimates I have made from October Current Population Surveys.

42. That is, I refer to the upward trajectory in the sawtooth pattern of rising test scores in the years following introduction of a new test.

43. Compare predicted distributions between table 1 and Betts and Danenberg's table 2.

44. These spreadsheets are available from the author by request.

Standards and Accountability in Washington State

PAUL T. HILL *and* ROBIN J. LAKE

In the early 1990s, Washington State was in the vanguard of the standards movement. Democratic governor Booth Gardner and leaders of the Washington Roundtable—a coalition of business leaders—agreed to press for a comprehensive statewide education reform package modeled after Kentucky's. David Hornbeck, who drafted the Kentucky consent decree that started the standards-based reform movement, advised on drafting of the state's reform bill. An omnibus reform package was passed in early 1993. By 1994, the National Business Roundtable rated Washington as one of four states that had enacted the most complete standards-based reform program.

Washington political and business leaders intended to transform public education from a bureaucracy controlled by mandates and enforced compliance into a performance-based system. They envisioned standards-based reform as a rational approach to improving public education. They sought to set standards that define what children need to know and be able to do, develop measurement systems to test performance against those standards, help schools find and use methods of instruction effective enough to allow them to meet the standards, give schools the freedom of action necessary to adjust their methods of instruction to meet student needs, and reward schools that meet standards and punish those that do not.

Like proponents of standards-based reform in other states, Washington State policy and business leaders assumed that establishment of a performance-based system would change the behavior of teachers, parents, school administrators, and students.[1] Teachers and parents, informed by the stan-

199

dards about what students need to know, would look for evidence that individual children were performing as expected. If a child or a group of children—say those in a particular classroom or school—failed to meet the standards, then teachers and parents would search for better methods of instruction. School administrators, expecting pressure from parents, political leaders, and district and state administrators if children could not meet standards, would carefully monitor school performance and lead staff efforts to improve instruction and measured results. Administrators and teachers would think boldly, knowing that old rules governing schools' instructional methods, staff assignments, and use of time had been eliminated. Children—at least the older students who could anticipate needing access to jobs and higher education—would take their test scores as evidence of what issues they needed to work on in school. The net result would be better schools, more imaginative and adaptive teaching, and improved learning for all students, particularly those now least well served by the schools.

In Washington, as in other states, these hopes are far from fully realized. However, results to date do not necessarily disprove the assumptions behind standards-based reform.[2] Like many other promising ideas, standards-based reform might work if it were seriously tried.

Though some key elements are in place, eight years after enactment Washington's standards-based reform is still under construction. Grade-level academic achievement standards for grades four, seven, and ten were established after a painstaking development process with much teacher involvement. Fourth graders took the new statewide tests (the Washington Assessment of Student Learning, or WASL) in reading, writing, mathematics, and listening for the first time in spring 1997, and seventh- and tenth-grade students took the tests for the first time in 1999 and 2000, respectively.[3] Each year since 1995 the state has allocated millions of dollars to pay for planning time so teachers and administrators could learn how to prepare students to meet the standards. The Office of the Superintendent of Public Instruction (OSPI) has also created numerous assistance programs, including teacher mentoring and a math helping corps, under which expert teachers advise schools in need of improvement. OSPI has created an excellent website on which anyone can inspect any school's test-score trends, and a business group, the Partnership for Learning, has sponsored creation of highly regarded how-to materials for teachers and parents.

Washington has also inched toward performance-based accountability. Beginning with the 1998–99 school year, the state required districts and schools to set reading and math achievement goals to be met within four years. The State Academic and Accountability Commission (A+ Commission) has designed an accountability system complete with rewards, assistance for struggling schools, and interventions in low-performing schools that fail to improve. All pieces of the reform are supposed to be in place by 2008, when all students must pass state tests leading to a Certificate of Mastery before receiving a high school diploma.

While most of the elements of the 1993 reform are moving forward, some are languishing. The omnibus reform legislation called for streamlining the state code to weed out regulations that interfere with school performance. But a legislative committee formed for this purpose was unable to find any rules not favored by some group. In the end, it recommended only minor amendments. Governor Gary Locke has since tried unsuccessfully to eliminate major portions of the code. State politicians have also been unable to agree on promised spending increases to support the reform. Working relationships between Republicans and Democrats in the legislature, and between pro-reform business groups and skeptical teacher and administrator groups, have frayed.

Perhaps most importantly, a left-right coalition, both in the legislature and among key Olympia interest groups, threatens to block the remaining steps in implementation of the reform. This coalition is composed of conservative Republicans who fear standards as a government effort to take away the freedom of families and small communities and Western Washington Democrats who want to protect unionized teachers from the rigors of being judged on the basis of performance. These groups, which together successfully blocked three efforts to enact a charter school bill, have staying power. The 2000 elections only strengthened it, and no reason exists to suspect that the coalition or its senior members will disappear in the foreseeable future. Work is unlikely to be completed on the social studies exams, high school Certificate of Mastery, or the accountability recommendations of the A+ Commission.

Thus, Washington State, long considered a leader in standards-based reform, may stop far short of full implementation. The political forces in favor of the official reform strategy are strong enough to prevent its repeal but cannot enforce the timetable for complete rollout by 2008.

With a stalemate among elected officials and interest groups, the future of standards-based reform probably depends on whether it can gain support at the grassroots level, and there the picture is divided. Some district administrators and principals claim that the standards, tests, and potential accountability pressures have strengthened their schools; some local parent groups are strongly behind the state's reform package. However, the statewide teachers union is critical of any effort to judge or intervene in schools on the basis of test results, and the Seattle teachers union has attacked the tests themselves as invalid and harmful. As in other states, high school students in the more elite public high schools have threatened to boycott the tests, charging that they are irrelevant for college admission and encourage dumbed-down teaching. Observers of all political persuasions predict a broad-based parent uprising if WASL scores are ever used to withhold diplomas from students who have completed twelve years of school.

The Good News: Standards Help Some Schools Improve

From 1999 to 2001, we conducted a series of studies, called *Making Standards Work*, in an attempt to understand and clearly describe the actions of schools that posted strong gains on the new state exams. We wondered whether the explanation for these schools' success was a result of teaching to the test and making superficial curricular changes, of having more advantaged populations of students or more qualified teachers, or of experiencing significant shifts in their overall approach to teaching and learning that were affecting students' testing outcomes.

The Study

The study's purpose was to learn how schools whose students do well on the early tests differ from schools whose students do less well and, by extension, to identify ways that struggling schools can get the help they need.

The study was based on a survey of two statewide samples of elementary schools whose students had taken the fourth-grade test in 1997 and 1998. The first was a group of thirty schools whose scores had improved significantly from one year to the next. The second was a group of ten schools that serve demographically similar students and are located in the same parts of the state as the first group, but whose scores had improved only slightly or not at all. The majority of schools in each sample were low income (as measured by the proportions of their students receiving free and reduced-price lunch), and all scored below the statewide average on the 1997 fourth-grade tests.

Rapidly improving schools were those whose scores increased at more than twice the statewide average. Elementary school reading and math scores increased at an average rate of 10 percent between 1997 and 1998. In rapidly improving schools, scores increased at a rate of 50 percent or greater.

We interviewed principals at thirty-five elementary schools. The interviews sought principals' ideas about why the students scored as they did on the state tests and, when appropriate, why scores had improved. In addition, principals were asked about

—New funding received beyond the normal school budget;

—Recent changes in instructional methods;

—Sources of help, advice, and teacher training;

—Sources of pressure for improved test scores;

—Changes in school-parent relationships; and

—Helpfulness of materials provided by the state and school district.

Finally, every principal was asked what advice he or she would give other schools that were struggling to improve student learning.

In the second year of our study, we expanded its scope to include middle-grade schools, which by that time were in their second year of testing. We used the same general approach to choosing improving and comparison schools, but we expanded the interviews to include focus groups with teachers, parents, and students. In addition, we interviewed the original sample of elementary principals from fast-improving schools after their third year of test results to see whether and how those schools were able to sustain their gains.

SUCCESSFUL RESPONSES TO STANDARDS. In general, we found that whether a school improved or not depended on what the adults in it did in response to the new standards and tests. In rapidly improving schools ("improving schools"), principals and teachers assessed strengths and weaknesses, set a limited number of priorities, focused on improving instruction, and took the initiative to find the help the school needed. To make sure planned improvements happened, principals and teachers reallocated funds, rearranged teacher work assignments and instructional schedules, and made sure all staff members coordinated their classroom work. These schools also continually—and candidly—assessed their own progress.

Schools that did not improve ("comparison schools") were passive and fragmented. Teachers often tried to improve instruction, but each went his or her own way. Schoolwide collaboration proved difficult and principals could not—or did not try to—overcome long-established patterns of teacher isolation. School leaders often took the attitude that someone else (that is, the district or the state) was responsible to show teachers how to improve and align instruction with the new standards and assessments. Some complained

that the technical assistance materials provided by the state were too volumi-
nous and varied to be useful.

Our findings make it clear that schools—and what the people who work in
them do—can make a difference in what students learn. This conclusion should
be no surprise. However, many critics of standards-based reform claim that
action at the school level either does not matter or cannot change enough to
increase students' test results. These critics note that student achievement is
highly correlated with family income and the presence of two educated parents.
Scores on state tests do correlate highly with family income and other indicators of socioeconomic status, but that does not tell the whole story. Children in
some low-income schools did relatively well on the state tests, and children in
some higher income schools did relatively poorly. Family income is an advantage for some schools and a problem for others, but in itself it does not cause
student learning. Further, some schools are clearly able to improve the effectiveness of the resources they have. Better family services, more investment in
instructional materials, and demanding teacher training and evaluation can
also help. But the reality is that schools can make a difference now.

Specifically, we found that the following actions characterized the improving schools in our study.

Improving schools focused time and resources on a few key goals. Improving schools made quality of teaching their first priority, not one of many
competing priorities. After reviewing their curriculum and instructional practices with the new state standards in mind, they made tough choices about
what to keep, what to cut, and what to adapt to help students reach the new
learning expectations. Schools whose scores did not increase were generally
less focused on skills and more reluctant to eliminate activities that teachers
enjoyed but were not clearly productive. A principal from an improving school
aptly described the difficult choices the staff at the school made.

> You could dump all your electives and focus solely on the WASL. But then you lose
> the arts, and if you lose the arts you lose the vehicle of culture so to speak. But at
> the same time you don't want to waste any energy. So we had to talk a little bit about
> for instance some pet projects that people like to do because they're nice, warm,
> fuzzy things and they've always done them. We really had to ask the question,
> "Well, does it get us where we need to go? Is time better used maybe in some other
> project?"

Improving schools stressed the importance of taking a thorough look at
teacher practice and how it related to the state and district standards. They
looked for ways they could improve instruction throughout the school, start-

ing with kindergarten and first grade. In improving schools, we repeatedly heard, "This is not just a fourth-grade test." Some schools unified teachers' efforts via group discussions. Others developed specific grade-level exit standards for students and put them up on the wall so that teachers, students, and parents all understood what was expected.

> We sat down with every teacher at every grade level and we decided which things we were going to teach at every grade level. We created a checklist coordinated exactly to the Essential Learnings and the teachers check off when they accomplish the essential learning component.

> When I took over in the school, it didn't make any sense to me that teachers didn't communicate clearly with each other what was expected in first grade, second grade, third and fourth grade. What is the written curriculum? What is it that we say we're teaching? What are we really teaching?

Principals from improving schools mentioned using a number of name-brand instructional programs, such as Six Traits of Writing, Accelerated Reader, and Reading Recovery. But these programs were almost never implemented in isolation. They were brought in after the school had identified its needs and aligned all resources toward its goals. In other words, new methods and programs were seen as ways to flesh out a school improvement strategy to make progress toward the standards, not as magic bullets that would solve all problems by themselves.

Improving schools operated as teams, not random associations. Improving schools did more than plan. Every day in every classroom they made sure that teachers at every grade level were coordinating their efforts and working toward a common goal. In effect, these schools were mapping backward, using the fourth- and seventh-grade standards to plan what skills students needed to master at each grade. Principals and teachers recognized that even the best-conceived strategies fail unless every teacher executes them even when the classroom door is closed.

Principals in almost all the improving schools said their improvement strategies were implemented schoolwide. Individual teachers were not left to decide how to improve student performance. Principals emphasized the importance of making sure that all teachers understood the strategy and were excited about it. As they explained, making the school into a team requires more than teacher motivation. Students, parents, and the community must understand and support the school's improvement strategy. As one principal from an improving school said,

During year one, we had no idea of what to expect or how to prepare kids. And after we got the scores back the first year, we knew our kids were better than this and refocused and created a plan [tutoring and small groups] to prepare kids; our whole building took it on, not just third or fourth grade; it was a schoolwide effort.

Among schools that showed little or no improvement, responses from comparison school principals were almost evenly split between those that said their strategy was implemented schoolwide and those that said it was left up to individual teachers. Some principals were frustrated at their inability to create a unified schoolwide strategy.

I wish I could say schoolwide—[but] some older teachers are having trouble changing. For the time being, I am letting them go at their own pace. If they continue being resistant, I will have to be more heavy-handed and go to a whole-school program. But our staff's not interested in that.

Improving schools used limited resources strategically. Improving schools focused all available funds on instruction by setting priorities closely linked to the standards and directing resources toward them. In some cases, this meant extending the school day or lowering class size in selected classes. In others, it meant hiring additional instructional assistants to provide direct tutoring for students who needed extra help. Many improving schools controlled their own budgets in ways that allowed them to set their own funding priorities.

Improving schools were no more likely than other schools to receive an influx of new funding. The difference was in how they used funds, whether existing or new. For those with new financial resources, the improving schools had definite strategies for improving teaching and learning and used their funds, as one principal said, "like gold" to support those strategies.

We blended our funding to hire tutors so we could put more than one adult in each classroom. We used our Title I funds to create an inclusive model and a solid block of time for small group instruction. Ninety percent of our Title I funding is now used [to increase] instructional hours.

In improving schools, professional development was school development. Improving schools had no more funding for teacher professional development than schools whose scores did not increase. In fact, all had the benefit of new unrestricted state staff development funds intended to prepare teachers to teach to the new standards. Improving schools, however, took much more initiative to find and use professional development programs designed to remedy their particular instructional weaknesses than other schools did.

Moreover, they prioritized their professional development time to support the school's improvement plan.

Sixty-one percent of the improving schools indicated some recent change in their staff development programs and the allocation of their staff development resources, as opposed to only 44 percent of the comparison group. The improving schools stressed that dedicating school time to serious teacher collaboration was an essential part of their strategy. By contrast, few comparison schools used staff development time to support a specific improvement strategy; instead their professional development programs often consisted of miscellaneous workshops and technology training.

The improving schools shared three key attributes of effective professional development changes in response to state standards.

1. Staff development time was focused on a few instructional goals that meshed with Essential Learnings (state standards).

2. Many used staff development resources to allow teachers to plan and integrate methods and materials across grade levels.

3. Staff development funds were treated as finite resources for implementing the school's strategy. They were not seen as bottomless pots of money that individual teachers could use as they pleased. One principal from an improving school explained:

> There's a paradigm shift that happens. When [state staff development] money first came out, teachers thought they were getting the money. We changed things so that we'd pay for them to take course work. Money didn't go to pay them any longer, but to pay for the services we needed.

Fewer comparison schools had made major changes in their staff development program in response to the new standards. One principal in our comparison group said,

> If a staff member wants to go to a conference, they ask the site council. Hopefully, it relates to the [state standards].

Improving schools reached out to kids most at risk of falling through cracks by engaging parents as partners. Efforts to help struggling students were an important part of improving schools' strategies. In middle-grade schools especially, improving schools not only monitored student progress closely, but they also targeted resources to address the needs of students who were struggling the most. They restructured their programs to allow for more individualized attention from teachers. They used time before, during, and after school to offer extra support in students' key deficit areas, such as reading. As one principal explained:

> We identify the lowest readers in each grade level, and they are pulled out a period a day and are given intensive reading strategies and an oral fluency program.

Though these schools decided to target resources toward the highest need students, we did not see improving schools focusing solely on the needs of struggling students. One school created an after-school tutoring program for the lowest reading level students as well as recruited adult mentors to work with students who did not qualify for the after-school program but who could benefit from extra reading time.

The hands-on, interventionist approach of improving schools often included working with parents, too, despite the challenges involved. One principal described this relentless work.

> We talk about kids every day. We look at those kids who are out on the edge. How can we make those kids feel connected, what can we do? We don't lose too many. We are working with parents constantly.

At one comparison middle school, the principal described more of a sink-or-swim attitude about student learning.

> The culture among the staff here is still very much the classic Junior High . . . kind of an attitude of, "Well, I've put out the content. It's up to the kids to get it." . . . I still have a lot of teachers that move through their curriculum and say, "Oh, well, you didn't get it."

Letting students slip by may be the norm in middle schools, but schools that made positive gains in response to Washington's new state standards realized that schools must improve personal connections to improve test scores and achievement.

In improving schools, goals and expectations went beyond a comfortable level. Almost all schools reported feeling pressure from their districts and the state as a result of standards-based reform. Some schools were targeted—either formally or informally—by their districts as low-performing schools. These schools felt immediate pressure to "improve or else." In several of the improving schools, the district brought in principals specifically to turn the school around.

The community came to the district and said, "We've got to improve." Now every school must have a plan to improve test scores.

We scored very low on the first test and were called the flat tire of the district. Having been a football coach, I know that the best thing you could ever do to create a championship team was to put them down and say disparaging things about them. Particularly if they had any pride about them. Well, this school has a huge amount of pride and dignity and they just said they weren't going to take that any more. And I think that added fuel to the fire; created a common enemy.

But the motivation to improve test scores clearly was often also internal, coming from either the principal's leadership or the teaching staff's desire to improve. As one principal said,

The philosophy when I came [to this school] was, we need to make kids feel good about themselves before we teach them, so there wasn't a lot of teaching before third grade. I said to my teachers, "We're going to teach kids and they will feel good about themselves because they're learning." And the people who stayed bought into that. When we had the chance to move people in and out, we brought in a strong first and second grade team. I knew the curriculum would challenge the kids and challenge the ... teaching staff. We paired newer teachers with older teachers, then fifth-grade teachers were impressed and motivated.

They [parents] felt pressure from me. I said to them, this isn't an education I'd want for my child, I can't imagine it's one you want for your child. It was a lot of warehousing of kids.

Whatever the motivation, many principals reported that improving their test scores was among their schools' highest priorities. Three quarters of the improving schools and two-thirds of the other schools in our study said that raising WASL scores was of high or the highest importance.

I believe absolutely in raising the bar and raising the standards. And so far as the WASL can assess how we move toward these new and better and increased standards, then it is the highest priority for my building.

Improving schools made improvement a way of life; they analyzed, anticipated, and adapted. Elementary schools that were able to sustain their impressive gains from the year before shared certain characteristics that went beyond the common strategies employed. For these schools, improvement was not a one-time effort; it became part of the culture of the school. Teachers and principals regularly analyzed test scores and student needs, got better at eliminating instructional activities that did not contribute to the school's primary goals, and refused to become complacent.

Schools that sustained their gains beyond one year did not sit back and relax. They looked deeper into instruction and individual students' needs to see how they could keep improving. These schools

—Got better at analyzing data and zeroing in on areas of need,

—Did deeper analysis of individual students' needs,

—Increased the use of ongoing assessments that reflect WASL expectations, and

—Introduced changes in curriculum and approaches to instruction and learning in earlier grades.

One principal described the process this way:

> We share our successes in formal ways through staff meetings and have looked at our weaknesses and dissected them to help us make changes. We've tried to identify the materials teachers need to help them make changes. It's not just a once a year thing that we talk about—it's brought up nearly every week in staff meetings and team planning.

Some schools assumed that the changes they made the year before would suffice. But in the current year, they had a different group of students with different needs. Some schools recognized these needs and adjusted their strategies to meet them. Others excused lower performance as a result of more challenging student needs. As a principal at one school that was unable to sustain its gains put it:

> Our staff expected [scores to fall]. They felt that last year's group was lower in ability than the year before. They were particularly slow in math.

Implications: How Standards Help Schools

We find that those schools in Washington that are most successful in raising scores are using the standards and WASL results to fashion their teaching methods and allocation of resources. This does not mean that the standards and tests caused these schools to improve. But they facilitated the work of schools that were inclined to improve.

SCHOOL ATTRIBUTES GIVE STANDARDS LIFT. Our study was not designed to identify whether the changes schools made were a direct result of the new standards and assessments. It was intended only to identify practices that enabled the schools to improve their scores. We did, however, gain some insight into the kinds of schools that made productive use of the standards and tests.

One small group of schools (approximately five of thirty) was already operating fairly well as a team and used time and resources in a fairly strategic way. For these schools, standards and the WASL provided guidance for how they could improve their practice and make adjustments in their technique. The primary changes were instructional, such as better focus on areas they discovered were weak after analyzing their test results.

The larger group consisted of schools that, before the WASL was in place, had many attributes of the nonimproving schools (that is, teachers were operating in isolation, a lack of urgency existed about raising performance expectations, and time and funding were used in a diffuse manner). In these schools, the principals and teachers we interviewed clearly attributed the organizational and instructional changes to the state standards. In many cases, the principal used the WASL scores as a rallying cry to build momentum for deep, schoolwide changes.

Given that most of the improving schools we studied looked a great deal like their nonimproving counterparts before the WASL, it is logical to wonder what made it possible—and likely—for some schools with similar characteristics, and even within the same district, to respond differently. The following are lift factors, attributes that seemed to increase the likelihood that a school would make the changes associated with improvement.

—Strong leadership. School principals in many improving schools were more likely than their nonimproving counterparts to see their role as setting clear, rigorous academic goals and supporting classroom implementation. Many of these principals expertly managed the transformation by building a sense of urgency, allocating staff development time and budget priorities, and providing feedback to teachers. In some improving schools, however, the leadership vision came from a core group of strong teachers, and the principal played a background role.

—Teacher willingness to change. In some cases principals at improving schools attributed their success to having a new corps of younger teachers who were either already trained to adapt their teaching to standards or were willing to change their instructional practices. Comparison schools, conversely, often had a more veteran teaching staff, and principals claimed they resisted the change strategy.

—Homogeneous staff. Whether or not the faculty was working together effectively before the WASL, schools that started with high levels of mutual respect and trust among teachers and the principal had an easier time putting a team instructional strategy together and building mutual accountability.

—Positive attitude toward the WASL. Not surprisingly, teachers and principals who saw the standards and the WASL as legitimate tools for improving student achievement were more likely to make changes in response to the state reform effort. Many comparison school principals and teachers expressed doubt about the appropriateness of the test and resentment about district or media pressure to improve.

—School-level control over funding and use of time. Principals of improving schools attributed their ability to make dramatic structural changes to the freedom they were granted by the superintendent to do what they needed to do. This often included counseling out teachers who resist change, rearranging schedules to carve out more time for staff development and collaboration, and reallocating funds to align with their schools' academic plans.

Positive performance pressure is critical to improvement. All of the schools that made strong gains on the new state tests felt some pressure to improve. Pressure to improve WASL scores often came from within the school building, from teachers and principals who felt responsible for their students' success. But that internal pressure was usually spurred by outside expectations generated by newspaper reports of test scores, district threats, or the belief that the state accountability system would come into effect soon. For these schools, the level of pressure they are experiencing is a critical factor in their success.

This pressure was sometimes intense, especially for fourth- and seventh-grade teachers who felt they had the burden of responsibility to raise WASL scores. In many cases, this public attention was usually what mobilized these schools to radically rethink their practice. None of the principals or teachers we interviewed complained that the level of pressure is too high right now, indicating instead that the amount of pressure was generally healthy and pushed them to reexamine their assumptions about student capabilities. They recognized, however, that sustaining a reasonable level of pressure that does not lead to burnout and frustration would be a challenge.

The schools that were able to sustain gains over three years were more likely to have practices in place that spread the responsibility for student achievement schoolwide. The pressure to change was distributed throughout the building and even went beyond school staff to include students and parents who took the school's strategy and requirements seriously.

Complacency is also a danger. Schools that made strong gains in the first round of testing but whose scores dropped in the second year often attributed that decrease to having assumed that a one-year effort would be all they needed. Conversely, schools that sustained their gains did not assume that what worked one year would necessarily work again the next.

Improving schools' relationships with their districts ran the gamut. Some were rooted in a history of cooperation and partnership. District leaders pressed for improvement but expected long-term, steady gains. In other districts, demands were blunt and immediate: "Improve or else," for example. For schools in the latter category, pressure to make significant annual gains was strongest. A school making strong gains in the first year but falling back the second told us, "Our district loved us last year and hates us this year."

Principals noted, however, that with each passing year the intensity of the pressure is increasing. When results are being made public; when schools' scores are more closely scrutinized by districts, parents, and their communities; and when the state is moving closer to defining how schools will be held accountable for their results, pressure mounts. If schools are to make sustained gains, they will need to manage their efforts in ways that encourage teachers, students, principals, and parents to take on their fair share of responsibility for student achievement. Schools that have managed to find this appropriate balance might help by serving as exemplars. Grade-level exit standards can also help spread responsibility so that teachers at the grades tested do not bear sole responsibility for student performance on the WASL.

Standards can prod school staff to coalesce around a clear mission, but there are trade-offs. Focus necessarily means giving something up, but the schools we interviewed seem to be giving up things that were unproductive, instead of lessons critical to student learning.

We did see some evidence that schools are putting arts and music and sometimes core areas such as science on the back burner or not teaching them at all. But it is not clear whether this is a temporary measure that will allow these schools to focus on helping students reach grade-level standards or whether pressures from the test will crowd out nontested subjects for the indefinite future.

In an attempt to hone their efforts, schools often chose to focus on one or two particular areas of need, such as reading or writing.[4] While this gave them an opportunity to teach some subjects more deeply, some schools saw their scores drop in other areas, such as math, as a result. Some of this seesawing in emphasis is to be expected as schools learn to set balanced priorities and use their time more wisely. Learning how to emphasize mathematics, reading, and writing while not abandoning other subjects is an important tension to recognize and address, but it is not reason to think the new standards will necessarily drive out all other important learning from the classroom. Many schools we studied are learning how to create that balance by making sure they teach WASL-related skill and content areas at the same time they teach other subjects, such as art and fitness.

Standards do not necessarily mean standardization. The concept of standards-based education often invokes fears that all schools will deliver the same curriculum with lock-step instructional methods, driving creative teachers away from what gives them most satisfaction in their jobs: professional judgment and freedom to craft meaningful lessons and learning experiences for students. This is a very real concern. Though our study was not designed to examine this issue thoroughly, we did raise this issue with teachers and principals, though they usually raised it first. The Washington State reform does not set a prescribed curriculum, so our findings should be considered in that context.[5]

In our sample of improving schools, the principals we interviewed did not complain that the gains they made came at the cost of creativity in their work. Many saw standards as a challenge that stimulated creativity in the classroom. By clarifying what it was they were supposed to focus on, some explained, the standards had allowed them to do a limited number of things very well. The creativity challenge came in integrating lessons to work in areas, such as art and music, that were too important to the school's goals to permanently set aside. In most of these schools, professional satisfaction came from the new collegiality involved in increased team effort and staff meetings that were newly oriented around problem solving and analysis.

One of the improving schools we studied implemented a whole school design that depended on some level of standardization in reading. Some teachers in the school told us that having a prescribed reading program allowed them greater opportunity for creativity in other subjects because they were using their reading time more efficiently. One teacher learned through a more coordinated approach to reading that she was not an especially effective reading teacher, though she was strong in other areas. Experimentation would not have given her that knowledge. The teachers at this school chose to implement this whole school design after going through a process of researching which programs were most successful with the high-needs population they served. So although their reading instruction is highly coordinated, the principal and teachers made the choice. Teachers at a school that was forced to adopt the same design would likely have very different perceptions.

What effect standards will have on professional creativity will likely depend on at least three factors: (1) the intensity of pressure to make immediate gains on test scores, (2) the level of improvement a school needs to make to succeed, and (3) how schools and districts respond to the challenge. For schools that need to make dramatic gains quickly, time probably is not available for much experimentation. The students at these schools do not have time to wait and to serve as subjects in adult experiments. Further, the least qualified teachers may need more intense directives and guidance. As Harold Levy, chancellor of New York City public schools, said about teaching tightly to standards, "Creative teachers hate it and bad teachers need it."

Sustaining gains depends on more than superficial change. Of the improving schools we have interviewed over the past two years, a small group was more successful than the others in sustaining gains. While some of the secrets to these schools' success can be described in terms of school action, other factors were outside their control: the ability to rearrange funding to support school goals and school-level staff development priorities; the existence of support from their districts to pursue the strategy of their choice and maintain stable leadership and staff; and the ability to rearrange school schedules. All these factors seemed to contribute to the schools' ability to succeed beyond an initial burst of improvement.

Some schools have so far been unable to make any progress, much less sustain it. Our study thus far has revealed little about the prospects for these schools. But we are in the middle of a new study of such stuck schools, and early results show that they fall into different categories. Some simply do not see the value of—or are even resistant to—orienting instruction around standards and thus are simply continuing what they have always done. In other stuck schools, however, principals and many staff members have reached basic agreement on an improvement strategy, but they are having trouble getting the entire staff on board or are encountering other issues that prevent them from making gains.

The bottom line from our series of studies is that state standards are promoting real improvements in the learning and teaching environments of many Washington schools. But even fast-improving schools have a long way to go to assure that every child can meet the academic standards set by state legislators in 1993. Many schools, maybe most, remain completely unaffected. It also remains to be seen whether additional testing and accountability pressures will set impossible burdens for schools or whether they will spur more schools to make the positive organizational and cultural changes we saw in improving schools.

The Bad News:
Standards-Based Reform Might Not Work Statewide

Our *Making Standards Work* series has profiled the fastest improving schools and offered proof that standards-based reform can lead to better instruction. But the schools we studied were a small minority with outstanding rates of improvement. The schools and districts described as part of the good news fit Richard F. Elmore's "connoisseurship" model.[6] Will standards-based reform lead to general statewide improvements in quality instruction and student learning? It is too soon to tell for sure. Though WASL scores are up statewide, the average rate of improvement resembles the learning curves that, as Daniel M. Koretz and others have shown, reflect increasing familiarity with a test.[7]

There are reasons to doubt whether standards-based reform will affect schools statewide. The most important is the state's apparent inability to draw a definite link between WASL scores and consequences for teachers, students, schools, or districts.

Though some Washington teacher groups denounce standards-based reform for its reliance on high-stakes testing, to date the stakes are anything but high. Eight years after enactment of standards-based reform, no school or district is obligated to do anything in response to low scores, and the state has required no punitive action of any kind toward a teacher or student. Some districts and schools have used WASL scores (and the distant and improbable threat that students will someday be required to pass tenth-grade WASLs to get a high school diploma) as a warrant for action on their own.

The 1993 reform bill anticipated a slow buildup toward a system of consequences for school performance. The 1999 legislature was to establish an accountability system that set performance and growth expectations for individual schools, backed up by rewards, penalties, and assistance. Instead of enacting accountability legislation, the governor and state legislative leaders in 1999 appointed a bipartisan accountability commission, composed of knowledgeable educators and professionals in other fields. The A+ Commission was led by a prominent banker, Patrick Patrick, who had successfully led other statewide planning groups.

After a year's study and consultation with groups throughout the state, the A+ Commission issued its recommendations to the legislature.[8] High points of the commission's recommendations included:

—Using school WASL scores to identify high- and low-performing schools.

—Not allocating rewards and penalties directly in response to WASL scores. Instead the commission recommended "looking beneath the numbers" to determine whether particular schools were improving on their own, likely to improve promptly in response to help, or stuck and unlikely to improve promptly.

—Negotiating two-year performance agreements between the state and school districts that oversee low-performing schools.

—Imposing state sanctions including abolition or reconstitution of school districts whose schools consistently fail to improve.

—Instituting a system of nonfinancial recognition for schools with high value-added and a system of targeted assistance and interventions potentially leading to closure and restarting for low-performing schools judged not likely to improve.

The latter two recommendations were highly controversial even before the commission issued its report. Pressure from teachers and administrators unions led the commission to adopt language that requires a five-year process of community consultation before any school could be closed and restarted, no matter what its level of performance.

The commission also identified barriers to school-based accountability: Contrary to the promises made in the 1993 reform bill, the state had done nothing to reduce regulation or increase school-level control of dollars or other resources needed to improve performance. The commission was particularly concerned about state and district policies on teacher assignments. Frequently, school leaders have no say about which teachers are assigned to their schools. To the business members of the commission, this made school-level accountability impossible: No organization can be responsible for performance if it cannot select staff members and control money. These comments, however valid, were treated by the legislature as *obiter dicta*. The commission was supposed to suggest ways schools could be judged and rewarded or sanctioned, not to identify flaws in the state code.

In response to the commission's comments about school-level control of resources, Governor Gary Locke floated a proposal to sunset much of the state education code. His proposal was motivated by findings, such as those reported in the *Making Standards Work* series, that lack of control of hiring, firing, and spending often stymies serious school improvement efforts. However, the governor's proposal did not survive preliminary consultations with Olympia interest groups.

Reception to even the watered-down version of the A+ Commission's recommendations was tumultuous. In 2001 the legislature was deadlocked on an accountability bill based on the commission's recommendations. The House passed a bill closely patterned on the recommendations, but a Democratic Senate committee leader promised to block any provision that could lead to teacher reassignment or job loss, and a prominent Republican senator tried to eliminate authorization for the Certificate of Mastery, the WASL-based high school graduation requirement. As of late 2001, no end to the legislative stalemate seemed likely. In the Senate, conservative Republicans and pro-union Democrats tacitly agree that the status quo is better than any accountability system.

Response to the proposed accountability system and other controversies suggests that standards-based reform might have reached its high-water mark in Washington. If it becomes clear that the WASL is only a test, and that district leaders and school staff are free to use or ignore its results, the positive trends might not continue.

Aside from the stalemate about accountability, these other threats may weaken the state's commitment to standards-based reform:

—Attacks against the WASL, charging that the fourth-grade test might be developmentally inappropriate and the seventh-grade test results might be useless as measures of junior high school performance.

—Growing fears that teachers might flee the fourth and seventh grades, when the elementary and middle school WASL tests are given.

—Active resistance to extending the WASL into history, science, social studies, fitness, and arts and to withholding high school diplomas from students who fail these tests.

ATTACKS ON THE WASL. The fourth-grade WASL exams in reading and mathematics were designed to emphasize thinking and problem-solving skills and to set the bar higher for overall academic performance at the fourth-grade level. From the beginning, Superintendent of Public Instruction Terry Bergeson, a former statewide teachers union leader, encouraged teachers to anticipate a challenge and promised state help for teachers needing to upgrade their methods. As predicted, many complaints were heard about the burdens placed on teachers. These complaints get attention in the newspapers, but they have not set off a general backlash against the WASL.

Complaints against the WASL have taken a more potent form, however, when stated in terms of children's welfare. The Seattle teachers union, for example, has based its opposition to the WASL on such a child welfare claim. Test items, critics allege, are too difficult for nine-year-old children and are likely to do psychic harm. These charges are backed up by newspaper stories including examples of word problems in mathematics. Many of the items printed in the newspapers are surprisingly difficult.

Test designers claim that many of these are experimental items or items designed to challenge the most advanced students. Like the creators of traditional norm-referenced tests, WASL designers claim to need a few very difficult items to distinguish between children at the very top of the achievement distribution and others.

To date, the debate about the WASL's appropriateness has been largely anecdotal. We are aware of no effort to judge the overall fourth-grade examination or to assess whether forcing children to struggle with difficult items does any harm. Pro-WASL teachers and principals simply say that responsible school leaders can calm students by saying "no one can get all the questions right, but you should always try your best."

Some indication of whether the WASL is a reasonable challenge for fourth graders can be drawn from the test results themselves. If few or no children meet the standards, the WASL might be set at too high a level. However, many children do meet the standards. Moreover, in some schools, over 90 percent of all children meet them. In 2000 majorities of children met the reading standards in 85.9 percent of Washington elementary schools. In more than half the schools, more than two-thirds of all students met the reading standards. Proportions are far lower for fourth-grade math. Majorities met the standards in 31.7 percent of schools and supermajorities (over two-thirds of all students) met the standards in only 9 percent of schools.[9]

These data make it clear that the WASL is very challenging, especially in mathematics. But the fact that large numbers of children meet the standards, and that those who pass cluster in certain schools, implies that educational experience, not age-determined capacity, is the key variable. Though in the aggregate the proportion of children meeting standards varies directly with family income, some poverty area schools beat the demographics significantly, preparing more than half their children to meet the standards.

Thus, high performance on the WASL is possible for nine-year-olds. But the tests are far from perfect. The mathematics test in particular confuses skills that should be tested separately. It relies heavily on word problems and exposition of problem-solving methods. Low reading performance therefore depresses WASL mathematics scores, so that low-income and immigrant children who lack age-appropriate reading skills do even worse on mathematics than on reading.

The WASL is not as good as it could be. Besides the problems already noted, the speed at which the test was developed and the lack of statistical analysis comparing WASL results with those of known tests raise the possibility that scores might emphasize some skills over some that are equally or more important. In the future, when students now in the schools graduate, the WASL might not prove to be as good a predictor of college or economic success as conventional norm-referenced tests.

TESTING EARLY ADOLESCENTS IN THE WRONG GRADE? Testing students at about age twelve makes sense for an assessment of readiness for study of literature, science, and mathematics. Seventh grade is also a reasonable time to assess the performance of the state's 255 middle schools, most of which receive students in sixth grade and, therefore, have them for nearly two academic years before they are tested. But seventh grade is a less appropriate time to assess the performance of the state's seventy-six junior high schools. These do not receive students until seventh grade, and their students are therefore tested less than seven months after they enter. Results in these schools arguably reflect elementary school learning more than junior high school experience.

To date, the state's standards-based reform has not put either middle or junior high schools under a great deal of performance pressure. Only two years of test results were available in late 2001, as this is written, but within fourteen months the performance of any seventh grade in the state could be tracked over four years. If these data are used to criticize—let alone intervene in—particular schools, a serious backlash is probable. Junior high school leaders are certain to point out that most responsibility for student performance rests elsewhere, and seventh-grade teachers are likely to resist abandoning regular course work in favor of heavy test preparation.

Ironically, the seventh-grade WASL is generally recognized as more age-appropriate than the fourth-grade exams.[10] State leaders responsible for standards-based reform might face some difficult choices—whether to abandon the least controversial of the WASL examinations, restructure junior high schools so that a seventh-grade test comes after all children are nearly two years out of elementary school, or abandon the idea of using WASL scores as a measure of school performance.

Business leaders and political supporters of standards-based reform will certainly oppose the third option, knowing that high school staffs could then claim their job was made impossible when the state decided it could do nothing about the low performance of middle schools. Mandating that all students leave elementary school at the end of fifth grade would lead to costly demands for school building and renovation. In the end, revising the test to be appropriate for the eighth grade might be the only feasible option.

FEARS OF TEACHER FLIGHT. In Washington, the battle of anecdotes sometimes focuses on the fate of teachers in the tested grades. Critics allege that teachers are discouraged, beset, and forced to abandon regular instruction in favor of test prep. Some also warn that teachers will petition to get out of fourth and seventh grades, and schools will have difficulty recruiting people to teach at those levels.

Undoubtedly, everything alleged has happened someplace. Newspaper stories have documented the months of toil put in by some fourth-grade teachers who have succeeded in raising students' scores. But in the absence of a careful analysis of teacher attrition, transfer requests, and recruitment, knowing whether this problem is real or only potential is impossible. Much depends on what happens within individual schools. In our interviews with principals and teachers, several acknowledged that fourth- and seventh-grade teachers were starting to experience special pressures. But in the improving schools we studied, school leaders quickly recognized the need for the WASL to be a schoolwide responsibility and made raising scores the responsibility of K–3 as well as grade four teachers.

Nonetheless, tested-grade teachers in struggling schools are likely to feel even more pressure than teachers in other grades, and weak principals are unlikely to offer them needed levels of support. Though Washington's testing system is now anything but high stakes (no intervention is offered in troubled schools other than continued help and support), some low-performing schools might eventually face some consequences. In that case teachers might well want to avoid the tested grades. New federal legislation requiring testing in all grades might spread the pressure. But teacher avoidance of tested grades could become a serious obstacle to continuation of standards-based reform.

RESISTANCE TO EXTENDING THE WASL. The standards-based reform law enacted in 1993 envisioned WASLs that would cover most standard academic subjects. From the beginning, the superintendent of public instruction had intended to start with tests in reading, mathematics, writing, and listening and to develop other tests later. Costs of test development have prevented investments in additional subjects. But state officials have also learned from California's bad experience in trying to develop a statewide social studies test, and they shied away from issues that might provoke a culture war over test contents.

Development of tests in science, social studies, arts, history, and fitness has been delayed indefinitely. Business and political supporters of standards-based reform have understood their good luck. Though many people criticize the existing basic skills tests, no real controversy arose about whether some form of assessment in these areas is appropriate.[11]

But can the state permanently avoid developing tests expressly required by the omnibus school reform law? Perhaps not. Puget Sound area business and technology leaders are adamant that science is a basic skill, and their support for the whole WASL concept is indispensable. Once the state moves to develop one additional WASL, however, pressure for the other tests will be hard to avoid. Arts and humanities are popular topics among the well-educated and prosperous citizens of metropolitan Seattle. Coalitions of university and K–12 educators, backed by small foundations whose donors value arts and humanities, believe that getting these subjects into the WASL is the only way to ensure they will be taught in public schools.

Expansion of the WASL into other areas will both shake up the coalition that has sustained standards-based reform and intensify opposition from the political right. Current supporters of standards-based reform do not all agree that science is as important as literacy, and they will not readily agree on what all students should know about history and social studies. Educators comfortable with the current emphasis on mathematics and literacy will not welcome new competitors for school time and spending. Nor will business leaders take comfort from the sight of educators arguing over whether every student should have certain skills related to dance or drama.

Opposition from the political right is sure to focus on history and social studies where, as in other states, groups will argue over whose story should be told and what interpretation should be put on key events in American and state history. The fact that the right is heavily represented in all parts of the state but Puget Sound, and that it controls the Republican Party in the legislature, makes this conflict particularly deadly.

Proliferation of WASL tests will also complicate judgment of school performance. Nothing in the authorizing legislation determines how the state or school districts will weight tests in different subjects. It is therefore not clear whether a school with low scores in reading and high scores in art should be judged any differently from one with the opposite pattern. Supporters of standards-based reform might hope common sense will prevail, but nothing is certain. Puget Sound is a hotbed of support for multiple intelligence believers, including plenty who would deny the priority of reading and mathematics over artistic expression or self-esteem.

Any of these tensions about expansion of the WASL could wreck the flimsy centrist coalition supporting it. To date, financial necessity has given supporters an excuse for avoiding very dangerous issues.

Conclusion

What happened to the big legislative majority that enacted a bold standards-based reform bill? There are two answers. First, time and political events larger than education have changed the legislature and the governorship. Centrists are relatively weak in Olympia. Business, always the core support for standards-based reform, cannot win all by itself.

Second, the pro-standards coalition is falling apart as key supporters discover that they had never truly agreed about the purpose of standards. The initial coalition included the business community, Superintendent of Public Instruction Terry Bergeson, and education associations. As recent events have proven, members of the coalition are deeply split about whether standards are

1. Negotiated agreements among education professionals about what, under optimal conditions, they will try to help all students learn; or

2. A set of empirically grounded statements of what every child must know at each stage of his or her education to be prepared for higher education, rewarding work, and active citizenship.

Even in 1993 these different views were evident in the state's discourse about education. Bergeson acted on the first view by convening groups of teachers to devise standard learning requirements from which the WASL tests were then constructed. Enthusiasts for different subjects—American versus world literature, various arts, and so on—made the case for including their materials in mandatory state standards, and the drafters of state Essential

Learnings requirements tried to accommodate them. The question of whether educators were confident that they could prepare most or all students to meet these standards never came up. Though many teachers were involved in the standard-setting process, nobody seriously asked, "Would we set the same standards if they were also guarantees, such that if a student did not reach a standard his teachers would have an obligation to work with him until he did?" In the absence of such a question, the standard-setters were free to dream, not burdened by resource questions or the specter of consequences for themselves.

In contrast, the business community consistently asserted that standards should establish what every child needs to know and be able to do. They regarded standards as guaranteed minima, not millennial aspirations.

Now that the legislature is under pressure to meet its own timetable in establishing an accountability system, the differences between these understandings of standards are obvious. Supporters of standards as professional aspirations, or as logrolled agreements among claimants on school time and money, are understandably skeptical about taking firm action toward schools or districts whose students are not meeting standards. Maybe the aspirations were too ambitious and should be amended or their application delayed. Maybe teachers need more training and experience. Maybe the contending groups would change their demands in light of experience about how difficult it is to educate every child.

People who take standards as empirically grounded statements of what every child must know at a certain age if he or she is to become a full participant in community and economic life take a harder line. By their logic, temporizing is irresponsible. If children in a school or district are not meeting standards, something must be done about it immediately. There is no time to wait until teachers and administrators come around.

Lawyer-principal Larry Rosenstock of San Diego's High Tech High makes the best case for empirically grounded standards. According to his reasoning, forcing parents to send children to school—as in Constitutional terms—is a taking of liberty, which is permissible only in a case of compelling state interest. Saying "kids should go to school" does not establish a compelling state interest. To justify the taking of liberty, the state needs both to say what children need to know and to demonstrate that by going to school children will learn what they need. Under this argument, standards are more than aspirations. From the state's point of view, standards are the grounds on which it has authority to compel school attendance. From parents' points of view, standards are promises made by the state, and the state has an obligation to provide schools that can teach students successfully. Under this argument the state has two burdens: first, to show that particular learning requirements are valid— that is, that children who do not meet these requirements at a particular age suffer lasting harm—and second, to do whatever is necessary to provide effective schools so that children learn what they need to know.[12]

Washington's ongoing debate about accountability can be traced to differences about the meaning of standards. Business supporters thought the 1993 standards-based reform bill obligated the state to determine what children need to know and create a system that would prevent or quickly remedy failures. Those who regard standards only as topics of professional conversation see no warrant for strong state intervention in low-performing schools.

Washington's existing standards, as represented by what the WASL measures and the cutoffs it establishes for acceptable performance, are not based on empirical evidence on what children need to know. Nor, to our knowledge, are the standards set by other states. Empirically based literacy and mathematics standards, particularly at ages nine and thirteen, could be created. But it is hard to see how any state could prove children must know particular facts about history, the arts, or even science at a particular age or suffer predictable consequences. Empirically based standards would almost certainly be more modest in scope than the more aspirational standards set by most states. But compared with aspirational standards, empirically based ones would be compelling warrants for sustained and dramatic state action toward school improvement.

To date, no state has taken standards as seriously as Washington's business community (and those who think standards are promises to parents that the state has an obligation to meet) intended. That is why it is so difficult to create accountability systems, to act on behalf of children in even the most persistently low-performing schools, and even to leverage state funds for teacher recruitment and training and for school improvement initiatives.

In the history of American public education, the standards movement might be seen as yet another loosely defined effort to stir up commitment and to exhort teachers to higher performance. Or it might be seen as a turning point after which states let goals for student learning, rather than political processes and custom, define public education. In Washington, and probably in the other states at the leading edge of standards-based reform, the next few years will tell.

Comment by Michael J. Petrilli

Criticizing this excellent paper by Paul T. Hill and Robin J. Lake is diffi-cult, because it achieves all of its aims. It contributes to the research base on effective schools, and it astutely analyzes Washington State's attempts at reforms. Instead of offering criticism, then, I would like to highlight a few findings that I believe are especially poignant.

The good news section of the paper is good news for the entire nation. Edu-cators and policymakers have known it for a long time, but it is worth repeating: Schools matter. Demography is not destiny; effective schools can improve student achievement regardless of how poor the students or chal-lenging the environment.

While many people know that schools matter, the message needs to be communicated to the world, because too many educators and political lead-ers continue to assume that poor children cannot learn. In President George W. Bush's words, they continue to practice "the soft bigotry of low expecta-tions." This paper says loud and clear that poor students can learn and that good schools are the key.

The bad news is bad, but not for all the usual reasons. Many commentators would look at Washington's experience and focus narrowly on the demise of its accountability provisions. Washington's original plan focused heavily on standards and testing. It did so because growing evidence from Texas, North Carolina, and elsewhere shows that standards-based reform, well imple-mented, works. The Bush administration strongly supports this approach, as evidenced by the president's education proposal.

However, standards, testing, and accountability represent only one side of the equation. The other side goes by various names—flexibility, freedom of action (as Hill and Lake call it)—but is equally important. According to Hill and Lake's account of the past few years, policymakers in Washington seem to have made a serious mistake by not taking the flexibility agenda seriously.

Why is flexibility so important? The current system is top-down, rule-driven, and process-oriented. The culture of education in this nation needs to be changed to a culture of achievement. Standards-based reform takes the sys-tem part of the way by focusing attention on results. But without clearing the underbrush of years of rules, compliance culture, and mandates, schools face an impossible situation. They are told that student achievement is what counts, but their hands are tied with rules and regulations. Society demands results, but at the same time schools are loaded up with nonacademic responsibilities.

The experience in Texas is instructive. While Texas's standards-based system gets considerable attention, part of its strategy was to dramatically increase flexibility at the local level. Political leaders cleared out the Texas education code. They demanded that districts give local schools greater autonomy. While Washington considered such moves early in its reform movement, the state quickly dropped them when resistance from the established interest groups became clear. This was just as great a loss as the failure to win meaningful accountability.

Furthermore, both Texas and North Carolina are weak union states. Their policymakers were able to create systems that held educators accountable for results and gave administrators power to shake things up. What happens to standards-based reform in states with hidebound union regulations and in schools with calcified union contracts? How does a principal shake up a school when he or she cannot bring in new talent or remove incompetent employees? How does he or she focus on academics when the recruitment pool is disturbingly shallow?

A major part of a flexibility agenda, then, would include a commitment to giving schools the tools to recruit talent from anywhere they can find it. Early on, Washington's reformers perceived the need to change the pipeline of new teachers, but efforts to reform teacher certification were quickly abandoned. Abandoned, too, were efforts to give principals control over teacher assignments and budgets. As Hill and Lake report, business groups held the view that "no organization can be responsible for performance if it cannot select staff members and control money." Education is a people business, and until the quality of the people going into schools is improved, the results are going to be disappointing.

If Washington cannot revamp its traditional certification system, then creating rigorous alternate route programs would be one good place for the state to start. A recent evaluation of the Teach for America program demonstrated that these young, untrained teachers are at least as effective in raising student achievement as teachers who complete traditional education school requirements. The groundbreaking news is that, all things considered, education school training and its process-oriented requirements do not seem to matter. Why not allow school leaders access to high-quality people who have not gone to education school?

In sum, I would urge policymakers and analysts to pay as much attention to flexibility issues as they do to accountability issues. Because Washington's reformers—like many throughout the nation—did not take the flexibility agenda seriously enough, most struggling schools likely will continue to languish under meaningless rules and red tape. Standards-based reform will fail if it does not attack compliance-based rules and the union-based regulations as a core component of the model.

The Bush administration is moving aggressively on the flexibility agenda as a part of standards-based reform. By consolidating discretionary programs, focusing on performance instead of compliance, and working to slash the reporting requirements of existing programs, the administration intends to untie the hands of local schools and educators. The testing and accountability provisions of "No Child Left Behind" rightly garner a great deal of attention, but the flexibility agenda is just as important.

Hill and Lake express disappointment that Washington did not implement the tough accountability provisions that would have put teeth into the system. I share their frustration, and I wonder if consequences for failing schools could have been created through other means. For example, if Washington had adopted a charter school law and supported the development of significant numbers of high-quality charter schools, the competition from these schools might have served as an effective check on failing schools. Today, parents with children in failing schools are told that their school is in trouble but they cannot do much about it. Imagine what might happen if a new charter school opened up next door. Competition could do some of the work that top-down sanctions would typically do in a standards-based system. In other words, the movement for greater parental choice should not be viewed as a rival to standards-based reform, but as an effective complement. Perhaps some of the business leaders who have fought so hard for standards and accountability should put equal effort into the battle for charter schools. In the quest to leave no child behind, educators and policymakers should embrace any strategy that works.

Comment by Michael Cohen

Paul T. Hill and Robin J. Lake have provided a provocative case study of key aspects of standards-based reform in Washington State. Overall it offers a sobering view of the challenges that must be faced in state after state if this decade-long strategy for increasing student achievement is to succeed. I want to focus my comments briefly on several related issues they highlight that are of significance nationally, not just in Washington.

Good News and Bad News in Washington State

Hill and Lake found a set of schools in Washington that has been showing consistent improvement in the years since the state's content standards were developed, and they have documented the factors that contributed to the schools' success. The common characteristics and strategies of the improving schools include a clear focus on a few key learning goals that stretched the capacity of the school; a coherent and coordinated effort on the part of the entire school instead of isolated responses of individual teachers; the strategic use of resources aligned with learning goals; a collegial approach to professional development that is integral to the school improvement strategy; an effort to monitor student progress and identify students at risk of falling through the cracks; and attention to building continuous improvement into the daily fabric and culture of the school. There is nothing magical about the factors in this list. With the right conditions and support, they are replicable in just about every school in America. And while important, they are not new research findings. They are consistent with what educators and policymakers began to learn more than twenty years ago from the research on effective schools and effective classroom teaching.

While the success of the improving schools Hill and Lake studied should be celebrated, excitement should be kept under control. A subset of schools in every state and community has always incorporated these findings into day-to-day practice, either because they are continuously implementing research-based practices or because they have figured out sound management and instructional practices through their own experimentation and learning. But it is almost always just a subset—rarely, if ever, an entire local or state system of schools. And so it is frustrating that common knowledge and common sense have not yet become common practice, on a large scale. In most states, the accountability system is supposed to help provide the incentives and pressure (and, if well designed, the support and flexibility) that schools need to focus on results and implement proven practices.

But in Washington State, accountability legislation has been stalled in the legislative process. As Hill and Lake describe, this legislation is being thwarted by a coalition of conservative Republicans and liberal Democrats, and there is no end to the stalemate in sight. Despite an early and promising start, a key component of the standards-based reform agenda enacted in 1993 is dead in its tracks. Those who oppose a stronger role for the state and those who oppose stronger accountability have apparently teamed up in favor of the status quo. Similar left-right coalitions have formed before, and no doubt they will again, especially as accountability provisions begin to take hold in other states.

Nothing is inevitable or irreversible about the movement to raise standards. It can be thwarted, blocked, and undone. Frequently its opponents are more powerfully motivated than its proponents, because they can see the specific losses they will suffer, while the gains are often more diffuse and distant, even for staunch proponents. Further, students will benefit the most from clear standards and strong accountability, but they count the least in the political arena. One clear lesson from the Washington State experience is that the centrist coalitions necessary to enact standards-based legislation at the state and federal level must be carefully nurtured and expanded if the movement itself is to have sufficient time to take root and work.

Limits of Federal Requirements on State Accountability Policies

While frustration with the status quo may not be evident in the Washington State legislature, it is certainly evident in the halls of the U.S. Congress. Frustration with the pace of education reform nationwide, including the failure of a number of states to establish tough-minded accountability systems of their own, has fueled an effort to substantially tighten accountability provisions in Title I. The 107th Congress is debating proposals that would require additional annual testing, significant annual improvements in measured achievement (for all subgroups of students) in each school, and forceful sanctions for schools that fail to improve.

But the Washington State experience also contains an important lesson—if not warning signal—to federal policymakers. At a minimum, it should at least give them some reason to think hard about the prospects of success in effectively driving accountability from the federal government to the school-house. The clear evidence from Washington and other states is that state education policymakers may not pay much attention to federal dictates.

According to Hill and Lake—as well as Washington State officials with whom I have spoken—the failure of the legislature to pass an accountability measure is understood to mean that there is no accountability for results in Washington. However, lack of action by the state legislature need not equate to an absence of accountability statewide.

The 1994 reauthorization of Title I requires every participating state to have a system of content and performance standards and aligned assessments, to use those to measure the progress of every school, and to identify and inter-vene in those not making adequate progress. More recently, Congress has targeted additional funds to help states turn around low-performing schools, through the Comprehensive School Reform Demonstration Program, the Title I School Improvement Fund, and the Reading Excellence Act. If a state edu-cation agency pays serious attention to these program requirements and resources—by publicizing their existence, aligning implementation with the state's overall approach to standards-based reform, setting and enforcing rea-sonable standards for adequate yearly progress, working with schools identified as needing improvement, and targeting financial and technical resources to them—a statewide system of school accountability would be in place.

But these steps are not automatic, and the federal requirements are not self-executing. In many states, the implementation of federal education pro-grams is separate from the development and implementation of the state's education reform policy, even within the same agency. Many legislators under-standably believe that when it comes to matters of testing and accountability, the state is solely in charge. In most state legislatures, typically almost no awareness is found of the Title I requirements, let alone automatic deference to them. Further, it is not clear that the federal government's small share of total elementary and secondary education spending gives it the leverage it needs to enforce federal requirements on reluctant states.

The implementation of the 1994 Title I testing requirements, which are less demanding on states than those under consideration now, is instructive. Only fifteen states fully complied with the assessment requirements by the imple-mentation deadline, the end of the 2000–01 school year. As assistant secretary for elementary and secondary education, I was responsible for ensuring state compliance with these provisions. While I am certain that all but a few will ultimately and fully meet the requirements, I am equally certain that governors, legislators, and other officials in a number of states either ignored or were unaware of the specific federal requirements while designing and implementing state testing policies.

Based on this experience, I believe that more consistent compliance with the new Title I provisions will depend on a number of factors. First, the final statutory provisions must be clear, understandable, feasible to implement, and seen as sound education policy by state officials and others. Second, the Education Department's implementation strategy must begin immediately upon enactment and include a sustained effort to publicize and explain the requirements to governors, legislators, and other state education policymakers, not just to state Title I coordinators. Third, the Education Department must arrange for the technical support and assistance states will plainly need for sound and effective implementation. Finally, the department must deftly combine a sustained effort to help states reasonably adapt new requirements to their own circumstances and approaches—without compromising on the fundamental principles underlying the new requirements—together with a clear signal that failure to comply will result in loss of federal funds.

Getting the Standards Right and Making Standards Count

Hill and Lake highlight a number of significant issues that undermine serious accountability and threaten to erode further the coalition that supported Washington's standards-based reforms in the first place. These include, for example, the difficulty of the state exams (the Washington Assessment of Student Learning), the appropriateness of using a seventh-grade exam for middle school accountability, and the subjects that should be included in the state testing program beyond reading and math.

As the authors insightfully point out, the most fundamental of these issues is the very nature and purpose of the standards themselves. Standards proponents appear split between those who view standards as primarily aspirational (statements of what Washington students should learn and schools should teach them, ideally) and those who view standards as empirically derived statements of the knowledge and skills each student much achieve to succeed at the next level of schooling or as preparation for citizenship, work, and further learning.

Only empirically derived standards can effectively serve as the basis for both school and student accountability. Where the standards accurately reflect the prerequisites for success in an important arena, state-attached consequences for meeting or failing to meet the standards are defensible because of the consequences individuals experience in the marketplace, higher education, and the broader society. Simply put, it is considerably more important and legitimate to hold schools accountable for equipping students with the knowledge and skills necessary for success in higher education and high skill jobs than for knowledge and skills that are simply nice to acquire.

In the main, in Washington State and elsewhere, the rhetoric of standards proponents leaned heavily toward the second (empirically based) view, while the procedure for developing standards embraced the first. Beginning with the development of national standards in the content areas and following with similar actions in each state, the process relied largely on getting groups of educators and other experts to reach agreement on the important knowledge and skills in each discipline. While most states involved representatives of higher education and business in the standards process, rarely was the process informed by clear, empirically based information on the literacy and math skills necessary for admissions into and success in the state higher education system or successful employment in high performance work organizations.

None of this is to fault the educators involved. Rarely do institutions of higher education specify the standards students must reach for academic success in the freshman year, and no common employment standard has been developed or used by employers nationally or within states.

State standards cannot be static; they must change as more is learned about the requirements of effective implementation. Most states will need to make various midcourse corrections. As they continue to implement systems of standards and assessments, and particularly as they extend them into the high school years, many must make midcourse corrections to ensure that exit standards are properly aligned with those of postsecondary education and work and that standards in the earlier grades are fully aligned with the exit standards.

Notes

1. The earliest source of this theory of action was David Hornbeck, whose Nine Essential Elements of standards-based reform was the basis of a 1989 court order establishing the Kentucky Education Reform Act (KERA), the first statewide standards-based reform. See *Rose* v. *Council for Better Education*, 790 S.W.2d 186, 60 Ed. Law Rep. 1289 (1989) Supreme Court of Kentucky. The clearest statement of the theory of action can be found in National Business Roundtable, *A New Architecture for Education Reform* (Washington: The Business Roundtable,

1995). See also Paul T. Hill and Mary Beth Celio, *Fixing Urban Schools* (Brookings, 1998), chapter 3.

2. One key assumption—that teachers will refocus their teaching in response to testing and public discussion of student performance—is well founded in evidence from other states. See Brian M. Stecher and Sheila I. Barron, *Quadrennial Milepost Accountability Testing in Kentucky* (UCLA, Center for Research on Evaluation, Standards, and Student Testing, 1998). See also Daniel M. Koretz and Sheila I. Barron, *The Validity of Gains in Scores on the Kentucky Instructional Results Information System (KIRIS)* (Santa Monica, Calif.: RAND Institute for Education and Training, 1998).

3. New tests covering social studies, history, and science are supposed to be phased in over the next few years.

4. RAND's study of the effect of Washington's reforms on classrooms confirms that teachers across the state have dramatically shifted instructional time toward areas tested by the Washington Assessment of Student Learning (WASL).

5. Some districts, however, do require new districtwide curriculum in response to the standards.

6. Richard F. Elmore, "Getting to Scale with Good Educational Practice," *Harvard Educational Review*, vol. 66, no. 1 (Spring 1996), pp. 1–26.

7. Koretz and Barron, *The Validity of Gains in Scores on the Kentucky Instructional Results Information System.*

8. We are deeply implicated in these proposals. See, for example, Paul T. Hill and Robin J. Lake, *Toward a K–12 Accountability System in Washington State* (Seattle, Wash.: Center on Re-Inventing Public Education, 1999). See also Sarah R. Brooks, *How States Can Hold Schools Accountable: The Strong-Schools Model of Standards-Based Reform* (Seattle, Wash.: Center on Re-Inventing Public Education, 2000).

9. Thanks to Mary Beth Celio for the original analysis that produced these statistics.

10. See Brian Stecher and others, *The Effects of the Washington State Education Reform on Schools and Classrooms* (Santa Monica, Calif.: RAND, 2001).

11. Nationally, some of the strongest critics of testing have come to agree that state-mandated reading and math exams are legitimate, though they continue to resist testing in history, social sciences, and other more elective areas. See, for example, Howard Gardner, "Stick to Testing the Basics," *New York Times*, April 21, 2001, p. A–25.

12. To our knowledge, no state has built its standards in this way. Doing so would be very demanding. States would have to work backward from the skill requirements of jobs and the knowledge prerequisites of higher education, to identify the habits, skills, and knowledge that all successful adults have in common. To set skill and knowledge requirements for children of a particular age, the state would have to analyze how and when key milestones are normally reached and demonstrate that children who did not reach particular milestones were unlikely ever to catch up. This analysis would be extremely challenging, but it might be the minimum basis on which a state could legitimately prescribe what a child should know and when. The costs and technical challenges of such an analysis mark it as a job for national institutions and an appropriate use of federal funds. However, no entity has taken this challenge on—not the federal government, individual states, multistate alliances, or the business community, despite their avowed commitment to standards-based reform. The closest approximation to the required analysis was done only on job requirements (and not for different student age groups) by the Labor Department in collaboration with the business community. See Department of Labor, Secretary's Commission on Achieving Necessary Skills, *Skills and Tasks for Jobs* (1992).

Volatility in
School Test Scores:
Implications for Test-Based
Accountability Systems

THOMAS J. KANE *and*
DOUGLAS O. STAIGER

B y the spring of 2000, forty states had begun using student test scores to rate school performance. Twenty states have gone a step further and are attaching explicit monetary rewards or sanctions to a school's test performance. For example, California planned to spend $677 million on teacher incentives in 2001, providing bonuses of up to $25,000 to teachers in schools with the largest test score gains. We highlight an under-appreciated weakness of school accountability systems—the volatility of test score measures—and explore the implications of that volatility for the design of school accountability systems.

The imprecision of test score measures arises from two sources. The first is sampling variation, which is a particularly striking problem in elementary schools. With the average elementary school containing only sixty-eight students per grade level, the amount of variation stemming from the idiosyncrasies of the particular sample of students being tested is often large relative to the total amount of variation observed between schools. The second arises from one-time factors that are not sensitive to the size of the sample; for example, a dog barking in the playground on the day of the test, a severe flu season, a disruptive student in a class, or favorable chemistry between a group of students and their teacher. Both small samples and other one-time factors can add considerable volatility to test score measures.

Initially, one might be surprised that school mean test scores would be subject to such fluctuations, because one would expect any idiosyncrasies in individual students' scores to average out. Although the averaging of students' scores does help lessen volatility, even small fluctuations in a school's score can have a large impact on a school's ranking, simply because schools' test scores do not differ dramatically in the first place. This reflects the long-standing finding from the Coleman report (*Equality of Educational Opportunity*, issued in 1966), that less than 16 percent of the variance in student test scores is between schools.[1] We estimate that the confidence interval for the average fourth-grade reading or math score in a school with sixty-eight students per grade level would extend from roughly the 25th to the 75th percentile among schools of that size.

Such volatility can wreak havoc in school accountability systems. To the extent that test scores bring rewards or sanctions, school personnel are subjected to substantial risk of being punished or rewarded for results beyond their control. Moreover, to the extent such rankings are used to identify best practice in education, virtually every educational philosophy is likely to be endorsed eventually, simply adding to the confusion over the merits of different strategies of school reform. For example, when the 1998–99 Massachusetts Comprehensive Assessment System test scores were released in November of 1999, the Provincetown district showed the greatest improvement over the previous year. The *Boston Globe* published an extensive story describing the various ways in which Provincetown had changed educational strategies between 1998 and 1999, interviewing the high school principal and several teachers.[2] As it turned out, they had changed a few policies at the school—decisions that seemed to have been validated by the improvement in performance. One had to dig a bit deeper to note that the Provincetown high school had only twenty-six students taking the test in tenth grade. Given the wide distribution of test scores among students in Massachusetts, any grouping of twenty-six students is likely to yield dramatic swings in test scores from year to year—that is, large relative to the distribution of between-school differences. In other words, if the test scores from one year are the indicator of a school's success, the *Boston Globe* and similar newspapers around the country will eventually write similar stories praising virtually every variant of educational practice. It is no wonder that the public and policymakers are only more confused about how to proceed.

Sources of Data

We obtained math and reading test scores for nearly 300,000 students in grades three through five, attending elementary schools in North Carolina between the 1992–93 and 1998–99 school years. (The data were obtained from the North Carolina Department of Public Instruction.) Although the file we received had been stripped of student identification numbers, we were able to match a student's test score in one year to their test score in the previous year using date of birth, race, and gender.[3] In 1999, 84 percent of the sample had unique combinations of birth date, school, and gender. Another 14 percent shared their birth date and gender with at most one other student in their school and grade, and 2 percent shared their birth date with two other people. (Less than 1 percent shared their birth date and gender with three or more students in the school, and no match was attempted for these students.) Students were matched across years only if they reported the same race. If more than one person had the same school, birth date, race, and gender, we looked to see whether any unique matches could be made on parental education. If more than one person matched on all traits—school, birth date, race, gender, and parental education—the matches that minimized the squared changes in student test scores were kept.

However, because of student mobility between schools and student retention, the matching process was not perfect. We were able to calculate test score gains for 65.8 percent of the fourth- and fifth-grade students in 1999. (The matching rate was similar in other years.) The data in table 1 compare the characteristics of the matched and the nonmatched sample of fourth- and fifth-grade students in 1999. The matched sample had slightly higher test scores (roughly .2 student-level standard deviations in reading and math), a slightly higher proportion female, a slightly lower proportion black and Hispanic, and a slightly lower average parental education than the sample for which no match could be found.

We mostly employ the test scores in reading and math used by the North Carolina Department of Public Instruction. However, a one-unit change in such scores does not have any intuitive reference point. To provide readers with an intuitive sense of the magnitude of such scores, we subtracted the mean and divided by the standard deviation in scores in each grade to restate test scores in terms of student-level standard deviations from the mean. However, because we used the overall mean and the overall standard deviation for

Table 1. Characteristics of the Matched and Nonmatched Sample of Fourth- and Fifth-Grade Students in 1999

Characteristic of sample	Nonmatched	Matched
Fourth- and fifth-grade students	34.2%	65.8%
Mean math score	153.8	156.5
Standard deviation in math score	11.1	10.5
Mean reading score	150.5	152.4
Standard deviation in reading score	9.5	9.1
Female	47.4%	50.1%
Black	35.1	27.7
Hispanic	5.4	2.2
Parental education		
High school dropout	16.6%	9.8%
High school graduate	47.1	43.7
Trade or business school	4.6	5.3
Community college	11.3	14.2
Four-year college	16.5	21.9
Graduate school	3.9	5.1
Sample size	69,388	133,305

Note: Each of the differences was statistically significant at the .05 level.

the whole period 1994 through 1999 to do the standardization, we allow for changes over time in the distribution of scaled scores. We also calculated student-level gains by taking the differences in these scores (standardized as above) from one year to the next. As a result, both test score levels and test score gains are in units of student-level standard deviations in levels. We also experimented with using quasi-gains, by regressing a student's score on his or her score in the previous year, and then taking the residuals as a measure of student improvements. However, because the results were similar, we are reporting only the results using gain scores and test score levels.

In a previous work, we also adjusted each individual student's score for race, gender, and parental education.[4] That has the effect of removing between-school differences due to differences in race and parental education. We use the unadjusted test score data here. (The exception is analysis presented in tables 5 and 6, which report the results of our filtering technique.)

We also use school- and grade-level data on California's Academic Performance Index (API) scores in 1998 through 2000. The Academic Performance Index is based upon school-level scores on the Stanford 9 tests. Schools receive 1,000 points for each student in the top quintile, 875 points for students in the next quintile, 700 points for students in the middle quintile, 500 points for students in the 20th to 39th percentiles, and 200 points for students in the bottom quintile. A school's average is based upon a weighted average of their scores in the reading, spelling, language, and mathematics portions of the Stanford 9 tests.[5] We use the California data to highlight the generality of the measurement issues we describe and to analyze some of the properties of that state's accountability system.

Sources of Volatility in School-Level Test Scores

Three characteristics of school-level test score measures are vital to the design of test-based accountability systems. First, a considerable amount of variation in test scores exists at the school level due to sampling variation. Each cohort of students that enters first grade is analogous to a random draw from the population of students feeding a school. Even if that population remains stable, performance will vary depending upon the specific group of students reaching the appropriate age in any year. Using standard sampling theory, we can directly estimate the amount of variation we would expect to occur. Given that only sixty-eight students per grade level are in the typical elementary school, such variation can be substantial.

Second, other factors produce nonpersistent changes in performance in addition to sampling variation. Possible sources of such variation would be a dog barking in the parking lot on the day of the test, a severe flu season, the chemistry between a particular group of students and a teacher, a few disruptive students in the class, or bad weather on test day. We cannot estimate the magnitude of this source of variation directly without explicitly monitoring each influence on scores. However, we can do so indirectly, by observing the degree to which any changes in test scores from year to year persist and, thereby, infer the total amount of variation due to nonpersistent factors. Any nonpersistent variation in test scores that is not due to sampling variation we put into this category.

Third, by focusing on mean gains in test scores for students in a given year or changes in mean test score levels from one year to the next, many test-based accountability systems are relying upon unreliable measures. Schools differ little in their rate of change in test scores or in their mean value-added—certainly much less than they differ in their mean test score levels. Moreover, those differences that do exist are often nonpersistent—either because of sampling variation or other causes. For instance, we estimate that more than 70 percent of the variance in changes in test scores for any given school and grade is transient. For the median-size school, roughly half of the variation between schools in gain scores (or value-added) for any given grade is also nonpersistent.

Sampling Variation

A school's mean test score will vary from year to year, simply because the particular sample of students in a given grade differs. But just how much it varies depends upon two things: the variance in test scores in the population of students from which a school is drawing and the number of students in a particular grade. In schools where the students are particularly heterogeneous or in schools with a small number of students in each grade, we would expect test scores to fluctuate more.

In 1999, nearly one thousand schools in North Carolina had students in the fourth grade. Averaging across these schools (and weighting by school size), the variance in math scores among students in a given school was nearly nine-tenths as large (.87) as the student-level variance in scores. The ratio of the average within-school variance in fourth-grade reading scores to the total variance in reading scores was .89. That is, the heterogeneity in student scores within the average school was nearly as large as the heterogeneity in scores overall.

This is not some idiosyncratic characteristic of North Carolina's school system. It reflects a long-standing finding in educational assessment research. In their classic study of inequality of student achievement published in 1966, James S. Coleman and his colleagues estimated that only between 12 and 16 percent of the variance in verbal achievement among white third-grade students was due to differences across schools. The remainder was attributable to differences within schools.[6] In other words, two students drawn at random from within a given school are likely to differ nearly as much as two students drawn at random from the whole population.

Applying the rules from elementary sampling theory, one would simply divide the average within-school variance by the sample size to calculate the expected variance in the mean test score for a given school due to sampling variation. According to the National Center for Education Statistics, schools serving the elementary grades had sixty-eight students per grade level on average.[7] Dividing .87 and .89, respectively, by 68, we would expect a variance of .013, simply from the effect of drawing a new sample of students.

In North Carolina elementary schools near the national average in size (between sixty-five and seventy-five students with valid test scores), the variance in mean reading and math scores was .087 and .092, respectively. Dividing the estimated amount of variance due to sampling variation for a school of average size (.013) by the total variance observed for such schools, we would infer that 14 to 15 percent of the variation in fourth-grade math and reading test scores was due to sampling variation.

Gaining a strong intuitive sense for the magnitude of sampling variation with a proportion of variance calculation is sometimes difficult. An alternative way to gauge the importance of sampling variation would be to calculate the 95 percent confidence interval for a school's mean test score. One would do so by adding and subtracting 1.96 times the standard error of the estimate for the mean $\sqrt{.013}$, which is equal to .223 student-level standard deviations. Among schools with between sixty-five and seventy-five students with valid test scores, such a confidence interval would extend from roughly the 25th to the 75th percentile.

Sampling Variation and Mean Gain Scores across Schools

North Carolina—like a handful of other states including Arizona and Tennessee—rates its schools by focusing on the average gain in performance among students attending a particular school.[8] Advocates tout the value-added methodology as a fairer method of ranking schools, by explicitly adjusting for the fact that some students enter school with higher scores than others. However, to the extent that schools differ less in their value-added than in their test score levels, such measures can be particularly vulnerable to sampling variation.

The point can be illustrated with a few simple calculations. The variance in the gain in test performance between the end of third grade and the end of fourth grade within the average school in North Carolina was .331 in math and .343 in reading (stated in terms of the student-level standard deviation in fourth-grade math and reading test scores). The variance in gains is smaller than the variance in test scores in fourth grade (or third grade), even though one imperfect measure of a child's performance is subtracted from another. The variance in gains is roughly four-tenths as large as the variance in fourth-grade scores within schools (.331 / .87 and .343 / .89). If no relationship exists between a student's third-grade score and fourth-grade score, we would expect the variance to double when taking the difference. However, because third- and fourth-grade performance for a given student has a correlation coefficient of approximately .8, the variance in the gain is only roughly four-tenths as large as the variance in the test score levels.

To calculate the variance in test scores we would expect to result from sampling variation for a school of average size, we would simply divide the within-school variance in gain scores (.331 and .343) by the sample size (68), yielding an estimate of .0049 for math and .0050 for reading. However, while the within-school variance in gains between third and fourth grades is four-tenths as large as the within-school variance in test scores in fourth grade, the amount of variance between schools drops even more when moving from mean test scores to mean gains—at least for reading scores. Among schools with sixty-five to seventy-five students, the variance in reading scores was .015. Put another way, the between-school variance in mean student gains among schools of roughly the average size is only one-fifth as large as the between-school variance in mean fourth-grade scores. Yet, the variance between schools due to sampling variation is two-fifths as large. As a result, the share of variance between schools in mean reading gain scores that is due to sampling variation is double that seen with mean reading score levels. Sampling variation makes it much harder to discern true differences in reading gain scores across schools.[9]

Sampling Variation in Small and Large Schools

In all of the above calculations, we limited the discussion to schools close to the national average in size. Sampling variation will account for a larger share of the between-school variance for small schools and a smaller share for large schools. For figure 1, we sorted schools in North Carolina by the number of test-takers and divided the sample into five groups by school size. We then calculated the variance between schools in each quintile in test scores. We did so for fourth-grade math and reading and for gains in scores between third and fourth grade in math and reading.

Several facts are evident in figure 1. First, for each measure, we observed much more variance in test scores among smaller schools than among larger schools. For math and reading test scores, the variance between schools was roughly 50 percent larger for the smallest quintile of schools than for the largest quintile. For math and reading gain scores, the between-school vari-

Figure 1. Between-School Variances by School Size

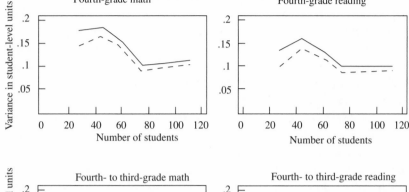

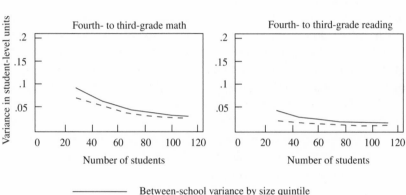

ance was roughly three times as large for the smallest quintile of schools than for the largest quintile.

Second, the dotted line in each panel of figure 1 identifies the between-school variance in each quintile after subtracting our estimate of the sampling variation. The sampling variation we estimated accounts for some portion of the greater variation among smaller schools, but even after subtracting our estimates of the sampling variation, the between-school variance is greater for smaller schools.

We ignored any peer effects in our estimate of the sampling variance. We assumed that having a disproportionate number of high- or low-test score youth would have no direct effect on the performance of other students in the class. However, if there were peer effects (for instance, if having a dispro-portionate share of low-performing youth pulls down the average performance of others or having a large number of high-performing youth raises the performance of all students through the quality of class discussions), we might expect the effects of any sampling variation to be amplified. If peer effects exist, we are understating the importance of sampling variation.

The peer effect need not operate through student test scores, however. A similar phenomenon would occur if any other characteristic that varied across samples had a direct effect on student test scores. For instance, Caroline Hoxby identifies substantial negative impacts on student performance from having a disproportionate share of boys in one's cohort.[10] Any time that a characteristic of the sample has a direct effect on the performance of each individual in that sample, our estimates of the magnitude of variance due to sampling variation are likely to be understated.

Third, very little variance existed between schools in the mean gain in reading scores between third and fourth grade. Even for the smallest quintile of schools, the between-school variance in the mean gain in reading performance was equal to .05 student-level standard deviations in fourth-grade reading scores. Moreover, a large share of this is estimated to have been due to sampling variation.

Small sample size is a particularly large problem for elementary schools. However, the problem is not unique to elementary schools. Figure 2 portrays the distribution of sample sizes by grade in North Carolina. School size is generally smaller in grade four. However, much more uniformity in school size is evident among elementary schools. While the size of the average middle school is larger than the size of the average elementary school, more heterogeneity is found in school size among middle schools. The same phenomenon is exaggerated at grade nine. High schools are generally much larger than elementary schools, but a number of small schools are enrolling ninth-grade students. In other words, elementary schools tend to be smaller than middle schools and high schools. However, they are also more uniform in size, meaning that schools have a more similar likelihood of having an extremely high or extremely low score due to sampling variation. Middle schools and high schools have larger sample sizes on average, but there is greater heterogeneity between schools in the likelihood of seeing an extremely high or extremely low test score due to sampling variation.

Variation in the Change in Test Scores over Time

The greater variability in test scores among small schools is not simply the result of long-term differences among these schools (such as would occur if all

Figure 2. Distribution of School Size by Grade Level

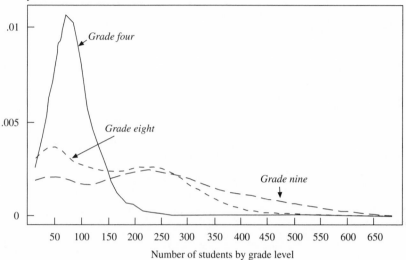

large schools were found in urban settings and if small schools contained a mixture of suburban and rural schools). Test scores also fluctuate much more from year to year among small schools than among large schools. Figure 3 plots the variance in the change in test scores between 1998 and 1999 by school size in North Carolina. The panel on the left portrays the variance in the change for fourth-grade math and reading scores and for gains in math and reading scores. The dotted line in both panels represents the result of subtracting our estimate of the contribution of sampling variation to the variance in the change. The variance in the change for fourth-grade test scores was three times as large among the smallest quintile of schools than among the largest quintile of schools (.079 versus .027). Moreover, the variance in the change for fourth-grade gain scores was five times as large among the smallest quintile of schools than among the largest quintile of schools (.060 versus .013).

A Measure of the Persistence of Change in School Test Scores

Sampling variation is only one reason that a school might experience a change in test scores over time. Sources of variation may be present at the classroom level, generated, for example, by teacher turnover, classroom chemistry between a teacher and the class, or the presence of a disruptive student

Figure 3. Between-School Variance in Annual Change

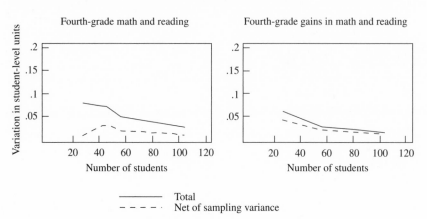

in a class. Sources of variation may affect a whole school, such as a dog barking in the parking lot on the day of the test or inclement weather, and could
generate temporary fluctuations in test performance. We can estimate the
amount of variation due to sampling variation by assuming that the succession
of cohorts within a particular grade is analogous to a random sampling
process. However, we have no similar method of modeling these other sources
of variation and anticipating a priori how much variation to expect from these
other sources. For instance, we would need a model of the time series process
affecting weather over time and have an estimate of the effect of such weather
on student test scores to approximate the variation in test scores stemming
from weather changes. We have neither. However, we provide a simple
method for estimating that fraction of the variation in test scores over time that
can be attributed to all such nonpersistent variation, even if we cannot identify the individual components as neatly. Subsequently, we will subtract our
estimate of the sampling variation to form an estimate of these other sources
of nonpersistent variation.

Suppose that some fixed component of school performance did not change
over time and suppose that fluctuations in school test scores fell into two categories: those that persist and those that are transient or nonpersistent. One
might describe a school's test performance, S_t, as being the sum of three factors: a permanent component that does not change, α; a persistent component,
v_t, which starts where it left off last year but is subject to a new innovation each
year, u_t; and a purely transitory component that is not repeated, ε_t. That is,

$$S_t = \alpha + v_t + \varepsilon_t,$$

$$\text{where } v_t = v_{t-1} + u_t.$$

One could write the changes from year t-2 to year t-1 and from year t-1 to year t as follows:

$$\Delta S_t = S_t - S_{t-1} = v_t - v_{t-1} + \varepsilon_t - \varepsilon_{t-1} = u_t + \varepsilon_t - \varepsilon_{t-1}$$

$$\Delta S_{t-1} = S_{t-1} - S_{t-2} = v_{t-1} - v_{t-2} + \varepsilon_{t-1} - \varepsilon_{t-2} = u_{t-1} + \varepsilon_{t-1} - \varepsilon_{t-2}.$$

Suppose that u_t , u_{t-1}, ε_{t-1}, and ε_t are independent.[11] Then the correlation between the change this year and the change last year could be expressed as

$$\rho = \frac{-\sigma_\varepsilon^2}{\sigma_u^2 + 2\sigma_\varepsilon^2}.$$

The numerator is the variance in the nonpersistent component (with a negative sign attached), and the denominator is the total variance in the change in test scores from one year to the next. With a little algrebra, the above equation could be rearranged to produce

$$-2\rho = \frac{2\sigma_\varepsilon^2}{\sigma_u^2 + 2\sigma_\varepsilon^2}.$$

The expression on the right side of the equation describes the proportion of the change in test scores that is attributable to nonpersistent factors. The expression on the left side of the equation is simply the correlation in the change in test scores in two consecutive years multiplied by –2. That is, given an estimate of the correlation in changes in test scores in two consecutive years, we can estimate the proportion of the variance in changes that is due to nonpersistent factors by multiplying that correlation by –2. If the correlation were zero, we would infer that the changes that occur are persistent. If the correlation were close to –.5, we would infer that nearly 100 percent of the changes that occur are purely transitory, such as sampling variation or a dog barking in the parking lot on the day of the test or inclement weather.

To explore the intuition behind the expression, suppose that the weather was particularly beautiful, the students were particularly well rested, and an unusually talented group of fourth-grade students was present on test day in 1999. Then the change in test scores for fourth-grade students between 1998 and 1999 would be large and positive. Because these factors were one-time phenomena that were unlikely to be repeated in 2000, we would expect a smaller than average change between 2000 and 1999. We would expect scores in 2000 to be back to the average and 1999 to still appear as a stand-out year. In other words, if changes were nonpersistent, we would expect a negative correlation between the change this year and the change next year. In fact, if all change were transitory, we would expect a correlation of $-.5$.

Suppose a school hired a new fourth-grade teacher in 1999 and improved facilities, thereby raising test performance. The school may make other such changes in the year 2000, but the magnitude of the changes one year provides no information about the expected magnitude of any such changes the next year. They may improve again, and they may decline, but to the extent that all changes are persistent, one would have no reason to expect any backsliding. If change in performance serves as the basis for subsequent improvements or declines instead of disappearing, we would expect a correlation of 0 in the change from one year to the next. If some changes are permanent, and some changes are purely transitory, one would expect a negative correlation between 0 and $-.5$.

The above estimator is focusing only on the transience of any changes in performance. Long-standing differences between schools do persist over time. But because any fixed trait of a school (α) drops out when we are focusing on changes, any unchanging characteristics are being excluded from our calculations. That is only fitting though, because we are interested in the proportion of change that persists, not the proportion of baseline differences that persist.

We calculated the mean fourth-grade scores in North Carolina (combining the scaled scores for math and reading) and calculated the correlation in the change in adjacent years, 1997–98 and 1998–99. We also calculated the mean Academic Performance Index scores in California for fourth-grade students and again calculated the correlation in the change in adjacent years. Figure 4 reports those correlations for each school size quintile in North Carolina and California. In North Carolina, the correlations ranged between $-.25$ and $-.4$. Using the reasoning above, this would imply that between 50 and 80 percent of the variance in the change in mean fourth-grade scores is nonpersistent. If one were to look for signs of improvement by closely tracking changes in mean scores from one year to the next, 50 to 80 percent of what one observed would be temporary—either due to sampling variation or some other nonpersistent cause.

Although the California schools tend to be larger, the data reveal slightly more volatility in the California Academic Performance Index for any given school size. For the smallest fifth of schools, the correlation in the change in

Figure 4. Correlation in the Change in Scores in Consecutive Years by Size of School in North Carolina and California

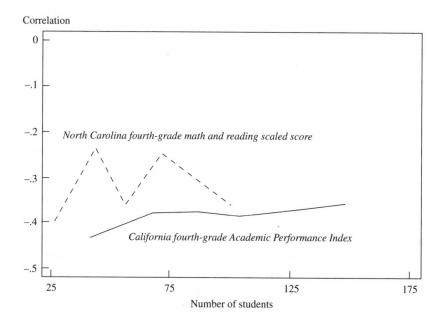

Correlation

adjacent years was –.43, implying that 86 percent of the variance in the changes between any two years is fleeting. For the largest fifth of schools, the correlation was –.36, implying that 72 percent of the variance in the change was nonpersistent.

In California, the correlations clearly rise (become less negative) for the larger schools. This is what one would expect if a source of nonpersistence was sampling variability. In North Carolina, the pattern is less evident. However, this is presumably because of the smaller number of schools within each size quintile in North Carolina relative to California.

Schoolwide Scores, Overlapping Cohorts, and the Illusion of Stability

Some states, such as California, reward schools based upon changes in the average performance across all grades in a school, instead of on a single grade. The use of schoolwide averages has two primary effects. First, combining data from different grades increases the sample size and, therefore, reduces the importance of sampling variation. Second, considerable overlap exists in the sample of students in a school over a three-year period. Failing to take account of such overlap can create the illusion that school improvements are more stable than they are. Consider an extreme example in which schools' long-term average performance does not change at all and any observed change in test performance is solely due to sampling variation. We would expect a correlation of $-.5$ in the change in performance in consecutive years for any given grade level, because any change would be nonpersistent. However, suppose we were using the change in a school's combined performance on fourth- and fifth-grade tests in two consecutive years (the change between years t-1 and t-2 and the change between year t and t-1). Now suppose that the fourth-grade cohort from year t-1 is a particularly stellar group of kids. If we were only looking at fourth-grade students, we would expect that the change from year t-1 to t would be smaller than the change from t-2 to t-1, because a great group of students is unlikely to appear two years in a row. However, because that stellar group of fourth graders in year t-1 will repeat again as a stellar group of fifth graders in year t, any falloff in performance is likely to be muted, because that group is still being counted in a school's test score. When one combines test scores from consecutive grades, one will have an illusion of stability in the year-to-year improvements, but only because it takes a while for a particularly talented (or particularly untalented) group of students to work their way through the educational pipeline. It is an illusion because only after the random draw of students has been made in one year is there less uncertainty for the change the subsequent year. A school is either doomed or blessed by the sample of students who enrolled in previous years, but before those cohorts are observed, there is considerable uncertainty.

Figure 5 portrays the correlation in changes in scores in consecutive years when combining two grades that would not overlap in three years, second and fifth grade, and when combining two grades that do overlap, such as fourth and fifth grade. Combining second- and fifth-grade scores is like expanding the sample size. The consecutive year changes are less negatively correlated. The correlation for the largest quintile of schools was approximately $-.3$, implying that 60 percent of the variance in annual changes is nonpersistent. The correlation for the smallest quintile was $-.37$. However, when combining fourth- and fifth-grade scores, there is a discontinuous jump in the correlation. Instead of having a correlation of $-.3$, the correlation for all quintiles was close to $-.15$. Using schoolwide averages, combining test scores across grades, leaves the impression of greater stability.

Figure 5. Correlation in Change in Scores in Consecutive Years with Overlapping and Nonoverlapping Cohorts

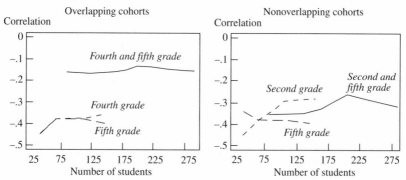

Disaggregating the Variance in Scores into Persistent and Nonpersistent Variation

Table 2 disaggregates the variation in school test scores into two parts: that due to sampling variation and that due to other sources of nonpersistent variance. We observe the total variation in mean test scores and mean gain scores among schools of different sizes. We also see the variance in their changes from one year to the next. We have an estimate of the proportion of the change that is due to nonpersistent variation. And we have an estimate of the amount of variation we would expect to result from sampling variation. Because sampling variation is by definition nonpersistent, we can use all these pieces of information to complete the puzzle and to generate an estimate of the variance due to nonpersistent factors other than sampling variation. The top panel of table 2 decomposes the variance in fourth-grade scores in a single year, the middle panel decomposes the variance in the mean gain in scores for students in a particular school, and the bottom panel decomposes the variance in the change in mean fourth-grade scores between years.

Three results in table 2 are worth highlighting. First, a school's average test performance in fourth grade can be measured reliably. Even among the smallest quintile of schools, nonpersistent factors account for only 20 percent of the variance between schools. Among the largest quintile of schools, such factors account for only 9 percent of the variance. However, when using mean test score levels unadjusted for students' incoming performance, much of that reliability may result from the unchanging characteristics of the populations feeding those schools and not necessarily from unchanging differences in school performance.

Table 2. Decomposing Variance in School Test Scores due to Sampling Variation and Other Nonpersistent Factors

School size	Average size	Total variance	Sampling variance	Other nonpersistent variance	Total proportion nonpersistent
Combined reading and math scores in fourth grade					
Smallest quintile	28	0.156	0.028	0.003	0.198
Middle quintile	56	0.137	0.015	0.005	0.144
Largest quintile	104	0.110	0.008	0.002	0.092
Combined reading and math gains between third and fourth grade					
Smallest quintile	28	0.053	0.008	0.022	0.575
Middle quintile	56	0.031	0.004	0.011	0.486
Largest quintile	104	0.019	0.002	0.003	0.286
Annual change in fourth-grade combined reading and math scores					
Smallest quintile	28	0.078	0.056	0.005	0.793
Middle quintile	56	0.055	0.030	0.009	0.728
Largest quintile	104	0.027	0.017	0.003	0.733

Note: All variances are expressed in units of student-level variances for fourth-grade scores. Sampling variance was calculated by dividing the average within-school variance (calculated separately for each school size quintile) by the sample size. The variance due to other nonpersistent factors was calculated as $-\rho_{\Delta_t \Delta_{t-1}} \sigma_{\Delta}^2 - \sigma_{Samp}^2$ for each quintile, where $\rho_{\Delta_t \Delta_{t-1}}$ is the correlation in adjacent year changes for that quintile, σ_{Δ}^2 is the variance in the change for that quintile, and σ_{Samp}^2 is the estimated sampling variance for that quintile. Sampling variance and other nonpersistent variance for changes in test score levels were estimated by doubling the variances in the top panel. For an alternative estimator and standard errors, see Thomas J. Kane and Douglas O. Staiger, "Improving School Accountability Measures," Working Paper 8156 (Cambridge, Mass.: National Bureau of Economic Research, March 2001).

Second, in contrast, mean gain scores or annual changes in a school's test score are measured remarkably unreliably. More than half (58 percent) of the variance among the smallest quintile of schools in mean gain scores is due to sampling variation and other nonpersistent factors. Among schools near the median size in North Carolina, nonpersistent factors are estimated to account for 49 percent of the variance. Changes in mean test scores from one year to the next are measured even more unreliably. More than three quarters (79 percent) of the variance in the annual change in mean test scores among the smallest quintile of schools is due to one-time, nonpersistent factors.

Third, increasing the sample size by combining information from more than one grade will do little to improve the reliability of changes in test scores over time. Even though the largest quintile of schools was roughly four times as large as the smallest quintile, the proportion of the variance in annual changes due to nonpersistent factors declined only slightly, from 79 percent to 73 percent. One might have the illusion of greater stability by combining multiple grades, but it is bought at the price of holding schools accountable for the past variation in the quality of incoming cohorts.

Instead of holding schools accountable for the level of their students' performance in a given year, a growing number of states are rewarding or punishing schools on the basis of changes in test scores or on mean gains in performance. Although either of the latter two outcomes may be closer conceptually to the goal of rewarding schools based upon their value-added or rewarding schools for improving student performance, both outcomes are difficult to discern. Schools simply do not differ much in terms of the change in their performance over time or in terms of the mean gain in performance achieved among their students. Moreover, changes over time are harder to measure. As a result, attempting to find such differences is like searching for a smaller needle in a bigger haystack.

Implications for the Design of Incentive Systems

According to *Education Week,* forty-five states were providing annual report cards on their schools' performance in January 2001 and twenty states were providing monetary rewards to teachers or schools based on their performance.[12] However, the incentive systems have been designed with little recognition of the statistical properties of the measures upon which they are based. Failure to take account of the volatility in test score measures can lead to weak incentives (or, in many cases, perverse incentives), while sending confusing signals to parents and to schools about which educational strategies are worth pursuing. We draw four lessons for the design of test-based incentive systems.

Lesson 1. Incentives targeted at schools with test scores at either extreme— rewards for those with very high scores or sanctions for those with very low scores—primarily affect small schools and imply weak incentives for large schools.

Each year since 1997, North Carolina has recognized the twenty-five elementary and middle schools in the state with the highest scores on the growth composite, a measure reflecting the average gain in performance among students enrolled at a school. Winning schools are honored at a statewide event in the fall, are given a banner to hang in their school, and receive financial awards.

One indicator of the volatility of test scores is the rarity of repeat winners. Between 1997 and 2001, 101 awards were given to schools ranking in the top twenty-five. (One year, two schools tied at the cutoff.) These 101 awards were won by 90 schools, with only 9 schools winning twice and only 1 school winning three times. No school was in the top twenty-five in all four years.

We have analyzed data for 840 elementary schools in North Carolina for which we had test score data for each year between 1994 and 1999. Of these schools, 59 were among the top twenty-five at some point between 1997 and 2000 (the top twenty-five each year included middle schools, which we are not analyzing here). Table 3 presents information on the mean gain scores in math in fourth and fifth grade, the variance in school mean gain scores, and the probability of winning a top twenty-five award by school size decile. Several results in table 3 are worth highlighting. First, the mean gain score is not strongly related to school size. Although the mean gain score over the period 1997 through 2000 among the smallest decile of schools was .032 student-level standard deviation units larger than the largest decile of schools (.021 – (–.011)), that difference was not statistically significant. Second, although mean performance varied little with school size, the variance between schools was much larger for small schools. The variance in mean gain scores among schools in the smallest size decile was nearly five times the variance among the largest decile of schools (.048 / .011). Third, as a result of this variability, schools in the smallest decile were much more likely to be among the top twenty-five schools at some point over the period. More than a quarter (27.7 percent) of the smallest decile of elementary schools were among the top twenty-five schools at some point over the four years the awards have been given. Even though their mean gains were not statistically different, the smallest schools were twenty-three times more likely to win a "Top 25" award than the largest schools (.277 / .012).

But, for the same reason, small schools are also overrepresented among those with extremely low test scores. Also beginning in 1997, the state assigned assistance teams to intervene in schools that had the poorest performance on the state tests and that also did not meet growth targets from the previous year. Table 3 also reports the proportion of schools in each school size decile that was assigned an assistance team because of extremely low test scores in a given year. All but one of the elementary schools assigned an assistance team was in the bottom four deciles by school size. (The smallest decile of schools would have received an even larger share of the assistance teams, except for a rule requiring the proportion of students scoring below grade level to be statistically significantly less than 50 percent.)

The North Carolina accountability system provides other rewards that do not operate solely at the extremes. For example, roughly two-thirds of the

Table 3. Awards and Sanctions among Elementary Schools in North Carolina

School size	Mean gain in math	Between-school variance in mean gain in math	Percent ever "Top 25," 1997–2000	Percent ever assigned assistance team, 1997–2000
Smallest decile	.020	.048	27.7	1.2
Second	-.007	.030	11.8	4.7
Third	.008	.028	8.2	7.1
Fourth	.009	.026	3.6	1.2
Fifth	-.002	.024	2.4	0
Sixth	.019	.018	3.6	0
Seventh	.007	.016	4.8	0
Eighth	.006	.016	7.1	0
Ninth	-.007	.015	0	1.2
Largest decile	-.011	.011	1.2	0
Total	.004	.023	7.0	1.5

Note: The table refers to the 840 regular public elementary schools for which the authors had data from 1994 through 2000. Charter schools are not included.

schools in 1999 were identified as having achieved exemplary growth and these schools received the lion's share of the award money. Therefore, we highlight the "Top 25" award not to characterize the North Carolina system as a whole, but to cite an example of the type of award program that is particularly susceptible to sampling variation.

In 2001 California planned to spend a total of $677 million on school and teacher bonuses. One component of the accountability system will provide bonuses of up to $25,000 to teachers in schools with the largest improvements in test scores between 1999 and 2000. (The state is expecting to spend $100 million on this component of the system alone.) Each school was given an overall target, based upon their 1999 scores. (Schools with lower 1999 scores faced higher targets for improvement.) To be eligible for the largest bonuses, a school had to have schoolwide scores below the median school in 1999, have no decline in test scores between 1998 and 1999, and have at least one hundred students.[13] Figure 6 plots the change in API scores by school size between 1999 and 2000 for those schools that met these requirements. One thousand teachers in schools with the largest improvements will receive $25,000 bonuses. Then, 3,750 teachers in schools with the next largest improvements in test scores will receive $10,000 bonuses. Finally, 7,500 teachers will receive $5,000 bonuses. The winners of the largest awards will generally be at smaller than median-size schools. Given the importance of sampling variation, this is hardly a surprise. Particularly when it comes to changes in test scores over time, the outlier schools will tend to be small schools.

Figure 6. Improvements in Test Scores among California Schools Eligible to Win Teacher Bonuses by School Size

Test score growth—target

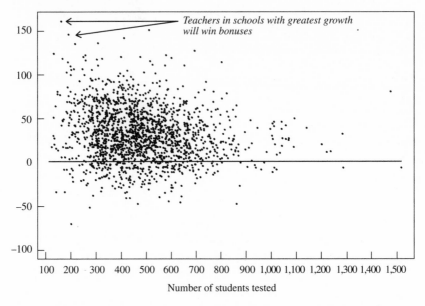

Number of students tested

Note: Reflecting program rules, the figure has been drawn only for those elementary schools in the bottom five deciles of Academic Performance Index scores in 1999, with non-negative changes in test scores between 1998 and 1999, with at least one hundred students tested.

Rewards or sanctions for extreme test scores or large changes in test scores have little impact on large schools, because large schools have little chance of ever achieving the extremes. Figure 7 illustrates the point with a hypothetical example. Suppose a small and a large school had the same expected performance. But because of sampling variation and other factors that can lead to temporary changes in scores, each school faces a range of possible test scores next year, even if they do nothing. As portrayed in figure 7, the range of potential test scores is likely to be wider for the small school than for the larger school. Suppose the state were to establish some threshold, above which a school won an award. If, as in figure 7, the threshold is established far above both schools' expected performance, the large school will have little chance of winning the award if it does nothing and the small school will have a non-negligible chance of winning the award if it does nothing. Because the probability of winning the award is represented by the area to the right of the threshold in the graph, the marginal effect of improving one's expected per-

Figure 7. Precision of Test Score Measures and Incentive Effects

Density function for observed performance

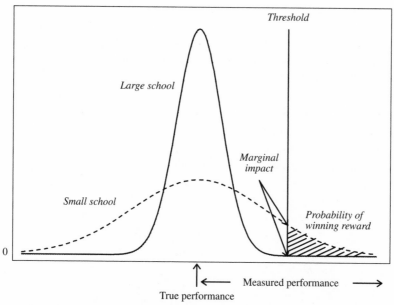

formance on the likelihood of winning the award is measured by the height of the curve as it crosses the threshold. In the hypothetical example portrayed in figure 7, the marginal incentive is essentially zero for the large school and only slightly larger for the small school. (Note that the opposite would be true if the threshold were established close to both schools' expected performance and that large schools would have a stronger incentive.)

A single threshold at either extreme is likely to be irrelevant for schools that are large, because the marginal effect of improving their performance on the likelihood of winning will be small. If the marginal costs of improving are also higher at large schools, the problem of weak incentives for large schools would only be compounded. While we do not observe the marginal costs of improving, the costs of coordinating the efforts of a larger number of teachers to implement a new curriculum likely would be larger.

A remedy would be to establish different thresholds for different size schools, such that the marginal net payoff to improving is similar for small and large schools, or offer different payoffs to small and large schools. For example, grouping schools according to size (as is done in high school sports) and giving awards to the top 5 percent in each size class tend to even out the incentives (and disparities) between large and small schools. An alternative solution would be to establish thresholds closer to the middle of the test score distribution, where the differential in marginal payoffs is less extreme.

Helen F. Ladd and Charles Clotfelter as well as David Grissmer and his colleagues report evidence suggesting that schools respond to incentives by raising student performance.[14] However, the long-term impacts of incentives may be substantially different from the short-term impacts. Even if school teachers are not sufficiently aware of the forces at work in an incentive system to analyze their incentives in a manner similar to that in figure 7, they may infer the magnitudes of the marginal incentives from their own experience over time. If their best efforts are rewarded with failure one year and less work the following year is rewarded with success, they are likely to form their own estimates of the value of their effort. Even if they do not fully recognize the statistical structure underlying their experience, teachers and principals are likely to learn over time about the impact of their efforts on their chances of winning an award. As a result, the long-term impacts on schools could be different from the short-term impacts.

Lesson 2. Incentive systems establishing separate thresholds for each racial or ethnic subgroup present a disadvantage to racially integrated schools. They can generate perverse incentives for districts to segregate their students.

The accountability system in a number of states, including California and Texas, establishes separate growth expectations for racial or ethnic subgroups. The presumed purpose of such rules is to maintain schools' incentive to raise the performance of all youth and to raise the cost to teachers and administrators of limiting their efforts to only one racial group. However, because the number of students in any particular racial group can be small, scores for these students are often volatile. For a racially integrated school, winning an award is analogous to correctly calling three or four coin tosses in a row, instead of a single toss.[15] As a result, at any given level of overall improvement, a racially integrated school is much less likely to win an award than a racially homogeneous school.

In California, to be numerically significant, a group must represent at least 15 percent of the student body and contain more than thirty students, or represent more than one hundred students regardless of their percentage. There are eight different groups that could qualify as numerically significant, depending upon the number of students in each group in a school: African American, American Indian (or Alaska Native), Asian, Filipino, Hispanic, Pacific Islander, white non-Hispanic, and socioeconomically disadvantaged students.[16]

Table 4. Proportion of California Elementary Schools Winning Governor's Performance Awards by School Size and Number of Numerically Significant Subgroups

School size quintile	Number of numerically significant subgroups				Total
	1	*2*	*3*	*4+*	*Total*
Smallest quintile					
Proportion winning	.824	.729	.587	.471	.683
Average growth in API 1999–2000	33.4	45.6	42.2	36.0	41.2
Number of schools	204	343	349	51	947
Second quintile					
Proportion winning	.886	.769	.690	.670	.749
Average growth in API 1999–2000	29.9	42.6	42.2	43.9	40.5
Number of schools	158	337	358	94	947
Third quintile					
Proportion winning	.853	.795	.708	.667	.756
Average growth in API 1999–2000	26.8	36.3	38.9	44.6	36.6
Number of schools	156	308	390	93	947
Fourth quintile					
Proportion winning	.903	.823	.776	.656	.799
Average growth in API 1999–2000	28.0	41.8	39.5	40.8	38.7
Number of schools	144	328	379	96	947
Largest quintile					
Proportion winning	.876	.776	.726	.686	.755
Average growth in API 1999–2000	29.5	37.9	36.9	40.5	37.0
Number of schools	89	370	387	102	948
Total					
Proportion winning	.864	.778	.699	.647	.749
Average growth in API 1999–2000	29.8	40.9	39.9	41.7	38.8
Number of schools	751	1,686	1,863	436	4,736

Note: API = Academic Performance Index. Reflecting the rules of the Governor's Performance Award program, the table was limited to elementary schools with more than one hundred students.

Table 4 reports the proportion of California elementary schools winning the Governor's Performance Award by school size quintile and number of numerically significant subgroups in each school. Among the smallest quintile of elementary schools, racially heterogeneous schools were almost half as likely to win a Governor's Performance Award as racially homogeneous schools: 47 percent of schools with four or more racial, ethnic, or socioeconomic subgroups won a Governor's Performance Award as opposed to 82 percent of similar-size schools with only one numerically significant group. This is particularly ironic given that the more integrated schools had slightly larger overall growth in performance between 1999 and 2000 (36.0 API points versus 33.4 points). Moreover, although the results are not reported in table 4 because of space limitations, such schools witnessed larger gains on average for African American and Latino students than for white students.

Because any numerically significant subgroups will be larger in size (and, as a result, their scores less volatile), the gap between homogeneous and heterogeneous schools is slightly smaller among larger schools. Among schools in the largest size quintile, homogeneous schools were 28 percent more likely to win a Governor's Performance Award (.876 / .686), even though the more heterogeneous schools had greater improvements in overall test scores (40.5 API points as opposed to 29.5).

The data in table 4 have at least two important implications. First, under such rules, a district would have a strong incentive to segregate by race or ethnicity. For instance, suppose there were four small schools in a district, each being 25 percent African American, 25 percent Latino, 25 percent Asian American, and 25 percent white, non-Hispanic. According to the results in table 4, a district could nearly double each school's chance of winning an award simply by segregating each group and creating four racially homogeneous schools.

Second, because minority youth are more likely to attend heterogeneous schools than white non-Hispanic youth, the rules put the average school enrolling minority students at a disadvantage in the pursuit of award money. For instance, in table 4, the addition of each racial or ethnic subgroup lowers a school's chance of winning an award by roughly 9 percentage points on average. The average number of subgroups in the schools attended by African American student was 2.8; the average number of subgroups in the schools attended by white non-Hispanic students was 2.2. If each school had an equal chance of winning an award, the average school attended by an African American youth would have a 74.9 percent probability of winning an award. Therefore, a rough estimate would suggest that the measure has the effect of taking 7 percent of the money that would otherwise have gone to schools attended by African American youth and handing it to schools enrolling white, non-Hispanic youth ((2.8 − 2.2) * (.09 / .749) = .072).[17]

Although the costs of the subgroup targets are clear, the benefits are uncertain. Policymakers might want to know whether the rules force schools to focus more on the achievement of minority youth. If so, some consideration of the test scores of racial or ethnic subgroups may be worthwhile, despite the costs. One way to estimate this impact would be to compare the improvements for minority youth in schools where they are just above and just below the minimum percentage required to qualify as a separate subgroup. We have done so with data from Texas. The trend in test scores for African American and Latino youth in schools where they were insufficiently numerous to qualify as a separate subgroup (in Texas, between 5 and 10 percent) was identical to the trend for African American and Latino youth in schools where their percentage of enrollment was high enough to qualify for a separate standard.[18] Despite the costs, the evidence does not suggest that such thresholds force schools to focus on the performance of disadvantaged minority youth.

Lesson 3. As a tool for identifying best practice or fastest improvement, annual test scores are generally unreliable. More efficient ways exist to pool information across schools and across years to identify those schools worth emulating.

When designing incentive systems to encourage schools to do the right thing, one cares about the absolute amount of imprecision in school test score measures and how that imprecision may vary by school size. The more imprecise the measures are, the weaker the incentives tend to be. However, policymakers and school administrators often are uncertain (or, at least, they disagree) about what the right thing is. The state may also have an interest in helping to identify the schools that are worth emulating.[19] If the goal of an accountability system is not only to provide incentives, but also to help identify success, the absolute amount of imprecision and the amount of imprecision relative to the degree of underlying differences determine the likelihood of success in the search for exemplars.[20]

Building upon work by Mark McClellan and Douglas Staiger in rating hospital performance, we have proposed a simple technique for estimating the amount of signal and noise in school test score measures and to use that information to generate filtered estimates of school quality that provide much better information about a school's performance.[21] Suppose that a school administrator is attempting to evaluate a particular school's performance based on the mean test scores of the students from that school in the most recent two years. Consider the following three possible approaches: (1) use only the most recent score for a school, (2) construct a simple average of the school's scores from the two recent years, and (3) ignore the school's scores and assume that student performance in the school is equal to the state average. To minimize mistakes, the best choice among these three approaches depends on two important considerations: the signal-to-noise ratio in the school's data and the correlation in performance across years. For example, if the average test scores for the school were based on only a few dozen students and school performance did not appear to vary much across the state, then one would be tempted to choose the last option—place less weight on the school's scores because of their low signal-to-noise ratio and heavily weight the state average.

Alternatively, if that school performance seemed to change slowly over time, one might choose the second option in hopes that averaging the data over two years would reduce the noise in the estimates by effectively increasing the sample size in the school. Even with large samples of students being tested, one might want to average over years if idiosyncratic factors such as the weather on the day of the test affected scores from any single year. Finally, one would tend to choose the first option and rely solely on scores from the most recent year, if such idiosyncratic factors were unimportant, if the school's estimate was based on a very large sample of students, and if considerable persistent change is evident over time.

Our method of creating filtered estimates formalizes the intuition from this simple example. The filtered estimates are a combination of the school's own test score, the state average, and the school's test scores from past years, other grades, or other subjects. Table 5 compares the mean performance in 1999 for North Carolina elementary schools ranking in the top 10 percent in fifth-grade math gains on two different measures: the simple means of math gains in 1997 and the filtered prediction that would have been made of a school's performance in 1999 using all of the data available through 1997. Thus, both predictions use only the data from 1997 or before. However, the filtered prediction incorporates information from reading scores and from prior years, and it reins in the prediction according to the amount of sampling variation and nonpersistent fluctuation in the data.

Table 5 reports the mean 1999 performance, cross-tabulated by whether or not the school was in the top 10 percent using the filtering technique and using the naive estimate based upon the actual 1997 scores. Sixty-five schools were identified as being in the top 10 percent as of 1997 using both the naive and the filtered predictions, and these schools scored .15 student-level standard deviations higher than the mean school two years later in 1999. However, among the schools where the two methods disagreed, there were large differences in performance. For instance, among the twenty-five schools that the filtering method identified as being in the top 10 percent that were not in the top 10 percent on the 1997 actual scores, the average performance on fifth-grade math gains was .124 student-level standard deviations above the average in 1999. Among the twenty-five schools chosen using actual 1997 scores that were not chosen using the filtering technique, scores were .022 standard deviations lower than the average school in 1999. The next-to-last column and row in table 5 report the difference in mean scores moving across the first two columns or first two rows. Among those that were not identified as being in

Table 5. Performance of North Carolina Schools in 1999 Identified as in the Top 10 Percent in 1997, Based on Actual and Filtered Test Scores

		Based on actual 1997 score				
		School not in top 10 percent	*School in top 10 percent*	*Row total*	*Difference between top 10 percent and the rest*	*Expected difference*
Based on filtered prediction of 1999 score (from 1997)	School not in top 10 percent	-0.016 (0.007) [N = 779]	-0.022 (0.066) [N = 25]	-0.016 (0.007) [N = 804]	-0.006 (0.043)	0.385 (0.034)
	School in top 10 percent	0.124 (0.050) [N = 25]	0.151 (0.026) [N = 65]	0.144 (0.023) [N = 90]	0.027 (0.052)	0.236 (0.036)
	Column total	-0.012 (0.007) [N = 804]	0.103 (0.027) [N = 90]	0 (0) [N = 894]	0.115 (0.024)	0.453 (0.019)
	Difference between top 10 percent and the rest	0.140 (0.042)	0.173 (0.059)	0.160 (0.023)		
	Expected difference	0.147 (0.013)	0.095 (0.012)	0.180 (0.007)		

Note: Within the box, the entries report the mean of the fifth-grade math gain score in 1999, along with standard errors of these estimates and the sample size in each cell. The columns of the table use actual scores in 1997 to assign schools to the top 10 percent and to calculate the expected difference between the top 10 percent and the rest. The rows of the table use filtered predictions of 1999 scores, based only on data from 1994–97, to assign schools to the top 10 percent.

the top 10 percent by the filtering method, knowing that they were in the top 10 percent on the actual 1997 score provided little information regarding test scores. The test scores were –.006 standard deviations lower on average holding the filtered prediction constant. In contrast, among those not identified as being in the top 10 percent on actual 1997 scores, knowing that they were selected using the filtering method was associated with a .140 standard deviation difference in performance. Apparently, the filtering method was much more successful in picking schools that were likely to perform well in 1999.

Moreover, the filtering technique provides a much more realistic expectation of the magnitude of the performance differences. As reported in the last column of table 5, the schools in the top 10 percent on the actual test in 1997 scored .453 standard deviations higher than the average school in 1997. If we had naively expected them to continue that performance, we would have been disappointed, because the actual difference in performance was only .115

standard deviations. Among those who were chosen using the filtering method, we would have predicted that they would have scored .180 standard deviations higher than the average school in 1999 based upon their performance before 1998. The actual difference in performance for these schools was .160 standard deviations.

Table 6 compares the R^2 one would have obtained using three different methods to predict the 1998 and 1999 test scores of schools using only the information available before 1998. The first method is the filtering method. The second method is using the actual 1997 score as the prediction for the 1998 and 1999 scores. The third method uses the four-year average of math performance before 1998 (1994–97) to predict 1998 and 1999.

Whether one is trying to anticipate math or reading levels or gains in fifth grade, the filtering method leads to greater accuracy in prediction. The R^2 in predicting fifth-grade math levels was .41 using the filtering method, .19 using the 1997 score, and .29 using the 1994–97 average. The filtering method also calculates a weighted average using the 1994–97 scores, but it adjusts the weights according to sample size (attaching a larger weight to more recent scores for large schools) and uses both the math and reading score histories in predicting either. In so doing, it does much better than a simple average of test scores over 1994–97.

In predicting math or reading gain scores in 1998, the second column reports negative R^2 when using the 1997 scores alone. A negative R^2 implies that one would have had less squared error in prediction by completely ignoring the individual scores from 1997 and simply predicting that performance in every school would be equal to the state average. One could probably do even better by not ignoring the 1997 score, but simply applying a coefficient of less than 1 to the 1997 score in predicting future scores. That is essentially what the filtering method does, while recognizing that the optimal coefficient on the 1997 score (and even earlier scores) will depend upon the amount of nonpersistent noise in the indicator as well as the school size.

Although it performs better than either the 1997 score or the 1994–97 average in predicting 1998 and 1999 gains, the R^2 using the filtering method is only .16 on math gains and .04 on reading gains. This hardly seems to be cause for much celebration, until one realizes that even if the filtering method were completely accurate in predicting the persistent portion of school test scores, the R^2 would be less than 1 simply because a large share of the variation in school performance is due to sampling variation or other nonpersistent

Table 6. Comparison of the Accuracy of Alternative Forecasts of 1998 and 1999 Test Scores Using North Carolina Data

	Unweighted R^2 when forecasting 1998 and 1999 scores being predicted under alternative uses of 1993–97 data					
	Predicting scores in 1998 (one-year ahead forecast R^2)			*Predicting scores in 1999 (two-year ahead forecast R^2)*		
Test score being predicted	*Filtered prediction*	*1997 Score*	*Average score, 1994–97*	*Filtered prediction*	*1997 Score*	*Average score, 1994–97*
Adjusted score						
Fifth-grade math	0.41	0.19	0.29	0.27	-0.02	0.13
Fifth-grade reading	0.39	0.13	0.33	0.31	-0.05	0.24
Gain score						
Fifth-grade math	0.16	-0.27	0.09	0.12	-0.42	-0.01
Fifth-grade reading	0.04	-0.93	-0.12	0.04	-0.85	-0.20

Note: The filtered prediction is an out-of-sample prediction, generated using only the 1993–97 data.

types of variation. Because of these entirely unpredictable types of error, the highest R^2 one could have hoped for would have been .75 in predicting math levels, .60 in predicting reading levels, .55 for math gains, and .35 in reading gains. For math gains, for instance, the filtering method was able to predict 16 percentage points of the 55 percentage points that one ever had a hope of predicting, implying an R^2 for the systematic portion of school test scores of .16 / .55 = .29.

One disadvantage of the filtering technique is that it is much less transparent.[22] The average parent, teacher, or school principal is likely to be familiar with the idea of computing an arithmetic mean of test scores in a school; the average parent or principal is certainly unlikely to be familiar with empirical Bayes techniques. However, a number of mysterious calculations are involved in creating a scale for test scores that are currently well tolerated. To start, parents are likely to have only a very loose understanding of the specific items on the test. (Admittedly, teachers and principals are probably better informed about test content.) Moreover, any given student's test score is generally not a percent correct, but a weighted average of the individual items on the test. Parents and all but a few teachers are unfamiliar with the methods used to calculate these weights. The filtering technique we are proposing could be used to provide an index of school performance, and beyond an intuitive description of the techniques involved, it might be as well tolerated as the scaling process is already.

Lesson 4. When evaluating the impact of policies on changes in test scores over time, one must take into account the fluctuations in test scores that are likely to occur naturally.

North Carolina in 1997 identified fifteen elementary and middle schools with poor performance in both levels and gains and assigned assistance teams of three to five educators to work in these schools. The next year, all of the schools had improved enough to escape being designated as low-performing. In summarizing the results of that first year, the state Department of Public Instruction claimed an important victory:

> Last year, the assistance teams of 3–5 educators each worked in 15 schools, helping staff to align the instructional program with the Standard Course of Study, modeling and demonstrating effective instructional practices, coaching and mentoring teachers and locating additional resources for the schools. As a result of this assistance and extra help provided by local school systems, nearly all of these schools made exemplary growth this year and none are identified as low performing.[23]

The value of the assistance teams was lauded in *Education Week*'s annual summary of the progress of school reform efforts in the states.[24] However, given the amount of sampling variation and other nonpersistent fluctuations in test score levels and gains, schools with particularly low test scores in one year would be expected to bounce back in subsequent years.

We had test score data from 1994 through 1999 for thirty-five elementary schools that won a "Top 25" school award in either 1997 or 1998 as well as for ten elementary schools that were assigned an assistance team in 1997 or 1998. Table 7 reports fourth-grade test scores the year before, the year after, and the year that each school either won the award or sanction. (For those assigned assistance teams, the help did not arrive at the school until the year after their low scores merited the assignment.)

For the average school winning a "Top 25" award, the year of the award is clearly an aberrant year. In the year of the award, their scores were .230 student-level standard deviations above the mean gain. However, in both the year before their award and the year after, their gain scores were slightly below the mean gain.

Moreover, the schools that were assigned assistance teams seem to have had a particularly bad year the year of their receiving the sanction. In the year before assignment, such schools had an average fourth-grade combined reading and math test score .668 student-level standard deviations below the average school. This reveals that they were weak schools the year before being sanctioned. However, in the year of assignment, their average score

Table 7. Fourth-Grade Test Scores before and after Sanction or Reward in North Carolina

Group of schools	Year before award or sanction	Year of award or sanction	Year after award or sanction	Year after– year before	Ratio of $S_{t+1}-S_{t-1}/$ $S_{t+1}-S_t$
"Top 25" in 1997–98					
Math + reading gain score	-.003	.230	-.064	-.062[a] (.164)[b]	.211
Assistance team in 1997–98					
Math + reading test score	-.668	-.786	-.523	.145[a] (.059)[b]	.551
Math + reading gain score	-.078	-.134	.078	.156[a] (.006)[b]	.735

Note: Test scores are in units of student-level standard deviations. The mean test scores across all schools in each year have been subtracted. If a single school won an award more than once, we used its first award. Thirty-five elementary schools in our sample won a "Top 25" award in 1997 or 1998 based upon their gain scores. Ten elementary schools in our sample were assigned an assistance team in 1997 or 1998 based upon a combination of low test scores and low gain scores.

a. Difference.
b. *p*-value.

was even lower, .786 student-level standard deviations below the average school. The year after assignment, their scores seemed to rebound to .523 student-level standard deviations below the mean.

Because the year of assignment was a bad year and because change is volatile, one is likely to greatly overestimate the impact of assistance teams by taking the change in performance in the year after assignment. In table 7, we estimate the impact of the assistance teams by taking the difference in scores in the year after assignment relative to the scores in the year before assignment. That estimate suggests that schools that were assigned assistance teams may have improved their performance over time, by a fairly sizable .145 student-level standard deviations. (Their mean gain also improved by .156 student-level standard deviations.) Both such estimates would be considered statistically significant at the .059 and .006 levels. However, as reported in the last column of table 7, such an estimate of the impact is between only 55 and 73 percent as large, respectively, as one would have seen using the year of assignment as the base year.

Conclusion

To date, school accountability systems have been designed with little recognition of the statistical properties of the measures upon which they are based. For instance, if there were little sampling variation and if changes in performance were largely persistent, one might want to focus on a school's mean value-added in the most recent year or on the changes in schoolwide scores over the most recent two years. However, such reasoning ignores an important trade-off: Changes in performance and mean value-added are very difficult to recognize and reward with only two years of test score data. An accountability system that seems reasonable in a world of persistent rates of change and easy-to-discern differences in value-added may generate weak or even perverse incentives when implemented in the world of volatile test scores.

The long-term effects on the morale and motivation of school personnel remain to be seen. Given the apparent role of chance in some of the incentive regimes being implemented, those effects could be significantly different from the short-term impacts. In 1967 psychologists Martin E. P. Seligman and Steven F. Maier published the results of an experiment in which one group of dogs was strapped into a harness and administered a series of electrical shocks through electrodes attached to their feet.[25] The dogs developed a strong aversion to such treatment. Later, the same dogs were transferred into a room in which they were administered similar shocks through the floor. The dogs merely had to jump over a shoulder-height barrier to escape from the shocks. However, rather than flee, the dogs lay down on the floor and accepted the shocks. Why the apparently self-destructive behavior? In addition to learning that they did not like being shocked, the first group of dogs apparently learned that they could do little to avoid the shocks. (A second group of dogs, which was able to stop the shocks during the first stage of the experiment by tapping a paddle, did flee the shocks in the second stage by jumping over the barrier.) In states' efforts to encourage school personnel to focus on student performance, it is not sufficient to create desirable rewards or noxious sanctions attached to student performance. Caution must be taken about the lessons teachers and principals are learning about their ability to determine those outcomes and about how their efforts will be rewarded.

However, the results of our research should not be interpreted as implying that all accountability systems are necessarily flawed. We provided four simple principles for improving existing systems. First, rewards and bonuses should not be limited to schools with extreme scores. To preserve incentives for large schools, states should either establish separate thresholds for schools of different sizes or, slightly less effective, provide smaller rewards to schools closer to the middle of the test score distribution. Second, rules making any rewards contingent on improvement in each racial group present a great disadvantage to integrated schools and generate a number of perverse incentives that may harm rather than help minority students. Third, when seeking to identify schools that are improving the most or to identify schools with the highest mean value-added, one can generate much more reliable estimates by pooling information across years and across outcomes. In earlier research, we describe an estimator that does that in a more efficient way than simply taking a simple mean across as many years as possible.[26] Finally, when evaluating the impact of policies that operate on schools at either extreme of the distribution, one has to recognize the importance of volatility and be careful about the choice of a baseline.

Comment by David Grissmer

The issue addressed by Thomas J. Kane and Douglas O. Staiger is whether schools can reliably be chosen for rewards or sanctions based on year-to-year test score gains. The question is whether picking schools based on gains identifies good or bad schools, or lucky or unlucky schools. The authors' analysis convincingly concludes that methods relying on gain scores at a given grade are mostly identifying lucky and unlucky schools, not good and bad schools. The reason for misidentification is that the variance due to sampling and other sources of noise can be a significant portion of the variance in gains across schools. In this area, standards-based reform is far ahead of statistical reliability.

This paper required several readings to extract the nub of the argument and analysis. I think the exposition can be improved. Basically the focus is on five quantities and their relationship and relative size: between-school score variance in annual scores, between-school variance in score gains from grade to grade, between-school variance in year-to-year score changes at a given grade, sampling variance, and variance from other sources of noise.[27] The basic argument is that to reliably identify good and bad schools by any criteria requires that the signal be much greater than the sources of noise. The signal in this case is the portion of a score or score gain that can be attributed to school effort. The noise is caused by sampling variability from a hypothetical student population and other sources of random noise.

The paper estimates these parameters using data from North Carolina and California, and it shows that the sources of noise are too large relative to the signal to allow reliable identification of good or bad schools. More often than not, the reason a school ends up near the top or bottom of a ranking can be attributed to random factors and not real improvement. Also because the sampling variation decreases with school size, small schools are disproportionately represented at both the top and bottom part of rankings. Perhaps as important, systems that use criteria involving separate consideration of scores by race or ethnicity are likely to make even poorer identification.

I like the way the paper is designed. The authors develop a statistical model, make estimations for parameters in the model, make predictions from the model, and use the data to verify the predictions. The authors draw out the important policy implications and provide guidance on how to improve the identification process.

The parameters are estimated using third- and fourth-grade data from North Carolina. The method used to estimate random sources of noise outside sampling variability is neat. The model and parameter estimations lead to predictions that use of year-to-year gain scores leads to small schools being disproportionately identified as good or bad schools. This prediction is verified in two ways. First, small schools in North Carolina have over twenty times the probability of being identified in the top distribution of rewarded schools. Second, rarely are schools that are rewarded in one year also rewarded in the following years. This nonpersistence of performance implies that nonpersistence sources of error are probably a major component of the actual gains.

The situation gets even worse if rewards or sanctions depend on score gains by racial or ethnic groups within grades, which is an increasingly common practice. The identification is then based on even smaller sample sizes, and the chances of high gains of all racial or ethnic groups become even more dependent on chance. The policy implications cited by the authors include all the morale issues arising from having rewards or sanctions based on factors other than real performance to misidentifying the reasons that schools are improving by focusing on the wrong schools.

The authors analyze possible solutions to the problem of increasing the reliability of the identification process. They analyze pooling scores schoolwide instead of using individual grade scores. The increased reliability from this type of pooling is not as large as one would expect from the increased sample size because student characteristics persist from grade to grade as a cohort flows through grades. Using score gains averaged over longer time periods— that is, sustained high or low performance—can significantly improve reliability. The authors also suggest a more sophisticated statistical filtering technique designed to improve the signal-to-noise ratio.

Overall, the paper is an outstanding contribution at three levels: the methodology, the quality of results, and the policy implications. The methodology—used more often in physics, statistics, and information theory—brings a new perspective and set of tools to analysis of achievement data. More of this kind of analysis and its logical extensions likely will be seen in the future. The results are robust and almost beyond argument. This paper may be one of only a few that would generate widespread consensus among researchers. Finally, this paper has immediate and important policy implications for educational policy. The questions addressed are important ones currently being considered in national legislation and across many states. Following the advice in the paper will improve public policy in education.

My comments are directed to making the statistical model reflect the more complex aspects of the educational system and to place the results in a wider perspective on the results of accountability systems across states. The current statistical models underlying the analysis do not yet reflect much of the complexity of the system. At least three other factors affect the variance of gain scores besides sampling that change with the number of students in a grade in a school. The first factor is that the variance in teachers will be different in schools with more students at a given grade. Small schools will have one teacher per grade while larger schools will have several classes and teachers per grade. Assuming that teachers are randomly assigned and have differential effects on achievement, then this teacher effect would narrow variance in larger schools.

The second factor is that the likelihood of being in a small class also varies by size of school. Schools with fewer students are more likely to be in smaller classes than schools with more students. Class sizes are often determined by setting a limit on class size, which requires the creation of another class if that limit is exceeded. For instance, if the limit is twenty-five but thirty students enroll, then two classes of fifteen will be created. As the number of students increases, the average class size will approach the limit. Compelling experimental evidence exists to suggest class size affects achievement, implying that more variance is introduced in smaller schools than larger schools as a result of this effect.[28] Finally, teacher turnover is higher in urban areas where school sizes are larger. Higher teacher turnover will increase variance in gain scores for larger schools.

The first two effects are intrinsic characteristics of small and large schools and largely independent of educational policy. Like sampling variability, they increase the variance in small schools and exacerbate the effects described by the authors. A more complex statistical model could capture these effects. The effect on variance of teacher turnover probably can be influenced by educational policy and cannot automatically be classified as noise instead of part of a real signal.

The question of separating effects into persistent and nonpersistent is also more complex than modeled in the present analysis, but the models can be extended to include this complexity. Some effects can persist over several years and then decay, and persistence can be different depending upon types of students. The Tennessee experimental results seem to imply that the effects persist if students are in small classes for three to four years, but not for one to two years.[29] A good teacher may also have an effect not only on students in the present grade, but also in future grades. A 2000 study by David W. Grissmer and others suggested that persistence effects can be captured only by interaction terms between schooling conditions in early years and later years.[30] Persistence may be easier to achieve with early interventions, but much more difficult with later interventions. The complexity of persistence effects makes modeling only adjoining years to separate persistence and nonpersistence problematic.

The current results are not very damaging to the standards-based accountability movement for two reasons. First, much of the problem can be fixed by using gains over several years. Second, financial rewards are not central to successful accountability systems. Successful accountability relies primarily on having more and better quality data linked to standards that can be used to diagnose problems from the student to the teacher to the school to the school district. The availability and informed utilization of the data by parents, teachers, principals, school districts, and state policymakers provide increased achievement. Standards together with these data allow better resource allocation from the student to the state and represent the central component of accountability, not financial rewards.

Finally, this is one of the few papers that I have ever read in education where I thought that a consensus among researchers is possible. However, no consensus mechanism in educational research would allow this consensus to be recognized. Other areas of research such as health have consensus panels that are able to generate an important dialogue about research results. The absence of such mechanisms in education is a significant problem for improving the quality of research and informing public policy.

Comment by Helen F. Ladd

Most states now have educational accountability systems based on student achievement as measured by test scores. Such systems can direct attention to districts, schools, individual teachers or students, or some combination thereof. In their excellent paper, Thomas J. Kane and Douglas O. Staiger treat schools as the unit of accountability. That is, they focus on accountability programs in which states measure the effectiveness of individual schools and then use those measures as the basis for providing awards, imposing sanctions, giving assistance, or identifying exemplars.

As the authors emphasize, many states have introduced such programs without a full understanding of the underlying statistical characteristics of relevant measures. In light of this observation, the primary contribution of the paper is methodological. Kane and Staiger explain and document the importance of one basic characteristic, the volatility of the measures, using data from North Carolina and California elementary schools. They then spell out the implications of that volatility for the design and use of measures of school performance. By combining sophisticated, but intuitively understandable, statistical analysis with clear and compelling applications to the policy debate, the authors provide some powerful new insights into an important current policy issue.

The Problem of Volatility

A school's performance can be measured in at least three generic ways: as the mean of student test scores in the school, as the mean of the gains in student test scores during a year, or as the average annual change in test scores in the same grade from one year to the next. Regardless of the approach, the measures will be subject to what the authors refer to as nonpersistent variation across schools. This nonpersistent chance variation, or noise, refers to variation that does not reflect true differences in performance across schools. Such noise has two sources: sampling variation that arises because of the characteristics of the particular samples of students being tested and other nonpersistent variation that arises because of one-time idiosyncratic factors that influence test results in any particular year, such as a disruption in the classroom or in the school.

The relevant policy question is how large the nonpersistent variation is relative to the true signal or, in practice, relative to the total observed variation. Determining how much of the total variation in student performance across schools is noise is not straightforward and requires various assumptions that Kane and Staiger spell out. The basic idea is that the noise share can be estimated from information about how the changes in test scores in each school are correlated over time. The more negatively correlated these changes are, the greater is the share of nonpersistent variation. Using this method, Kane and Staiger conclude that the nonpersistent variation sometimes accounts for a large share of the total variation.

The magnitudes emerge most clearly in table 2, which is based on data from North Carolina elementary schools. That table indicates that the nonpersistent variation accounts for almost 15 percent of the total variation in levels of fourth-grade test scores across schools, almost 50 percent of the total variation in gains in scores during fourth grade, and a whopping 73 percent of the variation in annual changes in fourth-grade scores. The table also shows that the size of the school matters: The ratio of noise to total variation across schools is significantly larger for small schools than for larger schools.

Are these large noise ratios plausible? Do the patterns make sense? To answer these questions, it is useful to split the nonpersistent variation into the sampling variance and other persistent variance. Based on standard statistical theory, the sampling variance can be calculated as the average variance within schools divided by the average sample size. Hence the sampling variation is larger for small than for large schools. Other persistent variation is then calculated as the residual difference between the total nonpersistent variance and the sampling variance.

The numbers in table 2 indicate that the sampling variation alone accounts for about 11 percent of the total variation for a medium-size school when levels of test scores are used as the performance measure, about 13 percent when mean gains are used, and 55 percent when annual changes are used. These estimates all seem plausible and hard to refute. Of particular significance is the large share for the annual change measure of performance. Sampling variation is large for that approach because of the two different cohorts of students involved, those in the fourth grade one year and those in the fourth grade the following year. In addition, the table clearly demonstrates the larger sampling variance in the smaller schools.

For schools of average size, other nonpersistent variation accounts for about 35 percent of the variation in the mean gains of third to fourth graders across schools, a far larger share than for the other two performance measures. This large share reflects two factors. One is the relatively small variation in mean gains across schools, and the other is the fact that two test scores are involved for each student and hence two opportunities for idiosyncratic effects to emerge. The authors, however, may be overstating the problem of volatility in this case. While volatility of this form is demonstrably a problem when policymakers focus on the gains of a single cohort of students in a single grade, such volatility could be less of a problem when multiple grades are combined at the school level. Only if all the idiosyncratic factors operated at the school level (such as a commotion outside the school during the testing period) and not at the grade level would the move to the school level not reduce the overall variation.[31]

Lessons for the Design of Accountability and Incentive Systems

Kane and Staiger spell out four lessons for the design of test-based accountability systems that emerge from the presence of volatility. I generally agree with all of them, but with some qualifications. In addition, I add a few more of my own.

First, the authors assert that incentive systems that provide rewards or sanctions for schools at the extremes of the performance distribution primarily affect small schools and provide very weak incentives for large schools. Given the smaller sampling variation in performance measures for large than for small schools—and hence the smaller probability that a large school will be at the extremes of the distribution—it is certainly true that, for any given level of true performance, small schools have a higher probability of being rewarded or of being sanctioned than large schools. Stated differently, with extreme cutoffs, a small school has a higher probability of being miscategorized as a success or failure than a large school.

How this difference between small and large schools translates into the power of incentives for schools of different sizes to improve, however, is less clear. As Kane and Staiger point out, the long-term incentive impacts on schools could differ from the short-term impacts as school personnel in small schools have trouble perceiving a clear relationship between their effort and the school's performance. The fact that noise plays such a large role in the classification of small schools means that a small school will have difficulty determining what to continue doing if it is deemed a successful school or what to stop doing if it is deemed a failing school. Thus, I would be inclined to emphasize that an accountability system that rewards and sanctions schools at the extremes is an ineffective means of inducing even the small schools to improve over time.

The main way to justify such a system would be in terms of the general signal that it sends to all schools about the state's interest in improving student performance. The hope then would be that all schools, not just the schools with a chance of winning an award, would respond to the public pressure to improve student achievement in a positive way.

Second, Kane and Staiger show that incentive systems that establish performance thresholds for each separate racial or ethnic subgroup put racially or ethnically diverse schools at a disadvantage with respect to being rewarded and also encourage districts to establish racially homogeneous schools. Their analysis of the California data provides support for this conclusion. The authors provide further analysis that shows there may be few, if any, offsetting benefits of such disaggregation. Their observations on disaggregated measures seem valid and are central to current policy discussions about congressional proposals relating to accountability.

Third, the authors emphasize that annual test results, mean gains, or changes in test scores are flawed as a tool for identifying schools worth emulating, and they argue that filtered estimates based on a Bayesian approach would better serve that purpose.[32] These filtered estimates are based on a combination of the school's own test score, the state average, and the school's test scores from past years, other grades, and other subjects. As the authors document, the filtering system is more successful than the simpler gains approach in predicting which schools are likely to perform well in a subsequent year. The authors convincingly argue that state policymakers could and should use measures in that spirit for determining which schools are worth emulating. However, unless they can be simplified in a way that makes them transparent to the school officials whose behavior state policymakers are trying to influence, such measures would be less useful for the purpose of providing direct incentives for improving school performance.

Finally, Kane and Staiger warn policymakers that they should pay attention to the natural fluctuations in test scores in evaluating the impacts of any policy interventions. In this context, they are raising the standard problem of regression to the mean. This lesson is fine for—and is also well known to—policy analysts. However, from the perspective of policymakers who want policies to look successful, the schools with unusually low performance one year are precisely the ones they may want to target given such schools are more likely to improve the following year in any case. Perhaps Kane and Staiger's lesson is more relevant for the media, which, with more statistical sophistication, could hold policymakers more accountable for true policy impacts.

To this list, I would like to add a few more policy-relevant observations.

1. *If the purpose of the rewards and sanctions is to generate incentives for schools to improve, the thresholds or cutoff scores should not be at the extremes of the distribution.*

The policy recommendation that thresholds for recognition and rewards not be at the extremes of the distribution is implicit in the Kane and Staiger analysis but is never stated clearly given their tendency to focus on the differences between large and small schools. To be sure, even with thresholds closer to the mean performance measure across schools, the problem of noise does not go away. However, setting thresholds closer to the mean would give more schools a chance to win recognition or rewards and hence would extend direct incentives deeper into the distribution. Moreover, compared with a system that bases rewards on extreme values, the incentives for school improvement from such a system are likely to be more powerful given that the larger schools, whose chances of winning would be increased, have more control over their measured performance than do the small schools, whose performance measures are subject to so much noise.

2. *Financial awards should not be large, and for some decisions, information other than test scores should be brought to bear.*

The volatility in test scores across schools inevitably means than any incentive program is going to mislabel many schools. This is not just a problem at the extremes of the distribution, but also one that applies to all schools regardless of where they fall in the distribution. Such mislabeling could be acceptable provided that it does not distort school behavior in highly undesirable ways or lead to gross inequities among schools. One option to avoid those undesirable outcomes is to keep the financial rewards for positive performance relatively small. In the case of sanctions for low-performing schools, where the stakes may be high, policymakers would do well to supplement the information from the test-based measures of performance with other information, such as from site visits, about the performance of the school.

3. *Volatility of measures is important, but low volatility should not be the only criterion for deciding among approaches for measuring school performance.*

Some policymakers might be tempted to conclude from table 2 that measuring school performance using average test scores would be preferred to other approaches on the grounds that it leads to the lowest nonpersistent variation relative to the total variation across schools and hence generates the clearest signal about school performance. That conclusion, however, would be inappropriate. Among the three approaches examined by Kane and Staiger, average test scores generate the least valid measure of school performance. As has been well understood since the Coleman report of the 1960s, average test scores are highly correlated with the socioeconomic status of students in a school.[33] Hence, a school's average test score indicates more about the composition of students in the school than it does about the effectiveness of the school in imparting learning. Only if that measure were adequately corrected for the socioeconomic status of the student body would it be a valid measure of school performance, but such adjustments are hard to make. For that reason, some form of gain or change measure is preferred.

The annual change measure can and should be ruled out on the grounds that sampling variation from one year to another generates an unacceptably large amount of noise relative to true signal.[34] The only remaining question is whether the ratio of noise to total variation is also too high for the school performance measure based on mean gains of a given cohort of students. That is a judgment call. Certainly the amount of volatility reported in table 2 suggests there may be a problem, particularly for small schools. However, the aggregation of several grades would reduce the volatility somewhat, provided that the idiosyncratic effects on test scores were not schoolwide.

More generally, many issues other than volatility arise in developing a valid measure of school performance or school effectiveness. Kane and Staiger have made an important contribution by focusing on volatility, but that focus should not keep policymakers from asking the other hard questions related to the measurement of school performance, including the purposes for which the measure is to be used and whose behavior it is designed to change.[35]

Accountability in North Carolina

Kane and Staiger use North Carolina data to illustrate many of their points. Data from North Carolina are particularly useful because the state has administered statewide end-of-grade tests to all students in grades three to eight since 1993. Because Kane and Staiger's main purpose is methodological, they use the North Carolina data to highlight certain conclusions about volatility, not to discuss the broader set of issues related to accountability in that state. As a result, a reader might come away from the Kane and Staiger paper with a misleading sense of the North Carolina accountability system.

North Carolina's program is sophisticated and is less subject to some of the methodological problems discussed by Kane and Staiger than it would be if it were more like the California system that emphasizes the extremes of the performance distribution. Although North Carolina does publicly recognize the schools with the highest performance and those with the greatest gains, most of the accountability program, and all of the financial rewards, are directed toward a larger group of schools that are identified based on the gains in their test scores relative to the predicted gains for the school.[36] For elementary and middle schools, any school whose gains exceed its predicted gains by more than 10 percent is designated an exemplary school and financial bonuses are given to the teachers and staffs of such school. In 1997, after the first year of the program, about one in three schools met the exemplary status. By 1999, more than one in two schools were exemplary. Thus, the North Carolina accountability program is targeted at a much larger proportion of schools than would be true of one focused only on the very highest performing schools.

At the bottom end of the distribution, North Carolina uses test scores to identify low-performing schools that receive both additional scrutiny and attention from state assistance teams. The criteria for being a low-performing school are twofold. One is that the school did not meet its expected growth in test scores during that year, and the other is that less than 50 percent of the students were at grade level. Thus, even this cutoff is more complex, and may be subject to less volatility, than some of the measures discussed by Kane and Staiger.

North Carolina's school-based accountability system has had a powerful effect on the behavior of one set of key adults in the education system— school principals. This assertion is based on evidence from surveys of a random sample of elementary school principals in 1997 and 1999.[37] Analysis of the survey responses indicates that most principals, including both supporters and nonsupporters of the state's overall goals, responded to North Carolina's accountability program in ways that were consistent with the state's goal of focusing attention on the basic skills of reading, math, and writing. For example, by 1999, most principals had redirected resources to math and reading, incorporated math and reading into other courses, increased their work with teachers to prepare for the end-of-grade tests and to improve instruction, and incorporated math and reading into extracurricular activities.[38] In addition, the program induced many principals to focus more attention on test-taking skills or on other activities that would improve a school's rating but not necessarily student learning. Thus, Helen F. Ladd and Arnaldo Zelli conclude that a well-designed accountability program can be a powerful policy tool, and for that reason, they urge that policymakers use it cautiously.

A follow-up analysis of some of the data presented in Ladd and Zelli shows that Kane and Staiger's emphasis on the differential magnitude of the incentives facing small schools relative to large schools does not apply to the North Carolina program. To test for differential effects, the survey responses were divided by size of school and statistical tests undertaken to determine whether principals of small schools responded more strongly to the incentives of the program than principals of large schools. Out of fourteen specific comparisons, only one statistically significant difference emerged. In that case, the larger schools responded more strongly than the smaller schools.

As the state moves forward with its accountability system and its efforts to reduce the black-white gap in test scores, state policymakers would do well to heed Kane and Staiger's second lesson about the dangers of basing rewards on test scores disaggregated by subgroup within schools and their third lesson about the need for care in choosing schools to use as exemplars of outstanding performance.

Notes

1. James S. Coleman and others, *Equality of Educational Opportunity* (Department of Health, Education, and Welfare, 1966).
2. Brian Tarcy, "Town's Scores the Most Improved," *Boston Globe*, December 8, 1999, p. C2.
3. In addition, the survey contained information on parental educational attainment reported by students. We use these data when attempting to control for the socioeconomic background of students.
4. Thomas J. Kane and Douglas O. Staiger, "Improving School Accountability Measures," Working Paper 8156 (Cambridge, Mass.: National Bureau of Economic Research, March 2001).
5. For a more detailed description of the California Academic Performance Index, see California Department of Education, Policy and Evaluation Division, "2000 Academic Performance Index Base Report Information Guide," January 2001 (www.cde.ca.gov/psaa/api/yeartwo/base/apiinfogb.pdf).
6. Coleman and others, *Equality of Educational Opportunity*, p. 326.
7. In 1996–97, 51,306 public schools in the United States had a third grade. (See Department of Education, National Center for Education Statistics, *Digest of Education Statistics*

(1998), p. 119, table 99.) This included 4,910 schools with grades prekindergarten, kindergarten, or first through third or fourth grade; 20,570 schools with prekindergarten, kindergarten, or first through fifth grade; 15,578 schools with prekindergarten, kindergarten, or first through sixth grade; 4,543 schools with prekindergarten, kindergarten, or first through eighth grade; and 5,705 schools with other grade-spans. Moreover, in the fall of 1996, 3.518 million students in the United States were enrolled in third grade. (See *Digest of Education Statistics*, p. 58, table 43.)

8. Darcia Harris Bowman, "Arizona Ranks Schools by 'Value-Added' to Scores," *Education Week*, February 9, 2000.

9. The impact on math gain scores is less pronounced, given greater variability in mean math gain scores between schools.

10. Caroline Hoxby, "Peer Effects in the Classroom: Learning from Gender and Race Variation," Working Paper 7867 (Cambridge, Mass.: National Bureau of Economic Research, August 2000).

11. In this section, we have sacrificed some generality for intuitive appeal. In some cases, it may not be reasonable to expect u_t and u_{t-1} or ε_{t-1} and ε_t to be independent. For instance, if there were ceiling effects such that a change one year bumped up against a limit (u_t and u_{t-1} and ε_{t-1} and ε_t were negatively correlated), we would overstate the amount of transience. (We observed no obvious evidence of ceiling effects in the data.) However, if there were schools that were consistently improving in a systematic way (u_t and u_{t-1} were positively correlated), we would understate the amount of transience. For a more general treatment of the issue, see Kane and Staiger, "Improving School Accountability Measures."

12. Ulrich Boser, "Pressure without Support," *Education Week,* January 11, 2001, pp. 68–71, table.

13. Schools also had to meet targets for each numerically significant racial or ethnic group.

14. See Helen F. Ladd and Charles Clotfelter, "Recognizing and Rewarding Success in Public Schools," in Helen F. Ladd, ed., *Holding Schools Accountable* (Brookings, 1996), pp. 23–64; and David Grissmer and others, *Improving Student Achievement: What State NAEP Test Scores Tell Us* (Santa Monica, Calif.: RAND, 2000). Nevertheless, whether the improvement in performance is real or the result of teaching to the test is unclear. See Daniel Koretz, "Limitations in the Use of Achievement Tests as Measures of Educators' Productivity," *Journal of Human Resources* (forthcoming), paper initially presented at "Devising Incentives to Promote Human Capital," National Academy of Sciences Conference, December 1999. Kane and Staiger, in "Improving School Accountability Measures," report that the schools in North Carolina that showed the greatest improvement on fifth-grade math and reading gains did not improve more on measures of student engagement (such as student absences, the proportion of students reporting less than an hour of homework, or the proportion of students watching less than six hours of television), even though these characteristics were related to gain scores in the base year.

15. However, because the threshold is higher, winning an award is probably a more accurate measure of true improvement for racially heterogeneous schools than for homogeneous schools.

16. A socioeconomically disadvantaged student is a student of any race neither of whose parents completed a high school degree or who participates in the school's free or reduced-price lunch program.

17. The number of subgroups in the average school attended by Latino students was 2.5; African American students, 2.8; Asian students, 2.7; American Indian students, 2.5; Pacific Islanders, 2.7; Filipino students, 2.8; socially disadvantaged students, 2.6; and white, non–Hispanic students, 2.2. The rough estimate of the impact of the rule on racial or ethnic differences

in spending is not precisely correct, because the marginal impact of the number of subgroups on a school's chances of winning an award depends upon the number of subgroups and the size of the school.

18. See Thomas J. Kane, Douglas O. Staiger, and Jeffrey Geppert, "Assessing the Definition of 'Adequate Yearly Progress' in the House and Senate Education Bills," University of California at Los Angeles, School of Public Policy and Social Research, July 2001.

19. Presumably, that is the point of identifying the "Top 25" schools in North Carolina and giving them a banner to identify that fact.

20. A similar point is made in David Rogosa, "Myths and Methods: 'Myths about Longitudinal Research' plus Supplemental Questions," in John Mordechai Gottman, ed., *The Analysis of Change* (Mahwah, N.J.: Lawrence Erlbaum Associates, 1995), pp. 3–65.

21. Mark McClellan and Douglas Staiger, "The Quality of Health Care Providers," Working Paper 7327 (Cambridge, Mass.: National Bureau of Economic Research, August 1999). See also Kane and Staiger, "Improving School Accountability Measures." The estimator is an empirical Bayes estimator in the spirit of Carl Morris, "Parametric Empirical Bayes Inference: Theory and Applications," *Journal of the American Statistical Association*, vol. 381, no. 78 (1983), pp. 47–55. However, the method employed for estimating the variance components is less computationally intensive than that proposed in Anthony Bryk and Stephen Raudenbush, *Hierarchical Linear Models* (Newbury Park, Calif.: Sage Publications, 1992) and can incorporate information on multiple outcomes and multiple years. Moreover, the filtering technique based upon these estimates is linear, offering additional computational advantages.

22. For a discussion of the merits of transparency, see Ladd and Clotfelter, "Recognizing and Rewarding Success in Public Schools."

23. North Carolina Department of Public Instruction, "ABCs Results Show Strong Growth in Student Achievement K–8," August 6, 1998 (www.ncpublicschools.org/news/abcs_results_98.html).

24. Kathleen Kennedy Manzo, "North Carolina: Seeing a Payoff, " *Education Week,* vol. 18, no. 17 (January 11, 1999), p. 165.

25. Martin E. P. Seligman and Steven F. Maier, "Failure to Escape Traumatic Shock," *Journal of Experimental Psychology*, vol. 74, no. 1 (1967), pp. 1–9.

26. Kane and Staiger, "Improving School Accountability Measures."

27. Sampling error in the context of sampling variance means something different from choosing a survey sample. The authors envision in each district a population of parents who produce children at random times making the mix of children in a given grade different from year to year. The variance is due to both intrafamily differences that are mainly random genetic differences (between siblings) and interfamily differences.

28. Jeremy Finn and C. Achilles, "Tennessee's Class Size Study: Findings, Implications and Misconceptions," *Educational Evaluation and Policy Analysis*, vol. 20, no. 2 (Summer 1999), pp. 97–109; and A. B. Krueger, "Experimental Estimates of Education Production Functions," *Quarterly Journal of Economics,* vol. 114 (1999), pp. 497–532.

29. Barbara Nye, Larry V. Hedges, and Spyros Konstantopoulos, "The Long-Term Effects of Small Classes: A Five-Year Follow-up of the Tennessee Class Size Experiment," *Educational Evaluation and Policy Analysis*, vol. 20, no. 2 (Summer 1999), pp. 127–42.

30. David W. Grissmer and others, *Improving Student Achievement: What State NAEP Scores Tell Us,* MR–924–EDU (Santa Monica, Calif.: RAND, 2000).

31. The authors argue that the use of multiple grades often does not reduce volatility as much as one might expect. Their example, however, relates to a different situation than the one discussed here in that it focuses on annual changes in which there are overlapping cohorts of students.

32. For the theory underlying the estimates, see Kane and Staiger, "Improving School Accountability Measures."

33. Coleman and others, *Equality of Educational Opportunity.*

34. Federal policymakers appear to have missed this basic point as is evident from the House and Senate versions of education bills passed during the summer of 2001. Those bills are designed to hold schools accountable for "adequately yearly progress," defined as changes in test scores from one year to the next.

35. Some of these issues are discussed, for example, in Ladd and Clotfelter "Recognizing and Rewarding Success in Public Schools"; Robert H. Meyer, "Comments on Chapters Two, Three, and Four," in Helen F. Ladd, ed., *Holding Schools Accountable: Performance-Based Reform in Education* (Brookings, 1996), pp. 137–45; and Helen F. Ladd and Randall Walsh, "Implementing Value-Added Measrues of School Effectiveness: Getting the Incentives Right," *Economics of Education Review* (forthcoming).

36. Kane and Staiger allude to this fact but do not elaborate. For a description of the state's methodology, see Ladd and Walsh, "Implementing Value-Added Measures of School Effectiveness"; and Helen F. Ladd and Arnaldo Zelli, "School-Based Accountability in North Carolina: The Responses of School Principals," Working Paper (Sanford Institute, 2001).

37. Ladd and Zelli, "School-Based Accountability in North Carolina."

38. Comparisons between some of the 1999 responses and the 1997 responses allowed the researchers to isolate the effects of the accountability system. See Ladd and Zelli, "School-Based Accountability in North Carolina."

Building a High-Quality Assessment and Accountability Program: The Philadelphia Example

ANDREW PORTER *and*
MITCHELL CHESTER

The purpose of implementing an assessment and accountability program in an urban school district is to improve student learning of worthwhile content.[1] Current levels of achievement in most U.S. urban districts are unacceptably low. Average achievement test results conceal the fact that achievement levels of students of color are substantially lower than those of white students. Improvements are urgently needed.

Assessment and accountability, by themselves, are unlikely to turn around the low levels of student achievement in urban settings.[2] Supports must be put in place so that students and schools can be successful. Such supports must be an integral part of an effective assessment and accountability program. Nevertheless, high-stakes testing can be a powerful policy lever in a more comprehensive reform initiative.[3]

Some education researchers and practitioners believe that high-stakes testing leads to a dumbed-down curriculum and unfair penalties for students and schools.[4] Others believe equally strongly that, without high-stakes testing, many schools will continue to provide inadequate opportunities to learn for students, especially students from low-income families. We believe that a

The research in this report was supported by the University of Wisconsin–Madison, School of Education, Wisconsin Center for Education Research and by the school district of Philadelphia. The opinions expressed are those of the authors and do not necessarily reflect the views of the Wisconsin Center for Education Research or the school district of Philadelphia.

285

carefully crafted and continuously refined assessment and accountability program can lead to more effective schools and higher levels of student persistence and achievement on content critical for future success.

A Framework for Building an Effective Assessment and Accountability System

An effective assessment and accountability program has many components. Much more is involved than simply administering a test and adopting a policy that says if students and schools do not achieve to a standard they will be punished. The most important statement for guiding the design of an assessment and accountability program is *Standards for Educational and Psychological Testing.*[5] Earlier versions of these standards have been in place for some time and have become the legal and industry benchmarks for test development and use.[6] Because the standards cover much more than student achievement testing and accountability, the American Educational Research Association (AERA) in 2000 developed a separate position statement concerning high-stakes testing in preK–12 education.[7] The AERA position articulates twelve conditions that every high-stakes testing program should meet.[8]

Those opposed to high-stakes testing use the standards for educational and psychological testing and AERA's position statement to critique assessment and accountability programs and find them wanting. For them, the standards and position statement are valuable insofar as they can be used to help put a halt to high-stakes testing. We see the standards and position statement in a different light. For us, they provide the criteria and guidelines for building an effective assessment and accountability program that will strengthen instruction and improve student achievement.

Essentially, the standards and the AERA position statement identify the following three criteria that any effective assessment and accountability program should meet.[9]

1. The assessment and accountability program should provide a good target for student and school effort. If assessment and accountability can focus effort, then they must focus effort in constructive directions.

2. The assessment and accountability program should be symmetrical. To produce high levels of student achievement, students and schools must work together. No school is so good that it can be successful without students who

are motivated and ready to learn. Similarly, even students who are motivated and ready to learn must be provided adequate opportunities to learn worthwhile content. Students from low-income families are especially dependent on school-based opportunities to learn. The assessment and accountability program should include stakes that schools and students share so that both have incentives to improve student achievement.

3. The assessment and accountability program should be fair. For students, fairness requires that schools provide an adequate opportunity to learn. For schools, fairness requires access to the resources needed to be successful. A fair assessment and accountability program must also include tests that are reliable and valid for the ways in which they are used.

Setting Good Targets

Those who argue against high-stakes testing believe that it will lead to a dumbed-down and narrow curriculum. In many urban schools, the curriculum is already dumbed down and narrow. Assessment and accountability can set a new and better target for instruction.[10]

The careful construction of district content standards is the first step. These content standards should call for a balanced curriculum, emphasizing students' mastery of key concepts and ideas and the ability to use those concepts and ideas to reason, communicate, and solve novel problems. Students should also master a foundation of facts and skills. The tests used in an assessment and accountability system must be aligned with these ambitious content standards.

Setting good targets requires that a number of factors be considered.

—A range of academic subjects should be tested. If, for example, only reading and mathematics are tested, the result may be to push school and student effort toward those subjects and away from other subjects, such as science and social studies.

—The whole school should accept appropriate responsibility for student success or failure. If only selected grades are tested (for example, fourth, eighth, and twelfth), an uneven assessment and accountability system may result, with undue pressure felt at grade levels that are tested and undue freedom felt at those that are not.

—Some content standards are not easily assessed in an on-demand paper-and-pencil test. If these standards are important, alternative assessment procedures should be put in place. Similarly, assessing students' ability to reason, communicate, and use their knowledge is more difficult and expensive than assessing their mastery of facts and skills. A test should be as balanced on these dimensions as the desired curriculum.[11]

—Achievement is lower for some groups than others. Setting a good target should involve reporting results disaggregated by groups (for example, males and females; African Americans, whites, and Hispanics).

—Performance targets should be set so that they require schools and students to raise the level of instruction and achievement to meet the expectations, yet with effort are attainable.

—A good assessment and accountability program focuses attention on the domain of content desired, as opposed to the specific sample tested. If the same form of a test is used repeatedly, undoubtedly the sample of content represented in that test form will become the target and lead to an inappropriate narrowing of the enacted curriculum.[12] Ideally, each time the test is administered, a different but parallel form should be used.[13]

—Holding schools and students accountable requires specifying standards for performance. For example, if test scores are to be used as the basis for promotion from one grade to the next or graduation from high school, minimum levels of satisfactory performance must be established. Similarly, if schools are to receive rewards for producing high levels of student achievement, qualifying levels of achievement must be identified.[14] Standards that are set too low will be too easily met, and standards that are set too high will be dismissed as unattainable; neither will have a positive impact. We do not argue against setting high standards in the long run, but we do argue against setting unreasonably high standards in the near term. Near-term standards should be set so that they put pressure on schools and students to exceed current levels of achievement. They should then be revisited periodically to see if they need to be revised and set higher.

—Finally, setting targets raises the question, what should be the size and nature of rewards and sanctions for students and schools?[15] We do not know the answer to this question. For students, promotion and retention represent large rewards and sanctions; using test performance as a component of grades is smaller. For schools, reconstitution is a large sanction. For teachers, a modest increase in salary or a bonus is a small reward. The goal is to set rewards and sanctions that are sufficient to focus attention on desired content and increase effort.

Symmetry

A surprisingly large number of assessment and accountability programs are not symmetrical. That is, they either hold schools accountable without holding students accountable or they hold students accountable without holding schools accountable. Such approaches are incomplete. If there are no stakes for students, students may not try their best on the test (especially at the upper grades). Even worse, students may not try their best in school. Either way, schools are left in the difficult position of having to raise the achievement of potentially unmotivated students. Similarly, if students are held accountable, they have the right to expect schools that are doing their best to meet student needs. School accountability may help.[16]

Our framework calls for symmetry not only of school and student accountability, but also of state and district accountability. If a state holds a district accountable for student performance on state tests, then those state tests should be a part of the district accountability program.

Fairness

The elements of a fair assessment and accountability program are opportunity to learn, adequate resources, and reliable and valid measures.[17] If students are to be held accountable, then schools must provide them with an adequate opportunity to learn the content for which they are being held accountable.[18] If schools are to be held accountable, then the state and district must provide those schools with adequate resources to be successful. Unfortunately, determining whether a student has an adequate opportunity to learn is not straightforward. Neither is it straightforward to pinpoint what resources are necessary for a school to be successful. Just because opportunity to learn and adequate resources are complicated concepts and difficult to measure in no way reduces their importance, however.

One approach to addressing opportunity to learn is to phase in accountability by holding schools accountable for a period of time before implementing the student accountability component of the program. School accountability would gradually bring the enacted curriculum into alignment with the district content standards and assessments. This alignment is crucial to providing students an adequate opportunity to learn. Instruction must not only be aligned with the content of the standards and assessments; it must be effective as well. Similarly, student accountability can be phased in by setting interim targets for achievement that are beyond current levels but short of levels ultimately desired. If schools are to be increasingly successful, they must be provided qualified staff, instructional materials including technology, high-quality teacher professional development, and reasonable class sizes.

In addition to providing adequate resources for schools and opportunity to learn for students, a fair assessment and accountability program requires that decisions be based on reliable and valid information.[19] Actually, reliability is probably not the most useful concept here; the real issue is one of decision consistency. For example, if a student's score falls below a criterion cutoff point, what is the probability that the student's true achievement level falls below that cutoff point? Validity is more complicated and concerns the appropriateness of inferences made. For example, if the decision is to promote or retain fourth graders based on mastery of the desired curriculum for kindergarten through fourth grade, then the assessments used to determine that mastery should be based on a representative sample of the desired curriculum. Alternatively, decisions to promote or retain fourth graders might be based on maximizing future success in school. For mastery, validity is more an issue of content validity. When the criterion is future success, validity is more an issue of predictive validity.

When high-stakes decisions are made about students, fairness requires that the decisions not be based on a single test administration or even a single test. Giving students multiple opportunities to demonstrate that they meet a standard improves the probability that a student whose true performance meets the standard will be judged as having met the standard. Providing multiple opportunities to meet the standard also creates a bias in favor of success. That is, the proportion of students certified as meeting the standard even though they did not will exceed the proportion of students certified as failing to meet the standard even though they did. For high-stakes promotion and graduation decisions, the bias should probably be in the positive direction.[20]

For schools, decision consistency is the probability that a school judged to exceed a standard and merit rewards has truly met the standard. Typically, a school performance index is defined by the average level of school performance tracked over time. Small schools have larger standard errors on this school performance index, and thus lower decision consistency, than large schools. Sometimes, standards are based on averages across multiple years of data to improve the decision consistency for schools.[21]

Finally, to ensure that an assessment and accountability program is as fair as possible, a district must be committed to evaluating the program over time. One part of this evaluation should address consequential validity. Is the program having the intended effects? Is the curriculum getting better and coming increasingly into alignment with district content standards? Are decisions about students leading to increased levels of achievement across all subgroups of students? Evaluation of the assessment and accountability program should also take impact into account. Are acceptable numbers of students being promoted from grade to grade and ultimately graduating from high school? Are reasonable numbers of schools reaching their targets and receiving rewards? Ongoing evaluation of an assessment and accountability program can guard against unintended negative effects and identify ways in which the program can be made more effective.

The Philadelphia School District

The Philadelphia school district serves approximately 215,000 students, making it the seventh largest school district in the nation. Eighty percent of the students served are of color, with 65 percent African American, 11 percent Hispanic, and 4 percent Asian American. Fifty-five percent of the students come from families on public assistance. There are 259 schools organized into twenty-two clusters, with each cluster consisting of a high school and its feeder schools (about eight to sixteen schools per cluster). Just over 10 percent of the students are labeled as having a disability. Student persistence is a serious challenge, with the district estimating it fails to adequately educate 70 percent of its students by the time they should graduate, with only 57 percent of first-time ninth graders graduating four years later.

Philadelphia created an accountability system designed to promote improved student reading, mathematics, and science achievement; attendance of staff and students; promotion rates; and student persistence rates. The baseline for the system was set in 1995–96. The long-term performance target is that within one student generation—twelve years—95 percent of Philadelphia students will be proficient on citywide measures of district academic standards, will graduate from high school, and will be prepared for further education or workplace employment.

The performance index is the composite measure of a school's scores in reading, math, and science; its promotion (grades K–8) or persistence rate (high school); and the attendance of students and staff. When calculating the achievement components of each school's performance index, the proportion of students scoring at each performance level (advanced, proficient, basic, and below basic) is multiplied by a weighting factor. Because the twelve-year goal is to have most students achieve at proficient levels, the proficient performance level is weighted 1.0; the advanced level, 1.2; the basic level, 0.8. The below basic level is divided into three performance bands to be sure that schools are credited for progress at the lower end of the achievement scale. These bands are assigned weights of 0.6, 0.4, and 0.2. Finally, the proportion of students who are untested is weighted zero.

Schools have two improvement targets. The first is to close the gap between their baseline and the twelve-year goal of a performance index score of ninety-five. Although many permutations will result in a performance index score of ninety-five, schools attaining that score must have roughly three-fourths of their students performing at proficient or higher levels across the index components. Schools that improve over the first two-year period at a rate that, if sustained, will result in attainment of the twelve-year goal have met the target for that first period. Every two years, a new baseline is established, and a new two-year improvement target calculated. In the second two-year accountability cycle, for example, schools had to gain one-fifth of the distance to the long-range goal, which was then ten years distant.

The second improvement target is to reduce the proportion of low-scoring and untested students. To meet this target, every two years schools must reduce by ten points the proportion of students who score at below basic levels or are untested. Schools for which the proportion is below 30 percent must reduce this proportion by one-third. This second target is an incentive for schools to attend to the achievement of all students, not simply those in the middle and upper achievement ranges.

Setting a Good Target

Setting a good target is the art of successive approximations. Maintaining the vitality and relevance of the accountability system requires a willingness to learn from experience and make refinements along the way.

MULTIPLE MEASURES. Philadelphia's accountability system incorporates both direct and indirect measures of student achievement, as well as noncognitive factors that facilitate student achievement. Through the first four years, achievement was measured directly through the Stanford Achievement Test,

Ninth Edition (Stanford 9). Reading, mathematics, and science achievement were assessed through both multiple-choice and open-ended formats. Student promotion rates in grades one through eight and high school persistence rates constituted the indirect measures of achievement. Student and staff attendance are particularly important to Philadelphia because the rates have been low historically, even in comparison to other large city districts.

From the start, Philadelphia realized that refinements in the performance index would be necessary to maintain the effectiveness of the accountability system. In particular, the district wanted to reduce its reliance on the Stanford 9 by incorporating assessments that provide better instructional targets for teachers and schools. The new assessments were to be systematically aligned with the district curriculum standards and frameworks, require strong communication and problem-solving skills, and reflect the cultural, racial, and ethnic diversity that characterizes Philadelphia's schools.

The first adjustment to the accountability system involved customization of the Stanford 9. Working with the test publisher, Harcourt Educational Measurement, the district developed and field-tested reading, mathematics, and science items that were culturally representative. On each form of the Stanford 9, the district supplanted off-the-shelf items with custom open-ended and multiple-choice items, using appropriate equating methodologies to ensure comparability of scores for the new and old test forms.

Beginning with the 2000–01 school year, the district replaced some of the Stanford 9 reading and mathematics testing with state tests in those subjects (the Pennsylvania System of School Assessment or PSSA). This decision responded in part to legislation that raised the stakes for Pennsylvania districts in which more than half of the students score in the bottom quartile on the PSSA. The decision also reflected a desire to reduce the amount of testing because in some grades reading and mathematics were being assessed through both the Stanford 9 and the PSSA.

By including PSSA results in the school district accountability system, Philadelphia achieves a degree of alignment among the criteria for judging school effectiveness. Overlapping district and state accountability systems can affect coherence, either positively or negatively. For example, because a strong correlation exists between school and student results on the Stanford 9 and PSSA, most schools that make gains on one assessment make gains on the other. Occasionally, however, this is not the case.

The contrast between the conclusions of the district and state accountability programs is sometimes dramatic. These inconsistencies happen because the district program is based on school gains whereas the state program is based on school levels of achievement. For example, in the fall of 2000, fifty-three Philadelphia schools that received rewards from the district were identified by the state as low performers.

Further adjustments to the accountability system are anticipated. Since 1998, the district has been developing proficiency exams at the middle and high school levels in English, mathematics, and science. These exams use multiple-choice, short-answer, and extended constructed response formats to assess student achievement on district content standards (for example, eighth-grade English, Algebra I, Living Environments). These exams are being phased in, with the first operational administrations occurring during the 2000–01 school year. Beginning with the 2001–02 school year, the district plans to use proficiency exam results in the performance index, thus reducing the reliance on the Stanford 9 and the PSSA.

An additional refinement was made to the accountability system after the first cycle. For the first two years that the performance index was in place, high school persistence was simply a measure of the proportion of first-time ninth graders who graduated within four years. In the third year, persistence was expanded to include calculations of the promotion rates of first-time ninth graders to tenth grade and the proportion of students who graduate in five or six years. The promotion rates from ninth to tenth grade were included to highlight the high failure rate that occurs in ninth grade and to provide an incentive for schools to focus on ninth-grade success. The five- and six-year graduation rates were included to reward schools that successfully engaged nongraduating students beyond four years. On-time, four-year graduation is weighted more heavily in the performance index than ninth-grade promotion and the five- and six-year graduation rates.

ACCOUNTING FOR ALL ENROLLED STUDENTS. From the start, the Philadelphia school district took a strong philosophical stand that schools are responsible for the achievement of all students and that, with few exceptions, all students can reach high levels of achievement in core subjects. This philosophy was put into operation by incorporating untested students into the performance index score, by exempting few students from the performance index calculation, and by instituting testing accommodations that were meant to maximize student access to the assessments. Many large-scale testing programs fail to take differences in participation and exemption rates into account when reporting results. Philadelphia has gone to great lengths to account for all enrolled students in its program.

The untested category is included to provide an incentive to focus on all students. The proportion of students who are untested is weighted zero when calculating the achievement components of the performance index. Because the percentage of students who take the tests varies considerably from school to school, the school district did not want schools that are reaching out to test all of their students to appear to have lower scores than schools that test only the more successful students. No matter how poorly students perform on the assessment, a school gets more credit if they are tested than if they are not.

Only 4 percent of Philadelphia students—the most severely disabled and English language learners who lack proficiency in both English and their native language—are excluded from testing. To accomplish this level of inclusion, the school district permits a range of test accommodations. Some examples are the provision of extra time, one-on-one testing in shorter time segments, and real-time translation of vocabulary on the mathematics and science sections.

For students who receive instruction in their native language, Philadelphia uses native language assessments. When possible, the school district has purchased existing assessments in the two languages for which bilingual programs exist—Spanish and Chinese. When existing native language assessments are not available, tests have been translated or native language versions have been developed in parallel with the English language version.

PERFORMANCE GOAL AND IMPROVEMENT TARGETS. When the accountability system was initially implemented, the Stanford 9 performance levels served as the benchmarks for setting the twelve-year goal and the two-year improvement targets. The Stanford 9 performance levels had features that supported the district's goal of having Philadelphia students achieve at levels that will allow them to compete with high school graduates anywhere. The performance levels were based on academic content standards developed with the input of national professional organizations. They represented achievement based on judgments about how students should perform. And the distribution of students from the norming sample across Stanford 9 performance levels paralleled the distribution of students nationally across the National Assessment of Educational Progress performance levels.

The Stanford 9 performance standards probably receive more attention by teachers and administrators than do other components of the performance index. Although student and staff attendance, grade one through eight promotion rates, and high school persistence rates contribute to the performance index score, the test score components are 60 percent of the total score.

Further, most schools attain higher scores on the nontest components, and therefore less room for improvement is found on these components than on the test components.

In the first two-year accountability cycle, 56 percent of Philadelphia's schools exceeded both their accountability targets (that is, their two-year improvement targets toward the twelve-year goal of attaining a performance index score of ninety-five and the required reduction in the proportion of low-scoring and untested students). Substantial performance gains have also been realized in the subsequent three years, but the rate of progress has slowed. Only 20 percent of schools exceeded both accountability targets in the second two-year accountability cycle.

The credibility and value of the accountability system are tied to educator and public perception of the reasonableness and appropriateness of the improvement targets. As the district has gained more experience with the targets, it has become apparent that the Stanford 9 performance levels that drive them are not realistic goals at this time for many Philadelphia schools. High schools, as well as many elementary and middle schools with very low baselines, are not succeeding in meeting their targets—often despite making substantial, consistent progress. Only two out of twenty-two comprehensive high schools have earned rewards since 1997, even though many have achieved strong and continuous gains. In part, this is an artifact of the way in which the performance levels are set on the Stanford 9. Nationally, the basic, proficient, and advanced levels are much more difficult to attain at the higher grades than they are at the lower grades, particularly in mathematics and science. This phenomenon contributed to much lower baseline performance index scores in high schools compared with other schools and thus much higher targets for improvement.

The Philadelphia school district is utilizing several strategies to set new improvement targets. First, the district is moving away from using the Stanford 9, replacing it with the state PSSA and district proficiency exams. Second, the district is studying gains achieved by schools over the first four years to help determine levels of improvement that are possible.

PROMOTING THE LEARNING OF WORTHWHILE CURRICULUM. Setting good targets requires that the academic components of the accountability system represent worthwhile content. This principle has several dimensions—the range of content areas assessed, the alignment of the assessments with curriculum standards, and the cognitive demands (including students' mastery of key concepts and ideas and their ability to use those concepts and ideas to reason, communicate, and solve novel problems).

The initial adoption of the Stanford 9 was based in part on content considerations. Stanford 9 reporting is based on rigorous performance standards, and the test assesses science as well as reading and mathematics. In addition, the test publisher permitted the Philadelphia school district to customize the assessments with items that were representative of the cultural backgrounds of its students. The district maximized the assessment's promotion of application of skills, problem solving, and communication by including the open-ended as well as multiple-choice components of the Stanford 9.

The district has been developing custom assessments that will reduce its reliance on the Stanford 9. These newer assessments include proficiency exams in middle and high school and a K–3 literacy and mathematics assessment system. The custom assessments are systematically aligned with district standards and curriculum. They emphasize higher order processing, including the application of skills to solve problems, communication of understandings, and explication of students' reasoning.

Nevertheless, high-quality, high-stakes assessments cannot be accomplished at low cost. Philadelphia spent approximately $7.5 million in development costs over the first three years for customized assessments.

REWARDS AND SANCTIONS. The accountability system's leverage is maximized through the application of rewards and sanctions. The rewards and sanctions are designed to motivate schools to focus on those outcomes that are most directly related to achievement and over which they have control. The first accountability cycle (school years 1996–97 and 1997–98) gave educators a concrete grounding in the reality of rewards and sanctions. Of the 259 district schools, 145 schools received a total of $11.5 million in reward funding for exceeding their two-year targets; 13 schools with declining performance participated in a quality review process that resulted in the identification of improvement initiatives and the establishment of timelines and benchmarks to be met; and 2 schools were slated for reconstitution (an arbitrator subsequently reversed the reconstitution decision on procedural grounds, although he validated the legality of reconstitution).

Schools that exceeded their targets and earned rewards are proud of their accomplishment. They boast of the achievement and prominently display the banners they were awarded. Philadelphia required that reward dollars, which averaged almost $80,000 per successful school, be reinvested in the school program; they could not be used for salary bonuses. Schools used the dollars to celebrate their success, support new professional development activities, fund new positions, and purchase new equipment and materials.

For some schools, avoiding sanctions is a stronger motivator than exceeding the targets and earning rewards. In schools that came close to meeting their two-year target after one year, the faculty rallied around a goal of exceeding the target. Schools that were still far from their two-year target after one year were likely to see their goal as avoiding designation as a low-progress school.

Improving Symmetry

Although symmetry primarily concerns the relationship between school and student accountability, it also encompasses the relationship between teachers of grades that are tested and teachers of grades that are not, and the degree to which each group feels responsible for student performance.

In the early years of the accountability system, not all educators perceived that they had equal responsibility for school performance. In the first two years, the achievement components of the performance index consisted only of test scores from grades four, eight, and eleven. Schools placed inordinate emphasis on programs and staff in tested grades, often at the expense of other grades. Beginning with the third year of accountability, the school district began to expand the grades that contributed to the achievement components of the performance index. By school year 2000–01, results from at least two grades per elementary, middle, and high school level were included, with plans to add more grades in 2001–02.

Initially, Philadelphia's accountability system held schools accountable; accountability for students began with the fourth year of the program. This sequence placed the initial responsibility on schools to improve. Educators unaccustomed to being held accountable for the achievement of students frequently lamented that students did not have a concrete stake in the outcomes. Yet these initial years of accountability encouraged educators to rethink what they were teaching, to whom, and how, before individual student stakes were implemented.

Beginning with school year 1999–2000, promotion from fourth to fifth grade required students to earn a passing mark from their teachers in reading and language arts, mathematics, science, and social studies; successfully complete a multidisciplinary project; and achieve a modest passing score in reading and mathematics on the Stanford 9 or on a second-chance assessment that the school district developed. Beginning in school year 2001–02, a combination of teacher marks and test score achievement in reading, mathematics, and science will be used to determine eighth-grade promotion and high school graduation.

As new promotion and graduation standards are implemented, the performance index is being modified to incorporate the new student requirements. Promotion and graduation rates will continue to be components of the accountability system. Proficiency exam scores that contribute to promotion and graduation decisions will be incorporated in the achievement components of the performance index. With these developments, both educators and students will have a stake in common measures, therefore providing the symmetry needed for students and teachers to work toward common academic goals.

A further dimension of symmetry concerns the overlap between the criteria by which individual teachers are evaluated and the criteria by which student progress and student achievement are assessed. The district is developing a pay-for-performance evaluation system that will reward teachers for demonstrating the knowledge and skills associated with effective teaching. To the extent that the criteria by which individual teachers are judged contribute to school improvement and student attainment of promotion and graduation requirements, the accountability system will promote coherent efforts by schools, teachers, and students.

Developing a Fair System

Fairness has both programmatic and technical dimensions. Programmatic dimensions concern the opportunities students have—to learn and to demonstrate what they know—and the resources schools receive to be successful. Technical dimensions relate to the quality of the instruments used and the inferences drawn about what students know and can do and about the status and progress of schools.[22]

SUPPORTS FOR STUDENTS. One of the most fundamental fairness considerations is whether students have had the opportunity to attain the performance levels for which they are being held accountable. In Philadelphia, adequate opportunities to learn have been fostered by implementing the school accountability component before the student accountability component. Because school accountability was implemented first, schools had four years to improve instruction and focus on test score measures of school performance that also serve as individual student measures.

An implementation of higher credit accumulation requirements for high school graduation is also improving student opportunity to learn. Still, there are problems. Some schools have not secured instructors to teach world language classes, even though students must earn two world language credits to graduate. In an effort to maintain the new graduation standards while not unfairly penalizing students, the school district is exploring a range of means of securing sufficient world language teachers, including contracting with community colleges and private language instructors.

Another way in which adequate opportunities to learn have been fostered is by phasing in the targets for student achievement. For example, Philadelphia initially held fourth graders responsible for meeting modest test score requirements while making plans to raise the passing standards in later years. Initially, eighth graders were required to achieve passing grades in English, mathematics, science, and social studies. In future years, test score requirements will be added. By setting low initial standards and raising them over time, and by periodically introducing new requirements, the district allows the gradual unfolding of opportunities to learn.

To further improve students' opportunities to learn, the district is identifying students who are at risk of failing to meet the standards at least one year before the promotion grades and three years before graduation. The district provides students with their first opportunity to meet the test score requirements for promotion and graduation in grades three, seven, and nine and identifies students with low grades at the same time. Extended time, intensive instruction, and summer programs are provided to students who are at risk of failing or who have failed the promotion and graduation standards. Philadelphia is also phasing in a kindergarten through grade three literacy and mathematics assessment system designed to identify students who need additional help. The K–3 assessments are instructionally embedded in ways intended to strengthen instruction and align instruction with the requirements for promotion to fifth grade.

SUPPORTS FOR SCHOOLS. The Philadelphia school district has experienced a teacher shortage that is not equally distributed. Certain subject areas—for example, mathematics, science, and world languages—have been harder to staff than others. Also, some schools are viewed as less desirable placements than others. One result is that many middle schools serving poor, minority populations have chronic teacher shortages that they must fill with emergency-credentialed or substitute teachers.

The school district must be diligent in seeking ways to provide adequate support for schools. Within the present context of district underfunding, low salaries compared with those in surrounding communities, often-neglected facilities, and large class sizes, the danger is that the accountability system will exacerbate low teacher and principal morale and commitment. When educators perceive that accountability for results is not balanced by support to achieve targets (for example, full staffing), the performance index may foster cynicism, not motivation.

ACCURACY OF DATA. The Philadelphia school district has made a number of adjustments to ensure that the data on which decisions are made are reliable and that the decisions themselves are consistent with the decision criteria. At the school level, achievement results from additional grades and tests have been included in the performance index to increase the probability that score increases and decreases reflect real improvement or decline and are not the result of cohort effects or measurement error.

To ensure the accuracy of inferences made about the gains and losses of schools, the district has calculated the standard error of the performance index score for each school and then used these findings to calculate standard errors for performance index change scores. The results have revealed that the standard error of the change score has never been larger than 1.5 performance index points. The standard error analyses are used to create a confidence band against which the district judges school growth. Schools are not sanctioned when an observed decline is smaller than can confidently be inferred to be a true decline.

At the student level, the school district has adopted two approaches to maximize decision consistency—the use of multiple measures and a compensatory scoring model. Wherever test scores are a requirement for promotion and graduation, Philadelphia provides students with multiple opportunities and uses multiple assessments to determine whether students meet the standard. To be promoted to fourth grade, for example, students must achieve a passing score in reading and math on the Stanford 9. As a second chance to meet the test score requirements, students are given an individually administered reading test or a small group–administered math test or both.

Test score requirements for promotion and graduation initially used a conjunctive approach, under which students had to meet the passing standard on each assessment. The district is now adopting a compensatory approach, which allows stronger performance in one subject to offset weaker performance in another and increases the reliability of the results.

The use of multiple measures has resulted in high levels of decision consistency. Fourth graders have not been retained for failing to meet the test score requirement unless they failed to meet standards on one administration of the Stanford 9 and on two administrations of the second-chance test (one administration in June, before the close of school, and a second administration using a different test form at the end of the summer). On the fourth-grade second-chance reading assessment, the 1999–2000 reliability index was .91.

Complexities and Interdependencies

Creating an effective assessment and accountability system for the Philadelphia public schools is not an easy task. The district's approach has been to wade in, doing the best that it can at the time, but with a commitment to continually improve the system. Perhaps not surprisingly, each new feature of the system and each change has a domino effect, requiring rethinking and adjustments throughout the system.

INCREASING HIGH SCHOOL GRADUATION REQUIREMENTS. The district is in the process of putting in place increased credit requirements for high school graduation and proficiency exams for many of the core academic courses that students are required to take. To graduate, students were previously required to obtain 21.5 credits, with 4 in English, 3 in math, 3 in science, 3 in social studies, 1.5 in health and physical education, 2 in arts and humanities, and 5 electives. By June 2002, however, students would be required to complete 23.5 credits, with 4 in English, 4 in math, 4 in science, 3 in social studies, 2 in world languages, 1.5 in health, 2 in art, and 3 electives. One-sixth of the final grade in the English, math, and science courses is to be based on the new citywide proficiency exams. At first glance, these increases in high school graduation requirements seem straightforward, although perhaps difficult to meet. Unfortunately, implementation is proving to be anything but straightforward.

First, the 23.5 credits create a very tight schedule for students, given that only 6 credits are typically earned per year. This has led the district to offer block scheduling, which enables students to complete a course in one semester instead of two. Block scheduling allows students to complete 8 credits per year, thus introducing greater flexibility.

Second, the proficiency exams were originally thought of as end-of-course exams that would count as one-sixth of the final grade in a course. But using the proficiency exams as part of the final grade requires quick turnaround time for scoring and reporting back to teachers. It soon became apparent that the proficiency exams could not be end-of-course exams; instead, they need to be given before the end of the course if results are to be available in time to be incorporated into course grades.

To shorten the scoring turnaround time, proficiency exams are being revised to be both shorter and more dominated by a multiple-choice format. At one point, consideration was given to using only the multiple-choice portion of the test for teacher grades, but that approach was rejected as setting a poor target for students and teachers. Not limiting the course grade portion of the exams to multiple-choice requires, in turn, that students' constructed response answers be scored either by the contractor in time to return scores to teachers before the end of the year or by teachers. If the latter option is selected, students' constructed response answers would be copied, with the originals taken away for external scoring and the copies left for the teacher to score and use as one-sixth of the students' grades. External scoring is necessary to ensure lack of bias when exam scores are used for high-stakes promotion and graduation decisions. This option drives an increase in test cost, because the constructed response items would need to be replenished annually. Teacher scoring, in turn, requires professional development for teachers to learn to score the exams, which may turn out to be a powerful and positive intervention. Professional development also drives cost, however, as the collective bargaining agreement in Philadelphia limits administrative control over teacher time.

A third complication arose from the need to administer the exams before the end of the course. Block-scheduled courses move at twice the pace of courses completed over two semesters. Because the proficiency exams are to be used as a part of the school performance index, how will results from block-scheduled courses be adjusted to be comparable to results from courses completed over two semesters? Clearly, less instruction will have been completed in a block-scheduled course at the time of administration.

Finally, questions came up about how the district should implement the requirement that proficiency exam scores count as one-sixth of the teacher's course grade. Ultimately, it was decided to provide information on how the teachers' students scored relative to the district and school distribution, and within that context each teacher would be allowed to decide how to implement the one-sixth requirement. This would result in differences among teachers in how much the performance examination scores count.

CREATING A NEW SCHOOL PERFORMANCE INDEX. The district decided to use state assessment scores as part of its school accountability program to reduce the total amount of testing time for students and to better integrate the assessment and accountability programs of the district with those of the state. This decision required the development of a new school performance index, however, because state testing was replacing Stanford 9 testing at various levels and in various subjects. Creating a new school performance index, in turn, requires setting new school targets. All of these changes are sure to cause confusion. At the same time, creating a new school performance index opens up the opportunity to correct flaws in the first index.

The initial school performance index was a function of students' moving into and out of various proficiency levels on the Stanford 9, as well as student and staff attendance and student promotion and persistence. The approach appeared to keep teachers and administrators focused on the lower end of the student achievement distribution. Further, the index was not easy for educators and lay people to understand.

The new index will be based on students' average scale scores across the various tests involved. The new index has several advantages.

—The index becomes a function of changes in each student's achievement and not simply changes in the performance level distribution.

—Calculating the index and determining its statistical properties are straightforward. It is hoped that the index will also be easier to explain and understand.

—Changing the metric for the performance index makes clear that the index is new. In contrast, an index that looked similar to the first index might be confusing, inviting inappropriate comparisons over time.

—A new index allows the district to move away from reliance on the Stanford 9 proficiency levels, which are inappropriately high, especially in the upper grades and in math and science.

In the initial index, the various components, with a couple of exceptions, were to be weighted equally. In fact, they were not. In the new index, each component will be standardized, with a common mean and variance in the baseline year. This will result in equal weighting or, for example, weighting student and staff attendance .5, as the policy requires.

District simulations revealed that the new and old performance indexes are correlated nearly 1.0, and correlations of school gains are a surprisingly high .8. This means that schools will be rank-ordered on the new performance index essentially as they were on the initial index, unless some schools become more productive than they were.

The district has not yet set final targets for school gains on the new index. Three approaches are under consideration. First is to translate standards set on the old index into the metric of the new index. Second is to regress student performance against year of performance for each school, setting standards in terms of some function of the slopes of these school regressions (for example, a school's target could be the average slope). Third is to take the slopes and intercepts from the school-by-school regressions, regressing slope on intercept. Each school's target is set as the predicted slope given their intercept.

Current school targets set the highest standards for the lowest performing schools, reflecting a commitment to bringing all students in all schools to the same high standard. Setting each school's target as the average of the rates of gain across schools would make each school have the same target, which might be fair to the lowest scoring schools but would be less fair to the highest scoring schools. Further, it would appear to step away from the commitment of bringing all students and schools to the same high standard. Taking advantage of the strengths of both these approaches, different schools could have different targets to reach in the short run. At the same time, at least in theory, the targets would be ones that schools have demonstrated are possible to reach. For schools distant from the mean slope and intercept, the predicted slopes will have large standard errors. Some predicted values might be inappropriate. The district is in the process of studying these various approaches to setting school targets.

MINIMIZING TESTING BURDEN. One of the high-profile issues in any assessment and accountability program concerns amount of testing time. Valid and reliable tests take time to complete. Offering students multiple opportunities to demonstrate that they have reached a standard also takes testing time. The best estimates of school value added to student achievement require longitudinal data on students, the generation of which, in turn, requires frequent testing.

The Philadelphia school district has struggled mightily with the conflict between creating good data for accountability decisions and keeping test burden under control. First, the district replaced some district testing with state tests. Second, the district uses cross-cohort data, not longitudinal data, to estimate school accountability. Third, testing time limits have been reduced. Unfortunately, evidence shows that, to some extent, tests have become difficult to complete in the time allotted. Fourth, the district has moved toward less reliance on extended response performance assessments and greater reliance on multiple-choice formats, which allow testing a wider range of content in a shorter period of time. But some student achievement is hard to assess with a multiple-choice format. Fifth, the number of pilot items included in each test form has been kept to a minimum. Creating equivalent forms of a test for future administration requires embedding pilot items in each assessment. The more pilot items embedded, the longer it takes for students to complete the test. To some extent, this problem can be addressed by using rotated forms. Nevertheless, fewer pilot items are embedded than would be ideal, which means fewer items are released to the public because fewer replacement items are available.

The many possible uses of test results—for example, benchmarking school and district performance against national performance, promoting instructional improvement, informing student placement decisions, judging school progress—cannot be met by one or even two tests. The reduction of test burden forces district officials to clarify the purposes and prioritize the uses of the testing program.

SETTING STANDARDS FOR HIGH SCHOOL GRADUATION AND GRADE-TO-GRADE PROMOTION. The district is publicly committed to increasing the standards for high school graduation and grade-to-grade promotion. District simulations of the impact of these new standards are sobering. For example, in school year 2001–02, without an opportunity for students to take a second-chance test, less than 50 percent of fourth-grade students were estimated to meet the standard for promotion to fifth grade, less than 25 percent of eighth-grade students were estimated to meet the standard for promotion to ninth grade, and less than 10 percent of seniors were estimated to meet the standard for graduation from high school. The impact differs by ethnic group, with African Americans and Hispanics the hardest hit. For example, slightly less than 15 percent of African American or Hispanic students were estimated to meet the standard for promotion to ninth grade, and slightly less than 4 percent were estimated to meet the standard for high school graduation.

These results are unacceptable. The district is caught between wanting to maintain a commitment to high standards, on the one hand, and realizing that its current announced plans will lead to unacceptable results, on the other. The district does not want to be seen as watering down its standards. At the same time, the district recognizes that students should not be inappropriately penalized by unreasonably high standards. Simulations have suggested alternative courses of action, leading the district to set interim standards.

One alternative would be to require students to meet the below basic 3 standard (the highest of the three below basic score bands), instead of the basic standard on the Stanford 9. Another possibility would be to move from requiring that students meet the standard in each separate subject (the conjunctive standard) to requiring that students meet the standard in an average across subjects (the compensatory standard). Two approaches to putting the compensatory standard into operation are being explored. One is to translate student scores into performance levels and then average across subjects. The other is to translate student performance into normal curve equivalents and then average. Students who are not tested would receive a zero under either approach. Simulations reveal that a higher percentage of students would meet the standards if they were set at below basic 3, they were based on the compensatory method, and they used normal curve equivalents.

The district is considering initially setting higher standards in the elementary school than in the middle and high school. This approach would reflect the fact that elementary schools are achieving higher levels of performance and would recognize that reforms need to be phased in, so that students will have benefited from a high-quality elementary, middle, and high school experience before they are required to meet demanding high school graduation standards. Clearly, the interim standards will be more demanding than previous standards. Thus, the district will be maintaining its commitment to increasing standards, but it will be implementing the increase in such a way as to allow time for the system to come into alignment instructionally and to ensure that the system is not unfairly penalizing students.

Evidence of Effects and Prognosis for Continued Impact

Estimating the impact of the accountability system in Philadelphia is difficult. Neither the results nor their interpretation is certain. A controlled experiment was not done; no comparison groups were in place. Further, the program is young and evolving. Still, judgments must be made. Overall, we conclude that the early effects of Philadelphia's assessment and accountability program have been positive on both student persistence and student achievement. Before presenting our analysis, however, three aspects of estimating effects that make the work difficult should be considered.

First, one must estimate what the true changes are in student persistence and achievement since the accountability program was initiated. The Stanford

9 achievement test is not only an indicator of student achievement, but also an integral part of the assessment and accountability intervention. There could be spurious gains on the Stanford 9, especially because the same form was used repeatedly, thus setting a narrower target than might be ideal. Given a good record-keeping system, statistics on persistence are less susceptible to inflation.

Second, assessing the effects of the program requires deciding what is included as a part of the program and what is not. On the one hand, charter schools were initiated in the district at roughly the same time as the assessment and accountability program. We see these two initiatives as separate. Further, a look at the results for the charter schools suggests that the schools are too few in number to affect district averages and too variable in their performance to have a large average effect on their own. On the other hand, given that fairness is one of our three criteria for a good assessment and accountability program, we do include as part of the program such supports to students as a summer school experience for those who score low on the Stanford 9 and such supports to schools as reduced class sizes for students who are retained.

Third, the Philadelphia assessment and accountability program is a work in progress. We cannot know yet what its ultimate effects will be. We hope that the program continues to improve indefinitely. On the near horizon are a number of important improvements. A new form of the Stanford 9 will set a better target, as will the new proficiency examinations and the curriculum-embedded early-warning testing system in kindergarten through grade three. High-stakes testing for students is being implemented in 2001 and will be phased in over the next several years. Our framework predicts that these and other changes will increase the positive effects on student persistence and achievement.

GAINS, BUT SLOWING IMPROVEMENT. The purpose of implementing an assessment and accountability program is to improve student learning of worthwhile content. Five years of Philadelphia data (from the 1995–96 school year baseline scores through the 1999–2000 school year results) reveal improving test scores at the same time that increasing numbers of students are participating in the testing program (see table 1). For example, in fourth-grade reading, the percentage of students scoring at the basic level or above increased from 43.5 percent to 59.6 percent. In fourth-grade mathematics, the percentages increased from 34.9 percent to 51.5 percent. Advances toward the long-term goal of having most students achieve at proficient levels were also realized. From the baseline year through 1999–2000, the percentage of

Table 1. Proportion of Philadelphia Students Scoring Basic or Higher on the Stanford Achievement Test, Ninth Edition
Percent

	School year				
Subject and grade	*1995–96*	*1996–97*	*1997–98*	*1998–99*	*1999–2000*
Reading					
Grade four	43.5	51.3	56.9	57.6	59.6
Grade eight	48.7	55.0	59.6	62.5	60.5
Grade eleven	25.9	34.9	34.1	37.2	38.7
Math					
Grade four	34.9	44.4	47.7	50.0	51.5
Grade eight	21.1	24.5	31.6	30.7	28.4
Grade eleven	12.0	14.8	16.5	15.8	17.2

Source: Based on authors' calculations.

students achieving at proficient levels districtwide improved from 7.7 percent to 12.2 percent. Although the rate of improvement was substantial, fewer than one in eight students had achieved proficient performance by 1999–2000.

Over the same period, assessment participation rates increased substantially, from 71.5 percent to 88.1 percent. The strongest increases in participation occurred in high schools (from 51 percent to 78 percent) and among special education students (from 31 percent to 70 percent) and English language learners (from 56 percent to 85 percent). This result is significant because in large-scale testing programs, increases in the proportion of participating students are typically associated with declines in achievement.

From 1995–96 to 1999-2000, on-time, four-year graduation rates increased from 49 percent to 57 percent, and promotion rates improved from 85 percent to 93 percent. Both staff and student attendance also improved over this period. For example, the proportion of staff attending at least 95 percent of the time increased from 54 percent to 63 percent from 1995–96 to 1999–2000.

Some may question whether the Stanford 9 changes represent real achievement gains. Unfortunately, these results are on repeated uses of the same form of the Stanford 9, so there probably is some inflation of gains that would not be found on a new form.[23] Daniel M. Koretz, Daniel F. McCaffrey, and Laura S. Hamilton concluded that validating gains under high-stakes conditions is not currently possible. Until methodologies are developed, they recommend examination of changes on external measures.[24] Fortunately, in Philadelphia, the state test presents just such an opportunity.

Philadelphia's advances on the Stanford 9 were also seen on the state test scale scores, with mean 1300 and standard deviation 200 (see table 2).

Table 2. Mean Philadelphia Scale Score on the Pennsylvania System of School Assessment

Subject and grade	School year				
	1995–96	*1996–97*	*1997–98*	*1998–99*	*1999–2000*
Reading					
Grade five	1090	1110	1090	1120	1140
Grade eight	1080	1140	1120	1130	1120
Grade eleven	1160	1140	1140	1140	1130
Math					
Grade five	1110	1130	1140	1140	1140
Grade eight	1070	1110	1120	1120	1130
Grade eleven	1170	1130	1120	1140	1160

Source: Based on authors' calculations.

District- and school-level performance generally improved on the PSSA from 1995–96 through 1999–2000, even though the test was not being used during that period for student or school accountability. Districtwide reading and mathematics scale scores improved in each grade except eleven, but in grade eleven the participation rate rose dramatically. The PSSA reading and mathematics scores improved over the four years in nine out of every ten Philadelphia schools.

To what should the increase in student persistence and achievement be attributed? Would the same level of improvement have been achieved without implementation of the assessment and accountability program? We find no alternative explanation for the gains that is as compelling as the district's aggressive and ambitious assessment and accountability program, together with its capacity-building initiatives, including targeted summer school and reduced class size. Before the implementation of the accountability and assessment program (for the first half of the 1990s), achievement and student persistence rates had been declining in Philadelphia.

Two factors are important to watch: the need to turn early achievement gains into continuous program improvement and the limitations of low funding levels. Both are related to the fact that although gains were achieved in each of the first four years of Philadelphia's accountability program, most of the gains occurred early, and the rate of improvement has slowed in successive years.

The pattern of strong early gains followed by slowing improvement is one that has been observed in other large-scale testing programs. In the early years of the program, schools learn to signal the importance of the tests to students and parents, create optimal testing environments, and ensure that students are familiar with test formats. Once these factors are optimized, the hard work of upgrading curriculum and improving instructional programs begins.

Evidence exists that curricular and instructional improvement is occurring where it was not happening before, although program improvement is not consistent across the district. In many places, students are being assigned work that requires them to communicate their understandings orally and in writing and to apply their understandings to solve real-world problems. In many places, teachers within and across grades are beginning to collaborate to develop curriculum and design instructional programs. The places where this work is happening systematically are the exception, however, and not the rule. These findings of changes in instructional practices are based on a number of studies, some conducted by the district, but most conducted by researchers outside the district.[25] Unfortunately, the set of studies has many gaps, leaving us less knowledgeable about assessment and accountability's effects on instructional practices than we would like.

THE SCHOOL DISTRICT CONTEXT. One factor in Philadelphia that has been an impediment to policy coherence is the range of initiatives implemented by the central office. Although the stream of policy initiatives may have emanated from a framework that was coherent to its architects, finding a school that implemented them coherently is rare. The pace of change has been frenetic, and the quantity of initiatives that were introduced (for example, small learning communities, new curriculum standards, new curriculum frameworks, comprehensive support process, school improvement planning, multidisciplinary project requirements, service learning project requirements, adaptive instruction) was too large for substantial organizational learning to occur. Few schools were able to incorporate the many new district initiatives in a manner that resulted in increased organizational capacity. Most schools have struggled to comply with the initiatives.

THE STATE CONTEXT. Another factor that bears watching is the intersection of accountability and inadequate funding. Low teacher and administrator salaries, high turnover of teachers and principals, old and poorly maintained facilities, and large schools and classes are artifacts of the Philadelphia school district's underfunding. The perception that accountability exists without matched support lowers morale and commitment. The district recognizes the conundrum: Philadelphia needs to show results before it can expect state-added support, but without added state support, the amount of improvement the district is able to attain is limited.

Summary and Conclusions

Student achievement in Philadelphia is low. Admittedly, large percentages of Philadelphia students come from low-income families; their achievement might be expected to be low. At the same time, the opportunities to learn available to Philadelphia students could be better. The content of instruction provided to students could be more ambitious, focused on key ideas in the academic subjects and balanced between communicating, reasoning, and problem solving, on the one hand, and mastery of facts and basic skills, on the other. Teachers could accept more responsibility for student achievement. At the same time, students could try harder than they do. In short, the Philadelphia school system was much in need of reform when Superintendent David Hornbeck took the reins in 1994, launching the assessment and accountability program.

Many argue that a high-stakes assessment and accountability program dumbs down the curriculum. This can be true and has, in some cases, been documented.[26] But an assessment and accountability program that pursues the three goals of setting a good target, making accountability symmetrical for schools and students, and achieving fairness in implementation is unlikely to dumb down the curriculum. Further, one must take into account a curriculum's starting point when initiating and evaluating an assessment and accountability program. In the case of Philadelphia, improvement clearly was needed. Doing nothing was not an option.

Some criticize high-stakes assessment and accountability for extinguishing students' intrinsic motivation to learn. This outcome also seems possible. However, if intrinsic motivation is already low, perhaps a little extrinsic motivation can help. The introduction of the accountability system jarred the prevailing culture and created opportunities for the Board of Education and educators to rethink the manner in which resources were allocated, the use of time, and student grouping practices. Based on the evidence, we conclude that, at least thus far, the assessment and accountability program in Philadelphia is having positive effects on the quality of instruction offered to students and, in turn, on the persistence and achievement of students. Additional components of the program are just coming on line, and our framework leads us to predict they will enhance the positive effect.

Although the early results from the assessment and accountability program are encouraging and the future of the program looks promising, much remains to be done. In particular, we are concerned about resources for instructional improvement. All too often, early gains in student achievement hit a wall after the first three or four years of reform. Once the most accessible inefficiencies have been corrected, will the assessment and accountability program in Philadelphia bring about continued improvements in the quality of instruction and student achievement? Will future resources be adequate to support continued improvements in instruction? Professional development, improved materials, summer programs, and reduced class size all cost substantial amounts of money. In short, will the assessment and accountability program be fair?

We have organized our analysis of the Philadelphia assessment and accountability program around the framework of setting a good target, symmetry for students and schools, and fairness. In many ways, the Philadelphia assessment and accountability program has strong characteristics when judged against these three goals. Still, there are weaknesses as well. Designing and implementing an assessment and accountability program for an urban school district requires a commitment to continuous improvement. We are convinced that the perfect system can never be realized. We are equally convinced that useful systems can be put in place and that they can be improved over time. That is what Philadelphia is doing, and what we hope it will continue to do in the future.

With regard to setting a good target, many positive outcomes of the Philadelphia assessment and accountability program can be cited. The district's movement away from the Stanford 9 and toward greater reliance on proficiency exams aligned with district content standards is a case in point. The district's commitment to testing in multiple subjects and multiple grades is another. The performance index gives schools incentives to test all students. Even for the Stanford 9, the district has replaced some items with culturally inclusive items, thus tailoring the test to the Philadelphia context.

But there are weaknesses in the targets set as well. First, the same form of the Stanford 9 has been used repeatedly. This undoubtedly has produced spurious gains in student achievement, though some of the gains are real. Second, although the district has struggled to set realistic targets for student achievement and school improvement, thus far the targets have been set too high. To the district's credit, it is working hard to revise these standards. Third, the emphasis on moving students out of the below basic category on the Stanford 9 may have taken attention away from improving student achievement at higher levels. Fourth, there is some reason to fear that testing only in selected grades has created difficulties in getting the whole school, all teachers at all grades, to accept responsibility for student achievement.

With regard to the goal of symmetry, Philadelphia is to be congratulated for holding schools accountable first, and then phasing in student accountability to make the program symmetrical. Nevertheless, school accountability is linked to Stanford 9 performance, whereas student accountability emphasizes proficiency exams. The district is working to bring student and school accountability into alignment to improve the symmetry of their program.

Similarly, with regard to the goal of fairness, a number of pluses and some minuses can be seen in the Philadelphia assessment and accountability program. First, the district has been committed to providing the support it believes necessary for schools to succeed with students. When the support has been lacking, the district has pulled back on the accountability expectations. But providing the necessary resources is a tremendous challenge that might not be met. Second, the district's decision to phase in student accountability after first instituting school accountability is likely to have facilitated improved opportunities to learn for students before holding them accountable. Moreover, student accountability allows students multiple attempts to reach a standard on a particular test, as well as opportunities to take different second-chance tests. In the interim, students are required to attend summer school to improve their knowledge and skills. Finally, throughout the implementation process, the district has expressed concern for the accuracy of its data and has worked to bring accuracy to acceptable levels.

But more work needs to be done to create fairness. The most important issue ahead concerns resources for schools and teachers to be successful. At the heart of the problem is attracting qualified teachers, who are in short supply, especially in urban settings. The accuracy of the school performance index is another issue. Accuracy might be improved if the index were created through use of two-year rolling averages, so that even small schools would have relatively small standard errors in estimating value added to student achievement.

Designing and implementing an assessment and accountability program often requires a careful balancing act. For example, tensions arise between

—the need to have assessments over time that are carefully calibrated, one to another, so that trends can be monitored and the need to improve the assessments, based on experience and shifting content priorities;

—the desire to include multiple-choice items in assessments, because such tests take less time, are more reliable, and are easier to equate over time, and the recognition that multiple-choice items may not measure the same content dimensions as performance assessment tasks;

—the desire to use assessments to leverage changes in classroom practice and the reality of working with assessments, at least initially, that do not have the best psychometric properties; and

—the need to use an assessment on which students are motivated to perform their best and the difficulty of meeting the psychometric and opportunity-to-learn requirements for a high-stakes test for students.

The Philadelphia school district has recognized these tensions and attempted to take reasonable and responsible positions on each. To evaluate the assessment and accountability program, the school board created an external Accountability and Assessment Advisory Panel. Initially, the school board wanted a panel that would come in, evaluate the program, submit a report, and leave. Wisely, we believe, the board decided instead to put in place a panel that would work with it over time, with the goal of building and implementing the best assessment and accountability program possible. Fortunately, the panel and the school district also formed a good working relationship.

The person who initiated the assessment and accountability program in Philadelphia, David Hornbeck, is no longer superintendent. Turnover in district superintendents is common, but it is also debilitating. As one extreme, the Kansas City, Kansas, school district has had twenty superintendents in thirty years. This revolving-door style of leadership makes sustained school reform impossible. We can only hope that when a new superintendent is found for Philadelphia, the leadership will continue the difficult and challenging work of using assessment and accountability to improve the quality of education for students.

Comment by Daniel Koretz

Andrew Porter and Mitchell Chester point out a number of positive aspects of Philadelphia's assessment and accountability program and make their case for them. A couple of aspects of the paper are particularly noteworthy. The authors' attention to decision consistency is laudable, but as Tom Kane suggested during his presentation at the Brookings conference, they probably have it wrong, and the decision inconsistency is probably much worse than a model based simply on sampling of kids suggests. But at least they are attending to the problem. Their use of normative data, which is a passing point in the paper, is an important improvement. Trying to base an accountability system solely on a priori standards, without reference to normative data, is asking for trouble. The authors found that it was not defensible to use only a priori standards and did make reference to normative data.

Despite these comments, I found the paper disturbing because it gives an unwarrantedly positive view of what has been done in Philadelphia, and I will criticize the paper on four grounds. First, Porter and Chester provide a series of assertions as if they were imperatives. These may or may not be reasonable assertions, but they are nonetheless assertions based in large case on, at best, informed judgment. They say that educators have to implement accountability in specific ways. The word "must" appears repeatedly. I do not think those claims are warranted. Second, they ignore most of the relevant research, which gives me at least a basis for being skeptical about some of the positive results that they cite. Third, the paper provides a cursory and misleading approach to the core problem of the validation of gains. Fourth, the paper therefore provides an overly sanguine view of the impact of the program.

I will take each of these in turn.

Porter and Chester say that one must test in all grades and one must have symmetric accountability; that is, there must be high stakes for both kids and teachers. Perhaps this is true. But, until recently, most systems, including, for instance, educational systems in Japan, did not have these features. So perhaps it is not absolutely necessary to have symmetric accountability and testing in every grade. The evidentiary basis for saying how good or bad it is to do is thin, because it is a new idea that has not been tried very often.

More important, the paper ignores relevant research, and I think this is a critical failure. The only way educators are going to avoid making the same mistakes over and over again is if knowledge about educational reforms is allowed to accumulate. Moreover, earlier research is what sets prior beliefs about what to worry about in looking at new research, and Porter and Chester did not take prior research into account in that way.

What are some findings of research to date about test-based accountability? The effects on practice are mixed. For a good overview of this, I would recommend the work of Brian Stecher.[27] It is not uncommon to find positive effects; for instance, an increase in writing. But it is also common to find undesirable effects. Narrowing of instruction is a common negative effect, research has shown that people also take other kinds of shortcuts to raise test scores, and they are inclined to take them if the goals are unreasonably high, which I suspect they were for low-achieving schools in Philadelphia. And most important, the available research, while not copious, fairly consistently shows inflation of scores—not modest inflation of scores, but egregious inflation of scores.

What do I mean by inflation of scores? I will use research carried out in Kentucky to illustrate this. The system in Philadelphia bears an uncanny resemblance to the system in Kentucky; both were designed by David Hornbeck. While there are some important differences, such as no stakes for individual kids in Kentucky, a large part of the systems is the same.

The Kentucky program generated an enormous amount of research, which set my expectations for looking at Philadelphia. Examples include the studies by Daniel Koretz and Sheila I. Barron, Daniel Koretz and others, Brian M. Stecher and others, and Brian M. Stecher and Sheila I. Barron.[28] I would have faulted Porter and Chester less for citing and rejecting this and other relevant research as either incorrect or inapplicable, but they simply made no mention of it. By ignoring negative findings from relevant studies of similar systems, Porter and Chester deprive the readers of perspective and bias their impressions of Porter and Chester's own findings.

One of the things that research about the Kentucky system showed was substantial score inflation. One example of this finding is shown in figure 1. KIRIS is the state's high-stakes test (the Kentucky Instructional Results Information System), and ACT is the ACT Assessment, which is the dominant college admissions test in Kentucky. Porter and Chester refer to the correlation between two tests as a reason to be optimistic that trends in scores will be similar on the two tests. The Kentucky Department of Education offered this argument in defense of KIRIS when parents of high-achieving students said that they did not want teachers focusing on the state's tests when the ACT is what affects students' admissions to college. The Kentucky Department of Education argued that because scores on the two tests correlate substantially in any one year, it is reasonable to expect that an increase on one will be mirrored by an increase on the second.

As indicated by figure 1, in the case of mathematics, a very large increase in the mean score on KIRIS was accompanied by no increase at all in average ACT scores. (This comparison was limited to students who took both tests, a bit under half of the total senior cohort.) Similar but less extreme disparities in trends were apparent in other subjects. At the time this divergence in scores was occurring, the cross-sectional correlation between ACT and KIRIS scores remained stable. There is no reason to expect otherwise; a correlation tells about similarities in rankings but is entirely insensitive to differences in means.

Figure 1. Trends in Mean Mathematics Scores in Kentucky, KIRIS and ACT

Standard deviation

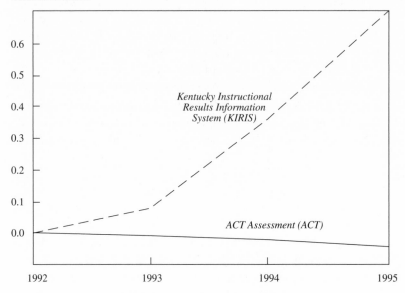

There are other examples of score inflation in the literature, but the clearest may be a study I conducted with Robert L. Linn, Steve Dunbar, and Lorrie A. Shepard over a decade ago.[29] One district included in this study had been under what is at most a moderate-stakes system by today's standards. The district had been using the test marked by a diamond in figure 2 for years. The district subsequently dropped it and began using a new test, indicated by squares in figure 2. Scores were much lower on the new test. The scores in the figure are third-grade math. Scores dropped by half an academic year immediately. Four years later, however, scores were back up where they had been.

At the end of the four years, Linn, Dunbar, Shepard, and I created a random sample of classrooms and gave the test that had been administered by the district until four years earlier. The scores on the test we administered were what they had been on the new test the first year the district had used it.

A final example comes from a study of Texas conducted by three of my colleagues.[30] It shows the importance of external validation of test score gains. Figure 3 depicts the differential score inflation found in Texas; that is, greater score inflation among minority students than among non-Hispanic whites.

Figure 2. Performance on Coached and Uncoached Tests

Grade equivalents

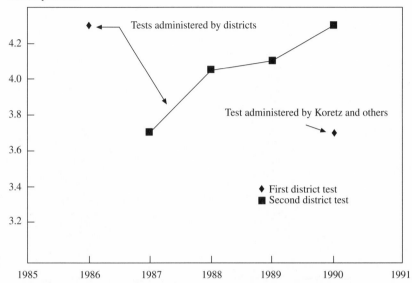

Source: Daniel Koretz and others, "The Effects of High-Stakes Testing: Preliminary Evidence about Generalization across Tests," presented at "The Effects of High-Stakes Testing," symposium conducted at the annual meetings of the American Educational Research Association and the National Council on Measurement in Education, Chicago, April 1991.

The black-white difference on the state's test shrank markedly, while the black-white difference on the National Assessment of Educational Progress did not shrink at all in the same years.

These studies suggest that one of the most serious threats to the validity of any inference about the effects of high-stakes testing programs is score inflation. Porter and Chester do mention score inflation. They attribute the possibility of score inflation primarily to the fact that the district has reused the same test year after year.

Reusing the same test is a good way to increase score inflation. There is no question about that. But the same test does not have to be used to get score inflation. Porter and Chester also suggest that dumbing down leads to score inflation and that this did not occur in Philadelphia. But score inflation can arise without dumbing down, just as it can arise without reuse of the same test. Furthermore, replacing the test with a new parallel form each year, which the authors recommend, will not solve the problem. For a test to be even approximately parallel, it has to be so close in content that the effects of inappropriate coaching are likely to generalize to some degree to the new form.

Figure 3. An Example of Differential Score Inflation from Texas: Differences between White and Black Mean Scores in Reading on NAEP and TAAS , 1994 and 1998

Standard deviation units

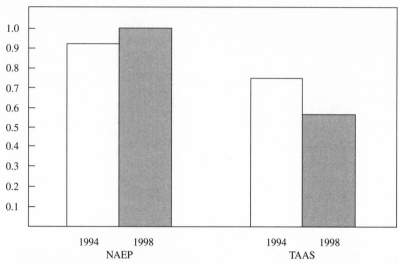

NAEP   TAAS

Source: Adapted from Stephen P. Klein and others, *What Do Test Scores in Texas Tell Us?* Issue Paper IP–202 (Santa Monica, Calif.: RAND, 2000) [www.rand.org/publications/IP/IP202/].
Note: NAEP = National Assessment of Educational Progress; TAAS = Texas Assessment of Academic Skills.

I started reading the Porter and Chester paper expecting to find evidence that score gains are meaningful in Philadelphia. The paper simply asserts that some of the gain is probably spurious but that the rest is meaningful. On what basis should these conclusions be believed? The paper does not have trends on the most recent state test results, placed on a comparable scale. The gains on the state test look small and erratic, but they may not be; one would have to know the scale to know how large the changes were. Validity is not an attribute of a test. It is an attribute of a conclusion or an inference based on scores. The question of validity, to simplify it, is the extent to which evidence from a test warrants the conclusions drawn from scores. When people are being paid or punished for changes in test scores, one key inference is whether students are learning more over time, commensurate with gains in scores.

Based on the evidence such as the findings above, I evaluate inferences of this sort with the presumption that a real threat to validity exists from possible score inflation. Something must be done to address and evaluate this threat to validity. None of this, however, is discussed well in the paper. The paper segues from a discussion of reliability into a discussion of validity without spelling out what the validity question is.

Figure 4. The Initial Rapid Gains in Test Scores: Evidence from Multiple State Assessments

Percentile rank

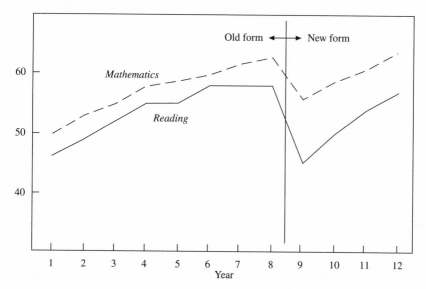

Source: Robert L. Linn, "Assessments and Accountability," *Educational Researcher*, vol. 21, no. 2 (2000), pp. 4–16.

Along similar lines, Porter and Chester also mention a problem with maintaining early, rapid initial gains in scores. This is presented not as a validity question, but as kind of a practical question of how to keep up the momentum. It is, however, another aspect of the validity of gains.

Psychometricians have known for many years that even in the absence of today's high stakes, test scores tend to rise rapidly in the first few years after a new test is introduced and then often plateau. In a recent paper on the uses of tests in accountability, Robert L. Linn presented a figure that shows this pattern, pooling data from a number of state testing programs (see figure 4).[31] Reading scores show the expected pattern: They rise for several years and then begin to plateau. Mathematics scores also show the rapid initial increase but show less of the later flattening out than one often sees in individual testing programs. Just as in the study by Koretz, Linn, Dunbar, and Shepard cited above, the gains vanish when a new test is introduced.[32]

What do the initial increases in scores mean about changes in student learning? The real problem of early initial gains is that absent some kind of confirmatory evidence from another source, it is impossible to know whether they mean anything. They might or they might not. Absent confirmatory data, no conclusions can be drawn.

The paper does not address what causes inflation of test scores, other than reuse of a test. Two of my colleagues and I recently put together a paper that presents a taxonomy of ways teachers respond to tests and then links how each of these responses might contribute to real and inflated gains.[33] We noted seven types of teacher responses:

—Teaching more,

—Working harder,

—Working more effectively,

—Reallocation,

—Alignment,

—Coaching, and

—Cheating.

The first three of these responses produce unambiguously meaningful gains in scores. The final response—cheating—can never produce meaningful gains and scores. The remaining responses can produce either meaningful gains or score inflation.

The response "reallocation" refers to shifting instructional resources from one place to another. These resources might be teaching time, a student's study time, or a parent's nagging emphasis. It can be any resource that contributes to learning. Thus reallocation is a shifting of whatever resources are thought to contribute to gains in student performance. Sometimes reallocation takes the form of greater alignment.

An essential aspect of score inflation is reallocation. People figure out what on the tests counts. Particularly if they have to show gains every year, they will worry about what specifically is on the test, because if they do not they are highly unlikely to have scores that move upward both rapidly and consistently, without occasional plateaus and downturns that have nothing to do with instructional quality.

Because the test is a small sample of what students should learn, the more people are encouraged to focus on the specific content of the test, the more likely it is that the rapid gains do not signal commensurate increases in student learning. That is, the more people focus on the content of the test instead of the domain it is supposed to represent, the more likely it is that score gains will be inflated.

Score inflation will not be solved by using tests that are worth teaching to or by using new forms every year. Measurement specialists know how to ameliorate the problem of score inflation, but they do not know how to solve it completely. No one yet has either a fix for the problem or a test-based accountability system that can fully avoid score inflation. Instead, researchers must ascertain, by the use of external evidence, case by case, whether the gains that are shown are meaningful.

These points show why I think the assessment of the accountability program's impact presented by Porter and Chester was a little credulous. I am more persuaded by their evidence such as changes in attendance rates. Those are hard to fake. Students are either present or not. The changes in attendance are remarkably positive, and Porter and Chester provide evidence of several other credible, positive changes.

But in terms of changes in test scores, I think more persuasive evidence is needed than Porter and Chester provide. Evidence must show what share of these gains is a sign of real improvement in student learning. Perhaps the state test scores could be used that way.

Finally, the paper does say strongly that programs of this sort need external evaluation, and I laud it for this. Very few such programs get a serious external evaluation, not only because it is expensive and time-consuming, but also because, unlike Philadelphia, most districts and states want no part of it. I have experienced this firsthand many times. I have had difficulty starting such studies, and I have had studies thrown out of districts and states. And I have also had one state demand (unsuccessfully) at the end of the process that I censor a report when the state's Department of Education did not like what the report said.

So Philadelphia is to be praised for allowing an evaluation, and the authors are to be praised for insisting on it. But evaluating these programs must be done from a different basis; that is, prior research must determine what are the most important or the most plausible threats to the conclusions to be drawn. Science is not a matter of proving what you want, but rather disproving threatening alternative explanations. Right now, given where recent research findings are, the single most threatening explanation, when you want to conclude that an accountability system is working, is the prospect of seriously inflated test scores. The evaluation of these programs ought to reflect that.

Comment by Theodore Hershberg

Americans in recent years have asked their schools to do something entirely unprecedented: educate all of their students, not only their top fifth, and educate all of them to levels far higher than were required in the past. The pedagogical vehicle introduced to achieve these goals—standards-based school reform—requires major changes in classroom instruction, in how schools are organized to support these changes, and in levels of funding. Although forty-nine states have embraced the standards movement, only a few have recognized the need for systems of accountability to accompany these reforms. The evidence available from around the country makes generally clear that accountability works. States showing the most significant gains in the National Assessment of Educational Progress—Kentucky, North Carolina, and Texas—are also the states that have increased school funding and implemented effective systems of accountability. The experience of those that have not, such as New Jersey, suggests the futility of standards reforms without accountability. More money alone wins the equity battle, but it loses the school reform war.

Andrew Porter and Mitchell Chester describe the accountability system used in Philadelphia as part of *Children Achieving*, the complex standards-driven reform agenda put in place by David Hornbeck, who came to Philadelphia in 1994 as superintendent of the public schools. The authors' account is a detailed and highly accurate portrayal of the system instituted by the school district. It is especially commendable for providing readers with a how-to primer as well as a rich description of the adjustments that were made in midstream as the system evolved in response to many specific challenges encountered along the way.

Daniel Koretz commented on the paper using a sophisticated psychometric lens, and while he found serious problems in the student test data, I remain convinced that real progress was made despite the shortcomings he identified. Ultimately persuasive are that student test scores continued to rise even though over time more students—particularly lower performing students—took the tests and that the scores improved on both the Pennsylvania System of School Assessment (PSSA) and the tests used by the school district (Stanford Achievement Test, Ninth Edition, or Stanford 9). Despite the methodological concerns raised by Koretz, these factors suggest strongly that some good things were happening in Philadelphia.

Given that psychometrics is not my field, my contribution is to establish the local and national contexts in which to understand the Philadelphia experience. *Children Achieving* included ten key elements—the tenth being an insistence that for the program to succeed all of the preceding nine had to be implemented. The record of standards-based school reform across school districts of all sizes and in all locations makes absolutely clear that success is difficult to achieve in the best of circumstances; that is, when adequate financial resources are available and all key stakeholders from the teachers unions and administrators to the school board and parents share the same goal. This was decidedly not the case in Philadelphia.

While separating out the individual contributions to student achievement from the overall reform effort provided by the accountability system is impossible, many factors external to the reform plan had an enormous impact on its outcomes. Given the opposition of the Philadelphia Federation of Teachers (PFT), the lack of adequate financial resources to support the reforms, the complicating role of race, and the resistance of those with vested interests in the noninstructional components of the status quo, what impresses most is that *Children Achieving* succeeded at all.

The Philadelphia Context

That Superintendent Hornbeck and the PFT got off to a bad start is undeniable. Why remains a matter of dispute. Union leaders insisted they were ignored from the outset—that the superintendent refused to open his plan to compromise. Hornbeck, a key architect of the standards-based reforms undertaken in Kentucky in the early 1990s and a nationally known educator, contended that he had a ten-point plan to reform the city's troubled schools and that he had been invited to Philadelphia by the school board and the mayor to implement it.

The plan's accountability system, however, did not sit well with the union. "Teacher performance and student achievement," argued Deborah Willig, the attorney representing the PFT, "have nothing to do with each other." And Jack Steinberg, the union's secretary, answered his own question on PBS's *Merrow Report*: "Can you evaluate a teacher on the performance of the students? No, you cannot." When the first teacher contract was negotiated in 1996, the school district hailed its accountability components, while the union applauded the absence of such provisions and declared accountability "dead."

Both the union and the district sought ways out of their impasse, meeting behind the scenes on repeated occasions. Sandra Feldman, national president of the American Federation of Teachers, came to Philadelphia at the behest of the mayor in an effort to bridge the gap. Labor-management consultants were hired to help the two sides find common ground, but all to no avail. As time passed the lines drawn early between them not only failed to close, but the distance separating them grew.

The union opposed *Children Achieving* almost from the start. The *PFT Reporter,* the union's monthly newsletter, kept up regular attacks on the reform plan. Depending on which side of the fence you sat, these could be characterized as a steady stream of compelling criticism or poisonous invective. By the end of Hornbeck's tenure in 2000, and despite improvements in test scores, attendance, and dropout rates, the large majority of Philadelphia teachers surveyed claimed they had no confidence in the reform plan or in the superintendent. So strong was the PFT's opposition that when Hornbeck announced his resignation, and the local media reflected on his accomplishments, the union refused to acknowledge the gains that had been made. The irony in so doing was to deny its own members credit for the substantial improvement in student performance their labors had produced.

Children Achieving also lacked adequate financial resources to make the reforms work. The school district needed more than $100 million to close an existing deficit, and Hornbeck estimated that an additional $350 million would be required annually to cover the costs of multiple interventions—full-day kindergarten, smaller class size in K–3, up-to-date technologies and facilities, after-school and summer school programs, and family centers, among many others—that children from low-income families would need to make and sustain academic gains. Philadelphia spends close to $2,000 less per child than the average of the school districts in the surrounding suburban counties, which means that in each classroom of thirty students there is roughly $60,000 less to spend for their education. Had the Philadelphia school district, with 215,000 children, been able to spend simply the same amount per child as the average in the suburban districts, the justifiably ambitious reform agenda of *Children Achieving* would have been more than fully funded.

Children Achieving never received the funding it needed, and the sources of the district's relatively inadequate per-pupil spending are found at both the local and state level. Although the city's school tax effort is low when compared with other communities in Pennsylvania, Philadelphians carry the highest overall tax burden in the Commonwealth, which is why the city is unable to raise the local real estate tax that supports its schools.

The major source of the problem is inadequate state funding. In 1975 the Commonwealth provided roughly 55 percent of total school funding. Since then it has fallen to 35 percent, which means that school districts have had to turn largely to local property taxes to make up for the shortfall. Although observers find it hard to believe because Pennsylvania ranks eighth in per-pupil spending nationally, its funding system is a nonsystem, no longer related to either enrollment or poverty or shaped by policy and principle. A Pennsylvania House of Representatives resolution (HR 42), which passed in June 2001 by a vote of 195-1, called the state's approach to school funding "nationally recognized as one of the most inequitable among the 50 states." *Education Week* gave Pennsylvania a grade of "D-" for its school funding system, which many describe as among the most regressive in the nation. Even the state Board of Education formed a subcommittee to examine the charges of inadequacy and inequity and to recommend changes.

Although Philadelphia receives 59 percent of its funding from the state, the problems with inadequate resources—for example, the district has received no additional per-pupil funding despite a growth in student enrollment of more than twenty-one thousand since 1991—explain the district's plight. In the last six years, the district's budget grew more slowly than inflation after accounting for the costs of safety and security, English speakers of other languages, charter schools, all-day kindergarten, and court-mandated placements in social service agencies. The district faces a projected budget deficit for fiscal 2002 of $233 million.

New funding remains a necessary, not a sufficient, means to raise student achievement—standards-based reform and accountability being the others. *Children Achieving* lacked the financial resources remotely commensurate to meet the unique challenges it faced in raising the academic achievement level of 215,000 students, the majority of whom were minorities living in poverty.

Other factors—race, media coverage, and the power of vested interests to protect their investment in the status quo—posed serious obstacles to the *Children Achieving* reform agenda. Some people felt that Hornbeck, who is white, should not have been given the job. The school board was split: Four minority members wanted an African American candidate and the four white members wanted Hornbeck. At the final tally, the tie was broken when a ninth and deciding vote was cast for Hornbeck by Ruth Hayre, an African American, reportedly because Hornbeck favored accountability. Some black activists insisted that a white superintendent was an inappropriate role model. Warren Simmons, president of the Annenberg Institute for School Reform and an African American, was publicly scolded by the African American City Council president and almost lost his job as president of the Philadelphia Education Fund, because he argued at an education conference session in New Orleans that race was in fact an important issue in Philadelphia school reform.

Although owned by the same parent company (Knight Ridder's Philadelphia Newspapers Inc.), the city's two major newspapers—the *Daily News* (its readers are primarily city residents) and the *Philadelphia Inquirer* (its subscription base is majority suburban)—chose opposite sides in the debate over Hornbeck and *Children Achieving*. The editor, reporters, and columnists at the *Daily News* found fault most everywhere, supporting the union and keeping the issue of race near the surface. The *Philadelphia Inquirer* was generally supportive of the superintendent and his reform agenda. This diet of daily argument in the city's press over the value of *Children Achieving* undermined efforts to forge a public consensus behind the reforms.

Finally, school reform of any significant stripe poses a challenge to the status quo. Roughly 30 percent of the school district's annual budget goes for noninstructional expenses, such as transportation, food services, construction, physical plant, and the like. In a district the size of Philadelphia, that means that almost half a billion dollars in contracts goes out each year to companies and vendors of all types for a wide array of support services. When Hornbeck divided the school district into twenty-two clusters—each with several elementary schools, two or three middle schools, and one high school (a feeder pattern)—and talked about budgetary independence down the road, many people felt the security of their business arrangements were threatened. School reformers have much to learn about how their efforts can be stymied by those with vested interests in the noninstructional component of the status quo.

The National Context

Given that the United States is the only developed nation that does not mandate federal standards, assessments, and curriculum, states should be applauded for the speed with which they have embraced reform. In less than a decade, forty-nine states have mandated standards. But how standards-based school reform is being implemented is of concern. A front-page story in the

New York Times on Labor Day 1999, while reporting on the rapid spread of the standards movement, did not discuss the need to provide extensive professional development so educators would be able to help their students meet the more demanding standards. The implicit assumption appeared to be that it was necessary only to "raise the bar," put in "high-stakes tests," and then kick all those lazy teachers and kids in the pants to close the skills gap separating American students from their future competitors growing up in the Pacific Rim and Western Europe.

That is patent nonsense. Standards-based reform will fail without fundamental changes in classroom instruction and in how schools are organized to support these changes. For well over a century, U.S. schools did their job well. But the existing school system, whose historic task was to educate the top fifth of its students and to socialize the rest for work in an industrial era, cannot reasonably be expected to succeed in educating all its students to the unprecedentedly high levels required by the high-tech and fiercely competitive global economy of the twenty-first century.

Large urban districts, such as Philadelphia, as well as rural districts and middle-class suburban districts, have serious capacity problems—pre-school, full-day kindergarten, smaller class size in K–3, after-school and summer school programs, and the like—that require significant new funding. But all school districts, even the well-heeled suburban ones where ill-founded complacency abounds fed by the results of norm-referenced tests that are highly correlated with family income, have need for massive professional development so that educators are able to teach the problem-solving pedagogy that lies at the core of standards reform.

Accountability as Catalyst for Fundamental Change

For some, accountability is punitive. It is a cudgel to beat up on the teachers unions and the educational establishment in general that resist vouchers and charter schools. For others, accountability is a catalyst for an indispensable conversation about the fundamental changes that will be necessary if schools are to succeed in helping students meet high standards. "If you are going to hold us accountable," educators should be arguing, "then we insist on changes in the laws that govern K–12 and in the level of resources required to get the job done." In this fashion, accountability becomes part of a critical quid pro quo that exchanges positive and negative consequences for educators in return for a new set of rules and the infusion of substantial new school funding.

A deserved sense of urgency should be widely shared. The failure of standards-based reform, when schools are unable to provide students with the problem-solving skills they must have to compete in the new economy, puts the middle-class basis of the nation at risk. Data for the last twenty-five years make clear that almost all the gains in income went to the top fifth of American families, in largest measure because of education. A panel of eighteen prominent economists convened by the Federal Reserve Bank of New York argued that half the growth in income inequality could be accounted for by "new technologies that favor the better educated."

The record of reform over the last quarter century is sobering. Despite considerable effort, student test scores, whether measured by the National Assessment of Educational Progress or the Third International Math and Science Survey, remain essentially flat. These trends should force everyone concerned about the future to recognize that real improvements will require fundamental changes.

Disconnect between Inputs and Outcomes

Many people in the private sector look at K–12 public education in puzzlement. Here is a $330 billion industry in which employees get paid to come to work, but no relationship exists between what their labors produce and their level of compensation. This disconnect between inputs and outcomes does not exist in other professions and represents a fatal flaw in the current system. While critics admit that teachers are not drawn to the profession because of the pay (which is often insufficient), they argue that unless the system is changed so that the most successful can be rewarded and those whose teaching hurts children can be remediated or released, the system will not improve. They acknowledge that merit pay systems have failed in the past but argue that incentives that will work can be created, including group- or school-based as well as individual-level incentives that do not put teachers in competition with each other to receive rewards. Required remediation for poor performers is a must, they contend, and those who fail to improve their teaching skills, following coaching and additional training, should be required to leave the profession. Raising teacher standards amidst a teacher shortage requires opening alternate sources of recruitment and flexibility to permit part-time teaching, not a retreat from quality. As John Grossman, president of the Columbus (Ohio) Education Association says, "Not everyone has the right to be a teacher in the 21st century."

The Culture of the Core

Richard Elmore describes the theory of "loose coupling" that joins the two parts of K–12: the "core," which consists of teachers and students, and the "administrative superstructure" around the core, which consists of superintendents, administrators, principals, and school board members.[34] When teachers close the door to their individual classrooms, what happens between them and their students is personal and intimate, and they believe even a bit magical and mysterious. But overall it is private, and they believe this is how it should be. Furthermore, it is the responsibility of the administrators to buffer the core from outside interference. Is it any wonder, then, Elmore asks, that when through innovation, creativity, and originality a teacher finds a better way for students to learn, the breakthrough is necessarily confined to that classroom, or to a few adjacent classrooms infected by the individual teacher, or on rare occasions is spread through an entire building because its principal has exceptional qualities as an instructional leader? Because normative behavior in the core supports isolated teaching as something good, right, and valuable to be protected, it should not be surprising that no mechanism exists in K–12 to identify best practices and to spread these models of effective teaching to all classrooms in the nation's sixteen thousand school districts so improvements in student achievement can be secured systemwide.

Collective Bargaining

No one vaguely familiar with American labor history should have any doubts about the importance of having unions to protect the interests of workers. Over the last thirty years, labor unions have won major gains for the nation's teachers, but collective bargaining in schools has come as a mixed blessing. The line drawn in the sand, dividing labor and management, gave the bread-and-butter issues to the unions—salaries, benefits, working conditions, job security—and all the others to management. Not only has this process hardened hearts on both sides, making collaboration exceedingly difficult, but this system also now stands squarely in the way of fundamental reforms. Whether one calls it "distributed leadership" or "power sharing," all educators—labor and management—must now share the responsibility for reform. How can the door to the classroom be opened, how can instruction be made public, without schools becoming places characterized by trust between teachers and administrators? Success in standards-based reform requires changing the culture of the core so that it becomes normative for teachers to share their talents and implementing systems of incentives and sanctions to promote quality teaching. But none of this will be possible in environments devoid of trust, where labor and management far too often play the roles of the Hatfields and McCoys in futile episodes of "us" versus "them" repeated at each contract negotiation. Teachers unions must want to become full partners in shaping reform, and they must be welcomed in this role by school boards and administrators.

Role of Value-Added Assessment

Among the significant barriers to improving instruction and for developing confidence among teachers that their craft should be made public is the widespread belief that no fair way exists to measure the impact of teaching on student performance. The work of William Sanders, the architect of Tennessee's value-added assessment system, challenges that notion. The system operates by projecting forward one year's growth based on a student's record of prior academic achievement. It then compares this expected growth with the actual growth to determine whether each student has achieved one year's growth from his or her own starting point in the teacher's classroom. Given that in this system each student serves as his or her own statistical control— family background, income, race, and other exogenous variables are constant in each student from September to June—the socioeconomic composition of students in a classroom does not affect the measurements. Thus the value-added approach genuinely levels the playing field for teachers. A decade of student achievement data in Tennessee linking all the students to the educators who taught them makes clear that effective teaching is ten to twenty times more powerful in predicting student achievement than any of the other variables, including race, family background, or class size. When tied to an annual test that measures higher-order thinking skills—that is, a test to which teachers can teach with confidence—value-added assessment, with its objective, empirical basis for measuring the impact of teaching on student learning, should be a critical component of successful standards-based school reform. The call by President George W. Bush for annual testing in grades three through eight provides an opportunity to build an assessment system that measures the appropriate knowledge and skills for the Information Society of the twenty-first century. States should resist the temptation to do this on the cheap, thereby undermining the purpose of assessment.

Accountability as the Quid Pro Quo for New School Funding

In well-off suburban school districts, where complacency characterizes the response to standards-based reform, accountability is required to command the attention of school boards and educators. Everywhere else accountability is required to secure the new funding necessary to build capacity and to underwrite the costs of the massive professional development needed by teachers to improve the quality of their classroom instruction and by administrators to succeed in their role as instructional leaders.

Americans who came of age at midcentury lived in communities with rich, poor, and middle-class neighborhoods, but their school taxes went to a single school district. After fifty years of suburbanization and the zoning game that guides and filters population by income, Americans have sorted themselves out into rich, semi-rich, middle-class, working-class, and poor communities. As a result, in the large majority of school districts (approximately two-thirds of those in Pennsylvania), the local real estate tax no longer provides an adequate base for school funding.

In the future new funding must come from broad state taxes such as the personal income tax or the sales tax (those with a narrow base, exempting food, clothing, and other necessities, are not regressive). Winning significant tax increases from state legislatures will require support from all constituencies, and the most likely way to achieve broad-base support is to offer the public a quid pro quo. In return for accountability, defined loosely here as holding educators responsible for what students learn, the state will provide school districts with the new funds they require. The tradition of local control is strong in America, but if the states put up the lion's share of school funding, they will insist properly that school districts adopt contracts with their educators that incorporate state-approved systems of accountability. Contracts can exploit teachers and administrators, and they can be co-opted by the same groups. The devil will certainly be in the details, but everyone will be well served by working to achieve a compromise on accountability that is acceptable to the teachers unions and the business community, the two groups with the power to veto such legislation. The systems of accountability that succeed will be fair to educators and credible to the public, and they will have as their central goal raising student achievement.

Notes

1. The framework draws from Andrew Porter's experiences as chair of the technical advisory panels for the assessment and accountability programs in Philadelphia and Missouri and as a member of the technical advisory panel in Kentucky, and from Mitchell Chester's experiences developing and implementing an accountability system in the school district of Philadelphia. In addition, the framework is grounded in the test standards developed jointly by the American Educational Research Association (AERA), American Psychological Association, and National Council on Measurement in Education and by AERA in *AERA Position Statement: High-Stakes Testing in PreK–12 Education* (Washington, 2000).

Educational Testing Service, *Using Assessments and Accountability to Raise Student Achievement* (Princeton, N.J., 2001); and Edward H. Haertel, "Validity Arguments for High-Stakes Testing: In Search of the Evidence," *Educational Measurement: Issues and Practice*, vol. 18, no. 4 (1999), pp. 5–9.

2. Robert L. Linn, "Evaluating the Validity of Assessments: The Consequences of Use," *Educational Measurement: Issues and Practice*, vol. 16, no. 2 (1997), pp. 14–16; and Robert L. Linn, "Assessments and Accountability," *Educational Researcher*, vol. 29, no. 2 (2000), pp. 4–16.

3. W. James Popham, *Modern Educational Measurement: Practical Guidelines for Educational Leaders* (Needham, Mass.: Allyn and Bacon, 2000). Statements of the desired curriculum are usually given in the form of content standards and curriculum frameworks. But these documents, by themselves, have neither provided students and schools with clear targets for instruction nor exerted much influence on teacher content decisions. Andrew C. Porter, "National Standards and School Improvement in the 1990s: Issues and Promise," *American Journal of Education*, vol. 102, no. 4 (1994), pp. 421–49. Assessment and accountability serve to focus the attention of schools (for example, administrators, teachers, and parents) and students on the content to be learned. At the same time as the assessments are intended to focus attention on the targeted content, accountability (rewards and sanctions) is intended to give the target weight, stimulating greater effort on the part of schools and students.

4. Linda M. McNeil, *Contradictions of School Reform: Educational Costs of Standardized Testing* (New York: Routledge, 2000); Lorrie A. Shepard and Mary Lee Smith, *Flunking Grades: Research and Policies on Retention* (Philadelphia: Falmer Press, 1989); and Mary Lee Smith, "Put to the Test: The Effects of External Testing on Teachers," *Educational Researcher*, vol. 20, no. 5 (1991), pp. 8–11.

5. American Educational Research Association, American Psychological Association, and National Council on Measurement in Education, *Standards for Educational and Psychological Testing* (Washington: American Educational Research Association, 1999).

6. Jay P. Heubert and Robert M. Hauser, eds., *High Stakes: Testing for Tracking, Promotion, and Graduation* (Washington: National Academy Press, 1999).

7. American Educational Research Association, *AERA Position Statement.*

8. The twelve conditions are (1) protection against high-stakes decisions based on a single test, (2) adequate resources and opportunity to learn, (3) validation for each separate intended use, (4) full disclosure of likely negative consequences of the program, (5) alignment between the tests and the curriculum, (6) validity of passing scores and achievement levels, (7) opportunities for meaningful remediation for students who fail high-stakes tests, (8) appropriate attention to language differences among students, (9) appropriate attention to students with disabilities, (10) careful attention to explicit rules for determining which students are to be tested, (11) sufficient reliability for each intended use, and (12) ongoing evaluation of intended and unintended effects of high-stakes testing.

9. Andrew C. Porter, "Doing High-Stakes Assessment Right," *School Administrator*, vol. 11, no. 57 (2000), pp. 28–31.

10. National Research Council, Division of Behavioral and Social Sciences and Education, Committee on the Foundations of Assessment, *Knowing What Students Know: The Science and Design of Educational Assessment*, edited by James Pellegrino, Naomi Chudowsky, and Robert Glaser (Washington: National Academy Press, 2001); and Norman L. Webb, *Criteria for Alignment of Expectations and Assessments in Mathematics and Science Education,* National Institute for Science Education and Council of Chief State School Officers Research Monograph No. 6 (Washington: Council of Chief State School Officers, 1997).

11. Eva L. Baker, "Model-Based Performance Assessment," *Theory into Practice*, vol. 36, no. 4 (1997), pp. 247–54.

12. Lorrie A. Shepard, "Inflated Test Score Gains: Is the Problem Old Norms or Teaching the Test?" *Educational Measurement: Issues and Practice*, vol. 9, no. 3 (1990), pp. 15–22.

13. At the same time, because the test and the accountability associated with testing results get the attention of educators, students, and parents, it is important to communicate the content being tested. Some representative fraction of items might be released to the public, following each test administration, as a mechanism for communicating the desired content.

14. Richard M. Jaeger and others, "Setting Performance Standards for Performance Assessments: Some Fundamental Issues, Current Practice, and Technical Dilemmas," in Gary W. Phillips, ed., *Technical Issues in Large-Scale Performance Assessments* (Government Printing Office, 1996), pp. 79–115; and Robert L. Linn and others, *The Validity and Credibility of the Achievement Levels for the 1990 National Assessment of Educational Progress in Mathematics*, CSE Technical Report No. 330 (University of California at Los Angeles, Center for the Study of Excellence, 1991).

There are many approaches to setting standards for testing programs (for example, bookmark, known groups, Angolf, Jaeger-Mills). There are many approaches to setting targets for school accountability as well. One approach is to set a long-term target that all schools are to meet or exceed, determine each school's present level of achievement (that is, its baseline), then take the distance between each school's baseline and the target and divide it into, say, twelve equal amounts (if each school is to reach the long-term target in twelve years). Because all schools have the same long-range target but different baselines, the lowest performing schools must progress at the fastest rate.

Another strategy for setting targets is to expect the same rate of growth for each school. This approach institutionalizes differences in school achievement, however, because low-performing schools are not expected to close the gap between their achievement levels and those of higher performing schools. Other approaches use criterion-referenced standards (for example, Virginia requires that at least 70 percent of students in each school meet the mastery level), norm-referenced standards (for example, Pennsylvania's Empowerment Act requires that no more than 50 percent of a district's students score in the bottom quartile of statewide performance), or a combination of norm- and criterion-referenced standards (for example, California generally requires gains of schools, but those performing above a mastery threshold may receive rewards regardless of their rates of progress).

15. Charles T. Clotfelter and Helen F. Ladd, "Recognizing and Rewarding Success in Public Schools," in Helen F. Ladd, ed., *Holding Schools Accountable: Performance-Based Reform in Education* (Brookings, 1996), pp. 23–63; and Craig E. Richards and Tian Ming Sheu, "The South Carolina School Incentive Reward Program: A Policy Analysis," *Economics of Education Review*, vol. 11, no. 1 (1992), pp. 71–86.

16. For school accountability, a value-added criterion is appropriate. Robert H. Meyer, "Value-Added Indicators of School Performance," in Eric A. Hanushek and Dale W. Jorgensen,

eds., *Improving American Schools: The Role of Incentives* (Washington: National Academy Press, 1996), pp. 197–223. Given the students with whom a school is working, what value does the students' school experience add to their levels of achievement? Ideally, school value added to student achievement is estimated based on longitudinal data, with each student serving as his or her own control. This approach requires testing at multiple grade levels, a cost in money and burden. Sometimes value added is estimated based on cross-cohort comparisons (for example, repeated testing at a single grade level). The assumption is that each cohort of students at a grade level is a fair comparison group for any other cohort of students at that same grade level. Whatever way value added is estimated, according to our framework the value added should be based on the same tests that are used for student accountability. In short, there needs to be alignment between the school and student accountability programs for them to work in concert.

17. Heubert and Hauser, *High Stakes.*

18. Andrew C. Porter, "School Delivery Standards," *Educational Researcher*, vol. 22, no. 5 (1993), pp. 24–30; and Andrew C. Porter, "The Uses and Misuses of Opportunity-to-Learn Standards," *Educational Researcher*, vol. 24, no. 1 (1995), pp. 21–27.

19. Samuel Messick, "Validity," in Robert L. Linn, ed., *Educational Measurement*, 3d ed. (Phoenix, Ariz.: Oryx Press, 1993), pp. 13–103.

20. An assessment and accountability program that is fair to students will have additional features. Students who are at risk of failing a standard, such as promotion from grade four to five, should be identified in the earlier grades. Those on a low trajectory should be given an early warning and receive appropriate support. Students with special needs should receive appropriate accommodations. Daniel M. Koretz and Laura S. Hamilton, "Assessment of Students with Disabilities in Kentucky: Inclusion, Student Performance, and Validity," *Educational Evaluation and Policy Analysis*, vol. 22, no. 3 (2000), pp. 255–72; Susan E. Phillips, "High-Stakes Testing Accommodations: Validity versus Disabled Rights," *Applied Measurement in Education*, vol. 7, no. 2 (1994), pp. 93–120; and Martha L. Thurlow, Judy L. Elliott, and James E. Ysseldyke, *Testing Students with Disabilities: Practical Strategies for Complying with District and State Requirements* (Thousand Oaks, Calif.: Corwin Press, 1998). For example, English language learners should be assessed in the language of their instruction. Students with disabilities should be provided accommodations that are construct irrelevant; that is, the accommodation should not change the construct being assessed but should allow the student to demonstrate his or her accomplishment on the construct.

21. An assessment and accountability program that is fair to schools requires still other features. There should be incentives for schools to test all of their students; a school should not have a higher probability of receiving rewards by not testing its weakest students. Neither should teachers score their own students' tests if the test scores are to be used for school accountability. The pressure for bias may simply be too great. More generally, a district must guard against cheating. Tests must be secure, and the administration protocol must be faithfully implemented.

22. Milbrey W. McLaughlin and Lorrie A. Shepard, with Jennifer A. O'Day, *Improving Education through Standards-Based Reform: A Report by the National Academy of Education Panel on Standards-Based Education Reform* (Stanford, Calif.: National Academy of Education, 1995).

23. Stephen P. Klein and others, *What Do Test Scores in Texas Tell Us?* Issue Paper IP–202 (Santa Monica, Calif.: RAND, 2000) [www.rand.org/publications/IP/IP202]; and Daniel M. Koretz and Sheila I. Barron, *The Validity of Gains in Scores on the Kentucky Instructional Results Information System (KIRIS)* (Santa Monica, Calif.: RAND, 1998).

24. Daniel M. Koretz, Daniel F. McCaffrey, and Laura. S. Hamilton, "Toward a Framework for Validating Gains under High-Stakes Conditions," presented at "New Work on the Evalua-

tion of High-Stakes Testing Programs," symposium conducted at the annual meeting of the National Council on Measurement in Education, Seattle, Wash., April 2001.

25. See, for example, Mitchell D. Chester, Margaret Orr, and Jolley Christman, "Consequential Validity of Philadelphia's Accountability System: Triangulating Four Years of Multiple Sources of Evidence," paper presented at the annual meeting of the American Educational Research Association, Seattle, Wash., April 2001; and Consortium for Policy Research in Education, Research for Action, and OMG Center for Collaborative Learning, *Children Achieving: Philadelphia's Education Reform Progress Report Series 1996–97* (Philadelphia, 1998).

26. Mary Lee Smith, "Put to the Test."

27. For example, Brian Stecher and others, *The Effects of Standards-Based Assessment on Classroom Practices: Results of the 1996-97 RAND Survey of Kentucky Teachers of Mathematics and Writing*, CSE Technical Report 482 (UCLA, National Center for Research on Evaluation, Standards and Student Testing, 1998); Brian M. Stecher and Sheila I. Barron, *Quadrennial Milepost Accountability Testing in Kentucky*, CSE Technical Report 505 (UCLA, National Center for Research on Evaluation, Standards and Student Testing, 1999); and Brian M. Stecher and others, *The Effects of the Washington State Education Reform on Schools and Classrooms*, CSE Technical Report 525 (UCLA, National Center for Research on Evaluation, Standards and Student Testing, 2000).

28. Daniel Koretz and Sheila I. Barron, *The Validity of Gains on the Kentucky Instructional Results Information System (KIRIS)*, MR-1014-EDU (Santa Monica, Calif.: RAND, 1998); Daniel Koretz and others, *The Perceived Effects of the Kentucky Instructional Results Information System (KIRIS)*, MR-792-PCT/FF (Santa Monica, Calif.: RAND, 1996); Stecher and others, *The Effects of Standards-Based Assessment on Classroom Practices;* and Stecher and Barron, *Quadrennial Milepost Accountability Testing in Kentucky.*

29. Daniel Koretz and others, "The Effects of High-Stakes Testing: Preliminary Evidence about Generalization across Tests," presented at "The Effects of High-Stakes Testing," symposium conducted at the annual meetings of the American Educational Research Association and the National Council on Measurement in Education, Chicago, April 1991.

30. Klein and others, *What Do Test Scores in Texas Tell Us?*

31. Linn, "Assessments and Accountability."

32. Koretz and others, "The Effects of High-Stakes Testing."

33. D. Koretz, D. McCaffrey, and L. Hamilton, *Toward a Framework for Validating Gains under High-Stakes Conditions*, CSE Technical Report (University of California, Center for the Study of Evaluation, forthcoming).

34. Richard Elmore, *Building a New Structure for School Leadership* (Washington: Albert Shanker Institute, Winter 2000).

Accountability and Support in Chicago: Consequences for Students

G. ALFRED HESS JR.

Accountability in Chicago in the 1990s derived from progressive reform legislation adopted in 1988 and 1995. The Illinois General Assembly in 1988 passed the Chicago School Reform Act (P.A. 85-1418), which included a set of goals, a redistribution of the school district's resources, and a decentralization of decisionmaking to the school level. The central goal of the legislation was for Chicago's students to achieve at levels comparable to students across the nation (that is, meet national norms in reading and math), both districtwide and at each individual school in the district.[1] Taking decisionmaking about school improvement out of the hands of a stultified and entrenched district bureaucracy was seen as a key strategy to encourage student achievement. The locus of accountability was moved from bureaucrats in a central hierarchy to local school councils, elected by parents and community members, with the power to hire and fire principals.

The 1988 reform act emphasized setting high expectations for student achievement, giving schools the opportunity to change, and fostering professional development that would enhance teachers' instructional capacities. It also tried to address the will to change by making principals' tenure subject to the decisions of local school councils composed primarily of parents, community representatives, and teachers.[2] The legislation had a very cumbersome mechanism for the central Board of Education to intervene in failing schools (a so-called educational bankruptcy provision then being pioneered in the state of New Jersey). However, these various restructuring mechanisms were not strong enough to overcome resistance to change in some faculties. By 1993, the Consortium on Chicago School Research had suggested that

339

roughly a third of the city's elementary schools were making serious efforts at change, a third had added multiple—and at times conflicting—new programs, and a third had not changed at all.[3] There was general agreement across the city, bolstered by declining achievement scores, that the school-based management reforms of 1988 were not working as well in the high schools.

About the same time that the consortium was putting forward its elementary school study, the Quest Center of the Chicago Teachers Union, with the support of several large foundations, initiated a partnership with the Council on Basic Education and the Chicago public schools (CPS) to develop a set of standards for student learning at the fourth, eighth, and twelfth grades. The first draft of these standards was developed by 1995 and printed on a large wall chart that was distributed to every Chicago public school for comment and response. Teachers working with the Quest Center to restructure their schools began to develop assessments to measure whether students were meeting these standards.

The General Assembly in 1995 adopted the second set of reforms by amending the 1988 reform act to place responsibility for the central operations of the school district more squarely in the mayor's hands while expanding the power of the district's central administration to control its own finances and to hold individual schools accountable for improving student achievement. On July 1, 1995, a new Reform Board of Trustees and a new administrative team headed by Chief Executive Officer (CEO) Paul Vallas took control of the school district. Both the board and the top five administrators were directly appointed by Mayor Richard M. Daley.

The first challenge facing the new administrative team was the fiscal insolvency of the district. Early in the reform years, the Board of Education had granted salary increases totaling 27 percent over four years, but it did not have the revenues to sustain those costs. By the fall of 1993, the district had accumulated such a large budget deficit that it could not open school. After a prolonged struggle, the General Assembly allowed the school district to borrow $400 million to balance its budget for two years, during which time both the governor and mayor would be seeking reelection.[4] Thus, a $350 million deficit faced the new administration in 1995, which included payments on the newly acquired $400 million in debt. Vallas, an acknowledged public finance expert who had directed the city's budget department and a fiscal commission for the state legislature, quickly restructured the district's debt, cut costs without curtailing school-level programs by privatizing a number of services and reducing by three quarters the number of union bargaining units, negotiated a four-year contract with the remaining employee groups, and utilized the increased flexibility provided by the amendatory act to balance the budget and to project three further years of balanced budgets—all before school opened in the fall.[5] Vallas then announced he was ready to tackle improving student achievement. During the prior two decades, no previous superintendent had asked to be judged, as Vallas did, on whether student achievement improved.

The 1995 amendments included a new set of accountability measures that had been advocated by the prior school administration. They included the authority to place schools on probation, to reconstitute faculties in failing schools, and to intervene directly in schools that continually failed to improve. The board was also given the power to declare schools in crisis for misman-agement. In the late fall of 1996, 109 schools (about 20 percent of the system's regular elementary and high schools) were placed on probation by the reform board for having less than 15 percent of their students reading or doing math at or above the national norm. At the same time, the district moved to end social promotion by telling students that they would have to achieve at accept-able levels on standardized tests or attend summer school. By the end of the 1996–97 school year, students who did not achieve at those levels at the end of summer school, and who were not waived into the next grade as a result of other educational considerations, would be retained in grade.

In the summer of 1997, the seven lowest performing high schools were reconstituted. None of these schools had more than 8 percent of their students reading at national norms. Four of the seven principals were replaced; two recently appointed principals were allowed to continue, as was one veteran principal who was forced to accept an almost coequal associate principal who had full responsibility for the school's instructional program. Thirty percent of the teachers in these seven schools were replaced.

In conjunction with sanctions on lower performing schools, the school dis-trict announced it was instituting promotion gates at the third, sixth, eighth, and ninth grades, when students had to achieve certain cutoff scores on the dis-trict's standardized reading and math tests to advance to the next grade. The cutoff scores were set low (a year below national norms at third grade, a year and a half below at sixth grade, and two years below the norms at eighth and ninth grades). Holding students accountable was important so that early edu-cational deficits would not impede later learning. Furthermore, it countered teachers' complaints that they should not be held accountable if students did not experience consequences for not making an effort to learn and to do well on the tests by which teachers and schools would be measured. In the fall of 1997, 12,122 students were not promoted to the following grade. Thus, within two years, the new administration and reform board had moved to put sanctions in place for both low-performing adults and low-performing students.

In 2000 the school district announced it was adding a report card for parents to its array of accountability measures. Previously, parents had been required only to pick up student report cards and have a conference with their child's teachers at the end of the first and third quarters. In 2000 teachers began sending home a checklist of activities reflecting parents' responsibilities in the education of their child.

The district became a national leader in establishing a system of high-stakes accountability for students as well as teachers and school administrators. Shortly afterward, the Illinois State Board of Education adopted its own, much weaker, version of sanctions on low-performing schools, without corresponding sanctions on individual students, though these may appear in the form of a statewide graduation exam in the next few years.

Completing the process begun under the previous administration, the Chicago public schools adopted a set of learning standards based on the initial work designed by the partnership between the school district, the Chicago Teachers Union, and the Washington-based Council for Basic Education (whose role had since been taken over by the Consortium on Chicago School Research). Once again, CPS acted before the state adopted its own standards but made the small modifications necessary to stay aligned with the state standards when they were promulgated. Flowing from the district's standards, a Program of Study (curriculum guide) was established for all grades and all subjects. Assessments designed to measure student achievement against the standards were developed for all core subjects in ninth and tenth grades.[6]

As a result of an evaluation by the Center for Urban School Policy, CEO Vallas decided to abandon the reconstitution process enacted in 1997. In its place, in the fall of 1999, twelve high schools started a process of reengineering, under which teachers at a school would help to judge the competence of their colleagues and would design and enact remediation programs.[7] Five of these schools made enough improvement in reading and math test scores to escape probation and were dismissed from the process at the end of the 1999–2000 school year. Six others began the judgment and remediation phase in the fall of 2000. In July 2000 the Board of Education placed five additional high schools into Intervention, under which an externally imposed supervisory team evaluated all teachers between that September and the following April.

Those judged to be inadequate were subject to summary dismissal.[8] Two of these high schools had been reconstituted in 1997 but had made little progress since; two probation high schools had improved enough to be removed from that status in 1999 but had fallen back to about 10 percent of their students at the norms in 2000; and one probation school had been in managerial chaos with low student scores for several years.

Accountability came with additional support. Schools placed on probation or remediation received funds to hire external partners to assist with professional development of the school's faculty. (Schools received full funding of about $100,000 in the first year, had to supply half the cost in the second year, and were to fully support the cost in the third year, though many were allowed to negotiate reduced service levels.) Probation managers were provided as supportive mentors for principals at schools on probation. Summer school was added for students not meeting prescribed promotion cutoff scores on standardized tests and for other students at risk of failure. By 2001, nearly half the students in the system were receiving six weeks of instruction during the summer. The Lighthouse after-school program provided tutoring, social programs, and an evening meal for many low-performing, low-income students. The district also entered its most extensive facilities upgrading since the end of the baby-boom construction era in the 1960s, as virtually every school facility received either major or minor rehabilitation and dozens of new schools or additions were built.

Thus the pre-1995 reform era could be characterized as a low-stakes, school-based voluntaristic improvement period, while the post-1995 era has been a high-stakes accountability era, featuring both severe sanctions for adults and students and extensive support for the district's lowest performing schools. While some have claimed credit for the improvement in student achievement on the basis of changes instituted in one or the other era, untangling the interweaving effects of these two reform efforts is probably impossible. In the data below, I do not distinguish the effects of these two different eras.

Improving Achievement in Chicago's Elementary Schools

Under the initial reform effort (1988–95), the major focus for student achievement was the Illinois Goal Assessment Program. During the administration of Argie Johnson, Vallas's immediate predecessor, the school district

Figure 1. Chicago Elementary School Achievement in Reading and Math

Percent at or above national norms

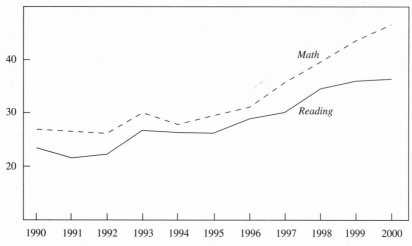

Note: Achievement of combined third through eighth graders.

had begun to report the percentage of students who scored at or above the national norms on the Iowa Test of Basic Skills (ITBS). This measure was directly tied to the goal of the 1988 legislation—that Chicago students achieve at levels comparable to other students across the nation. The incoming Vallas administration adopted this measurement in deciding on sanctions for schools. I also utilize this measure, as it relates directly to the 1988 goals and provides a common longitudinal framework for the whole reform decade.[9]

Student achievement in the city's elementary schools has improved significantly since 1990, when less than a quarter of the city's third through eighth graders read at the national norm.[10] By the spring of 2000, more than a third (36.4 percent) did so, as seen in figure 1.

Math scores improved even more dramatically, from just over a quarter of elementary students at the national norms in 1990 to just under half at the national norms in 2000. That means that the school district, as a whole, has nearly reached the 1988 goal in elementary math (50 percent at the national norm would mean Chicago students were performing at levels comparable with students across the nation).[11]

These scores indicate not only that significant improvement has occurred in student achievement in the elementary schools, but also that there is still a long way to go in reading. While 50 percent more students read at the national norms in 2000 than in 1990, the improvement brings the city's children only

Table 1. Performance Levels in Reading of Chicago Elementary Schools, at or above National Norms

Performance level	1990	1996	2000
More than 50 percent	36 (8.2%)	70 (14.5%)	107 (21.3%)
30 to 49 percent	81 (18.4%)	96 (19.9%)	168 (33.5%)
15 to 29 percent	183 (41.5%)	229 (47.5%)	209 (41.6%)
5 to 14 percent	134 (30.4%)	83 (17.2%)	17 (3.4%)
Less than 5 percent	7 (1.6%)	4 (0.8%)	1 (0.2%)

halfway to meeting the goal of the 1988 reform act, after a decade of improvement. Even more troubling is the flattening out of the achievement trend in reading in 1999 and 2000.

Despite the record of improvement, there is still a long way to go to meet the 1988 goal that every school should match the national norm in student achievement. In 1990, at the beginning of the reform decade, only 36 elementary schools (8.2 percent) had more than 50 percent of their students reading at national norms. By 1996, 70 schools (14.5 percent) had matched the national norms. In 2000, 107 (21.3 percent) had met the 1988 goal, but 78.7 percent had not.

As shown in table 1, only a quarter of the city's elementary schools in 1990 had as many as 30 percent of their students reading at the national norm. That figure had improved to a third (34.4 percent) by 1996 and reached more than half (54.8 percent) in 2000. While at the beginning of the 1990s a third of the elementary schools (141, or 32.0 percent) had less than 15 percent reading at the national norm (the level for which schools were put on probation in 1996), that number had dropped to 87 (18.0 percent) in 1996 when Vallas imposed sanctions on schools for such low student performance and included only 18 schools (3.6 percent) in 2000. Once again, the picture is one of significant improvement, but still a long distance from the 1988 goals for all Chicago elementary schools.

This positive picture of achievement improvement must be tempered with one caveat. As reported by the Consortium on Chicago School Research, the percentage of elementary students excluded from testing increased steadily between 1992 and 1999, rising from 17.7 percent to 26.1 percent.[12] The percent excluded dropped slightly in 2000 to 25.8 percent. Half of this increase had happened by 1996. About 60 percent of the students excluded in 2000 were due to special education categorization and 40 percent due to bilingual education enrollment.[13] The number of students excluded for being in bilingual education tripled in 1999 when CPS extended the exclusion from three to four years. The effect of this policy change was entirely at the third- and fourth-grade levels. If all of the additional excluded students had taken the test and their scores were included in the systemwide tally, and if they had all scored below the norm, the percent at or above the national norms in 2000 would be 3.6 percentage points lower (at 32.8 percent). This would still represent a significant increase over 1990 and 1996, but it would indicate that a larger improvement was needed to reach the 1988 goal of 50 percent at the national norms.

Effects on Individual Students

While overall achievement has been going up in the Chicago elementary schools, on virtually all measures (percent at or above national norms, median scores, average grade equivalent, or percent in the lowest quartile), some students still are not learning at the desired levels. These students are far below the systemwide or state learning standards, despite the best efforts of the district and individual schools to improve their learning opportunities and to motivate them to learn through incentives and sanctions.

Melissa Roderick and her colleagues at the Consortium on Chicago School Research have tracked the effects of the effort to end social promotion in Chicago's elementary schools.[14] The promotion policy was designed to assure that students moving to fourth, seventh, and ninth grades were ready to do appropriate work at those grades, by establishing promotion gates at the prior grade.[15] To be promoted, students in the prior year were to achieve certain cutoff scores on the Iowa Test of Basic Skills. The effect of these promotion gates was to dramatically increase the number of students retained in third, sixth, and eighth grades. But the policy also seems to have dramatically improved the performance of other previously lower performing students.

A number of students were not subject to the promotion policy, primarily those enrolled in bilingual education and special education classes. About a third of students in the third grade were thus excluded from the effects of the policy, as were a fifth of students in sixth and eighth grades.

Students who did not achieve the cutoff score during the normal spring testing period were required to attend summer school, at the end of which they had another opportunity to pass the test. Nearly half the third graders, more than a third of the sixth graders, and more than a quarter of the eighth graders

Figure 2. Chicago Elementary School Passing Rates

Percent passing by August

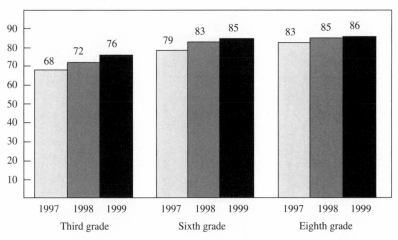

Source: Adapted from M. Roderick and others, *Update: Ending Social Promotion: Passing, Retention, and Achievement Trends among Promoted and Retained Students, 1995–1999* (Chicago: Consortium on Chicago School Research, 2000).

did not pass the cutoff score in the spring of 1997, the first year under the new policy. Most of those students (about 80 percent) attended summer school. About half of the students who went to summer school passed their second chance at the Iowa test, and some of those who did not pass received waivers and were promoted anyway. In all, more than twelve thousand students were retained in grade when school opened in the fall of 1997. In the two succeeding years, the percentage of students being retained fell only slightly at each grade level. Most of the retained students were promoted in the following year, but a few have been retained a second time.

While the promotion policy is designed to provide additional assistance to students not passing the cutoff score (additional time through summer school and after-school programs, smaller class size after retention, and other material resources), its primary target is to improve the achievement levels of previously low-performing students. Roderick and her colleagues have documented that the policy has been effective in that regard. The percentage of students passing the initial cutoff score at each grade improved for each of the first three years of the policy (see figure 2).

The fact that passing rates increased, while retention rates declined only slightly, indicates that fewer students were receiving waivers after not pass-

Figure 3. Chicago Elementary Students Reaching Promotion Cutoff Scores

Percent reaching cutoff by August

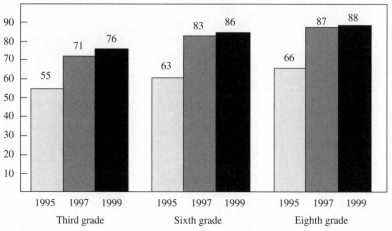

Source: Adapted from M. Roderick and others, *Update: Ending Social Promotion: Passing, Retention, and Achievement Trends among Promoted and Retained Students, 1995–1999* (Chicago: Consortium on Chicago School Research, 2000).

ing the Iowa test cutoff. Thus, more students were passing the test cutoffs in each succeeding year.

Roderick and her colleagues also compared the performance of lower performing students with the performance of lower performing students before the initiation of the promotion policy. The consortium team found a significant improvement in the percentage of students achieving at the cutoff level, when compared with the students at the same grade level in 1995 (see figure 3).

The school district has modified the promotion policy several times since 1997. One modification has been to raise the cutoff scores gradually. Originally the cutoff score for eighth grade was a grade equivalent of 6.9 (two years below the national norm for that grade), but by the fall of 2000, it had been raised to 7.4 (less than a year and one half below the national norm). Another modification resulted from the high initial failure rates at third grade. In 1997, 48 percent of students taking the ITBS had not achieved the cutoff score on the spring test administration. Starting in 1999, students more than a year below the national norm in first and second grade were required to attend summer school (though not mandated for retention). In addition, individual schools began to increase the number of students retained in first and second grade (systemwide, in first grade from 3.9 percent in 1992 to 6.6 percent in 2000 and in second grade from 2.6 percent to 4.1 percent). A third of the students retained once in these primary grades were still retained again at third grade in 1999, meaning that 2 percent to 3 percent of elementary school students in these cohorts would be two years older than their classmates.

Most students who were retained at one of the promotion gate years were promoted the following year. In 1998, 71 percent of previously retained third graders were promoted to fourth grade, 73 percent of retained sixth graders were promoted, but only 52 percent of retained eighth graders were promoted. Among the 1997 retained eighth graders, 29 percent had dropped out by the fall of 1999. However, when dropout rates were compared with those for students in eighth grade in 1995, they were only 2 percent higher for comparable students, and the overall dropout rate for the whole class had not increased. This indicates that some lower performing students were dropping out earlier in their school careers than had been the case before the promotion gate policy, but these students would not have been likely to graduate even in the absence of the promotion policy.

In the first two years of the promotion policy, many students benefited greatly from the summer bridge program, raising their achievement levels significantly. However, they made less progress during the ensuing school year, indicating that regular classroom instruction did not seem to be improving for these lower performing students. However, by 1999, the increases in achievement levels reflected higher performance during the school year, with fewer students requiring summer school. Students tended to maintain their higher learning trajectory after passing through one promotion gate. In 1999, 86 percent of the students who had been promoted after sixth grade in 1997 were promoted again at eighth grade. Three quarters of the students who had required the added instruction of summer school after sixth grade were promoted after eighth, though half of these again required summer school assistance. About two-thirds of those who had not passed the sixth-grade cutoff, but had been promoted through waivers, were promoted at the end of eighth grade.

In summary, Roderick and her colleagues found that the promotion policy had been successful in encouraging many lower performing students to improve their achievement levels enough to avoid retention. The percentage of students meeting the various cutoff scores increased by more than 20 percentage points over the performance of students in those grades in 1995. Many of these students took advantage of various support efforts provided by the school system, including added instruction during the summer. However, Roderick and her colleagues pointed out that a persisting group of very low performing students had not been successful in school before the promotion policy and continued to be unsuccessful under the new policy. The continued lack of success of this group of perhaps 10 percent of each elementary grade poses a difficult problem for the Chicago public schools and for other urban school districts with a similar group of hard to educate young people.

Improving Achievement in Chicago's High Schools

Between 1990 and 1996, the proportion of high school students reading at or above the national norms had fallen from 30.6 percent to 20.5 percent, while the proportion of students doing math at the norms had remained stable at about 21.7 percent (see figure 4). This dismal record of declining student achievement led CEO Vallas to constitute a task force to redesign Chicago's high schools. The task force was led by a steering committee of about thirty persons, supplemented by seven working teams, which each involved about thirty persons.[16] Thus more than two hundred teachers, principals, regional and central office administrators, academics, and citizen activists worked to develop and refine proposals for improving the city's high schools. The completed High School Redesign Plan was submitted to the Board of Education in December 1996 and, with some amendments, adopted by the Reform Board of Trustees in March of 1997. Student achievement in the city's secondary schools has improved steadily since 1996.

Reading scores exceeded their 1990 level in 1999 and further improved in 2000 to the point where more than a third of the tested students were at or above the national norm.[17] The proportion doing math at the norms had doubled to 45.0 percent.

One concern raised by focusing on the 1988 Reform Act's goal of meeting the national norm is that schools would focus only on students near the national norms, a concern reinforced by the explicit strategies of some external partners who were providing staff development assistance to schools on probation. Two additional measures provide evidence that the improvement in test scores is widespread and not limited to a few pupils previously achieving just below the national norms.

One measure is the median percentile on the standardized tests. The median describes the score at which half of the students taking the test scored above and half below. A rising median score, given a stable test population,

Figure 4. Chicago High School Achievement in Reading and Math

Percent at or above norms

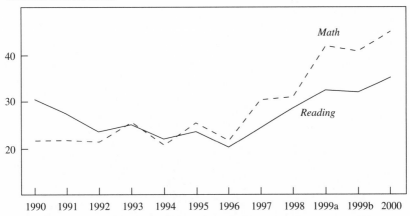

Note: Ninth and eleventh grades to 1999a; ninth and tenth grades in 1999b and 2000.

would indicate that students below the norm but above the previous median were improving their levels of achievement. The median scores of Chicago students have been consistently rising in both reading and math since 1996 (see figure 5).

In 1996, half of Chicago's high school students tested below the 25th percentile in reading and below the 22d percentile in math. By 1999, the median had increased to the 37th percentile in reading and the 42d percentile in math. Tenth graders tested slightly higher in reading in that year than did their eleventh-grade colleagues, so the ninth- and tenth-grade median was slightly higher, though fewer tenth graders were at or above the national norm. In 2000 the improvement in the median continued in reading, reaching the 41st percentile, while improving only marginally in math to the 43d percentile.[18]

The second measure of the breadth of improvement in student achievement is an examination of the quartile distribution of test scores. As implied by a 25th percentile median in 1996, half of Chicago high school students were in the bottom quartile of students nationally. For Chicago students to match the nation, 25 percent of Chicago's students should test in each quartile. In 1996, 51 percent were in the bottom quartile, 28 percent were in the second quartile (thus 79 percent were below the national norm of the 50th percentile), while 13 percent were in the third quartile and only 8 percent were in the top quartile. By 2000, a marked shift had occurred. Only 21 percent of tested high school students were in the bottom quartile in reading; 44 percent were

Figure 5. Median Percentiles in Regular High Schools

Percentile

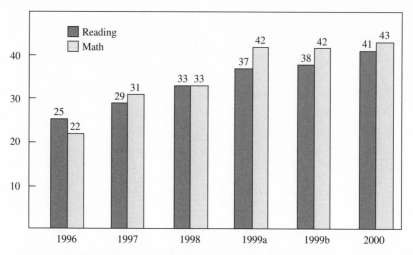

Note: Ninth and eleventh grades to 1999a; ninth and tenth grades in 1999b and 2000.

in the second quartile; 22 percent were in the third quartile; and 13 percent were in the top quartile. Chicago's students were still underrepresented in the top two quartiles and overrepresented in the second quartile, but in 2000 city high schools had fewer students in the lowest quartile than was true for the nation as a whole. In part, that is because promotion gates, installed in 1997, have kept out some of the poorest performing fourteen- and fifteen-year-olds. But the largest proportion of the shift (about 80 percent of the total) is the result of students graduating from the eighth grade reading at higher levels than was true in 1996. The dramatic shift in quartile distribution can be seen in figures 6 and 7.

Figures 6 and 7 clearly indicate that improved student achievement in reading was widespread and not limited to a few students whose prior achievement was near the national norm. Two thousand more students were reading in the top quartile of students across the country in 2000 than had been the case five years previously. Thirty-six hundred more were reading in the third quartile; six thousand more reading in the second quartile; and ten thousand fewer were reading in the bottom quartile. Thus, there were 5,647 more students reading at the national norms in 2000 than there had been in 1996. This increased number of students at the norm accounts for 80 percent of the improved percentage at the norms.[19] Furthermore, because the second quar-

Figure 6. Quartile Distribution of High School Reading Scores, 1996

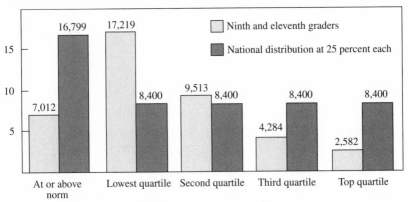

Figure 7. Quartile Distribution of High School Reading Scores, 2000

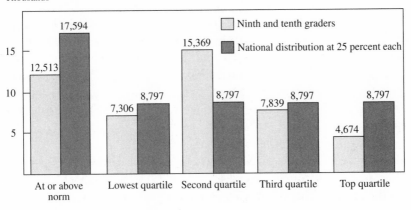

tile includes students generally described as low average to average, more than three quarters of Chicago's high school students were in the low average or higher category. These students were at grade level. They were within the range of achievement considered average for these grades. Chicago's high schools were no longer dominated by very low performing students, as was the case as recently as 1996, when more than 70 percent of students in reconstituted high schools tested in the bottom quartile.

Figure 8. Chicago High School Dropout Rates

Percent dropping out

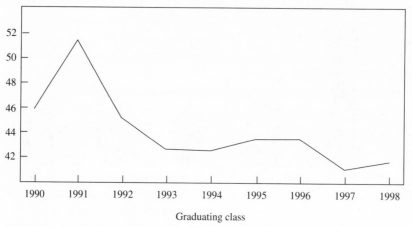

Graduating class

Note: Four-year longitudinal cohort rates.

However, dropout rates have not significantly improved, as might have been expected from the improved student achievement levels. In 1985 Diana Lauber and I found that four-year longitudinal dropout rates in the Chicago public schools were about 42 percent.[20] During the early years of implementing the 1988 reforms, the dropout rate had skyrocketed to 51.5 percent. By 1993, the rate had dropped back to mid-1980s levels and stayed at those levels through 1998, the last year for which CPS has computed the data (see figure 8).

Anthony Bryk and his Consortium on Chicago School Research colleagues Ellen Allensworth and Shazia Miller have suggested that the normal four-year cohort analysis, starting with students who enroll as high school freshmen, may not catch the effect of the CPS promotion gates. They have recalculated dropout rates for the most recent classes starting with students who are thirteen years old (the normal age for starting eighth grade). They claim that dropout rates for the graduating classes of 1998, 1999, and 2000 were between 42.7 percent and 43.3 percent, and that the students in the classes of 2001 and 2002 are on a pace for a similar dropout rate.[21] The chief accountability officer of CPS, Phillip Hansen, responded that, with higher standards, most observers would expect higher dropout rates, but that had not happened.

Unlike the many CPS elementary schools that improved enough to escape from probation, only a few high schools did so. There has been a wide range of student performance among the city's high schools, with one school having 92.3 percent of its students reading at the national norms in 1990 while another had no students at that level. In that year, six had more than 50 percent of their students reading at or above the norms while twenty-one had less than 15 percent at the norms. The largest group of schools (twenty-seven) were between 15 percent and 29 percent at the norms. This distribution shifted dramatically during the decade (see table 2).

By 1996, only eight of the twenty-seven schools were above 30 percent reading at the norm, while forty-three had less than 15 percent at the norms, and, of these, ten had less than 5 percent of their students reading at the norms.

The recovery since 1996 is demonstrated by the fact that ten high schools in 2000 were above the 50 percent level and twelve others had over 30 percent at norms. The number with less than 15 percent at norms had fallen from forty-three to twelve; within these numbers, there were no high schools with less than 5 percent reading at the national norm in 2000, whereas four years previously, ten schools had been in this condition. However, because the level for escaping probation was set at 20 percent reading at the norm, only seven high schools of the original thirty-eight had escaped that category by the end of 2000.

Citywide, there was a 14.8 percentage point increase in the number of tested high school students reading at or above the national norms between 1996 and 2000. Eighteen high schools exceeded the citywide gain, while thirty-five others had increases of at least half the citywide gain; thirteen had smaller increases, with four of these gaining an average of less than 1 percentage point per year.

What Accounts for the Improvement in High School Achievement?

Given the sequence of events (declining high school achievement, the adoption of a new Design for High Schools, subsequent widespread improvement in both reading and math scores), implementation of the Design for High Schools might account for the improvement. In lower performing high schools where scores were rising, leaders and teachers claimed that their hard work was paying off.

Significant changes were undertaken in the city's sixty-six regular high schools.[22] The Design for High Schools was intended to help achieve the

Table 2. Performance Levels in Reading of Chicago High Schools, at or above National Norms

Performance level	1990	1996	2000
More than 50 percent	6 (9.1%)	4 (6.0%)	10 (15.2%)
30 to 49 percent	21 (18.2%)	4 (6.0%)	12 (18.2%)
15 to 29 percent	27 (40.9%)	16 (23.9%)	32 (48.5%)
5 to 14 percent	20 (30.3%)	33 (49.3%)	12 (18.2%)
Less than 5 percent	1 (1.5%)	10 (14.9%)	0 (0.0%)

goals of the district's already adopted *Children First Education Plan,* which included, among other goals, increasing the percentage of students scoring at or above norms on standardized tests, increasing the high school graduation rate, increasing student attendance, decreasing the dropout rate, and decreasing the number of schools on the state's academic watch list. To reach these goals, the reform board believed that "it is necessary to fundamentally restructure the system's high schools."

Restructuring was to take place on the basis of two principles: increasing the academic press and enhancing personalization in high schools. The design document described these two principles: "Good schools engage students in learning and teachers in teaching through rigorous, consistent academic expectations and caring, personalized experiences and environments. . . . Both are essential. Both are integral parts of the larger vision as schools move forward with their school improvement planning."[23] Three of the design priorities through which these principles were to be enacted were heightened academic accountability, nurturing student development, and expanding paths to success. Two critical design reinforcements in the plan were expanding the development of people in the schools and providing additional management support for principals.

The Design for High Schools envisioned two main kinds of change that would occur in the city's secondary schools. Schools would increase the pressure for academic performance, and they would enhance the personalism by which students would be better known and would better know other students and teachers. Increasing the pressure for academic performance entailed adopting higher graduation standards and requiring all students to take a full load of courses that would produce credit toward meeting the graduation standards. Schools would also be judged on the basis of the level of student achievement on standardized reading and math tests, with the lowest performing schools placed on probation, provided extra instructional support, and threatened with the loss of jobs for the adults in the schools.

The Chicago Reform Board of Trustees did adopt higher graduation standards. Schools did require students to take credit-bearing courses in the core subjects. Lower performing schools were placed on probation and provided extra instructional support, and seven high schools were reconstituted in the summer of 1997, with four of the seven principals being replaced as well as 30 percent of the teachers. Promotion gates were established at ninth grade as well as elementary grades three, six, and eight and summer school was provided for students not meeting the grade-appropriate standard. However, in the high schools, not very many of the qualifying students attended the mandatory summer school and the meaning of retention in high school was unclear. In recognition of these realities, the ninth-grade promotion gate was eliminated after the first year.

In response to the higher graduation requirements and the core course emphasis, students began taking more ambitious course work. Between 1996 and 2000 there was a 55.2 percent increase in students taking world language courses and a 17.8 percent increase in students taking science courses, despite a 4.2 percent decline in student enrollment. There was a corresponding decrease in noncore courses of 14.9 percent. While the total number of students taking mathematics courses declined slightly, the percent taking advanced algebra increased by 59.0 percent (from 12,682 to 20,169) and the percent taking honors courses in math increased by 74.5 percent. The increases in science course taking were significant; environmental science replaced general science as the introductory freshman course; enrollments in chemistry increased by 29.8 percent (to 13,993 taking the course in 2000) and earth science tripled from three thousand to over ten thousand. Meanwhile, passing rates increased by 4.2 percentage points for all students, with comparable increases in most subjects: 4.3 points in English, 3.6 points in social studies, 2.8 points in science, 4.1 points in math, and 5.6 points in noncore subjects. Only foreign languages showed a decrease in the passing rates, down by 1.1 points, but at 84.5 percent passing, it still had the highest passing rate among the core subjects. The 55 percent increase in students taking foreign languages (32,880 students took a foreign language in 2000) was concentrated in Spanish (up 55.1 percent) and French (up 68.8 percent) with slightly more students passing French, but slightly fewer passing Spanish. Thus, in general, students were taking harder courses and more students were passing these courses than had been the case in 1996. Correspondingly, the average student's grade point average (GPA) increased from 1.87 to 1.99 on a 4.0 scale.

There were two primary strategies for enhancing the academic press in the city's high schools. These strategies were made available to all schools on probation or remediation (that is, those schools not on probation but still on the state's academic watch list).[24] The first major strategy was for principals to get additional managerial support. Probation managers were assigned to all schools placed on probation. While originally conceived of by many as managerial supervisors, a consensus developed during the first year of probation that these experienced former principals should function more as mentors than as overseers (though their signatures continued to be required on school improvement plans and budget documents). While many high school principals, especially those who were newly appointed, found the advice and networking ability of their probation managers to be very helpful, about half dissented from that opinion. Besides probation managers, all high schools on probation were given an additional position and provided with a business manager to run facilities operations and oversee the school's finances, freeing the principal to pay more attention to instruction.

The second major strategy to increase academic performance was aimed directly at the quality of teaching. The district solicited the assistance of universities, the federal regional educational labortory, national reform organizations, and other private individuals or groups to assist faculties to improve instruction. Individual schools could select which external partner they wanted; nine such groups were chosen to provide assistance to high schools. In the first year and a half, the district paid the entire cost of the external partners, which averaged about $100,000 per year per high school. In the second year, half the cost was provided by the district and half came from the discretionary funds of the individual schools. In the third year, schools were responsible for the full cost of the services but were allowed to negotiate for a reduced level of service to curtail additional costs. Schools were also allowed to change partners if they felt they were not being well served. About half the high schools stayed with the same partner between 1996 and 2000. One external partner, a national reform organization, was decertified as a qualified partner in 1999, and the school district formed its own internal partner to focus assistance on reading in a number of high schools. By 1999–2000, this team served more high schools than any other partner. Seven high schools saw student achievement improve enough to escape probation between 1997 and 2000.

The effort to enhance personalism to overcome the anonymity of large urban high schools was emphasized in several restructuring initiatives. Advisories were designed to provide students the opportunity to meet with a smaller group of their peers (usually about fifteen) and at least one teacher to explore issues of social and emotional development. A number of different initiatives were launched to create smaller learning communities within urban high schools. Junior Academies were designed as aggregates of 100 to 125 students assigned to a common group of four or five core subject teachers, all of whom would teach the same students, with the students assigned to homerooms in the same part of the building with the same teachers. Schools-within-schools were created in which students and teachers self-selected into smaller learning communities around some common learning theme. Career Academies were established in which students interested in a particular cluster of careers worked together with faculty members in ways that might look much like a small school or might resemble a program theme with teachers teaching students from different themes in different courses or periods. Other forms of restructuring were also encouraged. Unfortunately, most Chicago high schools avoided such restructuring following the adoption of the Design for High Schools.

The implementation of advisories, one of the key strategies in the Design for High Schools intended to enhance personalism in the city's high schools, has been fraught with difficulties. Initially, in 1997–98, despite frequent complaints from teachers that they were not trained or skilled in getting involved with the lives of their students, most high schools implemented this strategy. Many schools had advisories meet multiple times per week, with teachers working with students in this context for no extra compensation.[25] However, grievances about this uncompensated effort sharply curtailed the advisories in 1999. In 2000, as a result of new schedule options that included advisories within the compensated minutes of instruction (generally at the expense of shorter periods for academic subjects), all high schools visited as part of the Center for Urban School Policy (CUSP) evaluation were conducting advisories.

However, the meaning of "advisory" has been progressively diluted and the range of activities conducted under this label has been significantly expanded. A focus on character education and social development has progressively given way to more mundane division-like activities and an increasing focus on academic activities, particularly reading improvement and test preparation.

Junior Academies evolved from Freshman Academies, a feature of the original High School Design. Freshman Academies had been designed to create small learning communities to support and orient newly entering students.

A limited number of students were scheduled together, with four or five core subject teachers, and located in the same part of a school building. The idea was to create small learning communities in which students and adults would be well known to each other. Freshmen Academies were seen as a strategy to overcome the anonymity of large urban schools and to enhance personalism in Chicago's high schools. Senn Academy had pioneered the model as an experiment in 1996–97, and it was incorporated into the High School Design as one of the two primary strategies (with advisories) to enhance personalism. In 1998–99 the Freshman Academies were expanded to include sophomores and were renamed Junior Academies. With the expansion to include sophomores, a further criterion was included—that the learning communities created for new freshmen would continue, intact, for two years, through the sophomore year.

The idea of a Junior Academy met with resistance in many Chicago high schools. Only seven of the thirty-three high schools on probation in 2000 incorporated the major structural features of the Junior Academy, including utilizing a separate part of the building for freshmen and sophomores and assigning teachers who teach only this group of students. Some schools implemented some aspects of the design. Several schools, in conjunction with other efforts to create smaller learning communities either through small schools or career clusters, restricted the Junior Academy to the freshman year, while sophomores were included in specialized communities with juniors and seniors. Many schools simply began to call the freshman and sophomore classes the "Junior Academy." Most of these schools have none of the criteria included in the original description. Thirteen high schools indicated they did not have a Junior Academy, thus completely rejecting this aspect of the Design for High Schools.

In addition to advisories and junior academies, creating smaller learning communities within larger urban high schools has been a way to make these schools less anonymous. The initial effort in this arena in Chicago resulted from the movement to create small schools. A number of high schools had established small schools before the adoption of the Design for High Schools. The strategy was recognized within the design as one way to enhance personalism, one of the two central themes of the design. In some high schools, small schools existed side by side with a general education segment of the school, and the outcomes of students in the small schools were frequently compared favorably with the outcomes of students in the general program. In other high schools, all students were enrolled in a small school.

Small schools typically were organized with students physically located in a set of specific divisions, and their classes were taught by faculty members who were mostly devoted to those students alone (though frequently these students took physical education and specialized courses such as art or music with teachers not part of the small school faculty). Small schools were typically led by a teacher-director, and the faculty made significant organizational decisions, such as period length and course requirements, which might vary from the pattern in the larger school or from other small schools in the same building. Some high schools were organized into smaller units by grade levels, called "houses," with faculty designated to each house. Houses were generally led by deans, who played more of a disciplinary role than an instructional leadership role.

Since the adoption of the Design for High Schools, two other organizing features have emerged—career academies and special program academies. Career academies have largely replaced the previous vocational high schools and feature career clusters that frequently look much like small schools (and some high schools with small schools now look much like career academies), but career clusters may also take on the features of a program (or track) followed by various students. Unlike small schools, faculty may teach courses in several different programs.

In 1998–99 the Chicago public schools announced the initiation of a number of specialized programs in twelve neighborhood high schools. These programs were designed to attract better prepared graduating eighth graders to enroll in these nearby high schools, instead of enrolling in magnet or other elite schools outside their community. The two most frequent programs were the Math, Science, Technology Academies (MSTA) and military academies. This effort to attract better performing students to neighborhood high schools was the first initiative to reverse the pattern of educational triage of sending the highest achieving elementary graduates to magnet high schools or those in more white communities on the fringe of the city, while leaving only poorly prepared students to attend inner-city neighborhood high schools.[26]

In 1999–2000, four high schools on probation utilized the small schools approach. Twelve probation high schools operated as career academies. Two were military academies, and there were four math, science, technology programs. Eleven high schools on probation operated with no small schools or other organized smaller learning communities in 1999–2000. Very little other school restructuring was undertaken during 1999–2000.

Effects of the Effort to Redesign Chicago High Schools

The Center for Urban School Policy evaluation team concluded that little of this activity in the city's high schools had any effect on student achievement.[27] While some significant efforts were made to restructure the organization of some high schools, most high schools in June 2000 looked and felt very much as they had when team members first encountered them three years earlier. More important, despite the extensive efforts of external partners, probation managers, and school principals, the quality of teaching did not seem to have changed much.

CUSP staff observed more than eight hundred classes between 1997 and 2000 in more than thirty schools under probation, reengineering, or reconstitution. Some teachers were observed over a three-year period. Teachers' pedagogy had changed in two significant areas. Novice teachers had improved, in line with the expectations of a steep upward learning curve for new teachers. Because several of the reconstituted high schools replaced veterans with large numbers of novices, this improvement had a larger effect than if the novices were spread more widely across all high schools. It is not clear whether external partners accelerated or expanded this novice learning curve, because no comparison group of similarly placed teachers was available for analysis. The other change was a weeding out of the most egregiously poor teachers, which occurred most prominently in the high schools whose staffs were reconstituted but also was carried out in some other schools on probation. What was not seen was any significant change in the pedagogy of veteran teachers. The majority of teachers observed taught at very shallow levels, and this pattern worsened over the three years.

Unfortunately, only minor changes in teaching were observed in 2000. New content related to the effort to improve reading scores was fairly widely adopted: timed readings, bell-ringers, and word of the day. These alterations to teachers' practices could be fairly easily monitored, and the degree of compliance noted. In schools where principals included compliance with such requirements as part of their supervisory teacher evaluations, such compliance was nearly universal. However, utilization of these techniques had little effect on reading scores and did not significantly alter instructional practices for most teachers implementing them. Most teachers used the same pedagogical approach to these exercises as they utilized in the rest of their teaching, and they brought the same attitudes to that part of their lessons as to the rest of the class period. However, teaching in many classrooms did generally become

Figure 9. Appropriateness of Instruction

Percent of observations

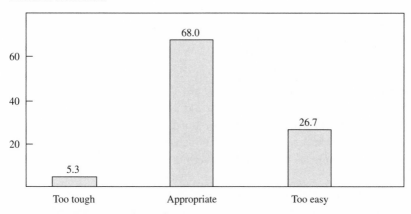

Note: Based on 1999–2000 classroom observations.

more interactive, with more teachers using a question-and answer-technique, supplemented with many brief lectures. But in too many, teachers used round-robin reading with teacher-delivered lectures after each paragraph read by the students.

CUSP researchers focused on three dimensions of teaching in their class-room observations: the appropriateness of the content, the depth of instruction, and the degree of engagement of students. In 1998 observers of reconstituted schools noted that many classes seemed to be conducted at a level of content far below what the course title would imply. This was confirmed in 1999 when classrooms in all schools on probation were visited.

In 2000, two-thirds of the classes (68.0 percent) were deemed to be focused on content that was appropriate to the course title. This was a significant improvement over 1999 and may reflect the wider use of Programs of Study, which spell out what content should be covered in each core subject to meet the Chicago Academic Standards. Still, in a quarter of the classrooms observed (26.7 percent), the content was not at a level deemed to be appropriate (see figure 9).

However, in a majority of classrooms observed, the material was being covered in a superficial way and only a minority of the students responded to discussions or teacher questioning.

In years two and three of this project, CUSP staff used a taxonomy of depth of questioning that was developed out of classroom observations in

1997–98. Questions were grouped by the kind of response required and organized hierarchically in terms of the depth of thinking required. The levels employed were:

Level 0—No real thought required; procedural or rhetorical questions or direction (for example, "Turn to page 33; will somebody please read the first paragraph aloud?").

Level 1—Fact-based questions or procedural operations, frequently repeated directly from the text (for example, "Who is the main character of *To Kill a Mockingbird?*" Or "How do you add 2x + 3x?").

Level 2—Subjective or relational questions; expressive of students' feelings or personal experience (for example, "Which character did you like or dislike in *Huckleberry Finn?*" or "Have you ever run away from anything like Huck and Jim did?").

Level 3—Inferential; answers must go beyond the text or presentation (for example, "What was the picture of slavery presented by Mark Twain in *Huckleberry Finn?*").

Level 4—Compare or contrast; seeks integration of different characters or texts or subjects (for example, "Compare the causes of World War I with the causes of World War II; how were they similar and how were they different?").

Level 5—Hypothetical; "what if" type questions that require postulations and hypotheses (for example, in studying *Romeo and Juliet*, "What would you do if you were told by your family that you could not date someone from a different racial or ethnic group?").

In a majority of classrooms observed in 1999–2000 (58.3 percent), the teacher never asked questions any deeper than Level 1, questions that requested facts or asked students to mechanistically implement some set of procedures, such as mathematical operations of addition or subtraction or specified steps in a science experiment. In another 8.7 percent of classrooms, students were asked about their own responses to the material being studied (Level 2) but were not asked to think more deeply about the classroom lesson. In 33 percent of the classrooms, teachers did ask students to make inferences beyond the textual material, or to make comparisons and contrasts between material studied, or to solve hypothetical problems related to the material. These numbers mean that shallow teaching was proportionally more extensive than in 1999, when 44.8 percent confined themselves to facts and procedures (see figure 10).

English teachers were more likely to ask their students to think more deeply than were teachers of other disciplines. Three quarters of observed English

Figure 10. Depth of Questioning

Percent of classrooms observed

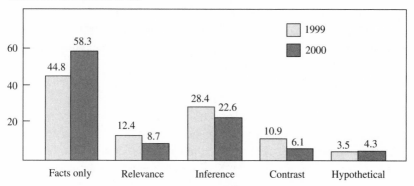

Levels of questioning

teachers asked their students to push beyond facts or procedures to deeper reactions or analyses. By contrast, 80 percent of science teachers and 72.4 percent of math teachers never asked their students to do anything but provide facts as answers to questions or carry out scientific or mathematical procedures. Surprisingly, a majority of social studies teachers (58.6 percent) also never asked their students to respond to more than fact-based questions.

As in 1999, classroom observations in reconstituted, reengineered, and probation high schools led to the conclusion that most Chicago students were not being asked to do more than regurgitate answers from texts. They were asked to remember facts (names, dates, places) and to carry out mathematical or scientific procedures, but they were not asked to think about these facts and procedures, to understand their relevance for their own lives, or to infer or analyze the deeper meanings of the facts and patterns. In some classrooms, teachers did not know how to lead students to think more deeply about the matters being covered and frequently gave little indication that they themselves had thought more deeply about the subject matter. In other cases, teachers felt that students needed to know the facts to do well on either standardized tests or the Chicago Academic Standards Exams (CASE). Too many teachers seemed to think their students were incapable of thinking deeply or of answering questions that required they do so.

In a 2000 study of five matched pairs of predominantly African American elementary schools, CUSP researchers discovered that in schools with larger gains in standardized reading scores over eight years, teachers taught to greater depth than their counterparts in schools with little or no test score gain. This means that the strategy of teaching to the test was less effective in boosting achievement levels on standardized tests than teaching for depth and for understanding. The applicability of this lesson from elementary schools to high schools is not demonstrable from data collected by the monitoring study team, but it is instructive that during the pilot phase of the CASE exams, students scored much higher on the English exams than on math, science, or social studies exams.

Finally, many teachers engaged only a small portion of their class. In nearly half the observed classrooms (48.3 percent), five or fewer students responded to teacher questioning or were engaged in classroom discussions. In only a quarter of the classes (24.1 percent) did teachers engage more than ten students (see figure 11). Teachers tended to offer undifferentiated instruction, despite wide variances of student preparation within their classrooms. Thus, in many classrooms, some students found the lesson was not challenging while others in the class found the work too hard. This was particularly true in classrooms when large numbers of special education students were included with regular education students.[28] The inability of teachers to provide different levels of instruction, through small group work or differentiated assignments for different students, meant that many teachers taught to the middle. The better prepared and the least well prepared students were thus left disengaged.

Why Did High School Test Scores Go Up?

Virtually all of the improvement in test scores reflected changes in preparedness of students entering the city's high schools, not differences in what these students encountered once they arrived in the city's secondary schools. Most of the credit for improved high school achievement belongs to the combination of higher performing elementary school graduates and the promotion gates that prevented the lowest performing students from entering the city's regular high schools. Since 1993, the percentage of eighth-grade students reading at or above the national norm has increased from 21.8 percent to 39.0 percent (see figure 12). The improvement of ninth-grade scores lagged several years behind improvement in eighth-grade scores.

As the number of entering freshmen with eighth-grade scores at or above the national norm increased, the number of ninth graders scoring at or above

Figure 11. Students Responding in Class

Percent of classrooms

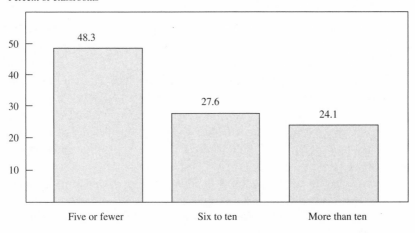

Note: Based on 2000 classroom observations.

Figure 12. Comparing Eighth- and Ninth-Grade Reading

Percent at or above norm

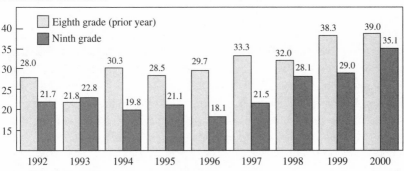

the norm in subsequent years also increased, with tenth- and eleventh-grade scores improving as these better prepared freshmen progressed through high school. Ninth-grade scores in 1998 and 2000 were closer to the scores these students had achieved in eighth grade than for other cohorts of students since 1994. In contrast to the improvement in preparation of freshmen, the number of students on subsequent tests added to those already reading at the norms in ninth grade has been small or, in the case of the last cohort, negative.[29] The lack of improvement of students after they were first tested in high school indicates the general ineffectiveness of external partners at teaching more high school students to read fluently, given the intensity of effort they could sustain on $100,000 per year per school. While some partners did increase the number of students reading at the national norm in some schools, in other schools these same partners had little or no success.

Thus, the good news is that high school students were scoring higher on standardized tests than were their predecessors, but that was not because schools had dramatically changed what they were doing with their students. Test score improvement was more a tribute to what the elementary schools had done with these students and, secondarily, a result of the policy that kept the very least prepared from enrolling in high school.

Yet this is not to say that nothing good came from the effort to improve Chicago's high schools. The effort, itself, has been very important as a testing ground for some of the proposed strategies for improving urban high schools. The lessons learned may help to fashion more effective strategies for the near future.

Implicit versus Explicit Standards

The improvement in student achievement on nationally standardized tests in Chicago during the 1990s has been encouraging. After a decade of stagnant scores in the 1980s, the improvement, especially in the last half of the 1990s, has been significant, even with all the necessary caveats. As the data indicate, the improvement has been more substantial in the city's elementary schools than in its high schools. Because most of the high school improvement represents enrolling better prepared freshmen, and because better prepared students still disproportionately attend the twenty highest performing high schools, the improvement in school level test scores not surprisingly has been more widespread among elementary schools than among high schools.

In 2000 there were 107 elementary schools (21.3 percent) and 10 high schools (15.2 percent) in which more than 50 percent of the students were at or above the national norms in reading. More than half the elementary schools (54.8 percent) and a third of the high schools (33.4 percent) had more than 30 percent of their students at the norm. This is a significant increase at the elementary level, but a much more modest improvement among high schools.

Given that high schools have not changed much since 1996, less improvement is seen in this category at the school level. Correspondingly, proportionately more elementary schools (74.6 percent) escaped probation than did high schools (20.5 percent). However, the vast majority of both elementary schools and high schools still have not achieved the 1988 goal that all Chicago schools would be at or above the national norm. Chicagoans are still waiting for that goal to be met.

While the improvement in achievement on standardized tests is important, it is not the same as meeting the district's learning standards. Something of a conflict exists between the implicit standards represented by the district's focus on standardized test scores in reading and math and the explicit learning standards adopted by the district. Learning standards were adopted in six different areas, but the focus of standardized tests has been limited to reading and math. In the elementary schools, students also take the ITBS in science and social studies, and the scores on these tests are posted on the district's accountability website, but little attention is paid to them.

Thus, in practice, at the city's elementary schools, the implicit reading and math standards of the ITBS have dominated the accountability system. The ITBS standards are, as the name implies, focused on basic skills. The concern of many Chicagoans has been that by focusing on these tests, and their implicit basic skills standards, the city's elementary schools would be narrowing their instructional focus from the wider array of formally adopted district standards. Many anecdotes report that this narrowing of focus has occurred in a number of elementary schools.

In this regard, the findings of the CUSP elementary school study provide an encouraging potential antidote to the narrowing of instructional focus. In that matched pairs study of ten elementary schools, the schools with the largest growth in achievement scores were also the schools whose teachers taught to greater depth. Frequently these schools also had more extensive after-school programs and were more widely engaged in their communities. From this small study, narrowing the instructional focus to the basic skills in reading and math does not seem to be the best strategy for improving scores on standardized tests. This finding directly contradicts the conventional wisdom about teaching to the test.

In the city's high schools, the conflict between the implicit standards of the tests and the explicit learning standards adopted by the Board of Education is more obvious. For accountability purposes, high schools have been judged on the basis of their test scores in reading and math. But at the same time, the district has been developing Programs of Study for each core subject course that are aimed at aligning these courses with the district's learning standards. Also based on the learning standards are the Chicago Academic Standards Exams, which have been developed for each core subject for ninth and tenth graders (and some for courses taken by juniors and seniors). The CASE exams are composed of 60 percent multiple-choice questions, scored by machine, and 40 percent constructed response questions, which are scored by teachers at each school. Thus, the CASE exams have the potential to examine students' comprehension and analytic capacity to a greater extent than do the standardized tests. This is particularly true in English and mathematics, where the standardized tests focus on fluency and general math skills, while the CASE exams focus more on literary analysis and algebra and geometry.

Because the district's focus on reading at the high school level had resulted in such meager improvement (an average of one more student per year per school reading at the national norms), CUSP recommended that the district base its accountability system on the CASE exams. The CUSP high school monitoring study suggested that the reading emphasis diverted a significant amount of time away from the core subjects, intruding on various subject periods for timed reading, word of the day exercises, and bell-ringers (supposedly short opening exercises to engage students, but frequently lasting well into the class period).

Shifting accountability to the CASE exams would bring a more explicit focus on the district's learning standards and would align assessment with what the district says students are supposed to know and be able to do. However, making that shift would create other problems. If high stakes were attached to CASE outcomes (currently the only stakes are for students, because the CASE results must count for at least 10 percent of their final grade), the portion of the test scored at the school level would be susceptible to corruption. A second problem is that the current Programs of Study generally focus on breadth of curriculum coverage, making it difficult for teachers to find the time to teach to greater depth. To encourage reaching the depth of thinking that the standards now imply, the Programs of Study probably would need to be more narrowly recast, with the CASE exams following suit. These two concerns would not be easily solved, but the rewards in better aligning the system's accountability efforts with its explicit standards would undoubtedly benefit the city's secondary school students.

Addendum: The End of the Vallas Era

One of the accomplishments of the Vallas-Chico era has been a restoration of confidence in the viability of public schools in Chicago. That confidence came, in part, from Vallas's unceasing boosting of the school system, at the same time that he took a hard-line approach to less successful schools and students. The confidence was reinforced by the significant improvement in student achievement scores and by solid operational and financial accomplishments.

However, as reports of the plateauing of student achievement began to emerge after the 2000 administration of standardized tests, Mayor Daley began a campaign to replace CEO Vallas and board president Gery Chico.[30] The first step in that campaign was to urge Vallas to become a candidate for the Democratic nomination for governor. After months of considering this option, during which time Chico made it plain that if Vallas did run he could not continue as CEO of the Chicago schools, Vallas declared he was not running. Daley then attacked the slowing of improvement in achievement, going so far as to schedule his own conference on reading without consulting either Chico or Vallas and inviting Vallas to attend only after the conference had been announced. When scores on the spring 2001 tests showed declines in both elementary math and high school reading, Daley increased the pressure on both Chico and Vallas to resign, while never publicly calling for those resignations. He suggested that perhaps someone else was needed for the next stage of reform. In late May, Chico resigned, followed two weeks later by Vallas. Thus the Vallas era ended on a sour note: mayoral dissatisfaction and the first declines in test scores since the mayor's team was installed in 1995.[31]

Vallas was replaced by one of his assistants, Arne Duncan, a young (thirty-six), white, Harvard graduate, and protege of Jonathan Rogers, an African American investment adviser who had served as president of the Park District Board for Mayor Daley. At the press conference announcing his nomination of Duncan, the mayor noted that perhaps too much attention had been focused on test scores and the district should look to other measures of student achievement. In so doing, he undercut the very argument he had been making to induce Vallas to resign. In all likelihood, slipping test scores only served as a rhetorical excuse for replacing his long-standing schools team. Daley's management style is to work his top appointees very hard and then to replace them after about three years. He also reacts poorly to underlings who get more press attention and credit than he does, a sin of which Vallas was frequently guilty. Because of Vallas's popularity in the city, and the conviction shared by many that he had performed a miracle in turning around the Chicago public schools, the mayor wanted to avoid the direct accusation that he was dumping this successful servant. Thus his campaign was carried out by underlings through off-the-record conversations with the press and advisers to Vallas and Chico. Two weeks after leaving CPS, Vallas announced the formation of an exploratory committee for a run for governor.

These events give support to Stanley S. Litow's suggestion that Chicago was at a transition point in 2001, with the turnaround phase completed and the next phase undefined. When, during the winter of 2001, the mayor asked for a plan for the next phase of improvement in CPS, Vallas quickly crafted a plan that many saw as more of the same. Linda Lenz, the publisher of *Catalyst*, pointed out that a February survey of education leaders and activists produced a "remarkable consensus" about what she called "Phase III" of school reform: "improving instruction by investing in good people."[32] Duncan, who had good contacts in the education reform community through earlier philanthropic work, could lead the district into this much more intractable campaign. A new president at the Chicago Teachers Union, Deborah Lynch-Walsh, who had previously led the union's professional development efforts, could be an enthusiastic partner for such an approach, but only if the district turns away from a blaming teachers approach that she saw underlying the district's sanctions on schools.

I support Litow's assessment that changes in governance had much to do with the success of the Vallas-Chico team. The 1995 amendments to the Chicago School Reform Act gave the CEO and the school board unprecedented power to control the district's finances and to privatize a number of its operations. It also, in an emergency measure, prevented union strikes for the first eighteen months of the new regime. These actions led the union to agree quickly to a four-year contract during Vallas's first summer and allowed Vallas to create a four-year balanced budget, which in turn led the bonding agencies to raise the district's bond ratings to investment grade. The improved ratings allowed Vallas to refinance the district's debt, significantly reducing debt service payments, thereby freeing up funds for programs to support the imposition of accountability. These actions, in turn, led to further improvement in bond ratings, which allowed the massive capital campaign of rehabilitation and new buildings to be successfully launched. Financial stability and labor peace were vital aspects of the Vallas era, as well as the strong mayoral backing.[33]

I also concur with Richard Elmore's concern that this next phase of reform is going to be asking teachers and administrators to do things they do not know how to do. The danger is that teachers and administrators will learn how to fake it, instead of changing. CUSP staff's experience observing the efforts to change high schools supports Elmore's concern, for it saw little real change during the three-year evaluation, though principals and teachers were quick to claim credit for improving test scores. However, I am less sanguine about Elmore's references to districts that are changing as having focused narrowly on only a few areas of instructional improvement. My concern is not on the necessity of narrowing the focus, but on the claim that teachers' instruction had widely improved in these districts. In the districts Elmore traditionally points to, teacher replacement has certainly played a prominent, though under-reported and underemphasized, role and may account for much of the modest improvements in instruction. Further, improvement seems easier in elementary and middle schools than in high schools. As Elmore says in several of his writings, changing the technical core of public education, what happens in the classroom between teachers and students, is not something with which great success has been achieved over the two decades since *A Nation at Risk* launched the current school reform effort.[34]

Elmore makes a reasonable sounding critique of the theory of action of standards-based reform when he suggests it is unfair to put stakes on students until after instruction has changed. That is, students should have the benefit of improved instruction before they are held accountable for their learning. While this criticism sounds reasonable, it ignores the chicken-and-egg nature of changing teacher instruction. As consequences were introduced for schools, teachers, with some justification, complained that they were being held accountable for the performance of students who cared little how they scored on achievement tests. Thus putting some consequences on students became an issue in assuring that the tests measured what students could do.

But it may be that consequences for students, as they began to play out in retentions and nonmatriculation from high school, were an important reason for change in the instruction offered by elementary teachers, who generally see themselves as teaching students, not subjects. Elementary teachers' own sense of efficacy is arguably tied to the success of their students, in ways that are less true for high school teachers. As long as student success was linked to graduating and going on to high school and virtually every student did that, teachers in the elementary and middle grades could be content with what their students were learning. When teachers began to see their students not graduating and not being promoted to the next grade, many felt compelled to work at higher levels or more intensely and to demand more of their students, so that they might meet the cutoff scores for promotion. Thus consequences for students could have had a larger impact on changing teacher classroom behavior than did threatened consequences for teachers. While this argument is speculative, it does offer a potential explanation for why more change appears to have occurred in elementary schools than in high schools. It does not dismiss, however, the moral responsibility for consequences for students when they have not had an improved opportunity to learn. It does suggest that this responsibility is one of the costs to be borne in changing instruction on a large scale, so that many students have more opportunity to learn than they did previously.

Overall, I concur with the concerns raised by Litow and Elmore, and I see their comments as adding to the understanding of the meaning to be drawn from the Chicago case study. Chicago seems to have completed the second phase of reform. (School autonomy to break the bureaucratic lethargy and engage local actors in reform was the first phase; standards, accountability, and support was the second.) The challenge facing the city's schools, as in many other urban school districts, is to address changes in what happens between teachers and students in classrooms. This phase promises to be more difficult than changing governance and public expectations and the locus of accountability for student learning.

Comment by Stanley S. Litow

Chicago's public schools were once dismissively dubbed the worst in the nation by former U.S. secretary of education William J. Bennett. They were held up as prima facie evidence of the failure of urban education in America. That may or may not have been true then, because no objective comparative analysis supported that charge, but it is certainly not true now. G. Alfred Hess Jr., a long-time and highly credible professional analyst on Chicago's version of the Great School Wars, turns out a well-researched and well-documented case as evidence of just how far the Chicago public schools have come. Certainly they are not the best in the nation, yet. But, compared against their own prior performance, Hess provides ample documentation of their successful turnaround. Were they a private company their stockholders would be pleased with the performance results to date, stock analysts would place a "buy" recommendation next to their name, and they might likely make the cover of *Business Week.* While Hess answers the question of whether or not children are hurt by standards-based reform with a convincing and resounding no, his analysis and conclusions in my view go much further. They provide a textbook case of how to begin an improvement campaign focusing on student achievement via standards, measurement, and accountability in the most difficult of urban settings, and they cry out for more complete analysis of the role played in this turnaround by political and leadership changes as well as by important governance and managerial change. All urban school systems, all big-city mayors, policy analysts, and education journalists ought to take note of Chicago's standards-based reform. It is not alchemy. It has worked so far, and with necessary midterm corrections it can continue to work. Though, given recent leadership changes, some important signals that there will be continuity may be in order.

The Chicago public schools suffered mightily through the 1970s and 1980s. Its mangled and unaccountable governance structure, poor financial and management controls, political strife, and labor-management conflicts, and the persistent urban woes of poor housing, health care, and disjointed and ineffective social welfare programs all contributed to substandard school performance and student achievement. By the early 1990s the system was mired in the muck of school decay. A controversial governance reform program shook the system to its core. It had lost its credibility with city and state leaders and especially with parents and teachers. It was nearly in the equivalent of Chapter 11. If it had not reached rock bottom, it was close to it.

The performance turnaround began in the mid-1990s. With the full support of Mayor Richard M. Daley, the Chicago public schools got a new noneducator chief executive officer (CEO), Paul Vallas, who had an impatient and tough managerial and strategic style. The schools also got a new coherent and accountable governance structure, an atmosphere of political stability via the mayor's leadership and support, and a stable financial outlook significantly early into Valla's tenure that he was able to achieve long-term labor peace and, most significantly, he was able to adopt a coherent school reform playbook that the school system could follow. The Chicago public schools bypassed rhetorical flourish and concentrated on standards-based reform—the steak not the sizzle, that is, standards, measurement, and accountability. Following close behind was a commitment both to reengineering and restructuring that provided added support to both teachers and students. As with many big-city school systems, prior governance structures and years and years of tried-and-failed school reforms had given just enough power to every special interest to halt reforms from being implemented and not enough power to any one locus of power to get anything of a substantial nature done. Moreover, the system was left with a risk-adverse culture that was pervasive within middle management, a defensiveness and resistance to change, and a predilection to kick even the most minor decisions up the chain of command. What resulted was a hidebound and insular bureaucracy, slow to respond even to the most urgent of issues. It is an understatement to say that the last five years have represented a stark departure from the past.

An examination of the available data reveals that performance results from 1995 to 2000, while significantly improved, are not perfect. But, some would argue that those seeking perfection ought not even attempt to engage in school reform at all, let alone urban school reform. Improvement in the high schools, while marked as Hess points out, does not keep pace with the gains in elementary and middle schools, this is true. And, the impressive lower school gains came with a price—the exclusion of too many special education youngsters from the testing program. Most significant, a small percentage of students, about 10 percent at each elementary grade, continue to persistently underperform. And the entire reform would benefit greatly from better alignment of curriculum, standards, and measurements and, especially, higher quality teacher professional development. All this is true. But, while important, they ought simply to provide areas for further work. They ought not distract from the major conclusion and the larger truth, which is that the Chicago school reforms worked and are working. The performance gains are substantial. Moreover, every turnaround in the public or the private sector needs interim goals, strategies, and measurements. While keeping the goals intact, strategies and tactics must shift to encompass different approaches over time.

Elementary school achievement in both math and reading has improved in Chicago over the last five years and the improvement is significant. In 1990 reading achievement in grades three through eight showed that less than a quarter of students read at the national norm. In the first five years of the decade of the 1990s there was little measurable improvement. But in the five year period from 1995 to 2000 the percent of students in grades three to eight reading at national norm jumped, markedly, by nearly 40 percent—to well over a third. The gain in math achievement is even more impressive. In 1990 only 27 percent of Chicago students in grades three to eight were at the national norm in math. Again by 1995 little progress was measurable. But in the five-year period from 1995 to 2000 students doing math at national norms jumped by about 80 percent—from 29.8 percent to 46.7 percent. As Hess points out, there is still a long way to go. But the facts are clear: The five-year gains are impressive and significant. Contrasted with the stagnant performance of the 1980s, they are very significant. Hess is careful not to attribute the leap in performance totally or even directly to Vallas and indicates that it is impossible to successfully untangle the interweaving effect of the five-year period before Vallas and the five-year period under his watch. Perhaps, yet he does note that the shift in outcomes correlates directly with the shift by Vallas from what is characterized as a low-stakes voluntaristic five-year period (during the first half of the decade) into the later high-stakes approach developed by Vallas. It is hard to conclude anything other than the fact that "high stakes" work and "not stakes" do not.

Hess also documents the data on promotional policy by analyzing research by Melissa Roderick and her colleagues at the Consortium on Chicago School Research. By establishing promotional gates to ensure that students moving into fourth, seventh, and ninth grades were ready to do work at these grades as opposed to being socially promoted, the number of students retained in grades three, six, and eight increased. Students were provided with both added services and investments, with the following result: "The promotional policy had been successful in encouraging many lower performing students to improve their achievement levels to avoid retention." Furthermore, with more services in the summer, many students improved and were placed on the right trajectory. And, while retention policies might effect dropout rates, they did not in Chicago, as ending social promotion did not lead to increased dropout rates. Though the continued lack of success of a group representing about 10 percent of each elementary grade is noted, it ought not detract from the large-scale success with limited fallout.

In the high schools, reform efforts began later and are, by many experts' estimation, tougher to achieve. The results according to Hess are less conclusive though the data in the high schools do reveal evidence of substantial improvement. Student achievement in secondary schools has improved steadily since 1996. High schoolers reading at national norms went from 20 percent to 35 percent, and math achievement more than doubled from 1996 to 2000, going from 21.7 percent to 45 percent. Dropout rates in the high school did not skyrocket as many predicted would occur. Significant changes were undertaken in the city's high schools—restructuring, added resources, and policy changes at the system level, which resulted in more students taking and passing rigorous course work. According to Hess, this is more due to the cumulative impact of changes in elementary and middle schools than in the high school restructuring per se. Maybe so. This last conclusion is based on a review that determined that in a majority of classrooms material was more often than not being covered in a superficial as opposed to an in-depth fashion with only a minority of students responding to either discussion or teacher questioning. This would clearly dictate a more effective effort at teacher professional development.

In his conclusion, Hess asks the system to move on from its obvious successes and to tackle the most daunting and elusive challenge in standards reform, that is, aligning standards, curriculum, tests, and accountability systems. From there, it must move on to the vitally important changes in teaching and learning that will yield results. To be fair, the Chicago public schools, Vallas, and his successor ought to be able to savor the incredibly strong start they have already made. They have turned student performance around, while others have stumbled. They reversed over two decades of educational drift. They have sustained and built upon their gains. Clearly, this is not a one- or two-year bump. They have achieved the support of the business and political establishment both in Chicago and increasingly nationwide. But, the challenges of sustaining that effort and support over the next five years will be daunting.

IBM's Reinventing Education initiative, conceived under the leadership of CEO Louis Gerstner, has been part and parcel of the Chicago reform, developing and implementing scalable strategies designed to influence math instruction, especially in the middle schools. In these efforts, the system has been willing to work in full partnership with the private sector in ways that have produced real change in teaching practice and a professional development system that supports teachers. Standards have provided the vehicle that permits all of these reforms to be coherent and connected as opposed to the earlier efforts in which every reform was a special project and depended too heavily on out-of-system technical help. From firsthand knowledge, I would say that standards-based reforms have been the reason for the success of IBM's public-private partnership in Chicago and arguably many others, too. While the school system clearly needs further reengineering, as is necessary in every corporate turnaround, after the initial five-year period, Chicago schoolchildren have been helped, not hurt, by the move toward accountability. Furthermore, earlier policies that resulted in too few children reading or doing math at national norms hurt far too many children and did so for a long time. But another nuance to the story is probably worth more attention. While not explicitly researched by Hess, it remains an intriguing subtext in his paper. What effect did the new style of leadership have on the success of the school reform? What, if any, impact does a noneducator serving as superintendent have on either pupil performance or overall district operations? How much or how little did a new governance system contribute to the success? What was the impact of Vallas's efforts to create a more centralized system of accountability? How significant was the vocal and consistent support of Mayor Daley in providing for the school system and its leadership the air cover that permitted the reform to take hold? What role did stable labor relations negotiated early on by Vallas with Daley's support play? What role did the economic recovery of the 1990s and a stable school budget play in achieving the successes to date?

The coherent governance structure, political support, and fiscal and labor peace were vital in achieving success to date. The contrast with New York City's splintered board structure and lack of mayoral support or Philadelphia's tense labor situation that has brought it to the brink of state takeover is significant. Both of these big-city systems attempted standards-based reform. While they experienced some modest successes, one wonders how successful they might have been had their CEOs, like Vallas, had the support needed to be effective. Both New York City and Philadelphia as of late 2001 have noneducator leaders. So do Los Angeles, Seattle, and San Diego. What impact, if any, does this have? Clearly there is room for further study. With the most recent change in leadership in Chicago and the selection of a key member of Vallas's team as CEO, it is useful to ask the system to provide continuity and for its political supporters to demand it. They must also take up the challenge so well articulated by Hess, that is, to concentrate on structural and systemic changes that affect teaching and learning.

For policy analysts and educators, answers to these questions and others posed by Hess's study are vitally important—but for the public they are essential. They are worthy of further study and need clarity so that those charged with improving education in America's urban schools do not miss the full significance of what has taken place along Lake Michigan.

Comment by Richard Elmore

In commenting on G. Alfred Hess Jr.'s paper, I use Chicago as an example to highlight what the Consortium for Policy Research and Education, the organization where I do my work, calls the second-generation problems of standards-based reform. That is, if the principle of continuous improvement is applied to an accountability system, what sort of problems has arisen in Chicago? First, however, I would like to make a couple of contextual remarks. Chicago, as a case, is a powerful model in ways that have not been explicitly stated. The Chicago experience is one of a relationship between the academic community and the school system around issues of reform. This relationship has not been altogether smooth. In fact, it has often been highly troubled. But the best academic minds in Chicago, which are among the best academic minds in the country, have worked on school reform there. This unusual situation has reached only tepid approximation in Boston. When the likes of Anthony Bryk, Alfred Hess, and others are willing to devote substantial amounts of their time to making reform work, a unique set of circumstances is created.

Hess is an authority on accountability. His paper contains a certain smoothness of narrative that glides over many historical and substantive complexities of Chicago school reform. Such a conceit develops when an author gets into a historical voice. Things tend to get smoothed out. Some issues discussed in the paper address how the narrative is constructed.

Hess has written a kind of teleological paper, communicating a sense of manifest destiny. Things are generally getting better in Chicago, and progress is based on a rational, straight-ahead model.

So, if my remarks reveal some questioning of the inevitability of success and the flawlessness of how the pieces fit together, they are not a critique of Hess but an allusion to the saying about how legislation, like sausage, is best not seen in the making. History is best not seen in the making, I suppose is the analogy.

The first problem with Chicago's accountability system is purpose and focus. Based on the evidence, Chicago is a classic case of mixed signals. Part of the second-generation reform must be focusing the signal more clearly and dealing with the consequences of focusing the signal.

Chicago must bring its students up to the national norms on the Iowa Test of Basic Skills (ITBS). As Hess suggests in his conclusion about implicit and explicit norms, this is what I would characterize as the "Lake Good Enough" phenomenon. Lake Wobegon ("where all the children are above average") anchors one end of the distribution, and Milwaukee and Kansas City anchor the other end. The problem with a norm-referenced standard for success is that it is an artificial idea. However, having test results to use as a benchmark for performance does make a certain amount of sense. But the ITBS is an inappropriate choice for Chicago. So the problem is not so much with using the ITBS or any norm-referenced test. The problem is with the target and with the idea of a norm-referenced standard as the target. It is an artificial and inappropriate construct for improvement.

Sooner or later, this is going to become a huge problem. An indication is the talk about end-of-course tests (which are geared to the standards developed outside of the school system), ways of validating those tests and standards, and how to think about alignment of the curriculum to the performance measures. All of those are imperative second-generation changes for Chicago. If, five years from now, ITBS scores are the focus of discussion in the case of Chicago, reform will not have worked.

Another issue arising from the mixed signals is the tremendous institutional conflicts embedded in the system between the first-generation and the second-generation reform. I have characterized the 1988 reform not as a reform, but as a return to ward politics in Chicago. Local school councils were created, which for two-thirds of the schools in Chicago turned into little patronage organizations. The local school councils were compatible with the old social and political structure of Chicago. Part of the subsequent 1995 reform was to mow down that structure.

However, the institutional structure still exists in some senses, and it is sending mixed signals about the locus of authority and responsibility and control for what are fundamentally instructional decisions. The absence of focus on instruction and the obsession with governance structure in the first reform created a long hiatus during which the school system floundered. The system thought it was doing school reform without ever touching teaching and learning.

Urban school systems essentially represent a conglomeration of reforms from the last hundred years. Maris Vinovskis could provide a detailed inventory of the two hundred or so strata, and they are all present. That is the point. They are all still present in the organizational structures of urban school systems.

So, the first problem is mixed signals. The second-generation reforms must define a clear purpose, determine how instructional practice connects to that purpose, and show how to fulfill that purpose. The second problem is reciprocity of capacity for accountability. Teachers and administrators in Chicago, Philadelphia, and elsewhere are asked to do what they do not know how to do. Part of the validity problem is distinguishing between faking it—pretending that something is being done or that teachers and administrators know how to do it—and learning how to perform differently. What do teachers and principals need to implement reform?

The only successful systems I have seen focused on a single or, at most, two instructional areas at once. Furthermore, they instituted the instructional practice across the entire system. As a result of the 1995 reforms, the capacity issue in Chicago was addressed by external providers and then with intervention teams. The proportion of people who know anything about instructional practice is small. They are, for the most part, coming from the kind of witch doctor community of educational reform that focuses on sort of improvement by levitation.

Over the long term, educators and policymakers must deal with instructional issues, not theories of educational improvement. That requires focusing on the text and on teaching practices. It therefore is essential for the academic partners in the school reform effort to continue to do research on instructional practice.

The third problem is that the theory of action behind standards-based, performance-based accountability is weak and not specific enough. This is the way public policy works; that is, with a ready, fire, aim principle of policymaking by those who act as if they know what they are doing.

A general shift in policy is launched with big political rhetoric. A theory is then invented that makes the change seem to work. Theory-of-action problems have to be solved if reform is going to go anywhere. One is the role that expectations of teachers and students play in the process of producing performance.

Part of the issue is that teachers are carrying the expectations that they have of students with a new expectation of what they are going to teach. What they communicate to kids are the expectations they used to have in the guise of the new instructional practice. As a result, expectation drives performance and not the practice.

So, changed practice with low expectations produces low performance. Charter schools have not solved this problem. I have never heard such incredible attributions to students as in some charter schools. Part of this has to do with the missionary zeal of people who claim they know what is wrong with instructional practice. In reality, they would not know instructional practice if they fell over it in the street.

I subscribe to a kind of behavioral theory of changing expectations. Teachers must be engaged in instruction. Someone must watch them and make suggestions regarding what they are doing. Teachers have to see the improved performance of students as a consequence of the change of instruction. That increased performance changes a teacher's expectation and causes a teacher to engage in a higher level of performance—which produces a higher level of instruction; which, in turn, produces a higher level of performance; which, in turn, produces a higher level of expectations. A behavioral theory of action must be developed to make reform work.

Hess claims that the Chicago system is symmetrical by Andrew Porter and Chester Mitchell's standard. It is not. A fundamental design problem of school reform is that stakes are placed on kids before they have gotten instruction. Most of the retention and failure in the Chicago system is a consequence of bad instruction. That should be acknowledged. The kids should not have to pay the price for that.

A theory of action is needed that indicates an appropriate point at which adults have discharged their responsibility. From there, the stakes are equalized and kids are engaged in the action.

Consider what it is like to be a student in a system undergoing reform. In some high schools in Texas, the kids who fail the algebra section of the Texas Assessment of Academic Skills (TAAS) have to be advanced to the next level of math, because they must meet course-taking requirements to graduate. So, they take the next level of math—while they are taking a remedial algebra course. They then have after-school instruction and, later on, the TAAS preparation course in the subject that they failed. The instruction that they are getting is the same instruction that caused them to fail the test in the first place, only they are getting four times as much of it. This is not just the louder-and-slower method; this is the deeper-the-rut method. It is a miracle that any of these kids are still in school.

The question is what does remediation consist of, where do the stakes fall, and at what point do stakes kick in for kids.

The fourth problem is about validity. To the extent that policy discourse focuses on quartiles in the ITBS, a huge problem is going to be created over the long term. Part of the responsibility of those who run the school system and the academics who do research on it is to shift policy discourse toward measures and interpretations of measures that make sense in terms of the accountability structure. This should be done sooner rather than later. The infrastructure inside the system must be built up to run the accountability system.

A big design principle is whether a curriculum-embedded assessment can be invented, which focuses on end-of-course objectives, content area by content area. The instructional focus must be kept tight enough so that some sort of behavioral response can be set up for teachers, principals, and students to improve instruction.

If these things cannot be done, all the organizational changes in the world around the instructional core are just going to be distractions from the work itself. They may ultimately support the core, but in the short term, no one will be able to determine what organizational changes will work to support the core until there is a core to support. If there is no instructional core to support, incentives and organizational changes are not going to create one. The way to increase the quality of instruction is to focus on the structure.

Notes

1. See G. A. Hess Jr., *School Restructuring, Chicago Style* (Thousand Oaks, Calif.: Corwin Press, 1991), for a complete listing of the ten goals included in the legislation and for a fuller account of the initial school reform effort in Chicago.

2. For a fuller treatment of this analysis, see G. A. Hess Jr., "Expectations, Opportunity, Capacity, and Will: The Four Essential Components of Chicago School Reform," *Educational Policy*, vol. 13, no. 4 (September 1999), pp. 494–517.

3. A. S. Bryk and others, *A View from the Elementary Schools: The State of Reform in Chicago* (Chicago: Consortium on Chicago School Research, 1993).

4. See G. Alfred Hess Jr., *Restructuring Urban Schools: A Chicago Perspective* (New York: Teachers College Press, 1995), for a fuller account of the school-based management reform years and the district's financial mismanagement during that period.

5. Stanley S. Litow correctly notes the importance of fiscal stability and labor peace as key conditions for the effort to improve achievement. Creating those conditions was an early success of the new administration, based on elements of the 1995 reform amendments.

6. The Chicago Academic Standards Exams (CASE) were piloted for three years and began to count toward students' course grades in 2000–01.

7. Reengineering was an adaptation of the Toledo Peer Review Plan proposed by the American Federation of Teachers (AFT) affiliate in that city and adopted by its Board of Education in the late 1980s. The Chicago Teachers Union is also an AFT affiliate.

8. Only seven teachers in these five intervention high schools were recommended for possible dismissal, but by July 2001, none had been dismissed. See Mario G. Ortiz, "Intervention Year End Review: Amid Dismal First Year Results CPS Plans for Year Two," *Catalyst*, vol. 12, no. 9 (June 2001), pp. 22–23.

9. Similar achievement trends are evident when tracking other measures as well, such as median grade equivalent scores for each grade, percent of students in the lowest quartile, or

average percentile ranking. However, different forms of the standardized tests were used in different years, creating something of an uneven scale of measurement. The Consortium on Chicago School Research performed a series of equating studies to establish a common achievement scale for the early years of reform, but the effort was too costly to maintain and did not indicate significant variances with the general trends reported here. See A. S. Bryk and others, *Academic Productivity of Chicago Public Elementary Schools* (Chicago: Consortium on Chicago School Research, 1998). Richard Elmore correctly questions the use of norm-referenced tests to measure the effects of standards-based reforms. However, a dearth of reliable criterion referenced assessments is generally available to urban school districts, and even fewer that match particular state and district adopted standards. Chicago public schools (CPS) did embark upon a four-year process to develop CASE, now in use for most core subjects in grades nine, ten, and eleven.

10. Schools in Chicago are mostly organized as kindergarten through eighth grade (elementary schools) and ninth through twelfth grade (high schools). However, many elementary schools have fewer grades. There are about thirty middle schools of sixth through eighth grade (or seventh and eighth grade), only a few of which subscribe to the middle school philosophy. Some schools only serve primary grades (K–2 or K–3). Many schools also provide prekindergarten programs, funded by federal Chapter I, a state prekindergarten program, Head Start, or local district support. In recent years, a number of elementary and middle schools have added ninth and tenth grades as an alternative to sending their graduates to larger, anonymous, and lower performing high schools.

11. To truly match the national performance level, Chicago students also would need to match the bell curve distribution of the national norm. Another way to approximate that criterion would be to see if 25 percent of students did math in each of the four quartiles. In 2000 more students scored in the third quartile (between the 50th and 75th percentile) and fewer were in the top quartile.

12. J. Q. Easton, T. Rosenkranz, and A. S. Bryk, *Annual CPS Test Trend Review, 2000* (Chicago: Consortium on Chicago School Research, 2001).

13. There were 22,069 special education and 14,018 bilingual students excluded in 2000, with another 2,799 excluded who were both special education and bilingual education enrollees.

14. See M. Roderick and others, *Ending Social Promotion: Results from the First Two Years* (Chicago: Consortium on Chicago School Research, 1999); and M. Roderick and others, *Update: Ending Social Promotion: Passing, Retention, and Achievement Trends among Promoted and Retained Students, 1995–1999* (Chicago: Consortium on Chicago School Research, 2000). Both studies can be accessed from the consortium's website: www.consortium-chicago.org.

15. The original promotion policy included ninth grade as a promotion gate. Resistance of high school students to attending summer school, combined with the uncertainty of what retention meant in high school, forced the district to drop the ninth-grade gate.

16. I was privileged to serve on the High School Redesign Steering Committee. After the Design for High Schools was adopted by the Reform Board of Trustees, I was asked to develop a plan to evaluate its implementation. Under my direction, the Center for Urban School Policy (CUSP) conducted a monitoring project from 1997 to 2000 under contract to the Chicago public schools. A summary of the report on that project is available. See G. A. Hess Jr. and S. Cytrynbaum, *The Effort to Redesign Chicago High Schools: Effects on Schools and Achievement* (Chicago: Center for Urban School Policy, 2001).

17. In 1999, in preparation for the launching of the Prairie State Exam for eleventh-grade students in 2000, the Chicago public schools began a shift toward testing ninth and tenth

graders on the Test of Achievement and Proficiency (the high school companion of the Iowa Test of Basic Skills). In that year, scores were available for ninth and eleventh graders (1999a on figure 4), completing the longitudinal sequence for those grades from 1990, and for ninth and tenth graders (1999b), which began a new sequence carrying into 2000. Because some lower performing students tested in tenth grade would be likely to drop out before the eleventh-grade testing, it would generally be expected that ninth- and tenth-grade scores would be slightly lower than those for ninth and eleventh grade. This was the case districtwide in 1999, but not for many individual high schools.

18. While some testing experts (for example, Daniel Koretz) have suggested rising test scores may be the result of increasing familiarity with the test by students and teachers, the same form of the Iowa Test of Basic Skills was used in Chicago every year during the 1980s with no increase whatsoever in median grade equivalents. Test familiarity, by itself, does not automatically lead to higher test scores, though becoming accustomed to a new test may result in score improvement.

19. The other 20 percent reflect the artificial reduction in the number reading in the bottom quartile due to retention in eighth grade or diversion to Transition Centers.

20. See G. A. Hess Jr. and D. Lauber, *Dropouts from the Chicago Public Schools* (Chicago: Chicago Panel on Public School Policy and Finance, 1985).

21. See "New Student Dropout Report Shakes Up Biz," *Crain's Chicago Business*, March 19, 2001, pp. 1, 60–61.

22. In addition, the district opened fifteen charter schools (the most ambitious embracing of Illinois's new charter legislation), contracted with a number of private providers for new alternative schools for students with special needs, and established a set of nine Transition Centers to assist fifteen-year-olds who had not passed the eighth-grade cutoff in preparing for entry into high school.

23. *Chicago Public Schools Design for High Schools* (Chicago: Chicago Public Schools, December 1997, revised), p. 1.

24. These strategies were also available to elementary schools on probation or remediation.

25. In 1997–98, forty-three of forty-eight high schools visited by CUSP staff had implemented advisories: eighteen conducted them daily; twelve conducted them between two and four days per week; thirteen held them once a week. In 1998–99, only thirty conducted advisories: nine held them daily; nineteen held them one day per week; two held them less frequently than weekly.

26. The pattern of educational triage was first identified in Hess and Lauber, *Dropouts from the Chicago Public Schools.*

27. The 1999–2000 research team was composed of the following members: Solomon Cytrynbaum (co-primary investigator), Theodorea Regina Berry, Rebecca Gould, Karen Granda, Leswin Laubscher, Susan Lee, Theodore E. Moran Jr., Derrick McNeil, and John Schwartzman. Analytic and logistical support was provided by Ronit Bar Orion, Emily Buser, and Dionne Brown.

28. The number of special education students in high schools increased from 11 percent to 14 percent in five years. In addition, as a result of a settlement of litigation, nearly 85 percent of these students were included in mainstream classrooms, starting in 1998–99. Special education students were disproportionately enrolled in the high schools with the lowest performing students.

29. See Hess and Cytrynbaum, *The Effort to Redesign Chicago High Schools.*

30. See G. Alfred Hess Jr., *Achievement Trends in Illinois and Chicago* (Brookings, 2000).

31. Reading scores on the Iowa Test of Basic Skills improved, from 36.4 percent of third through eighth graders at the norm to 37.7 percent in 2001, but declined on the Test of Achieve-

ment and Proficiency (TAP) from 35.3 percent at the norm in ninth and tenth grade to 31.8 percent. Elementary math scores also declined, from 46.7 percent at the norm in 2000 to 43.7 percent. No TAP math test was given in 2001, as the system prepared to shift to an American College Test (ACT)-based set of high school assessments. The district initiated use of PLAN (ninth grade) and EXPLORE (tenth grade) in the fall of 2000 and began utilizing the state's Prairie State Exam, which has the ACT at its core.

32. See Linda Lenz, "Solid Footing for City's New School Leaders," *Catalyst,* vol. 12, no. 9 (June 2001), p. 2.

33. For a further explication of these issues, see Hess, "Expectations, Opportunity, Capacity, and Will"; and G. Alfred Hess Jr., "Community Participation or Community Control? Reform Movements from New York to Chicago," *Theory into Practice*, vol. 38, no. 4 (Autumn 1999), pp. 217–24.

34. National Commission on Excellence in Education, *A Nation at Risk: The Imperative for Educational Reform* (Government Printing Office, 1983).